Markets, information, and uncertainty

Essays in economic theory in honor of Kenneth J. Arrow

Markets, information, and uncertainty is a collection of essays by leading theorists offering powerful new insights on the role of uncertainty and information in today's market. This book features Kenneth Arrow on information and the organization of industry, Roy Radner on new technologies, Graciela Chichilnisky and Frank Hahn on human-induced uncertainty, Geoffrey Heal and Walter Heller on the creation of new markets, and Edmund Phelps on unemployment, among topics investigated by other eminent practitioners. It is an authoritative collection offering imaginative and fresh approaches to economic theory.

Graciela Chichilnisky holds the UNESCO Chair of Mathematics and Economics at Columbia University and is Director of Columbia's Program on Information and Resources. In 1995 she was awarded the Lief Johansen award from the University of Oslo and was the 1994–5 Salimbeni Professor at the University of Siena. Professor Chichilnisky is recognized as one of the world's leading applied and theoretical scientists, having originated the concept of "basic needs," which is widely used in economic development and was explicitly adopted by 150 nations in the UN Agenda 21 at the 1992 Earth Summit. She has served as advisor to organizations including the Organization of Economics Cooperation and Development, the United Nations, and the Organization of Petroleum Exporting Countries (OPEC), in the areas of international economics and environmental policy. Professor Chichilnisky is a member of the board of directors of the Natural Resources Defense Council and is the author of eight books and some 160 scientific articles.

T0318309

Kenneth J. Arrow

Markets, information, and uncertainty

Essays in economic theory in honor of
Kenneth J. Arrow

Edited by
GRACIELA CHICHILNISKY
Columbia University

CAMBRIDGE
UNIVERSITY PRESS

CAMBRIDGE UNIVERSITY PRESS
Cambridge, New York, Melbourne, Madrid, Cape Town, Singapore, São Paulo, Delhi

Cambridge University Press
The Edinburgh Building, Cambridge CB2 8RU, UK

Published in the United States of America by Cambridge University Press, New York

www.cambridge.org
Information on this title: www.cambridge.org/9780521553551

First published 1999
This digitally printed version 2008

A catalogue record for this publication is available from the British Library

Library of Congress Cataloguing in Publication data
Markets, information, and uncertainty: essays in economic theory in
honor of Kenneth J. Arrow / edited by Graciela Chichilnisky.

p.   cm.

Includes index.

ISBN 0-521-55355-5

1. Economics.   2. Arrow, Kenneth Joseph, 1921–.   I. Arrow, Kenneth
Joseph, 1921–.   II. Chichilnisky, Graciela.
HB71.M29   1999   97-25548
330 – dc21   CIP

ISBN 978-0-521-55355-1 hardback
ISBN 978-0-521-08288-4 paperback

Contents

Section III. Market externalities and justice

Preface

This book emerged from the celebration of Kenneth Arrow's 70th birthday at a workshop entitled "Columbia Celebrates Arrow's Contributions" in October 1991. This took place at Columbia University, where he studied between 1941 and 1950, and obtained his PhD degree under the supervision of Harold Hotelling and Albert Hart. The papers presented at that workshop to a most enthusiastic audience were special. It was a heartwarming event. It was later suggested that those papers, and those of other authors closely related to Ken Arrow, be compiled in a volume in his honor to memorialize this happy occasion. Uncharacteristically for such a volume, the book starts with a paper by Arrow himself, which he presented at the Columbia workshop. His piece on information and uncertainty reflects upon the future of industrial societies in a most original and thoughtprovoking manner. Each subsequent author reflects on an aspect of the uncertainty-information axis, which, as argued below, is a representation of a tug-of-war between the individual, whose life is short and whose capacities to predict are limited, and society, which exists in a more atemporal world.

Many thanks are owed to the authors who kindly helped with the process of producing this book, and to close associates and colleagues at Columbia who provided invaluable support: Drs. Yun Lin and Yuqing Zhao, Geoffrey Heal, Bruce Greenwald, Ned Phelps, David Krantz and Duncan Foley; also to colleagues at Stanford University where some of the work was completed: Paul Milgrom, David Starrett, and Paul Ehrlich, and to my daughter Natasha Chichilnisky-Heal, and Kim Stack and Grace Fernandez of the Program on Information and Resources (PIR) at Columbia. Thanks also to Scott Parris and Louise Calabro of Cambridge University Press who provided continued support, and Shirley Kessel who kindly compiled the indexes. The UNESCO Chair at Columbia University offered research facilities to PIR for producing this book, supported warmly by UNESCO Director General Federico Mayor and by Drs. Jorge Werthein and Pierre Lasserre of UNESCO, by Jonathan Cole, Provost of Columbia University, and by Vice Provosts Michael Crow and Peter Eisenberger. Many thanks are owed to them all. Research support from the U.S. National Science Foundation and the

Sloan Foundation to Columbia University were very valuable in completing this book.

In the process of putting this book together I learned a great deal from the authors. I found all the chapters interesting and at times challenging. Some are pathbreaking. It is my pleasure to offer this book in honor of the man who inspired them.

Graciela Chichilnisky, New York, July 1998

Contributors

Kenneth J. Arrow
Joan Kenney Professor of
Economics, Emeritus
and Professor of Operations
Research
Department of Economics
Stanford University
Stanford, CA 94305-6072
USA

Graciela Chichilnisky
UNESCO Professor in
Mathematics and Economics
Director, Program on Information
and Resources
Columbia University
405 Low Memorial Library
New York, NY 10027
USA

Tito Cordella
Professor, CORE
Université Catolique de Louvain
34 Voie du Roman Pays
B-1348 Louvain la Neuve
Belgium

Peter Coughlin
Professor, Department of
Economics
University of Maryland
College Park, MD 20742
USA

Vladimir I. Danilov
Professor, Central Institute of
Economics and Mathematics
Russian Academy of Sciences
Krasikova 32 Moscow 117418
Russia

Jacques Drèze
Professor, CORE
Université Catolique de Louvain
34 Voie du Roman Pays
B-1348 Louvain la Neuve,
Belgium

Frank Hahn
Professor, Faculty of Political
Economy
University of Siena
53100 Siena
Italy

Peter Hammond
Professor, Department of
Economics
Stanford University
Stanford, CA 94305
USA

Geoffrey Heal
Garrett Professor of Public Policy
and Corporate Responsibility
Columbia University
Graduate School of Business
New York, NY 10027
USA

Walter P. Heller
Professor, Department of
Economics
University of California at San
Diego
9500 Gilman Drive
La Jolla, CA 92093-0508
USA

Peter H. Huang
Professor of Law
University of Pennsylvania
Law School
3400 Chesnut Street
Philadelphia, PA 19104
USA

USA Gleb Koshevoy
Professor, Central Institute of
Economics and Mathematics
Russian Academy of Sciences
Krasikova 32 Moscow 117418
Russia

P. B. Linhart
Information Sciences Center
AT&T Lab-Research
Florham Park, NJ 07932
USA

Enrico Minelli
Professor, CORE
Université Catolique de Louvain
34 Voie du Roman Pays
B-1348 Louvain la Neuve
Belgium

Edmund S. Phelps
Professor, Department of
Economics
Columbia University
1004 International Affairs
Building
Mail Code 3308
New York, NY 10027
USA

Heracles Polemarchakis
Professor, CORE
Université Catolique de Louvain
34 Voie du Roman Pays
B-1348 Louvain la Neuve
Belgium

Roy Radner
Professor, Stern School of
Business
New York University
44 W. 4th Street
New York, NY 10012
USA

Alexandr I. Sotskov
Professor, Central Institute of
Economics and Mathematics
Russian Academy of Sciences
Krasikova 32 Moscow 117418
Russia

Ross M. Starr
Professor, Department of
Economics
University of California at San
Diego
9500 Gilman Drive, Dept. 0508
La Jolla, CA 92093-0508
USA

David A. Starrett
Professor, Department of
Economics Building #235
Stanford University
Stanford, CA 94305
USA

Maxwell B. Stinchcombe
Professor, Department of
Economics
University of Texas, Austin
Austin, TX 78712
USA

Hirofumi Uzawa
Professor, Research Center on
Global Warming, RICF
The Japan Development Bank
1-9-1 Otemachi, Chiyoda-ku
Tokyo 100
Japan

Ho Mou Wu
Professor, Department of
Economics
College of Law
National Taiwan University
Taiwan ROC

Information and markets

Introduction

Graciela Chichilnisky

The mystery of brilliant productivity will always be the posing of new questions, the anticipation of new theorems that make accessible valuable results and connections. Without the creation of new viewpoints, without the statement of new aims, mathematics would soon exhaust itself in the rigor of logical proofs and begin to stagnate as its substance vanishes. Thus, mathematics has been most advanced by those who distinguished themselves by intuition rather than by rigorous proofs.[1]

Few people fit this description. Kenneth J. Arrow is one of them. Who is Kenneth Arrow?

Although very well known, Arrow remains somewhat of a mystery. His brilliant productivity over a period of about fifteen years – from 1950 to the mid-1960s – spanned the most interesting fields in economics, bringing the power of mathematics and statistics to bear on novel approaches to economic analysis and important issues of economic policy. He left an important mark on the fields of market economics, social choice and welfare economics, the economics of uncertainty, information, and mathematical programming. After that period the fountain of innovative ideas shifted ground. The shift took him away from pathbreaking innovation and into somewhat more conventional thinking,[2] and increased his professional ascendancy. Since the late 1960s Arrow's role as an editor and intellectual organizer has been consolidated in several books and edited volumes offering the last word on contemporary history of economic thought. The shift was somewhat surprising. Why this change in gears? The change has been attributed to his professional generosity – his proclivity for never saying no to a request – and for concentrating mostly on

---

[1] Herman Weyl reproduces this quote from Felix Klein's lectures on the history of Mathematics, in his *Unterrichtsblätter für Mathematik und Naturwissenschaften* 38, 177–8 (1932).

[2] Without, however, changing the level of mathematical formalization of his work.

3

the work of others. There is, however, an alternative interpretation. Innovation, some say, is costly and can lead to professional unease. This is particularly true in economics, a field where dissidence and cynical values abound. Arrow's originality and creativity had a cost. Is it possible that Arrow decided to follow the smoother road – a safer road which leads to professional acceptance, preeminence, and influence?

Arrow's multifaceted personality may explain the mystery. He always appears to reflect back what the observer projects upon him. A man at home in the most staid and conservative academic institutions, Arrow has nevertheless won over many of those who have sought to change the academic rules. Kenneth Arrow was always an insider in the clothes of an outsider. His economics appealed to those who prefer raw and free markets, as well as to those who prefer restrained markets, or even justice and planning. Ned Phelps's chapter in this book touches on this facet of his personality. Arrow's work appealed to those who prefer realism to elegance, and also to those who prefer elegance over realism. On a personal level this made him a very popular figure to very different audiences. His disarmingly candid and charming demeanor has a cautious streak. Arrow's beautiful blue eyes reflect wonder, and shine with intelligence and humanity while incisively measuring up the personality and weakness of the opponents. Arrow does not win an argument. He seeks to win the other side over. Often he succeeds.

The source of this somewhat unusual personality may be found in his life experience growing up in New York City. The Depression left on Arrow an indelible mark. His father was a victim of the largest and most severe wave of unemployment recorded in this country, and this may have created deep insecurities which meshed with remarkable intellectual clarity and strength. This combination could have originated an unusual and appealing personality.

Born in 1921 in New York City to Harry and Lillian Arrow, young Kenneth was raised in the city and did his undergraduate studies at that remarkable educational institution: City College of New York. After graduating in 1940, he went in 1941 to Columbia University where he studied under its great original thinker, Harold Hotelling. Columbia was at this stage the top U.S. institution in economics. Yet little enthusiasm existed at Columbia for what is now known as neoclassical price theory, the field on which Arrow's contributions are based. All attempts to introduce formal or rigorous thinking at Columbia have met with hostility during the years, even at present. In this context Arrow's Ph.D. dissertation, filed in 1950 under Albert Hart, was hardly recognized as a contribution to economics. Instead it started a new era in the field now called social choice theory.

Arrow says that he was led to study social welfare functions at Rand and through this he discovered results on elections at the same time as Duncan Black. He went on to formalize an axiomatic theory in his dissertation-monograph, "Social Choice and Individual Values," which appeared in 1951. His contribution was in a way small, but in another, decisive. His generalization of famous voting paradoxes in an accessible yet formal manner attracted widespread attention from unexpected quarters. His result, called an "impossibility theorem," was mysterious and teased the imagination of the reader. Here is Kenneth Arrow proposing something so simple that surely it can be solved. Yet he shows it cannot. His elementary techniques teased the reader even more. Everyone could read his results, without even knowing calculus, everyone could try his or her hand at the problem. The mystery propelled many to write and rewrite Arrow's results in different forms and variations, leading to what some critics called a combinatorial patchwork. But the sheer volume of the field prevailed and became known as social choice theory.

Several factors delayed Kenneth Arrow's completion of his graduate studies. A major one was World War II. Arrow served with the Weather Division of the Army Air Force where he wrote his first scientific paper, "On the use of winds in flight planning." In 1946 Arrow returned to Columbia for doctoral studies with Harold Hotelling; in 1947 he joined the Cowles Foundation at the University of Chicago where Jacob Marschak, Leo Hurwicz, and Tjallings Koopmans were on the faculty. Arrow considered becoming an actuary but Koopmans advised him against it.

In 1947 Kenneth Arrow married Selma Schweitzer, then a graduate student at the University of Chicago. In 1950 he completed his Ph.D. dissertation at Columbia, published in 1951 under the title *Social Choice and Individual Values*. Immediately thereafter he published *An Extension of the Basic Theorems of Classical Welfare Economics*, developed for the Berkeley Symposium on Mathematical Statistics and Probability, proving formally that a competitive equilibrium is Pareto efficient. Kenneth Arrow joined Stanford University in 1949, as an assistant professor of economics and statistics.

In the early 1950s he collaborated with Gerard Debreu in the formalization of Walrasian general equilibrium theory and the proof of the existence of a competitive equilibrium. Both were working on the same problem, each facing different difficulties, when Tjallings Koopmans brought them together. Their work is a triumph of simplicity and generality, and is based on a simple but crucial insight: that a market equilibrium is no more than a balance between supply and demand. They never explain how the market behaves outside of equilibrium, or how it adjusts toward an equilibrium. This has puzzled many scientists from other disciplines, where an equilibrium is the rest point of a dynamical system. The work of Arrow and Debreu defines an equilibrium without defining a dynamical system. Prior to their work, a market equilibrium was formalized as the "rest point" of price or quantity adjustments processes representing trade. Their approach is different. It is obviously weak in explaining the dynamics of the system – how markets come to equilibrium – but as often happens its weakness is also its strength. It cuts short the unending arguments about how trading occurs outside of equilibrium which had plagued the mathematical foundations of the theory of markets. That supply must match demand was, however, never debated; therefore their work cut the Gordian knot. They solved the problem by bypassing it. Concentrating only on the uncontroversial market clearing conditions, supply matck demand, they followed Nash and Von Neumann and proved the existence of a market clearing equilibrium by fixed point methods. This led to their paper, "Existence of an Equilibrium for a Competitive Economy," and to the successful adoption of what is now called the Arrow–Debreu model as an abstract standard with respect to which market behavior is measured. With Leo Hurwicz, Arrow collaborated during the mid-1950s on issues connected with mathematical programming, decentralization, and the stability of competitive equilibrium.

In 1962 Arrow served on the research staff of the Council of Economic Advisers; he was a visiting fellow at Churchill College, Cambridge, in 1967, where he collaborated with Frank Hahn, leading to the production of his book *General Competitive Analysis*. He also collaborated on studies on continuous time optimal control with Mordecai Kurz, resulting in his book *Public Investment, the Rate of Return and Optimal Fiscal Policy*. Arrow taught at Harvard University from 1968 to 1979, a period during which his productivity slowed down. He received the Nobel Prize in Economic Sciences in 1972, at the age of 51. In 1974 he set an agenda for the future in his presidential address to the American Economic Association and in his Fels Lectures, *The Limits to Organization*, published about the same time. It was in this year that I met him. Invited by Kenneth Arrow to Harvard University as a research associate, I dedicated myself to research and then turned to teaching as a lecturer, until 1978. This period did not appear to be specially productive at the time, but during those four years I completed my second Ph.D. dissertation, this one in economics, and produced new research on what would become recurrent themes of my work, introducing and developing the concept of basic needs, creating a model of North–South trade, introducing Hilbert spaces in infinite economies, developing an alternative topological theory of social choice, and laying the foundations of limited arbitrage as a unifying conceptive resource allocation. The latter two results establish that two seemingly unrelated strands in Arrow's work, his impossibility theorem of social choice and his theorem on the existence of a competative equilibrium, are so closely related as to be one and the same. Based on this, I introduced[3] a new concept of social diversity, defined in terms of endowments and preferences of the traders of an Arrow–Debreu economy. A limitation on social diversity (limited arbitrage) is both necessary and sufficient for a resolution of the social choice problem and for the existence of competitive equilibrium. This relation between social choice and markets was not known to Arrow himself. I did not realize this as I began to develop the topological approach to social choice which is at the foundation of this work. The question came to me as a surprise: Could one find such a close connection between two parts of Arrow's work market equilibrium and social not apparent to their author? The mystery remains today.

Did Kenneth Arrow have an influence on my work? Yes. But in a rather unusual way. He never suggested a problem, and seemed extraordinarily interested in topics of which he knew little and on which he had never worked – an unusual trait. His attitude, at the time and even now, was that of an enthusiastic Ph.D. student rather than that of a professor. I do not know how he elicited from me the intellectual production he did. Except that he faithfully and patiently had lunch with me once a week at the Harvard Faculty Club which had then opened its doors to women for the first time; he endured all my bouts of enthusiasm, shared my despair about the referees and editors who rejected my work, and corrected and offered criticisms of my writing. He even proofread my early papers. This behavior, I now know, was somewhat extraordinary. I have been trying to imitate Arrow with my own students, on the grounds that one thanks one's intellectual parents by giving more of the same to others, and it has proven difficult. Those years at Harvard researching with Kenneth Arrow's support were happy and fruitful. Can one ask for more?

I left Harvard for Columbia University just at the time that Arrow returned to Stanford University, where he became Joan Kenney Professor of Economics and Professor of Operations Research in 1978. He retired in 1991.

Despite his urban origins, or perhaps because of them, Arrow always sought suburban life. He lives on the Stanford campus with his wife. They adopted two sons, David and Andrew. Both followed artistic careers,

---

[3] G. Chichilnisky, "Arbitrage, gains from trade, and social diversity: A unified perspective on resource allocation," *American Economic Review* 84, No. 2, May 1994, 427–34.

which Arrow considers more risky than the academic road. Since his retirement in 1991 Arrow has embarked on an ambitious traveling schedule, becoming part of many policy oriented institutions and committees, including the Intergovernmental Panel on Climate Change (IPCC) and the Blue Ribbon Committee created to evaluate the damages done by the Exxon *Valdez* oil spill in Prince Andrew Sound. Both dealt with environmental issues, the former on a global scale.

This book follows another, *Essays in Honor of Kenneth Arrow*, volumes I, II, and III, edited by W. Heller, R. Starr, and D. Starrett (1986), in that it contains the contributions of friends and students of Kenneth Arrow who write in his honor on topics on which he inspired them.

The present book has a somewhat different origin and purpose, however. It emerged from the celebration of Arrow's seventieth birthday at a workshop entitled "Columbia Celebrates Arrow's Contributions" which took place at Columbia University in October 1991. The papers presented at that workshop to a most enthusiastic audience were special. It was a heartwarming event. It was then suggested that the papers, and those of other authors who could not attend, be compiled in a volume in Arrow's honor to memorialize the happy occasion.

Since I have been puzzled by Arrow's recent reluctance to offer pathbreaking ideas, I insisted on a piece from him. His chapter, Information and the Organization of Industry, is based on a lecture, *Lectio Magistralis of the Laurea Honoris Causa*, which he gave when he received an honorary degree from the Universita Catolica of Milano, on April 12, 1994. It is published with the permission of the Universita Catolica. Arrow's paper makes tantalizing assertions which are not proved or developed fully. The paper could lead to seminal developments, but Arrow said he would have preferred it to contain a formalization of its concepts. His view of formalization is that it helps develop a subject. In this he is correct. Formalization lays the foundations on which others can build solid edifices. In any case the future holds the key: His piece belongs to the future.

Arrow's paper is about the economics of information and the organization of industry, a subject which has interested him for many years. Arrow reminds us that information is a rather unusual commodity in that the same piece of information can be used over and over again, by the same or different producers. Once created, information is not scarce in the economic sense, so it is difficult to make information into property. Furthermore, the use of information leads to the most extreme form of economies of scale, the existence of fixed costs. Information therefore challenges the basic concepts on which markets are constructed. Two social innovations, patents and licenses, are designed to create artificial scarcities where none exist naturally. These scarcities are needed to create incentives for undertaking the production of information in the first place. This is because information can be very costly to produce. Arrow's paper walks us through the far reaching implications of the peculiar properties of knowledge for the structure of markets and the stability of the firm. It explains his perception of the shift in today's industrial societies. Information is becoming one of the most valuable "commodities" in the industrial world. Though costly, once produced it should be distributed as widely as possible for efficiency, because it can be shared without diminishment. The informational content in software, an extremely important sector of today's economy, is used to exemplify the issues. Arrow develops this theme, explaining how an information theory of value could be developed, and the impact this could have on the theory of the firm and property rights. His piece is somewhat futuristic: It maps out the main problems the "knowledge intensive" economy is likely to meet as it proliferates.

Kenneth Arrow's chapter and the one that follows, by Vladimir Danilov, Gleb Koshevoy, and Alexandr Sotskov, emphasize the need for a new algebra to understand the economics of information. As already pointed out, information is an unusual good in that it can be used time and again without exhausting itself. The chapter by Danilov, Koshevoy, and Sotskov moves matters forward by defining an algebra that formalizes this characteristic and studies the existence of prices that clear markets with information goods such as software. The three authors define an algebraic structure, a semilattice, to deal with the unusual features of information. In their economy every consumer is a producer. They prove the existence of a market equilibrium and show that it belongs to the core, namely, it is an allocation of information goods from which no coalition of traders would wish to deviate.

These two essays are building blocks for the new economics of information. They are about an issue leading to a major change in the world economy, one which Arrow anticipated in his work many years ago. I called this change the "knowledge revolution," because I believe the most important input to production now is knowledge, rather than capital and labor as in an industrial society, or land, as in an agricultural society. Knowledge can be encoded in books or on electronic equipment but it is mostly held in human brains and is thus often called human capital. Information is not the same as knowledge. Information is the medium in which knowledge is processed, stored, and communicated. Knowledge is the content. And it is the content, aided by radical technological changes in the medium, that is driving change today.

The transition from the industrial to the knowledge society is not even, but it is deep and swift. One may say that we are undergoing a

social and economic revolution which matches the impact of the agricultural and industrial revolutions. I like to call it the *knowledge revolution*.[4] Information technology is the most obvious manifestation of this
change, but the real change is in human knowledge, its creation and distribution, and the corresponding changes in the organization of society.
Knowledge has always been the force driving change in the world
economy. However, by releasing the constraints on the ability to reproduce, store, and communicate knowledge, information technology fuels
knowledge today as never before. Information fuels the engine of economic progress, knowledge. The dynamics in the world economy today
is in computers and software, in telecommunications and biotechnology,
in entertainment and financial markets. It is not, as was previously
thought, a transformation from industrial production to services. It is
a transformation from a resource-intensive to a knowledge-intensive
economy. This revolution can lead to the advent of the knowledge society, a society global in nature, deeply innovative in and dependent on the use of human knowledge and, it can be argued,
conservative in environmental use: a society centered on human capital
where diversity is the foundation of innovation and where knowledge is
power.

The first part of this book is about knowledge, uncertainty and information, and the challenges which they pose to economic theory today.
Uncertainty is lack of information. As Arrow said, "What information
does do is reduce uncertainty." Thus information and uncertainty are two
sides of the same coin.

The problem of uncertainty is part and parcel of the human condition. It originates in the fact that time is a dimension in which we are
short. Humans live only for a few years and cannot travel across time. In
geometrical terms, we are "flat" in the time dimension. Because we
cannot observe well through time, we cannot predict. Due to this lack of
information, we are uncertain.

The short span of a human's life contrasts with the long life of the
human species. Humans fit into their species as cells fit into an organism.
We are important parts of a larger animal and even as the parts die, the
whole survives and grows. The part and the whole share common interests but on occasion they have contrasting goals and needs.

All this creates a fascinating tension often perceived in economic
organizations. It is the tension between decentralization, the pursuit of

---

[4] See also G. Chichilnisky, The Knowledge Revolution, Columbia University Discussion
Paper 1995 and *Journal of International Trade and Economic Development*, 7(4):39–54,
1996.

the individual interest, and centralization, the pursuit of the interests of the whole society. Sometimes they meet and sometimes they pull apart.

One can say that an essential feature of human societies is the tension between the interests of the individual and those of the group. Economics inherits the tension between individual interests and social interests. Centralization and decentralization, markets and planning are examples. Kenneth Arrow's work illustrates this well. Starting from his work on social choice and individual values, he moved swiftly toward the study of that quintessentially decentralized organization, the competitive market. Throughout he kept his eyes firmly on the fundamental issues of uncertainty and information. Both are at the root of the tension between individuals and society.

In this book each author reflects on an aspect of the uncertainty-information axis, which, as I argued above, is simply a representation of the tug-of-war between the individual, whose life is short and whose capacities to predict are limited, and society, which exists in a more atemporal world.

Each writer has a close connection with Kenneth Arrow through life and work, and reflects on the aspects that most deeply touched him or her. Each contributor offers a scientific contribution in the spirit of a first step toward a new theoretical development. Each seeks a better understanding of how the economy works. The essays are not just technical but often profound. It is a pleasure for me as an editor to offer this book in celebration of Kenneth Arrow's contributions.

The first part of the book deals with markets and information, and is followed by the other side of the coin: markets and uncertainty. There are several chapters dealing with "endogenous uncertainty," uncertainty partly caused by nature and lack of information, and partly by human action. Discussed minimally for several years, this interesting subject was introduced formally by Partha Dasgupta and Geoffrey Heal[5] in the context of development paths where present actions alter the environment and thus future productivity, and treated informally by Mordecai Kurz in a comment on the Kester–Stigum model.[6] Optimal growth paths with endogenous uncertainty were first studied by Heal.[7] The first theo-

---

[5] P. Dasgupta and G. Heal, *Economic Theory and Exhaustible Resources*, Cambridge University Press, 1979.

[6] Kurz, The Kesten-Stigum Model and the Treatment of Uncertainty in Equilibrium Theory, in M. Balch, D. McFadden, and S. Wu (eds.), *Essays in Economic Behavior under Uncertainty*, North Holland, 1974.

[7] G. Heal, Economics and Climate: A Framework for Policy Design under Uncertainty, in K. Smith and Ann Dryden (eds.), *Advances in Applied Macroeconomics*, Greenwich: J.A.I. Press, 151–8.

rems on the existence of a general equilibrium in markets with endogenous uncertainty are in Chichilnisky and Wu,[8] Chichilnisky, Dutta, and Heal,[9] and Chichilnisky.[10] Several chapters on the subject are included in this book and are discussed below.

Jacques Drèze's contribution is an insightful discussion of uncertainty, starting from Arrow's 1953 paper to the most recent literature on endogenous uncertainty. Drèze's chapter is useful because it discusses several ways in which the general equilibrium theory of markets has incorporated uncertainty and lack of information. He discusses temporary equilibrium models of markets in which forward markets are not active and expectations about prices are used to make decisions. Drèze includes a short but interesting discussion linking this with the theory of general equilibrium with incomplete markets, in which certain markets are not open.

Frank Hahn's chapter presents a model of a two-period economy where traders take into consideration that there are several possible equilibrium prices in the second period. This contrasts with the "rational expectations" literature in that here expectations about the second period equilibrium prices are a set-valued, as opposed to a single-valued, function. Hahn shows that this leads to rather different behavior. In particular, if rational agents predict correctly the set of possible market clearing prices in the second period, the economy will never reach an equilibrium.

My own chapter takes a step in formalizing Arrow–Debreu markets to include uncertainty about prices. Aware of our uncertainty, we introduce markets for hedging against unfavorable consequences of price changes. I introduce formally and discuss the concept of endogenous uncertainty which is caused by a combination of nature and human actions. Price uncertainty is a typical example of endogenous uncertainty. But how to hedge against the risks that we ourselves cause? Not perfectly. We introduce new markets, markets where the securities hedge against endogenous risks. This is precisely the role of derivative markets, which hedge against the negative consequences of changes in crucial indices. I define a concept of general equilibrium in which the state space and the asset markets are defined as part of the equilibrium. Traders do

[8] G. Chichilnisky and H. M. Wu, Financial Innovation and Endogenous Default in Incomplete Asset Markets, *Stanford Institute for Theoretical Economics Technical Report No. 50*, 1991.

[9] G. Chichilnisky, J. Dutta, and G. Heal, Price Uncertainty and Derivative Securities, Working Paper, Columbia Business School, 1993.

[10] G. Chichilnisky, Markets with Endogenous Uncertainty: Theory and Policy, *Theory and Decision*, 1996, 99–131.

not know the equilibrium prices a priori. An equilibrium consists of a state space, the corresponding asset markets, and prices yielding fully insured and Pareto efficient allocations which clear the markets. The essay proves the existence of a market equilibrium building on recent results in Chichilnisky, Dutta, and Heal (1993).

Following the work of Jacques Drèze, Frank Hahn, and myself, the chapter by Ho-Mou Wu and Peter Huang studies a general equilibrium model of an economy where traders also have uncertainty about prices. Using a somewhat different approach, the authors discuss how investors can hedge against spot price uncertainty by trading in complete markets for European options when they know the equilibrium price correspondence, and when they do not. They discuss in general terms what conditions may be needed to ensure the existence of equilibrium.

Chichilnisky and Heal's chapter deals with markets facing unknown risks and suggests how a new type of instrument can hedge these risks efficiently. The essay is concerned with individual risks whose frequencies are unknown, perhaps because they are relatively new – such as the health effects of a recently discovered environmental hazard. Opinions may be widely different about how the population is affected, and there are no reliable actuarial data. Under these conditions, we study financial instruments that suffice to reach efficient allocations of risk bearing. The problem is formalized in a general equilibrium economy with incomplete markets. Introducing simultaneously an array of mutual insurance policies to cover individual risks and security markets for the correlated part of the risks leads parsimoniously to an efficient allocation. The results – explained less formally in a previous essay by the same authors[11] – suggest the creation of derivative instruments called "catastrophe futures." These instruments came into existence soon after our first article was published, and are now traded in the Chicago Board of Trade. This chapter also anticipates the emergence of another instrument, a hybrid combining insurance and security elements, called "catastrophe bundles," which is now coming to existence. The results anticipated the recent trend for securitization in the insurance and reinsurance industries worldwide.

Turning the coin over, we pass on to the subject of markets with imperfect information. The next chapters deal with this issue. Ned Phelps presents a model of intertemporal equilibrium with unemployment based on the maximization of expected lifetime utility when workers and managers have imperfect, differential information. In this setting, an enterprise is a firm in the sense that it offers continuing employment to every

---

[11] Chichilnisky and Heal, Global Environmental Risks, *Journal of Economic Pespectives*, 1994.

current employee, subject to honest performance and some provisos concerning retirement and downsizing. In this sense Phelps's view of the firm is the same as that in Arrow's chapter. The goal is to discover an equilibrium path of the rate of interest, wage rates, actual time worked, labor force participation – which in this model is equivalent to determining retirement – and unemployment. The main purpose of the chapter is to show how the accumulation of wealth by employed workers leads inevitably to mandatory retirement of the rich alongside the involuntary unemployment of the poor.

Peter Linhart and Roy Radner also deal with information in the firm. A firm can choose among several techniques of production. New technologies are more efficient as their use increases, and as users become more knowledgeable – this is reminiscent of Arrow's learning-by-doing. Which of two techniques should be used, and when? The problem is formulated as follows. A known time-dependent output stream can be produced by either of two technologies. What mixture of these technologies should be used to minimize the discounted present value of the cost of production? Each technology has a unit cost that declines with experience, a form of "knowing by doing." Typically, one technology starts out with "higher" costs, but has a lower cost in the long run than the other, older technology. Linhart and Radner show that there exists an optimal policy that is "extreme," that is, it never uses both technologies simultaneously. If the two cost functions cross at most once, then there exists an optimal policy that switches at most once. Depending on the parameter values, several optimal policies are displayed: The role of a good knowledge of the parameter is crucial.

The next chapters concentrate on the other axis of the same problem: the issue of centralization versus decentralization. Geoffrey Heal makes an interesting contribution on the formation of markets, the quintessential decentralized organization, which he explains as networks. He studies the emergence of markets through the formation of coalition in networks. In his innovative essay Heal addresses the economics of certain value added networks (VANs) that are common in the financial markets, and which are becoming widespread in other sectors. He studies different pricing regimes and their impact on efficient allocations, as well as the nature of competition between vendors of these services. Heal shows that VANs appear to be a classic case of natural monopoly, although this is not dependent on increasing returns on their technologies. The point is that there are strong externalities among users: the VAN is more valuable the more users it has on line. Together with fixed costs this implies that a VAN is only economically viable after a certain critical mass of users is achieved. Standard prescriptions for achieving efficiency in such situations, such as marginal cost pricing and interconnection, are of limited value. This chapter is related to Arrow's work on information and uncertainty, and draws important conclusions about an economic activity that is rapidly expanding in economic importance.

Ross Starr and Maxwell Stinchcombe have a similar network structure. They seek conditions on trade – the structure of transaction costs – which can explain why monetary trade is the preferred way of conducting transactions. In this sense, they justify money by the optimization of transaction costs. Starr and Stinchcombe formalize a view expressed earlier by James Tobin, that sees a standard of transaction – such as money – as a public good. The use of a certain type of money by one individual increases its value to others, leading to increasing returns. This limits the number of moneys in a society, and explains the tendency for one type of money to monopolize the field. The formal structure of their model is that of a network and therefore has close connections with Heal's chapter on markets as networks. They formalize the problem as follows: There are trading posts and direct trades among them lead to more transaction costs than a hub-and-spoke network because of increasing returns to scale. Trade thus goes through a unique "hub" – a unique "money" – to take advantage of the declining average cost of per unit transaction. The monetary commodity is represented by the network hub. Thus they explain the use of money.

Walter Heller's chapter seeks to explain how markets emerge. Kenneth Arrow was one of the first to point out that markets are not a fixture of the economy but the results of decisions made by private economic agents as well as government agencies. Heller points out that markets exist only if there are gains to be made from them. With fixed costs, this introduces an interesting start-up problem, which is alleviated by the increasing returns caused by the fact that markets benefit from having more traders. This introduces a feature also picked up in Heal and in Starr and Stinchcombe: Markets are like networks. They are more useful when they have more traders. Reciprocally, Heller points out that if two markets are complementary, and each of them needs the other to be profitable, the nonexistence of one can prevent the existence of the other. For example, markets for future labor do not exist because of laws prohibiting slavery. Any market requiring the trading of future labor – such as markets on property rights on inventions – will be affected by nonslavery laws. Heller extends available results explaining why markets may not emerge, and thus provides an endogenous explanation of why markets are incomplete. In this sense the chapter is complementary to those on endogenous uncertainty by Hahn and Chichilnisky in this volume, which also explain why markets are incomplete. In both cases there is a common feature: externalities. Each trader produces positive externalities on others which is why market creation, according to Heal, is a network problem. Endogenous uncertainty is also about externalities: Each trader changes the risk profile of society and produces externalities on others.

The three chapters by Heal, Starr and Stinchcombe, and Heller view markets as networks. In addition, Heal and Heller view the emergence of markets as a problem of capturing externalities of the trading activity. The matter can be taken one step further. Concentrate on a special case, competitive markets. One can view the services provided by competitive markets as a "public good," in the sense that the competitive conditions require that these services be available to all equally.[12] Otherwise the market ceases to be competitive. Markets may be privately or publicly produced public goods. Some markets are organized by the state and the subject of government policy and others are organized or "produced" by private traders. Heal and Heller consider the latter case. This confirms the intuition behind Heal and Heller's essays, since public goods offer a simple form of externality among the traders.

Hirofumi Uzawa's chapter also deals with externalities, but in this case the externalities arise from the natural environment or from social infrastructure. He formulates an analytical framework in which the economic implications of intertemporal allocation of social overhead capital are examined together with the conditions for intertemporal allocation of privately owned resources. He focuses on the following question: Is it possible to devise an institutional framework within which the pattern of resource allocation over time, both for privately owned factors of production and for social overhead capital, is optimal from a social point of view? Using standard techniques of optimization theory, he shows that there exist prices that guide the management of both private and social inputs toward the achievement of a social optimum.

Starrett's chapter is also about externalities: in his case, caused by population crowding and the measurement of social costs. Its contribution is on consolidation and applications, including some interesting examples. David Starrett reconsiders the social rate of discount in the context of population crowding. Its main objective is to find an appropriate way to measure the costs of crowding. Considering the earth as a fixed factor, it follows logically that we will observe diminishing returns for adding variable population. Consequently, increasing population is an externality

[12] See, e.g., "The market as a public good", G. Chichilnisky, Program on Information and Resources, Columbia University, Working Paper, 1998.

that can be offset only by another externality, technological change. As long as technological progress is independent of population size, a proposition that seems reasonable in a world of our size where research and development effort is widely duplicated, the presence of the population externality will not depend on technological progress. With or without such progress, output per person will be lower. This externality can be thought of as added congestion on the environmental commons. The externality imposed is equal to the "value" per person of the global commons. Is this a small or a large number? Starrett introduces an equity criterion that can justify imposing a "child tax" on prospective parents. If the costs imposed on future cohorts are undiscounted, there is a positive external cost, and the extra child is justified only if the private benefits outweigh its costs. Starrett provides a systematic discussion and defense of improvement rules based on partial orderings (equity criteria) and explores the implications for social intervention in a range of decision problems where public action is subject to debate.

The chapter by Tito Cordella, Enrico Minelli, and Heracles Polemarchakis raises an interesting problem involving markets and welfare. It provides an example of a standard market in which there may be no transfers across traders which ensures that all individuals are better off when moving from autarky to international trade. The standard belief is that, although international trade may not make everyone better off, it is always possible to redistribute endowments so that it does. The authors look at this classical question from a different point of view and belie this standard belief. They remark that for an equilibrium to exist one needs certain conditions on endowments and preferences to ensure nonzero income. This property is sensitive to the distribution of endowments. The authors remark that a move from autarky to a trade equilibrium may lead to a new set of endowments where this condition fails. Some individuals may end up with nothing that others value. In such a situation there may be no equilibrium. International trade may therefore fail to improve everyone's welfare because, after redistribution, an equilibrium does not exist.

Peter Hammond offers an analysis of market games and welfare economics. The expectation of future income redistribution affects current behavior, and this constrains what can be achieved by the center through redistribution. The main focus of the chapter is to point out some problems in applying the Arrow–Debreu methodology in intertemporal economic models. Hammond asks what happens when markets cannot be prevented from reopening in later periods, and if a benevolent welfare maximizing government cannot commit itself in advance not to make transfers at a later date. It turns out that the Nash equilibria will correspond to Walrasian equilibria that requires noncredible responses by the auctioneer or the redistributive agency and is therefore of a questionable nature.

Finally, Peter Coughlin's chapter belongs to the public choice literature. It studies justice in a government's reallocating role. He has an original angle: the introduction of uncertainty about the choices that voters face. According to Buchanan, redistribution via government in representative democracies fails to be just. Coughlin shows that this assertion is correct under certain assumptions, but false under others. He shows that uncertainty changes matters. If voters are uncertain about their choices, Buchanan's conclusions fail, and representative democracies may lead to just redistribution.

The reader will find all these chapters interesting, and at times challenging. Some are pathbreaking. It is my pleasure to offer this book in honor of the man who inspired them.

CHAPTER 1

Information and the organization of industry

Kenneth J. Arrow

About 15 years ago, my friend, the distinguished sociologist Daniel Bell, suggested to me that I should consider an "information theory of value," to play the role in the modern economy that the "labor theory of value" played in classical economics. I am afraid that I made light of the suggestion. I explained patiently, with the usual attitude of superiority of the economist to other social scientists, that the labor theory of value was supposed to explain relative prices and that information, however defined, could hardly play the same role. Surely goods did not exchange in proportion to their information content. I argued that in fact goods with high information content were likely to be very inexpensive, because information could be reproduced cheaply, even if the initial production was expensive; and every neoclassical economist knew that it was the marginal cost, the cost of reproduction, that is relevant.

There was nothing wrong with the specifics of my reply, but I had missed the essential point of Bell's comment. Facts are beginning to tell against my view. What is startling is that information is almost the exclusive basis for value in computer software and some other goods. These are extreme cases, but the role of information as a source of productivity and as a source of value is increasingly exemplified in many markets and is increasingly an important component of economic analysis. I therefore want to link two concepts, both indeed explored in the literature but neither fully satisfactorily: (1) the role of information as an economic commodity, and (2) the identity of firms as loci of knowledge and claims to wealth.

Delivered as *Lectio magistralis* at the Università Cattolica del Sacro Cuore, Milan, Italy, in 1994.

1   Characteristics of information as an economic commodity

Economic analysis in the last 30 years has been devoted in good measure to the analysis of the strategic implications of differences in information among economic agents. This work has been very important in providing insight into the functioning of many economic institutions which do not fit into the framework of general competitive equilibrium theory, but this is not the aspect of information I want to stress. (Parenthetically, it is my view that the literature in this field relies too heavily on effectively monopolistic or monopsonistic considerations. Many of the surprising outcomes, though by no means all, tend to disappear under competitive conditions.)

There is a basic assumption about the nature of information contained in the economics of asymmetric information which I certainly wish to retain: that information is scarce to the individual, as well as to society as a whole. Asymmetric information arises because one party cannot obtain freely (or at all) information available to another.

Information is indeed then a commodity in some ways like other economic commodities; it is costly and it is valuable. It is surprising then that mainstream economics, of the classical or neoclassical variety from Ricardo through Arrow and Debreu, has made virtually no explicit reference to information. There are exceptions and they are related to increasing returns. Some of Adam Smith's arguments for the superior efficiency obtained by division of labor refer to the acquisition of skills due to practice and Alfred Marshall also alludes to the acquisition and transmission of information as among the causes for a downward-sloping industry supply function.

The reason for this chariness is not hard to find. Competitive equilibrium is viable only if production possibilities are convex sets, that is, do not display increasing returns. This point was first made by A. A. Cournot in 1838. No one read Cournot for many years, but John Stuart Mill gave the same argument ten years later. Marshall reconciled competition with increasing returns, whether due to information or other causes, by introducing the even more striking doctrine of externalities. This is not an adequate solution, but it points in the right direction.

Even though information is an economic commodity, then, it clearly has many properties different from others. Although increasing returns can occur for reasons apart from information, one can at least imagine that, with ordinary goods, constant returns is typical. With information this is impossible. The algebra of information is different from that of ordinary goods. The latter can be added according to the usual rules of arithmetic. Two tons of steel can be used as an input to produce more in a given productive activity or for two separate activities. But repeating a given piece of information adds nothing. On the other hand, the same piece of information can be used over and over again, by the same or different producer(s).

The usual logic of the price system depends on the ordinary algebra of commodities. The buyer can buy more or less at the given price (or close to it if there is some element of monopoly). But information is different. In particular, technical information needed for production is used once and for all. It makes no difference whether one unit or one million units are to be produced; the same amount of information is required. Hence, the use of information leads to the most extreme form of economies of scale, the existence of fixed costs.

There is a possible complication in the analysis which should be mentioned explicitly. The technical information needed to produce goods is not necessarily a fixed message, which one may choose to buy or not buy (in the latter case, there is no production). It is usually true that there is better or worse information and that better information can be obtained at a higher price. "Better" here may mean more reliable information, or it may mean production of the given product at a lower cost, or it may mean production of a product of somewhat higher quality. It can be shown, however, that the ability to choose among various qualities of information does not affect the general proposition that the need for information in production leads to increasing returns.

The peculiar algebra of information has another important implication for the functioning of the economic system. Information, once obtained, can be used by others, even though the original owner has not lost it. Once created, information is not scarce in the economic sense. This fact makes it difficult to make information into property. It is usually much cheaper to reproduce information than to produce it in the first place. In the crudest form, we find piracy of technical information, as in the reproduction of books in violation of copyright. Two social innovations, patents and copyrights, are designed to create artificial scarcities where none exists naturally, although the duration of the property is limited. The scarcities are needed to create incentives for undertaking the production of information in the first place.

These property rights have a very limited power. The acquirer of information may also try to keep it secret, but there are many paths by which knowledge is diffused. One is labor mobility; technical personnel who have worked on research and development in one firm may at some stage want to leave for another. They cannot avoid bringing with them knowledge acquired at the previous firm, although there might be some legal restrictions on their use of that knowledge. Second, the appearance of a product on the market automatically conveys the information that it can be produced. This will certainly stimulate imitation and reverse engineering. When the first fission bomb was developed and used by the United States, there were great fears (in fact, justified) that the Soviet Union would acquire the "secret" of the bomb through espionage. Wiser physicists pointed out, however, that the truly important secret about the bomb was that it was feasible (by no means self-evident, as the experiences of both the German and the Soviet bomb projects showed). It pays to invest more heavily in research and development when it is known that there is some feasible solution. Third, obviously, a great deal of information is spread in the form of written material, disseminated with motives of income from royalties or sheer pride and scientific reputation. Finally, much is learned from others through informal contacts. That is the usual explanation for agglomeration economies in high-technology industries.

As a side comment on the current economic literature, there has been much emphasis in rational expectations equilibrium modeling on inferring information known to others from prices. But one can learn from many other observables, for example, product quality.

To sum up, there is a tension between property incentives to innovate (produce information) and diffusion of innovation. The latter is socially optimal ex post, though not ex ante. As frequently happens in economics, this normative conflict also manifests itself descriptively, as a pressure difficult to resist.

There is one important point: Knowledge inheres to a large extent in individuals, whether the knowledge is directly acquired or acquired from others. Knowledge may also be embodied in other forms, libraries and data bases.

2   The firm in law and economic theory

The firm is a basic concept both in law and in economic theory, yet its exact definition in either realm remains elusive for reasons that reflect a fundamental ambiguity.

Legally, incorporated firms are defined by the legal control and residual claims of stockholders. We will examine below what it is that they have claims to. But even at an elementary level, there are questions in this definition, especially for large limited liability public companies. It has been noted for a long while that management is frequently only weakly responsive to stockholders. In fact, the management is more nearly the essential definition of the firm. Stockholders are investors who trade their holdings with considerable frequency and have no close relation to the firm.

Let me turn to the role of the firm in economic theory: We ordinarily expect formal entities to correspond to underlying economic determinants, as in the case of the household. In economic theory, the firm is thought to be a locus of knowledge, as embodied in a production possibility set.

Where is this knowledge located and in what sense is it characteristic of the firm? Partly, indeed, technical knowledge may be owned by the firm like other property, in the form of written material and a data base. Clearly, however, the knowledge that is most important is largely embodied in individuals, not in mechanically or electronically reproducible form. New workers and even older ones acquire knowledge in the broadest sense in part from others in the firm and in part from sources outside the firm, perhaps general knowledge, perhaps market relations which are by no means always conducted at arm's length (a supplier of capital goods, for example, is a major source of operating information).

A firm then has an *information base*. Typically, it is *distributed*; not everyone in the firm has every piece, and there is some cost to transmission. There is likely to be specialization within the firm to economize on transmission of information. (I am neglecting for the moment the acquisition of new knowledge, for example, innovation or knowledge leading to it. Consideration of acquisition of information new to the firm or to society as a whole would reinforce the picture I am drawing.)

3 Dilemmas in the definition of the firm

In the neoclassical model, workers are not part of the firm. They are inputs purchased on the market, like raw materials or capital goods. Yet they (or some of them) carry the information base, even though not permanently attached to the firm. They are neither owners nor slaves. There is therefore a dilemma in defining the firm as a locus of productive knowledge. What knowledge is peculiar to the firm?

The essential point in resolving this dilemma is that workers in general have durable relations with the firm. Mobility is not zero, but it is not infinitely rapid. Even though some part of the firm's information base may leave with a worker's departure, the *expected* decay (and possibly competitive gain by others) is moderate and can be anticipated. Hence, a firm can treat its information base as an asset, not as well defined as a piece of land but not without content.

This helps to explain the value of a firm. It is a very old observation indeed that the value of a firm as *a going concern* considerably exceeds the value of its physical assets. The information base embedded in workers, managers, and technical personnel is an important part of the market's valuation of the capital of a firm, although not property in the usual sense.

An extreme case is the valuation of computer software firms, some of which are giants comparable to large industrial corporations. Essentially, their physical assets are trivial, and indeed so are their marginal costs of production. Their expenditures are for acquisition of information, but this information is held essentially in the minds of their employees. It has to be asked why the forces of competition do not erode the profits and therefore the value of these firms.

The analysis so far is incomplete. The explanation that embedded information is capital depends on slow mobility of information-rich labor. Clearly we want to explain this lack of mobility, not simply assume it. A possible answer is that old idea of Becker's, *firm-specific human capital*. Its very existence is a serious critique of standard value theory. Why should different firms competing with each other have qualitatively different contents to capital? The concept has itself to be explained. One way of looking at it is that the information base of a firm does not consist only (may not even mainly consist) of recipes for production. Much is simply knowing how to communicate with others in the same firm, knowing how decisions are made.

One might say that each firm has a way of *coding* information, and this code is itself part of the firm's information base. A good classically trained economist will immediately say that since every firm (at least in the same industry) has to choose its code to solve the same communication problem, there should be just one code. In fact, there are many optima, choice among which is neutral. (Also, the code is capital, accumulated over a period of time, so there is path-dependence.) Let me take a parallel. Peoples all over the world have invented many languages to solve the same communication problem, and these languages differ very considerably. A striking example is the differentiation of the Romance languages from their common base in Latin. This process lost an advantage, that of easy international communication.

4   A final reflection: Stability of the firm

Information, one of the fundamental determinants of production, leaps over from one firm to another, yet the firm has so far seemed reasonably sharply defined in terms of legal ownership. It seems to me there must be increasing tensions between legal relations and fundamental economic determinants. Small symptoms are already appearing in the legal and economic spheres. There is continual difficulty in defining intellectual property. The United States courts, at least, have come up with some strange definitions of property. Copyright law has been extended to software, although the analogy with books is hardly compelling. There are emerging problems with the mobility of technical personnel; previous employers are trying to put obstacles in the way of future employment which would in any way use skills and knowledge acquired previously. These are yet minor matters, but I would surmise that we are just beginning to face the contradictions between the systems of private property and of information acquisition and dissemination.

CHAPTER 2

Equilibrium in an economy with information goods

Vladimir I. Danilov, Gleb A. Koshevoy,
and Alexandr I. Sotskov

1   Introduction

Arrow's chapter in this volume, Makarov (1991), and Chichilnisky (1996)
have considered economies in which information plays an important role.
Makarov (1991) suggested an approach for modeling an economy with
intellectual goods (see also Danilov et al. [1994a]). Arrow discusses an
"information theory of value." Here we study the problem from the point
view of value in general equilibrium theory as in Chichilnisky (1996).

Like ordinary economic commodities information goods are costly
and valuable, but there is a crucial difference. Ordinary goods are counted
according to the usual rules of arithmetics. Information goods are different. It makes no difference whether one unit or many units are to be produced or consumed; the same amount of information is presented.
Furthermore, an information good can be used by others (if production
is costless) even though the original owner has not lost it. Once created,
an information good is not scarce in the economic sense: It can be used
over and over again. This means that information goods are added
according to an "idempotent sum" operation, that is, the result of
summing an object with itself is itself. (One can find a similarity to what
Arrow's chapter says about the algebra of information.) If we assume that
this operation is commutative and associative, the set of information
goods with such a sum operation is a semilattice (Gratzer [1978]).

A semilattice is an ordered set; that is, one speaks of the information
good as "better" or "worse." One good is better than another; if the latter
does not add something new to the first one, the sum of these goods
equals the first good.[1]

---

[1] Arrow (1994) said about better or worse information: "Better here may mean more reliable information, or it may mean production of the given product at a lower cost, or it
may mean production of a somewhat higher-quality product."

We assume that the economy has one perfectly divisible good – money. Thus, the space of commodities in the model is the product of a semilattice and real numbers. There are consumers and producers in the economy. Producers create information goods. Having created a good, the producer becomes owner of its copies. Consumers buy copies of information goods. (Consumers are understood in a broad sense to be people purchasing videocassettes, computer games, firms purchasing innovations for their products, and so forth.) We are interested in the general equilibrium of such a model.

Here is an elementary example. Assume there are one information good, one producer, and two consumers. Production cost equals $18. The first consumer wishes to pay no more than $5 for a copy, the second wishes to pay no more than $15. Let $4 be the price for the first consumer and $14 for the second. Each consumer buys a copy and the producer covers his or her production cost: $4 + $14 = $18. This is an equilibrium state.[2] It was assumed here that a consumer can buy a copy only from the producer and cannot resell it. Otherwise, the consumer could reproduce the good freely and sell copies at a still lower price. The producer would thus have no incentive to create goods and there is no equilibrium.[3]

In this chapter we establish the existence of equilibrium with information goods and show it belongs to the core. To simplify the model, we assume that copying is costless and utilities are transferable. A general model was considered in Danilov et al. (1993; 1994b).

2   A model

The set $\mathbb{D}$ describes all information goods. $X, Y, \ldots$ denote elements of $\mathbb{D}$. The goods are added as follows: If we have two information goods, it is natural to assume that there exists an information good in $\mathbb{D}$ which can be called the "sum or join of these goods." What do we know about this summing operation? As noted in the introduction, the sum of any information good with itself is itself. This property is the crucial difference between information goods and ordinary ones. It is natural to assume that the sum is commutative and associative as with ordinary goods. We now have a new summing operation (denote it $\vee$) with the following properties:

1    $X \vee X = X$ for any $X \in \mathbb{D}$ (idempotentness)

---

[2] Notice that equal prices are not equilibrium prices.
[3] Arrow (1994) pointed out: "There is a tension between property incentives to innovate (to produce information) and diffusion of innovation."

2   $X \vee Y = Y \vee X$ for any $X, Y \in \mathbb{D}$ (commutativeness)
3   $(X \vee Y) \vee Z = X \vee (Y \vee Z)$ for any $X, Y, Z \in \mathbb{D}$ (associativeness)

A set $\mathbb{D}$ endowed with such a sum operation becomes a semilattice. Such an operation is said to be a *join*. The set $\mathbb{D}$ is an ordered set, that is, there is a sense in which goods are better or worse. An information good X is said to be better than Y if $X \vee Y = X$, that is, one good is better than another if the latter adds nothing to the first one.

We assume that $\mathbb{D}$ is a finite set. $\mathbb{D}$ is thus indeed a lattice, that is, another operation – *meet* (denotes $X \wedge Y$) is also defined. ($\mathbb{D}$ is a finite semilattice with zero element **0** (the empty information good); it is therefore also a lattice (Gratzer [1978].) This meet operation is defined automatically and we are not especially interested in its interpretation. One can understand information goods as indivisible goods, but understand the sum as the join.

There is also one perfectly divisible good – money. One could assume that the economy of information goods is a part of a larger economy, which includes ordinary goods. In the model we interpret ordinary goods with the aggregated good, which can be called money. Thus, in the model, the commodity space is $\mathbb{D} \times \mathbb{R}$.

There is a set J of firms which produce information goods. Each firm produces one information good. Having created an information good, the firm can produce any number of copies costlessly. This leads to the most extreme form of economies of scale – fixed costs. The jth producer is described by its cost function $a_j : \mathbb{D} \to \mathbb{R} \cup \{\infty\}$. It can create an information good $X \in \mathbb{D}$, having spent at least $a_j(X)$ units of money.

We assume that $a_j(\mathbf{0}) = 0$, $a_j(X) \geq a_j(X')$ if $X \geq X'$ (the cost function is a monotone function with respect to the lattice ordering $X \geq Y$ if $X \vee Y = X$). That is, better goods are more costly to produce; $a_j(X) = \infty$ means that the firm j cannot create the good X. Other assumptions about the cost function are considered later. If it creates good X, the jth firm, $j \in J$, sells copies to consumers.

Let I denote a finite set of consumers (a consumer can be thought of as a group of homogeneous agents). A consumer $i \in I$ is described by utility function $u_i : \mathbb{D} \to \mathbb{R}$ which specifies the utility of information goods. Here, we assume that the value of utility is measured in money units. We also assume that a consumer's purchase is not more than one copy of each information good. Hereafter, the utility functions are assumed to be monotone and normalized by $u_i(\mathbf{0}) = 0$.

A state of economy is a tuple $((X_i)_{i \in I}, (Y_j)_{j \in J})$, where $(X_i)_{i \in I}$ are consumption bundles and $(Y_j)_{j \in J}$ are production outputs; X_i and Y_j belong to $\mathbb{D}$. A state $((X_i)_{i \in I}, (Y_j)_{j \in J})$ is said to be *feasible* if

$$\bigvee_{j \in J} Y_j \geq \bigvee_{i \in I} X_i$$

that is, the supply equals or exceeds the demand. To be realizable, a feasible state has to be economically accessible; we introduce the corresponding concept in the next section, where we define the notion of equilibrium.

3 Concept of the equilibrium

We consider a market in which information goods are produced and their copies distributed. The peculiar algebra of information goods requires an adequate notion of price system. A *price* is a monotone modular function on a lattice, which equals zero in the zero element. A function $p : \mathbb{D} \to \mathbb{R}$ is said to be *modular* if

$$p(X) + p(Y) = p(X \vee Y) + p(X \wedge Y) \qquad \text{for any} \qquad X, Y \in \mathbb{D}$$

According to this definition of prices, we get $p(X) \geq p(Y)$ if $X \geq Y$ and $p(X) + p(Y) \geq p(X \vee Y)$, that is, a better good costs more and the good $X \vee Y$ is cheaper than the pair of goods X and Y ($X \vee Y$ is the sum of X and Y, that is, as an information good it is equivalent to the pair X, Y). Prices of ordinary goods are linear functionals on a Euclidean space. Modular functions are analogs of linear functionals for lattices.

Prices are supposed to be individual for each consumer. For a consumer i, a price is a monotone modular function $p_i : \mathbb{D} \to \mathbb{R}_+$. To purchase a good X, the consumer i should pay the sum of money $p_i(X)$. Denote by p the price for producers. This is the sum of individual prices p_i, that is, the price for producers is a modular function $p = \Sigma_{i \in I} p_i$. If producer j creates an information good X, then he or she expects to sell copies to all consumers and obtain the sum of money $p(X) = \Sigma_{i \in I} p_i(X)$.

Individual prices are similar to those in a Lindahl model with public goods. The cost of producing an information good does not depend on the number of copies. In this sense an information good is like a public good. But there is a difference between information and public goods. Once produced, a public good is available to all. A consumer can obtain a copy of an information good only from the owner. Producers have all the property rights.

All participants are price takers. Given individual prices of information goods $(p_i)_{i \in I}$, the jth producer, $j \in J$, maximizes the profit:

$$\max_{Y \in \mathbb{D}} \left(\sum_i p_i(Y) - a_j(Y) \right) \tag{3.1}$$

Here $p_i(Y)$ is the amount of money the producer expects to receive from the ith consumer and $a_j(Y)$ is the cost of production. Therefore, $\Sigma_i p_i(Y) - a_j(Y)$ is the net return of the jth producer at the given individual prices.

A consumer i wishes to maximize his or her gain, which is, according to the assumption of transferability, of the form

$$\max_{X \in \mathbb{D}} u_i(X) - p_i(X) \tag{3.2}$$

Consumers' budgets are taken into account within their utilities.

A tuple $((X_i)_{i \in I}, (Y_j)_{j \in J}, (p_i)_{i \in I})$ is said to be an *equilibrium* if each Y_j is a solution of $j \in J$ and each X_i is a solution of $i \in I$; the state $((X_i)_{i \in I}, (Y_j)_{j \in J})$ is feasible and the balance with respect to money holds:

$$\sum_{j \in J} a_j(Y_j) \le \sum_{i \in I} p_i(X_i) \tag{3.3}$$

The total sum of money obtained from all consumers is thus enough to cover all producer costs.

4   Equilibrium and the core

Suppose we have an equilibrium. Can a coalition of the participants organize its interaction differently and be better off? We show that this is impossible.

First, we describe feasible allocations. Let K be a coalition of consumers and producers who have decided to produce and consume separately within themselves. An allocation within the coalition is the following: Consumer $i \in K$ obtains a good X_i and spends amount of money τ_i; producer $j \in K$ creates a good Y_j and obtains amount of money σ_j. An allocation is feasible if

i $\bigvee_{j \in K} Y_j \ge \bigvee_{i \in K} X_i$ (balance of information goods)
ii $\Sigma_{j \in K} \sigma_j \le \Sigma_{i \in K} \tau_i$ (balance of money)

Let $(X_i, \tau_i, Y_j, \sigma_j), i \in I, j \in J$, be a feasible allocation of all consumers and producers, $K' = I \cup J$. We say that it is (Pareto) dominated by a coalition K if there exists a feasible allocation $(X_i', \tau_i', Y_j', \sigma_j'), i, j \in K$, such that

$$u_i(X_i') - \tau_i' \ge u_i(X_i) - \tau_i \qquad \text{for each consumer} \qquad i \in K$$

$$\sigma_j' - a_j(Y_j') \ge \sigma_j - a_j(Y_j) \qquad \text{for each producer} \qquad j \in K$$

and at least one inequality is strict. We say that a feasible allocation not dominated by any coalition *belongs to the core*. This is the usual definition, but we take the producers into account. The producer's utility is his or her profit. Obviously, redistribution of profits would not affect the allocation of information goods in an equilibrium because of the property of utility transferability.

Theorem 1: *Any equilibrium allocation* $(X_i, \tau_i, Y_j, \sigma_j)$, $i \in I$, $j \in J$ *(where* $\tau_i = p_i(X_i)$ *and* $\sigma_j = p(Y_j)$*) belongs to the core.*

Proof: Clearly, each equilibrium allocation is feasible. Assume that a coalition K dominates it by an allocation $(X_i', \tau_i, Y_j', \sigma_j')$, $i, j \in K$. Then, for each consumer $i \in K$, we have

$$u_i(X_i') - \tau_i' \geq u_i(X_i) - p_i(X_i)$$

In view of the optimality of the right-hand side, we obtain $\tau_i' \leq p_i(X_i')$ for each $i \in K$. Summing up these inequalities, we have

$$\sum_{i \in K} \tau_i' \leq \sum_{i \in K} p_i(X_i') \tag{4.1}$$

Similarly, $\sigma_j' \geq p(Y_j')$ for each $j \in K$, and hence

$$\sum_{j \in K} \sigma_j' \geq \sum_{j \in K} p(Y_j') \tag{4.2}$$

Let X' be the join of X_i' over all $i \in K$, $X' = \bigvee_{i \in K} X_i'$; we have

$$\sum_{i \in K} p_i(X_i') \leq p(X') \leq \sum_{j \in K} p(Y_j') \tag{4.3}$$

In the last inequality we used (i) and the monotonicity property of nonnegative modular functions. Combining inequalities (4.1), (4.2), and (4.3) and taking into account that at least one of the inequalities (4.1) and (4.2) is strict, we have

$$\sum_{i \in K} \tau_i' < \sum_{j \in K} \sigma_j'$$

contradicting (ii). So the equilibrium allocations are not dominated.   QED.

5   Existence of an equilibrium

To establish the existence of an equilibrium we make certain assumptions about utilities, cost functions, and a lattice of information goods.

General equilibrium theory usually assumes concave utilities and production sets and consumption sets that are separable and convex. A separability and convexity requirement of a consumption set is the following assumption.

> **Assumption 1:**   *The space of information good $\mathbb{D}$ is a finite distributive lattice. A lattice $\mathbb{D}$ is said to be distributive if the following equation holds*
>
> $$\left(X \vee Y \right) \wedge Z = \left(X \wedge Z \right) \vee \left(Y \wedge Z \right) \qquad \forall\, X, Y, Z \in \mathbb{D}$$

Distributive lattices may be thought of as separable spaces in the sense that modular functions separate its elements. It follows from a crucial fact in lattice theory (see Section 6.1) that a finite distributive lattice can be obtained as the set of all minor subsets of some ordered set.[4] Elements of this set can be interpreted as properties of information goods. The set of all minor subsets has a geometric realization with nice properties (see Section 6).

The following example shows that "convexity" assumptions of utility and cost functions are needed for the existence of equilibrium.

> **Example 1:**   *Consider one consumer and one producer with the Boolean lattice $2^{\{l,m\}}$ of information goods, that is, there are three goods l, m, and $\{l, m\}$. The utility function u is defined by $u(\emptyset) = 0$, $u(l) = u(m) = u(\{l, m\}) = 1$. Let the cost function a equal u. We assert that equilibria do not exist here. Let (X, Y, p) be an equilibrium. From Pareto optimality of equilibria one may assume $X = Y$. By definition of equilibrium, the functions $u - p$ and $p - a = p - u$ attain maximum at the point X. This means that $u - p$ is a constant obviously equal to zero and u is a modular function, but this is not the case.*

We consider utility functions of consumers that satisfy the following condition:

> **Assumption 2:**   *The utility functions $u_i : \mathbb{D} \to \mathbb{R}$, $i \in I$, are supermodular nondecreasing functions specified by $u_i(0) = 0$.*

Recall, that a function $u : \mathbb{D} \to \mathbb{R}$ is said to be *supermodular* if $u(X \vee Y) + u(X \wedge Y) \geq u(X) + u(Y)$ for all $X, Y \in \mathbb{D}$. Mathematically, this assumption is akin to the requirement of concavity in utility functions on $\mathbb{D}$ (we explain this in the next section). The supermodularity

---

[4] Sets such that with every element they contain all smaller ones.

requirement of a function on a distributive lattice $\mathbb{D}$ is equivalent to the requirement

$$u\left(X \vee Z\right) - u\left(X\right) \geq u\left(Y \vee Z\right) - u\left(Y\right)$$

for any $X, Y, Z \in \mathbb{D}$, such that $X \geq Y$ and $X \wedge Z = Y \wedge Z$. Such an information good Z is said to be *additional* to a pair $(X \geq Y)$ ($X \wedge Z = \mathbf{0}$ is a particular case of this property). Good Z thus adds equally to X and Y. Economically, it means that each piece of additional information brings more pleasure if it is achieved by adding a better good than a worse one.

We make the following assumptions about cost functions.

Assumption 3: *The cost functions $a_j : \mathbb{D} \to \mathbb{R}_+$ are nondecreasing, $j \in J$, $a_j(\mathbf{0}) = 0$.*

Assumption 4: *The aggregate cost function A of all producers, that is, their convolution $A = *_{j \in J} a_j$, is submodular, that is, $A(X) + A(Y) \geq A(X \vee Y) + A(X \wedge Y)$ for every $X, Y \in \mathbb{D}$.*

Let us recall the definition of convolution of functions on a lattice. The *convolution* of a set of functions $f_t : \mathbb{D} \to \mathbb{R}$, $t \in T$, is a function (denoted $(*_{t \in T} f_t)$) defined by the rule:

$$\left(*_{t \in T} f_t\right)\left(X\right) = \min_{\vee_t X_t = X} \sum_{t \in T} f_t\left(X_t\right) \qquad \text{where} \qquad \left(X_t\right)_{t \in T}, X \in \mathbb{D}$$

A may be thought of as the aggregate cost function. Consider a *technology* as a closed subset $Q \subset \mathbb{D} \times (\mathbb{R} \cup \{\infty\})$. Its elements are pairs $(X, t) \in Q$, where t is an amount of money allowing production of the good X. We assume that all technologies satisfy the free disposal condition:

$$\left(X, t\right) \in Q, X \supset X' \qquad \text{and} \qquad t' > t \Rightarrow \left(X', t'\right) \in Q$$

A technology Q defines the corresponding cost function $f(X) = \min_{(X,t) \in Q} t$, which is monotone. If there are two technologies Q_1 and Q_2, then their sum is defined by the following rule:

$$Q_1 + Q_2 = \left\{(X,t) \middle| t = t_1 + t_2, X = X_1 \vee X_2, \right.$$

$$\text{where} \qquad \left(X_1, t_1\right) \in Q_1, \left(X_2, t_2\right) \in Q_2 \right\}$$

Obviously, the cost function f of the technology $Q_1 + Q_2$ is of the form

$$f\left(X\right) = \min_{X_1 \vee X_2 = X} \left(f_1\left(X_1\right) + f_2\left(X_2\right)\right)$$

where f_1 and f_2 are the cost functions for Q_1 and Q_2, that is, $f = f_1 * f_2$.

Submodularity of the aggregate cost function is due to the convexity of the technology. Economically, it can be explained as follows: The aggregate cost of production of an additional information good decreases as additional goods are produced.

$$A(X \vee Z) - A(X) \leq A(Y \vee Z) - A(Y)$$

for all $X, Y, Z \in \mathbb{D}$, such that Z is additional to the pair $X \geq Y$. This means that the producer of information goods has a "decreasing return to scale" technology.

The following theorem establishes the existence of equilibrium.

Theorem 2: *Let Assumptions 1–4 hold. Then there exists an equilibrium at which all producers have zero profit.*

For proof, see the Appendix (Section 6) and Danilov, Koshevoy, and Sotskov (1994a).

Why do we require convexity of the aggregate technology but not of the individual ones? The answer is: Equilibrium can fail to exist even if all individual technologies are convex. This can be illustrated by the following example.

Example 2: *There are two producers and one consumer; the set of information goods is the Boolean lattice $2^{\{1,2,3\}}$. The cost function a_1 is specified as follows:*

$$a_1(\emptyset) = 0, a_1(\{1\}) = a_1(\{2\}) = a_1(\{3\}) = a_1(\{1, 3\}) = 1$$

$$a_1(\{1,2\}) = a_1(\{2, 3\}) = a_1(\{1, 2, 3\}) = 2$$

The cost function a_2 is defined by equalities

$$a_2(\emptyset) = 0, a_2(\{1\}) = a_2(\{2\}) = a_2(\{3\}) = a_2(\{1, 2\}) = 1$$

$$a_2(\{1, 3\}) = a_2(\{2, 3\}) = a_2(\{1, 2, 3\}) = 2$$

The utility function u is defined to satisfy:

$$u(\emptyset) = u(\{2\}) = (\{3\}) = 0, u(\{2, 3\}) = 1$$

$$u(\{1\}) = u(\{1, 2\}) = u(\{1, 3\}) = 2, u(\{1, 2, 3\}) = 3$$

One can check that u is a supermodular function and a_1, a_2 are submodular functions. The values of the convolution $A = a_1 * a_2$ are

$$A(\emptyset) = 0,\; A(\{1\}) = A(\{2\}) = A(\{3\}) = A(\{1,2\}) = A(\{1,3\}) = 1$$

and

$$A(\{2,3\}) = A(\{1,2,3\}) = 2$$

The function A is not submodular. Let us check that equilibrium fails to exist. Suppose that (X, Y, p) is an equilibrium. By Pareto optimality of equilibria, one can assume that $X = Y$. Then, as mentioned above, the function $u - A$ attains maximum at the point X. The function $u - A$ equals 1 at the points $\{1\}, \{1, 2\}, \{1, 3\}, \{1, 2, 3\}$ and is nonpositive at all other points. So the point X has the form $\{1, \ldots\}$. At this point the function $u - p$ attains a maximum and the function $A - p$ attains a minimum. But on the set of points of the form $\{1, \ldots\}$, the function u equals $A + 1$. The function $u - p$ is therefore a constant on this set and hence u is modular on it. But this is not the case. In this example the convolution $A = a_1 * a_2$ of two submodular functions a_1 and a_2 is not submodular.

6   Appendix

The proof of Theorem 2 is in Danilov et al. (1994a). Its plan is as follows. First, we show that distributive lattices have a geometrical realization with a "nice" triangulation. Supermodular functions on a distributive lattice can be extended to concave functions which are affine on simplexes of the triangulation. Second, we aggregate the model, that is, consider one aggregate consumer with utility function $U = \Sigma_i u_i$ and one aggregate producer with aggregate cost function $A = *_j a_j$. The function $U - A$ is supermodular, therefore its convexification reaches maximum at a point on the lattice. After finding the maximum, we find supporting "subgradients" of the functions $u_i, i \in I$, and $- A$. These subgradients are prices at which agents choose optimal plans.

6.1   Distributive lattices and ordered sets

A lattice $\mathbb{L}$ is a set endowed with two operations: *the meet* $u \vee v \in \mathbb{L}$ (u, $v \in \mathbb{L}$) and *the join* $u \vee v \in \mathbb{L}$ ($u, v \in \mathbb{L}$) which are idempotent: $u \wedge u = u$ ($u \vee u = u$); commutative: $u \wedge v = v \wedge u$ ($u \vee v = v \vee u$); and associative: $(u \wedge v) \wedge w = u \wedge (v \wedge w)$ $((u \vee v) \vee w = u \vee (v \vee w))$. A lattice $\mathbb{L}$ is said to be *distributive* if the following equation holds

$$(u \vee v) \wedge w = (u \wedge w) \vee (v \wedge w), \qquad \forall u, v, w \in \mathbb{L}$$

In such a case the dual equation is also fulfilled (see, for example, G. Gratzer [1978]). One can characterize completely the structure of any finite distributive lattice. Ordered sets play a central role here. An *ordered set* is a set equipped with an *order* $\leq$, that is, a reflexive, transitive, antisymmetric binary relation. Let $(A, \leq^A)$ and $(B, \leq^B)$ be ordered sets; $f: A \to B$ be a function. f is said to be *monotonic* (or a *morphism*) if $a \leq^A a'$ implies $f(a) \leq^B f(a')$. The set of all morphisms A in B is denoted by $\mathrm{Mon}(A, B)$.

The set $\mathrm{Mon}(A, B)$ becomes an ordered set if we set the order $f \leq g$ by the rule: $f(a) \leq^B g(a)$ for all $a \in A$. If B is a lattice, then the set $\mathrm{Mon}(A, B)$ is a lattice. If B is a distributive lattice, then $\mathrm{Mon}(A, B)$ is a distributive lattice too. In particular, the set $\mathrm{Mon}(A, \{0, 1\})$ of all monotone functions of an ordered set A in the lattice $\{0, 1\}$ ($0 \wedge 1 = 0, 0 \vee 1 = 1$) is a distributive lattice. It is convenient to consider the set of nonincreasing maps from A to $\{0, 1\}$, that is, the set of functions such that $a \leq a'$ implies $f(a) \geq f(a')$. Let $\mathcal{D}(A)$ be the set of such functions. It is a distributive lattice (finite, if A is finite). A crucial factor of lattice theory is the structure of any finite distributive lattice. To explain this we show how to construct an ordered set (base) for $\mathbb{L}$.

The base of a lattice consists of join irreducible elements. A nonzero element $e \in \mathbb{L}$ is said to be *join irreducible* if a relation $e = a \vee b$ implies either $a = e$ or $b = e$. Denote as $\mathcal{P}(\mathbb{L})$ the set of all join irreducible elements in $\mathbb{L}$; $\mathcal{P}(\mathbb{L})$ is said to be the *base* of $\mathbb{L}$. This set is naturally endowed with the lattice order. Therefore it is an ordered set. For each $a \in \mathbb{L}$, define the *base* of a as the set $B(a) = \{e \in \mathcal{P}(\mathbb{L}), e \leq a\}$. It is easy to check the following (see, for example, Gratzer [1978])

1   $a = \sup\{e \mid e \in B(a)\}$ for all $a \in \mathbb{L}$.
2   $B(a \wedge b) = B(a) \wedge B(b)$ and $B(a \vee b) = B(a) \vee B(b)$.

Therefore, the map B embeds the lattice $\mathbb{L}$ in the lattice of subsets of $\mathcal{P}(\mathbb{L})$. It is easy to describe the image $B(\mathbb{L})$. It is evident that sets like $B(a)$ are minor subsets in $\mathcal{P}(\mathbb{L})$, that is, with any element, they contain all the smaller ones. Taking into account 2, we have

3   Any minor set M in $\mathcal{P}(\mathbb{L})$ has the form $B(a)$ where $a = \sup M$.

Thus, any finite distributive lattice $\mathbb{L}$ is isomorphic to a lattice $\mathrm{Min}(\mathcal{P}(\mathbb{L}))$ of minor subsets of an ordered set $\mathcal{P}(\mathbb{L})$. We thus receive the canonic embedding $\mathbf{i}: \mathbb{D} \to 2^{\mathcal{P}(\mathcal{D})}$ of a distributive lattice $\mathcal{D}$ into the Boolean one.

Finally, consider the characteristic function of each *minor* subset. We can state

Any finite distributive lattice $\mathbb{L}$ is isomorphic to a lattice $\mathcal{D}(\mathcal{P}(\mathbb{L}))$.

This shows that a (finite) distributive lattice is equivalent to a (finite) ordered set. Moreover, we can say that the *category* of (finite) distributive lattices is antiequivalent to the category of (finite) ordered sets.

6.2 Geometrical realization of distributive lattices

Consider the set of all nonincreasing maps of an ordered set A in the segment $[0, 1]$. The set of all such functions is denoted $C(A)$. $C(A)$ is a convex subset in the Euclidean space $\mathbb{R}^A$. Moreover, $C(A)$ is a convex polyhedron and $\mathcal{D}(A)$ is naturally embedded in $C(A)$.

> **Lemma 1:** *The set $\mathcal{D}(A)$ is identified with the set of vertices of the polyhedron $C(A)$.*
>
> *Proof:* It is evident that $\mathcal{D}(A)$ is a subset of the extreme elements $C(A)$. Check the converse: If a monotone function $\phi : A \to [0, 1]$ is an extreme element of the convex set $C(A)$, then its values are in $\{0, 1\}$. Suppose ϕ has a value $\alpha \in (0, 1)$. Let $X = \phi^{-1}(\alpha)$. Consider functions ϕ^+ and ϕ^- given by the formula $(\varepsilon > 0)$:
>
> $$\phi \pm \left(x\right) = \phi\left(x\right) + \varepsilon, if\ x \in X$$
>
> $$\text{otherwise} \quad \phi \pm \left(x\right) = \phi\left(x\right)$$
>
> If ε is small, then functions $\phi^\pm$ would be monotone functions and are elements of $C(A)$. But if $\phi = \frac{1}{2}\phi^+ + \frac{1}{2}\phi^-$, that is contradictory and ϕ cannot be an extreme element. QED.

The set $|\mathbb{D}| := C(\mathcal{P}(\mathbb{D}))$ is said to be the *geometric realization of a distributive lattice* $\mathbb{D}$. For example, for a trivial ordered set A, $C(A)$ is the unit cube $[0, 1]^A$. (Therefore, the canonic embedding $i : \mathbb{D} \to 2^{\mathcal{P}(\mathbb{D})}$ corresponds to the inclusion $|\mathbb{D}| \subset [0, 1]^{\mathcal{P}(\mathbb{D})}$.) $C(A)$ of a completely ordered set A is the simplex in the unit cube $[0, 1]^A$.

6.3 The natural triangulation of C(A)

Here we stress an important property of the geometric realization of a distributive lattice: for any A, there exists *natural triangulation* $\Sigma(A)$ of $C(A)$. This means that $C(A)$ is a union of simplexes that are correctly joined together.

The set of vertices of the triangulation $C(A)$ is $\mathcal{D}(A)$. A simplex of the triangulation is defined by a *chain* in $\mathcal{D}(A)$. A *chain* is a tuple $x_1 < x_2 <$

$\ldots < x_n$ ($n \le |A| + 1$) of elements in $\mathcal{D}(A)$. Elements of a chain are linearly independent. Therefore $\text{co}(x_1, x_2, \ldots, x_n)$ is a simplex in $C(A)$. (A chain of maximal length $|A| + 1$ defines a simplex of maximal dimension.) An element $f \in \text{co}(x_1, x_2, \ldots, x_n)$ has the following form. Let x_i be the characteristic function of a minor set $X_i \subset A$ (recall that $x_i : A \to \{0, 1\}$), $i = 1, \ldots, n$. Then f looks like a staircase: f has the maximum value at X_1, next downward on $X_2 \backslash X_1$, then downward on $X_3 \backslash X_2$, and so on. If f belongs to the simplex interior, then it always jumps at each step. Consider the set $\text{Ch}(A)$ of all chains in $\mathcal{D}(A)$ and consider the union of all simplexes which are defined by these chains. The union of these simplexes is the set $C(A)$. Check that any element in $C(A)$ belongs to the interior of a unique simplex of the triangulation. Consider an element $f \in C(A)$. Then the set of values of f defines a simplex in the union. Reorder values of f in an increasing manner: $\alpha_1 > \alpha_2 > \ldots > \alpha_n$. Set $X_i = \{a \in A : f(a) \ge \alpha_i\}$ and let x_i be its characteristic function. This set of characteristic functions x_i defines the chain, that is, the simplex in triangulation. The union of such simplexes over the set $\text{Ch}(A)$ of all chains in $\mathcal{D}(A)$ realizes the natural triangulation $\Sigma(A)$. The triangulated space $C(A)$ is an example of the more general construction of the geometrical realization of simplicial sets (Gabriel and Zisman [1967]).

6.4   Functions on distributive lattices

Let $\mathbb{D}$ be a distributive lattice, $f : \mathbb{D} \to \mathbb{R}$ be a function, $x \in |\mathbb{D}|$, and let σ be the minimal simplex which contains x; let $x = \Sigma_s \alpha_s Y_s$, $\Sigma_s \alpha_s = 1$; $\{Y_s\}$ is the set of vertices of σ. Set

$$\hat{f}(x) = \sum_s \alpha_s f(Y_s) \tag{6.1}$$

The important property of submodular and supermodular functions is the following:

Lemma 2:   *Let $\mathbb{D}$ be a distributive lattice. Then*

    a   *A function f on $\mathbb{D}$ is submodular iff $\hat{f}(x)$ is a convex function on $|\mathbb{D}|$.*

    b   *A function f on $\mathbb{D}$ is supermodular iff $\hat{f}(x)$ is a concave function on $|\mathbb{D}|$.*

For proof of this lemma see Danilov et al. (1993) or Lovász (1983).

The following extension operation is also important in the proof of Theorem 2. Let $\mathbf{g} : \mathbb{D} \to \mathbb{L}$ be a homomorphism of lattices, that is, $\mathbf{g}(X \vee Y) = \mathbf{g}(X) \vee \mathbf{g}(Y)$ and $\mathbf{g}(X \wedge Y) = \mathbf{g}(X) \wedge \mathbf{g}(Y)$. We assume that $\mathbf{g}(\mathbf{0})$

$= \mathbf{0}$ and $\mathbf{g(1)} = \mathbf{1}$. Let $h:\mathbb{D} \to \mathbb{R}$ be a function. Define the following two functions h_g and h^g on the lattice $\mathbb{L}$.

$$h_g(l) := h(X_l) \quad \text{where} \quad X_l = \bigwedge_{\{X \in \mathbb{D}: g(X) \geq l\}} X, X_l \in \mathbb{D} \quad (6.2)$$

$$h^g(l) := h(X^l) \quad \text{where} \quad X^l = \bigvee_{\{X \in \mathbb{D}: g(X) \leq l\}} X, X_l \in \mathbb{D} \quad (6.3)$$

Sets $\{X \in \mathbb{D}: g(X) \leq l\}$ and $\{X \in \mathbb{D}: g(X) \geq l\}$ are nonempty sets since $\mathbf{g(0)} = \mathbf{0}$ and $\mathbf{g(1)} = \mathbf{1}$. Therefore, functions h_g and h^g are correctly defined.

Lemma 3: *Let* $g:\mathbb{D} \to \mathbb{L}$ *be a homomorphism of distributive lattices. Let* $u:\mathbb{D} \to \mathbb{R}$ *and* $v:\mathbb{D} \to \mathbb{R}$ *be nondecreasing supermodular and submodular functions correspondingly. Then* $u^g:\mathbb{L} \to \mathbb{R}$ *and* $v_g:\mathbb{L} \to \mathbb{R}$ *are nondecreasing supermodular and submodular functions correspondingly.*

Proof: Check the following properties of elements X_l and X^l.

$$X_l \vee X_m = X_{l \vee m} \quad X_l \wedge X_m \geq X_{l \wedge m} \ \forall l, m \in \mathbb{L}$$

$$(6.4)$$

$$X^l \vee X^m \leq X^{l \vee m} \quad X^l \wedge X^m \geq X^{l \wedge m} \ \forall l, m \in \mathbb{L}$$

$$(6.5)$$

In fact, $X_l \wedge X_{l \vee m} = X_l$, because $g(X_{l \vee m}) \geq l \vee m \geq l$. Therefore, $X_{l \vee m} \geq X_l \vee X_m$. But, $g(X_l \vee X_m) = g(X_l) \vee g(X_m) \geq l \wedge m$. That yields $X_l \vee X_m = X_{l \vee m}$. $X_l \geq X_{l \wedge m}$ and $X_m \geq X_{l \vee m}$ ensure $X_l \vee X_m \geq X_{l \wedge m}$.

Equation (6.5) can be similarly established. According to (6.5), for any nondecreasing supermodular function $u:\mathbb{D} \to \mathbb{R}$ we get

$$u^g(l) + u^g(m) = u(X^l) + u(X^m) \leq u(X^l \vee X^m)$$
$$+ u(X^l \wedge X^m) \leq u(X^{l \vee m}) + u(X^{l \wedge m})$$
$$= u^g(l \vee m) + u^g(l \wedge m)$$

Analogously, using (6.4) we get the statement for submodular functions. QED.

The following lemma shows that if the convolution of a set of functions is a submodular function, then the value of the convolution is achieved at a disjoint union.

Lemma 4: *Let $\{f_t\}_{t \in T}$ be strictly monotone functions ($f_t(\mathbf{0}) = 0$) on a distributive lattice $\mathbb{D}$, $F = (*_{t \in T} f_t)$ be their convolution, $X \in \mathbb{D}$ and $X = \bigvee_{t \in T} X_t$ be the optimal realization of X, that is, $F(X) = \Sigma_{t \in T} f_t(X_t)$. If $F = (*_{t \in T} f_t)$ is a submodular function on $\mathbb{D}$, then $X_t \wedge X_{t'} = \mathbf{0}, \forall t \neq t'$ (that is, $X = \amalg_t X_t$ is a partition).*

Proof: Proceed by induction. Let $|T| = 2, f_1$, and f_2 be functions such that their convolution $f_1 * f_2$ is a submodular function. Suppose there exists an element $X \in \mathbb{D}$ such that $X = X_1 \vee X_2$ is an optimal partition, that is, $(f_1 * f_2)(X) = f_1(X_1) + f_2(X_2)$, but $X_1 \wedge X_2 \neq \mathbf{0}$. Then, according to the definition of convolution, $(f_2)(X_1) \leq f_1(X_1), (f_1 * f_2)(X_2) \leq f_2(X_2)$ and $(f_1 * f_2)(X_1 \wedge X_2) > 0$. The following sequence of inequalities holds:

$$\left(f_1 * f_2\right)\left(X\right) + \left(f_1 * f_2\right)\left(X_1 \wedge X_2\right) > f_1\left(X_1\right) + f_2\left(X_2\right)$$
$$\geq \left(f_1 * f_2\right)\left(X_1\right) + \left(f_1 * f_2\right)\left(X_2\right)$$

which contradicts the submodularity. Therefore $X_1 \wedge X_2 = \mathbf{0}$. The convolution $*_{t \in T} f_t$ of a set of functions can be considered as the convolution of two functions, f_s and $*_{t \in T \setminus \{s\}} f_t$ for each $s \in T$. Therefore, according to the proof for $|T| = 2$, for any optimal partition $X = \bigvee_t X_t$ and any $s \in T$ we have $X_s \wedge (\bigvee_{t \in T \setminus \{s\}} X_t) = \mathbf{0}$. Thus, according to distributiveness, $X_t \wedge X_{t'} = \mathbf{0} \ \forall t \neq t'$.

QED.

Finally, consider modular functions. We want to stress the similarity of modularity on distributive lattices to linearity on Euclidean spaces. Any linear function on Euclidean space is defined by its values in vertices of a full dimension simplex. Similarly, any modular function on a distributive lattice is defined by its values on vertices of any simplex of maximal dimension in the natural triangulation Σ.

6.5   Proof of Theorem 2

Denote $D := \mathcal{P}(\mathbb{D})$. Consider a function W of the form

$$W = \left(\sum_i (u_i)^i\right) - A_i$$

where $\mathbf{i} : \mathbb{D} \to 2^D$ is the canonic embedding. It is a homomorphism, therefore A_i and $(u_i)^i$ are functions defined by equations (6.2) and (6.3) correspondingly.

According to Lemma 3, W is the supermodular function on the

Boolean lattice 2^D. Consider its continuation $\hat{W}$, according to (6.1), on the unit cube $C = [0, 1]^D$. According to Lemma 2, there exists a point $X \in \{0, 1\}^D$ at which $\hat{W}$ reaches maximum. Let us demonstrate that we can choose $X \in \mathcal{D}(\mathbb{D})$. In the case of canonic embedding, according to (6.2) and (6.3), there are $Y_1 \geq Y_2 \in \mathbb{D}$ such that $(u_i)^1(X) = u_i(Y_2)$, $i \in I$, and $A_i(X) = A(Y_1)$. Therefore,

$$\sum_i u_i(Y_2) - A(Y_2) = W(Y_2) \geq W(X) = \sum_i u_i(Y_2) - A(Y_1)$$

that is, Y_2 belongs to Argmax $\hat{W}$. Therefore we can find $X \in \mathbb{D}$. There exist corresponding subgradients x_i^*, x_A^* and a functional x_C^* such that

$$\sum_i x_i^* + x_C^* = x_A^* \tag{6.6}$$

We have

$$x_A^* \geq 0, \; x_A^*(X) = A(X) \qquad \text{and}$$

$$x_A^*(X') \leq A(X') \qquad \text{for any} \qquad X' \in \mathbb{D} \tag{6.7}$$

$$x_i^* \geq 0, \; x_i^*(X) = u_i(X) \qquad \text{and}$$

$$x_i^*(X') \geq u_i(X') \qquad \text{for any} \qquad X' \in \mathbb{D} \tag{6.8}$$

$$x_C^* = \left(\lambda_1, \ldots, \lambda_{|D|}\right) \qquad \text{where} \qquad \lambda_t \geq 0, \qquad \text{if} \qquad (X)_t = 0$$

$$\text{and} \qquad \lambda_t \leq 0 \qquad \text{if} \qquad (X)_t \in 1$$

$$\tag{6.9}$$

Set $p_{it} = x_{it}^* + \delta_{it}$, where $\delta_{it} = x_{Ct}^* \cdot x_{it}^* / \Sigma_i x_{it}^*$, $t = 1, \ldots, |D|$ (if $\Sigma_i x_{it}^* = 0$ we set $p_{it} = x_{Ct}^*/L$); $p = \mathrm{x}_A^*$. It follows from (6.6–6.8) that $p_i \geq 0$ and $\Sigma_{i \in I} p_i = p$. From (15) it follows that δ_i separates C and X. Hence, we have:

$$\delta_i(X) \leq \delta(X') \qquad \text{for any} \qquad X' \in C, i \in I$$

In addition, property (6.8) implies that

$$u_i(X') - x_i^*(X') \leq u_i(X) - x_i^*(X)$$

Summing up these inequalities, we find that p_i supports X for the ith consumer.

It remains only to show that the price p is the supporting price for each producer. Let $X = \amalg_j Y_j$ be an optimal partition of X among the producers. According to Lemma 4, this partition exists (if a_j are not strictly monotone functions, deal with their small variations by adding a small positive modular function and take the limit). So $A(X) = \Sigma_j a_j(Y_j)$. For any j and all $Z \in \mathbb{D}$, we have $p(Z) - a_j(Z) \leq 0$, because otherwise $p(Z) - A(Z) > 0$, which contradicts (6.7). On the other hand, we have $p(Y_j) - a_j(Y_j) = 0$ for all j because the whole sum is equal to 0. So, for any $j \in J$,

$$0 = p(Y_j) - a_j(Y) \geq p(Z) - a_j(Z) \qquad \text{for any} \qquad Z \in \mathbb{D}$$

Finally, since the sets Y_j are disjoint, we have:

$$\sum_{j \in J} p(Y_j) = p(X) = \sum_{i \in I} p_i(X)$$

The budget equation is satisfied. Thus, $((X_i = X)_{i \in I}, (Y_j)_{j \in J}, (p_i)_{i \in I})$ is an equilibrium. The proof is complete.

References

Arrow, K. J. 1994. Information and the organization of industry, this volume.
Chichilnisky, G. 1996. Markets with knowledge, Program on Information and Resources, Columbia University. Invited adress to the National Academy of Sciences Forum on Biodiversiy, Nature, and Human Society, October 27–30, 1997.
Danilov, V. I., G. A. Koshevoy, and A. I. Sotskov. 1993. Equilibrium in an economy with intellectual goods (in Russian). *Economika i Mathematicheskiei Metody*, 29:607–16.
Danilov, V. I., G. A. Koshevoy, and A. I. Sotskov. 1994a. Equilibrium in a market of intellectual goods. *Mathematical Social Sciences*, 27:133–44.
Danilov, V. I., G. A. Koshevoy, and A. I. Sotskov. 1994b. Equilibrium analysis of economies with innovations. Mimeo.
Gabriel, P., and M. Zisman. 1967. *Calculus of fractions and homotopy theory*. Berlin and New York: Springer-Verlag.
Gratzer, G. 1978. *General Lattice Theory*. Berlin and New York: Springer-Verlag.
Lovász, L. 1983. Submodular functions and convexity. In *Mathematical Programming: The State of the Art*, ed. A. Bachem, M. Gretschel, and B. Korte. Berlin and New York: Springer-Verlag, pp. 235–57.
Makarov, V. L. 1991. About economies of intellectual goods and its modeling, Report at Sixth Congress of the European Economic Association, Cambridge, UK.

Uncertainty and finance

CHAPTER 3

The formulation of uncertainty:
Prices and states

Jacques H. Drèze

1 The states revolution of 1952

The seven-page paper by Kenneth Arrow (1953) "Rôles des valeurs boursières pour la répartition la meilleure des risques"[1] has changed the formulation of uncertainty in economic theory, and has led to significant advances in our understanding of resource allocation under uncertainty. Earlier discussions, including, for instance, those of Hicks (1931), Marschak (1938), or Tintner (1941), introduced as primitives *probability distributions* for some characteristics of the environment (technology, resource, tastes, etc.), and *also for some economic variables* (prices, incomes, production rates, etc.). The revolution initiated by Arrow consisted in exploiting fully the clarification permitted by the concept of "states of the environment."

In the theory of resource allocation under certainty, we start from a given environment: commodities, with associated initial resources; consumers, with associated consumption sets, preferences, and property rights; producers, with associated production sets. Arrow had a genial perception. (I guess he was inspired by his familiarity with statistical decision theory – providing a notable instance of transfer of concepts across disciplines.) Uncertainty means that the environment is not given; instead, there exists a set of alternative, mutually exclusive "states of the environment," one and only one of which will materialize. The results obtained for a given environment apply to an uncertain environment, if a commodity is defined not only by its physical properties (including the time and place at which it is available), but also by an event (set of states) conditional on which it is available. Commodities thus become "contin-

---

[1] Paper presented at the Conference "Fondements et Applications de la Théorie du Risque en Économétrie," organized by Maurice Allais in Paris, May 12–17, 1952.

gent claims." Initial resources, preferences, and technologies are defined in the enlarged commodity space.

The fact that the new formulation permitted in one stroke the extension to uncertainty of the theory of resource allocation under certainty was to prove extremely helpful, as we now realize.[2] The new approach frees the formulation from explicit reliance on probabilities as primitive data; the existence of (subjective) probabilities on the states will eventually (but not necessarily) follow from suitable assumptions about preferences.[3] The new approach also separates neatly exogenous uncertainties (the states) from economic parameters or decisions (prices, incomes, production plans, etc.).

Arrow's paper did not contain a discussion of the concept of "state." The use made of it, however, brings out implicitly two essential attributes. Because *traded* commodities are state-contingent claims, the states must be defined with *interpersonal objectivity* (so agents will agree whether a given state has occurred or not); and the states must reflect *exogenous uncertainties*, not influenced by the agents themselves (to avoid moral hazard problems).[4]

Arrow later explained that a state is "a description of the world so complete that, if true and known, the consequences of every action would be known" (1971, p. 20); in particular, "it would completely define all endowments and production possibilities" (Arrow and Hahn, 1971, p. 122).

Some of us have wondered whether, under that interpretation, the *prices* prevailing at a given date-event should be included in the definition of the event. Kurz (1974, p. 398) concluded from his extensive discussion of price uncertainties "that we should extend the notion of the state of the world to include future prices." When I brought up the question casually with Kenneth Arrow many years ago, he responded that he too had wondered. Taking advantage of the opportunity offered by this special volume, I wish to reappraise the question in light of new work by Chichilnisky (1992) and Chichilnisky, Dutta, and Heal (1991) which is discussed in the Appendix. Forty years of research within the new formulation point to some definite conclusions worth collecting. Trust readers will forgive me for treading over familiar ground. My reappraisal

---

[2] The significance of that fact was apparently not fully appreciated at once. The proceedings of the conference reveal extensive discussion of most papers – but a single comment (by Allais himself) on Arrow's paper!

[3] Savage's theory of personal probability (1953, 1954) was presented for the first time at the same session as Arrow's paper, in Paris, May 1952.

[4] These two attributes are also essential to Savage's theory of individual decision.

inevitably bears on the comparison between the theories of temporary equilibrium and of general equilibrium with incomplete markets. There, too, some definite conclusions seem to emerge.

2 Economizing on markets

An important aspect of Arrow's paper was to show that, in an economy with S possible states and C physical commodities, the SC markets for contingent claims to commodities (to "real insurance contracts") could be replaced by S markets for contingent claims to a numeraire, plus C spot markets for commodities once the true state is known. *If the spot prices associated with every state were known to the agents*, then operating S elementary insurance markets would suffice for risk-sharing purposes.

Arrow (1953) comments as follows on that proposition (his theorem 2): "Socially, the significance of the theorem is that it permits economising on markets; only $S + C$ markets are needed to achieve the optimal allocation, instead of the SC markets implied in Theorem 1." (Theorem 1 asserts the efficiency of an allocation sustained by competitive prices for the SC contingent claims to commodities.)

That comment fails to mention explicitly the requirement that spot prices of commodities, conditionally on any event, should be *known to all agents*. The economizing on markets is genuine if, and *only if*, these conditional spot prices are known. But how would they be known, in the absence of markets?

Two answers to that question have been offered. In Chapter 7 of Debreu's *Theory of Value* (1959), all markets are clearly simultaneous – either as markets for contingent claims to commodities, or as a mixture of markets for contingent claims to a numeraire and conditional markets for commodities given any state. There is thus no "economizing on markets." In the work of Radner (1968; 1972), the simultaneous clearing of all *conditional* markets is replaced by an assumption of *single-valued common rational expectations* about conditional prices.[5]

In both cases, it is assumed that, once the state is observed, spot markets *will effectively clear* at the relative prices given by the contingent prices or by the common expectations. In Debreu's case, these transactions simply consist in carrying out contingent contracts. In Radner's case, they are genuine spot transactions.

---

[5] Other authors, like Magill and Shafer, reserve the term "rational expectations" to the case where all agents assign identical probabilities to all events, referring otherwise to "perfect foresight."

·

3   Observability of states

Whether one assumes that spot prices given a state are determined ex ante through contingent or conditional trading, or that all agents hold ex ante single-valued common rational expectations about the prices that will clear spot markets ex post, *the definition of the states or events must be comprehensive enough that market-clearing spot prices are well defined.* Yet, the states must be defined with interpersonal objectivity, and they must be exogenous. These requirements cannot be realistically reconciled, because some of the determinants of market-clearing prices do not have the required properties of observability and/or exogeneity.

Numerous authors have noted the difficulties associated with uncertainty about *tastes* (individual preferences) – so many that I refrain from any references for fear of missing seminal ones. An individual i who has just signed up for flying lessons does not know yet whether he will enjoy the experience to the point of acquiring an airplane next summer. The demand for airplanes next summer is thus hard to predict. It is difficult to define the states not knowing whether or not individual i will become an airplane addict. "For individual i to expect delivery of some commodity if his tastes call for it is equivalent to expecting delivery if he should so desire, and one may hardly conceive of such conditions being entered in a contract!"[6] Lack of observability is compounded by moral hazard.[7]

The argument about tastes can be repeated for productivity or effort, on the supply side. It can be extended to decisions made by business firms or public authorities.

Difficulties of the same order affect *transactions*. Many participants to market transactions at future dates are not in a position to express their supplies and demands today; children or unborn persons illustrate the point. In addition, transaction costs discourage most of us from seeking to trade in claims contingent on any but a few elementary events – and then typically for money or purchasing power.

Thus, either states (events, rather) are described so comprehensively that conditional prices are well defined, but are not objectively observable, or states are objectively observable, but conditional price cannot be taken as known. We cannot have it both ways. We can, however, choose which of the two requirements is dropped.

---

[6] Quoted from Drèze (1971, Section 3.2).
[7] Revelation of tastes through market behavior, hence prices, is discussed in Section 5.

4 Two models

The two natural extensions were developed more or less simultaneously, under the respective names of "general equilibrium with incomplete markets" (GEI) and "temporary general equilibrium" (TGE).[8]

4.1 Incomplete markets

The first approach[9] sticks to the abstract concept of states defined so comprehensively that conditional (spot) market-clearing prices are well defined, but recognizes that not all markets for contingent claims are active, hence the reference to "incomplete markets." (The reasoning to the effect that comprehensive states are not an operational support for contracts becomes an explanation – among others – of why markets are incomplete.) Implicit or explicit reference is made to Radner's concept of single-valued common rational expectations to justify the assumption that conditional spot prices are known to all agents. In the GEI literature, these spot prices are invariably assumed to clear markets. (I return to that aspect under Section 8.2.) Expectations about the states themselves are allowed to remain idiosyncratic.

One possible interpretation is that there exists a set of events defined with operational objectivity; given any such event, there exists a set of alternative states, not distinguishable for operational objectivity, but defined *conceptually* with enough detail that a unique equilibrium is associated with each state. *This comes close to associating with each event a set of alternative equilibria, over which individuals are allowed to hold idiosyncratic expectations.* The reference to states provides some additional generality, allowing for state-dependent preferences. On the other hand, the reference to a *unique* equilibrium is problematic, given that multiplicity of equilibria is the rule rather than the exception – an issue to which I return in Section 6. Section 5.3 deals with work allowing explicitly for probabilistic expectations about conditional prices.

4.2 Temporary equilibrium

The "temporary equilibrium" approach[10] is not very different, but still quite distinct. It, too, deals with spot markets and incomplete asset

---

[8] I abstract here from specific topics, like the decision criteria for business firms discussed by GEI theorists or the demand for (and price of) money studies by TGE theorists.
[9] See Geanakoplos (1990) for a survey.
[10] See Grandmont (1982, 1988) for surveys.

markets. Instead of modeling the future through exogenous states with associated known market prices, Stigum (1969), Grandmont (1974), and others typically work with probabilistic expectations on future prices. (In more ambitious formulations, the expectations concern other variables as well, like quantity constraints.) There would, however, be no difficulty in introducing explicit exogenous uncertainties through alternative states of the environment, conditional on which the agents might have either probabilistic or single-valued price expectations. Consumer preferences could also be state-dependent. *The temporary equilibrium model with state-dependent expectations and preferences comes close to an incomplete markets model with probabilistic price expectations given the state.*

4.3   An incomplete and temporary distinction

What are the remaining differences? Let us first read the assessments offered by proponents of the two approaches.

In his survey of TGE, Grandmont (1977) writes:

The *perfect foresight* approach to the modeling of sequence economies is very useful as a tool for indicative planning or for the description of stationary states, where it appears natural to assume that agents do forecast accurately their future environment. It can also be used to check that an economic proposition does not depend upon people making mistakes. It is surely, however, an improper approach to the modeling of actual economies. By contrast, the approach that I am going to describe in this essay allows economic units to make mistakes when forecasting their future environment. It therefore takes into account a "disequilibrium" phenomenon which appears important in actual economies, which is the fact that at a given date the agents' plans for the future are not coordinated and, hence, may be incompatible.

In contrast, Geanakoplos (1990) surveying GEI theory writes:

Of course, there is the alternative view, held in temporary equilibrium theory (TGE), which puts almost no restrictions on the compatibility of agents' forecasts (except for a mild restriction on the non-disjointness of the supports of the expectations; observe that in GEI, the supports are identical). There is a modeling trade-off here. The TGE approach seems to strain less the credibility of the implicit powers of calculation of the agents. This power is specially significant in the GEI model in that at time 0 there is not even an imaginary auctioneer who is supposed to be calling out the prices of commodities for states of nature at time 1. On the other hand, in the TGE model the price expectations are fixed exogenously (perhaps as an arbitrary continuous function of time 0 market conditions). To the extent that they are allowed to differ from the GEI expectations, they are wrong. In such circumstances, it is difficult to make sense of efficiency questions, because every possible answer is confounded with the irrationality of agent's plans.

Magill and Shafer (1990) describe the distinction between the two approaches as follows:

> In a model in which time and uncertainty enter in an essential way, a concept of *market equilibrium* involves two subordinate concepts: one regarding *expectation formation* and one regarding *market clearing*. Agents must form expectations about future prices in order to determine their market demand decisions: Their demand decisions are then used via market clearing to determine prices. In a *temporary equilibrium* agents form expectations (ex ante) about future spot prices which are not necessarily fulfilled (ex post): in addition, at a given date, only the current spot markets are required to clear, no condition being imposed on the future spot markets. This framework provides a natural and powerful tool for analysing the consequences of incorrect and hence changing price expectations: it has been the subject of an extensive literature which is surveyed in Grandmont [1982, 1988]. However when financial markets enter in an essential way (that is when arbitrage and information are important), a richer theory can be developed if the much stronger assumption regarding expectation formation is made that agents correctly anticipate future prices and all future markets are also cleared. This leads to the concept which Radner [1979, 1982] has called an *equilibrium of plans, prices and price expectations* which forms the basis for the analysis that follows. It should be noted that this concept permits agents to hold different probability assessments regarding future events. In the special case where all agents hold common probability assessments this concept reduces to what is referred to in macroeconomics as a *rational expectations equilibrium*.

The precise nature of the difference must be properly understood. By allowing agents to hold idiosyncratic expectations about *events*, GEI theorists allow for a species of "incorrect" expectations. When events are described so comprehensively that conditional prices are well defined, the expectations about events entail expectations about prices. *In that sense*, GEI theorists do not rule out "incorrect" price expectations and "incompatible forecasts." What they rule out is an incorrect (in the sense of economic theory) *association between the description of an unobservable event and the conditional prices*. In contrast, TGE theorists are not explicitly concerned with that association.

The ultimate implication, on this score, is that GEI theorists assume that the support of price expectations consists of conditional equilibrium prices,[11] whereas TGE theorists admit an arbitrary compact support. (In

---

[11] A devil's advocate might argue that, under uncertainty about the environment, no restrictions are placed on the set of equilibrium prices; see Shafer and Sonnenschein (1982). I am not playing the devil's advocate here.

a nonmonetary economy with normalized real prices, compactness is automatic; in a monetary economy, it is an important assumption. I return to nominal prices in Section 8.1.)

I add two side remarks. First, Grandmont refers to compatibility of *plans*, whereas Geanakoplos refers to compatibility of *forecasts*. My reading is that both refer to the same phenomenon, namely expectations about ability to trade at specific prices (plans), which are expectations about the prices at which one will be able to trade (forecasts). Referring to (the consequences of) idiosyncratic expectations about "states and associated prices" as a "disequilibrium" phenomenon is a choice of terminology. It becomes a matter of subtance only when the "equilibrium concept" is modified (for instance, to introduce quantity rationing) – an issue to which I return in Section 8.2. (But my reading may be incorrect.)

Second, Geanakoplos argues that, under incorrect expectations, "it is difficult to make sense of efficiency questions." GEI theorists have treated the efficiency issue quite definitively, by establishing the generic inefficiency of rational expectations equilibria. (See the more specific statement in Section 8.2.) The ground is thus clear to proceed with the positive analysis, without being held back by the possible side complications surrounding efficiency analysis.

5   Price-dependent expectations

5.1   Observability of prices

The issue of observability does not concern states and events alone. It also concerns prices. There are two sides to that issue, both of which are relevant to the present discussion. On the one side, it is definitely unrealistic to assume that economic agents know all the prevailing prices. More realistically, agents know some prices, hold probabilistic expectations about some other prices, and are totally unconcerned about most. Allen (1987) has introduced "noisy price observations" in GEI-models and proved the existence of rational expectations equilibria. Search theory deals with decisions to observe (or not) additional prices before trading, consuming, or producing. Which prices are known to an agent, and what expectations the agent holds about other prices, is part of a comprehensive description of the environment.

On the other side, prices are sometimes more directly observable than the underlying exogenous realizations from which they result. This second obvious remark has some well-known implications.

Let me first digress to recall that the informational role of prices is at the heart of our theory of resource allocation through the price system. In an Arrow–Debreu economy, agents are unconcerned about technology, resources, consumer tastes, or transactions; prices provide them with sufficient information to guide their own decisions, granted that they also know their own feasible set and motivations.

A formulation of uncertainty where agents are assumed, and in a sense required, to use information about the state of the environment (and not only about market prices) to choose an action is logically at odds with the spirit of relying on prices to guide resource allocation in an informationally efficient way. That paradox already arises in a "complete markets" framework, like that expounded in Chapter 7 of *Theory of Value* (Debreu [1959]). Households choosing a state-dependent consumption plan are not only concerned about conditional preferences among consumption vectors given a state; they are also concerned about the likelihood, or probability, of alternative states. (I shall for ease of exposition refer to probabilities.) The probabilities of future events and states are conditional on current information. The more complete is that current information, the more accurate are forecasts of future developments. The formulation introduced by Arrow in 1953 reminds us that comprehensive information about the current environment is useful to consumers. Behind the formal analogy between the certainty and uncertainty theories is hidden a major logical difference regarding the channels of information.

5.2   *Price-dependent information*

In Chapter 7 of *Theory of Value* (Debreu [1959]) prices for contingent claims provide no additional information about the probabilities of future events. A major step toward greater realism was introduced by Radner (1967; 1968), who extended the analysis to the case where different agents receive different information signals. The characteristics of an agent then include an *information partition*, defining for each date the events observed by that agent. That extension logically entails the possibility that additional information about the environment accrues through prices rather than through direct observation of resources, investments, or transactions. In such a case, individual probabilities of future events are also revised on the basis of current prices. That feature can be incorporated into the analysis in either of two ways. First, one can model explicitly the way in which agents translate observations about prices into information about the environment. Alternatively, one can enter prices directly as arguments of the individual utility functions. The first approach is exemplified by the work of Radner (1979) and others on "revealing equilibria." The second is followed in TGE theory.

5.3   (Partially) revealing equilibria

Radner, and others (see Radner [1982, Section 4.2] and Allen [1987] for surveys) have formally analyzed economies where agents receive differential information and observe market prices. The pooled information of all agents defines an event (state of the environment). The set of events is finite and the agents' expectations are represented by idiosyncratic probabilities over that set. If the true event were known to all agents, equilibrium prices would be uniquely defined. The mapping from events to equilibrium prices is known to all agents. That mapping is called "revealing" if it is one-to-one.

When agents trade under differential information but the mapping from events to prices is revealing, a price vector is an equilibrium price vector if and only if (1) all markets clear at the individual demands conditional on the event for which the price vector is an equilibrium, and (2) that event is consistent with the private information of each agent (hence is the true event). Radner (1979) provides sufficient conditions for generic[12] existence of a revealing mapping with that equilibrium property (which he labels "rational expectations"). That result illustrates the logical consistency of the first approach.

Of course, "revealing" mappings from events to equilibrium prices are a remote possibility. In general, observed prices provide *some* information about the current environment, but that information is only partial – even under the extreme GEI assumption that all agents know the mapping from events to prices. The extension of the work just surveyed calls for modeling explicitly the information of agents as a function of the prices which they observe, and defining equilibrium conditionally on that information – through properties analogous to (1) and (2) above.

Radner (1978), summarized in Jordan and Radner (1982), models such an extension by assuming that each agent a holds probabilistic expectations about the market-clearing prices associated with a given state – say $\psi(p|s)$, with support $\Delta^l\{p \in R^l_+|\Sigma_k p_k = 1\}$.

This important step, by itself, provides the bridge between GEI and TGE evoked in Section 4 above. Probabilistic expectations regarding conditional spot prices are associated with each event a set of alterna-

---

[12] "Generic" with respect to the idiosyncratic prior probabilities of the events.

tive equilibria, over which individuals are allowed to hold idiosyncratic expectations; they permit a potentially incorrect association between an event and the conditional prices.

This step also permits a formal analysis of the partial information conveyed by prices. Upon observing p, agent a learns that the state belongs to the inverse image $\psi_a^{-1}(p)$, and revises his expectations accordingly. A partially revealing equilibrium, where individual demands maximize expected utility given observed prices and markets clear, exists generically under suitable assumptions – including in particular the assumption that the support of $\psi(p|s)$ is equal to Δ^l for all s (so that no agent ever observes the impossible).[13]

5.4   Price-dependent utility

The alternative approach developed by TGE theorists is not logically different, but embodies a modeling shortcut. The more natural formulation rests on expected utility. The (subjective) probabilities of future states are revised on the basis of current observations, in particular of prices. The (state-dependent) utility of future consumption need not depend on prices. But the expected utility of a state-dependent consumption plan depends on current prices, through the probabilities of the states. And when preferences over such plans are represented by a general "utility" function, without explicit reference to probabilities, observed prices should appear as arguments of that function. One may thus characterize this approach as calling for "price-dependent utility."

Once the influence of currently observed prices on information and expectations is taken into account, the remaining differences between the GEI and TGE approaches strike me as of second order. At this state I would recommend a flexible, nondogmatic methodological stance. Under either GEI or TGE, the same issues must be faced. They concern the formation of expectations, including the processing of information coming possibly from noisy market prices and from economic theory. They also concern the dependence of resources, tastes, and technology on future exogenous events. Each of these aspects has been treated in the literature, at one place or another. We must rely on the union of our knowledge, and not confine ourselves to one element of a methodological partition.

It is somewhat surprising (to me!) that GEI theorists seem to hold the information content of prices in "temporary" disregard. The surveys by

---

[13] See also footnote 11 above.

Geanakoplos (1990) or Magill and Shafer (1991) are "incomplete" on that point. Yet, the canonical model they are using lends itself to a natural extension incorporating that element. The extension in the form of price-dependent utilities, in particular, is not likely to raise forbidding technical difficulties, if we reason by analogy with the "complete markets" model.[14] Being insufficiently familiar with the mathematical arcana of GEI, I cannot make definite claims here, but I draw the attention of GEI theorists to this well-defined problem, to which they could meaningfully apply their skills.

To avoid ambiguity, let me repeat that my (Radner's) point concerns the information conveyed by current prices about individual probabilities of *exogenous events*; for instance, the information conveyed by the price of potatoes on June 30 about the probability that the year's crop as of July 31 will exceed T tons.

6   Price-dependent states

6.1   A flexible methodological stance

Where prices belong in the definition of the information partitions of agents, does it follow that prices *necessarily* belong in the definition of the events themselves? I think that the work reviewed above answers that question. The models of revealing and partially revealing equilibria illustrate the possibility of modeling uncertainty in terms of exogenous events, in an economy where the information partitions of agents are defined in terms of market prices (and of differential information about events). It is thus not *necessary* to include prices in the definition of events. The logical separation of exogenous uncertainties from economic parameters, introduced in Arrow (1953), holds on in the literature under review.

The claim by Kurz (1974, 1993) that price uncertainties imply "that we should extend the notion of the state of the world to include future prices" would then seem to require a more sophisticated argument. I have been unable to reconstruct that argument, and should like to hear more on the subject.

Yet, for practical purposes, the logical distinction between observed prices and the underlying events often seems contrived. If agents know that they will observe prices rather than attributes of the underlying environment, they form expectations about prices, and choose price-

[14] See, for instance, Shafer and Sonnenschein (1975).

contingent strategies. Why not model their behavior directly in these terms?

I see no reason to be dogmatic about that question. A flexible methodological stance is more appropriate at this stage. We can model an economy (conditionally on observed events) in terms of alternative states, not observable but defined with enough detail that a unique equilibrium is associated with each state, with individuals holding idiosyncratic expectations about the states. Or we can model it in terms of idiosyncratic price expectations. Convenience and suitability to research objectives should direct the choice of formulation, not methodological dictates.

6.2 Multiple equilibria

Entering prices in the definition of events is perhaps not inocuous. One pitfall has been brought out recently in the context of multiple equilibria. Although this pitfall seems specific to this context, it raises issues of greater generality, especially in non-Walrasian contexts.

The points made by Hahn (1991), Chichilnisky et al. (1991), and Chichilnisky (1992) are illustrated in the Appendix for two commodities and two agents by means of an Edgeworth box depicting an exchange economy with no real uncertainty but two competitive equilibria, a and b. A proposed parable postulates two auctioneers, Ann who would implement equilibrium a and Barbara who would implement equilibrium b. Which of the two auctioneers will be on duty is uncertain: Ann is scheduled to appear (state a), but there is a positive probability that she will be unavailable and replaced by Barbara (state b).

As documented in the Appendix, a market for claims contingent on these exogenous states (Ann's availability) cannot eliminate completely the uncertainty about the final allocation, hence cannot sustain an efficient allocation. The apparent contradiction with Arrow's theorem 1 is explained by the fact that the example introduces a *restriction on admissible prices given the state*. (If Barbara were allowed to implement equilibrium a, the uncertainty would be resolved, and an efficient allocation would result, with the market for contingent claims becoming redundant.) By imposing restrictions on admissible prices given the states, one introduces a fundamental modification of the model, which significantly affects its properties.

The more general issues related (though not reducible) to this example concern efficient ways of dealing with price uncertainties.

7   Price-dependent contracts

When events are not fully observable, *contracting conditionally on price offers additional possibilities of risk sharing*. These possibilities, also exploited in some theoretical work, have not escaped the attention of practitioners. On the one hand, *trading in options* is a well-established practice on developed commodity and financial markets. On the other hand, *indexing contracts* on the general price level is an established practice in many countries, especially for wages and house rentals. It is now recognized by TGE and GEI theorists alike that *price-contingent contracts* belong naturally in a realistic asset structure; this is not a controversial issue. What is perhaps controversial is the extent to which price-contingent contracts make the market structure "complete." I offer two remarks, which illustrate the simple principle that some of the standard reasons invoked to justify incompleteness of markets for state-contingent claims to commodities apply to markets for price-contingent claims as well.

7.1   Options and economizing on markets

Kreps (1979), then Harrison and Kreps (1979) among others, have shown that markets for options on a few assets are perfect substitutes for either spot markets for a richer class of assets, or markets for contingent claims to commodities. It should be clear, however, that no prospect for "economizing on markets" is offered by that substitution. In order to "span" a given event tree, a basis of given dimensionality is required. It makes no difference whether the basis comes from prices of options, from assets, or from insurance contracts.

If there is "economizing," it should be at the level of transaction costs. Understandably, a set of N option markets for a single instrument may be less costly to organize than spot markets for N assets. One should understand, however, that applying "derivative pricing" formulae to activate additional markets does not produce additional spanning – except possibly (I am not sure, and again invite specialists to answer the question) in situations where the assumptions underlying the formulae are violated in the real economy, so that the financial intermediaries are taking unmeasured risks.

More significantly for my purpose here, an evaluation of transaction costs should include the processing of information by traders. Whether it is more convenient to buy weather insurance, shares of stock in farming enterprises, or corn options depends on who you are and what risks you wish to hedge. In general, I discount the possibility that option markets (useful as they are) lead to complete markets: Our understanding of the relationship between asset prices and states of the environment is too limited, and too many individual contingencies are not insurable.

7.2 *Incomplete options markets*

Theoretical work on general equilibrium with price-contingent contracts is still in its infancy but seems to be developing along two distinct avenues. One avenue adopts the standard GEI framework, including specific options among the assets, with attention concentrated on the existence and efficiency of equilibria. Results from five articles are summarized by Magill and Shafer (1991, p. 1608). So far, the results seem to be sensitive to the precise specification of the asset structure. For instance, the robust example of nonexistence constructed by Polemarchakis and Ku (1990) hinges on the presence of a market for options (on the future bond price) *with a prespecified exercise price*, which could be ill-chosen relative to other parameters of the economy. One expects agents to choose or adjust exercise prices on the basis of available information. Why would they stick to an ill-chosen price? The merit of Polemarchakis and Ku is to show that a *finite* (not infinitesimal) adjustment may be needed. It is difficult to disagree with the conclusion by Magill and Shafer (1991, p. 1608): "Clearly, much research remains to be done to properly integrate options into the GEI model."

The other avenue, *intellectually* closer to the TGE tradition, was opened in an innovative article by Svensson (1981). It is also the avenue followed in the work of Kurz (1993), which gives technical content to some of the views expressed here. The distinctive feature of the second avenue consists in introducing *a full set of markets for options on future prices*, where an option is "any continuous function from price vectors to commodity vectors." (Svensson shows that, in such a full set of markets, there is much redundancy: Nothing is lost if all claims are settled, conditionally on future prices, in some always desired numeraire.)

Continuous functions from price vectors to a numeraire, say from the unit simplex of R^l to R, define an infinite-dimensional commodity space. Although the associated technicalities are taken in stride by theorists, the realism of the model is open to question.

Thus, Svensson analyzes a two-period exchange economy with no exogenous uncertainty. With l physical commodities, it takes $2l$ markets at the beginning to provide full exchange opportunities and sustain a first-best allocation. Svensson assumes that only the l markets for spot deliveries are active, but adds the continuum of markets for options on the vector of future spot prices. It is clearly much more demanding (costly) to organize these options markets than to organize the *l* forward markets. Yet the resulting allocation is in general less efficient, because agents choose their initial consumption under uncertainty about future prices, whereas there is no exogenous uncertainty.

It is interesting that forward markets are nested in Svensson's options markets. For commodity *k*, a forward contract is represented by an option contract stipulating, for each realization of the price vector, a payment equal to the price of *k*. Why do agents not limit themselves to that subset of options markets? An earlier essay by Svensson (1976) offered an answer. Agents know in period 1 that spot markets will open in period 2. If they anticipate that spot prices in period 2 will be proportional to forward prices, they have no incentives to transact on the forward markets rather than on the spot markets in period 2. The efficiency of the forward markets is then lost.

The analysis of Svensson and Kurz is a useful addition to our understanding of the economics of price-contingent contracts. It should, however, be extended to the case of incomplete markets for options.

8   Two extensions

Before concluding I wish to add two remarks about extensions of the analysis beyond the framework introduced in Arrow (1953) and used thus far.

8.1   Nominal prices

Although Arrow (1953) refers to "money," he deals with a real economy; his money is an always desired numeraire, with no specific role as either a means of transactions or a store of value.

Money has figured prominently in TGE theory since Grandmont (1974). It is also working its way into GEI theory, as can be seen from the surveys of Geanakoplos (1990) or Magill and Shafer (1991). These developments reflect the demand for money, rooted in the specific roles mentioned above. They do not, however, deal with the inflationary process itself. That is, they do not include a "positive theory of inflation"[15] explaining the level of money prices at each date-event. Such a theory

---

[15] This expression is borrowed from Drèze (1993), where the notion is discussed and illustrated.

might, for instance, associate well-defined nominal prices with specific assumptions about central bank decisions, wage negotiations, and the like.

In models incorporating a "positive theory of inflation," it would seem natural to describe events so comprehensively that *nominal prices* are well defined. Everything written above would then apply to a monetary economy. Short of that progress in our thinking, there may be no alternative to including nominal price levels directly in the description of events.

8.2   Noncompetitive prices

As noted is Section 4.3, any concept of market equilibrium rests on a concept of market clearing. Whereas GEI has dealt exclusively so far with market clearing through competitive prices, TGE has explored alternatives involving quantity constraints or monopolistic price setting (see section 4 of Grandmont [1977]).

It is interesting to note that GEI theory has established that allocations associated with competitive clearing of incomplete markets are generically dominated by other allocations satisfying the same feasibility constraints (that is, are "second-best inefficient" or "constrained inefficient"); see section 5 of Geanakoplos (1990) or Magill and Shafer (1991). Although some of the results remain abstract, the application to second-best wage rigidities is transparent.[16] Extending GEI theory to noncompetitive market clearing would thus be a natural step but one that remains to be taken.

The introduction of additional endogenous parameters, like quantity constraints, calls for an extension to these parameters of the discussion centered here on prices. I feel confident that everything written here about prices would apply to these additional parameters as well. In such an extended framework, the pitfall identified by Hahn (1992) and the results of Chichilnisky (1992) and Chichilnisky et al. (1992) on multiple equilibria would seem to deserve special attention.

9   Conclusions

I draw the following conclusions from my rambling discussion.

1   The conceptual device of defining states comprehensively enough that market clearing prices are uniquely defined is con-

---

[16] See Drèze and Gollier (forthcoming).

sistent and useful, provided one recognizes that many events are unobservable, so that markets are inescapably incomplete.

2   Whether one models the residual uncertainty associated with unobservable events through idiosyncratic expectations about states or about prices themselves does not seem to matter. There is no reason to be dogmatic.

3   Greater realism is obtained when it is recognized that prices are not observed perfectly, that different agents have different information, and that prices convey information.

4   The revision of expectations on the basis of price observations is an essential feature in market economies. It can be modeled through information partitions or through price-dependent utility; there is again no reason to be dogmatic.

5   A GEI model with residual price uncertainty and price-dependent utilities is formally analogous to a TGE model with state- and price-dependent utilities.

6   Much work remains to be done on GEI/TGE with incomplete price-contingent contracts.

7   A positive theory of price-level determination and an extension of GEI to noncompetitive market clearing and endogenous uncertainty figure prominently on the research agenda.

A   Appendix

It may be helpful to provide a simple explicit illustration of the recent work by Hahn (1991), Chichilnisky et al. (1991), and Chichilnisky (1992) on economies with multiple equilibria. Having never before constructed an example with multiple equilibria, I resort to the simplification of non-smooth preferences.

Consider an exchange economy with two risk-averse agents, i and j, and two goods. Endowments are $\omega^i = (0, 4)$, $\omega^j = (4, 0)$. Consumption vectors are (x^i, y^i), (x^j, y^j). The preferences of i and j are represented by the following utility functions:

$$u^i = \begin{cases} \left[\min\left(x^i, y^i\right)\right]\alpha & \min\left(x^i, y^i\right) \leq 1 \\ \left[\left(x^i - 1\right)^{1/2}\left(y^j - 3\right)^{1/2} + 1\right]\alpha & x^i, y^i \geq 1 \end{cases}$$

$$u^i = \begin{cases} \left[\min\left(x^i, y^i\right)\right]\beta & \min\left(x^i, y^i\right) \leq 3 \\ \left[\left(x^i - 3\right)^{1/2}\left(y^j - 3\right)^{1/2} + 3\right]\alpha & x^i, y^i \geq 3 \end{cases}$$

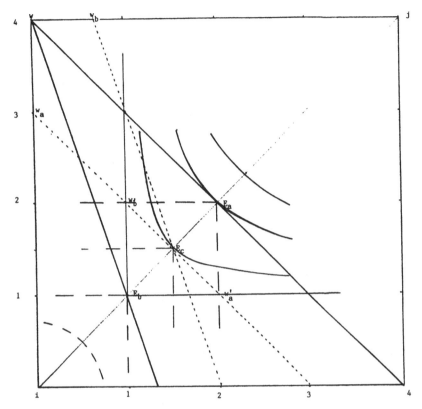

Figure 1. The indifference curves of i are solid lines, those of j are dashed.

The exchange economy is depicted in Figure 1. It has two competitive equilibria, at E_a with prices $p_x = p_y$ and at E_b with prices $p_x = 3p_y$. I normalize prices by setting $p_x = 1$ and write $p_y = p_a = 1$ at E_a, $p_y = p_b = 1/3$ at E_b.

In the absence of other information, let both agents assign equal probabilities to p_a and p_b. Then, agent $i(j)$ expects to consume either $x_a^i = y_a^i = 2$ ($x_a^j = y_a^j = 2$) or $x_b^i = y_b^i = 1$ ($x_b^j = y_b^j = 3$) with equal probability. Both agents would definitely be better off if they exchanged this uncertain prospect for its mean at E_c, where $x_c^i = y_c^i = 1.5$ ($x_c^j = y_c^j = 2.5$).

Hahn (1991) rightly points out that trading in claims contingent on p_a or p_b will not implement E_c (or for that matter, any point on the line segment $E_a E_b$) as a competitive equilibrium. Thus, let i promise to transfer 1 unit of y to j in case p_a obtains, against j's promise to transfer 2/3 units of x to i in case p_3 obtains – thereby transferring the endowment point to either ω_a or ω_b as the case may be. In my example, E_c is a competitive allocation at p_a with endowment ω_a, but E_c, though feasible, is not a competition allocation at p_b with endowments ω_b.

As noted in Section 6.2, this apparent contradiction with theorem 1 in Arrow (1953) is explained by the restrictions on admissible prices implicit in the definition of the events "a" and "b."

Chichilnisky, Dutta, and Heal (1991) make the interesting point that E_c could be implemented through trades contingent on *having realized* either E_a or E_b, rather than contingent on either p_a or p_b *being announced*. Thus, i could promise to transfer to j 1 unit of x (or 1 unit of y, or 1/2 unit of both) if E_a is realized, against j's promise to transfer to i 1 unit of x (or of y, or 1/2 of both) if E_b is realized. Trading from either ω_a' or ω_b' at prices $p = 1$ would lead to the *unique* equilibrium at E_c. That is, with two rounds of trading,[17] and a contract contingent on the outcome of the first round, an efficient allocation can be implemented.

Chichilnisky, Dutta, and Heal (1991) show that, *in a general context, a finite number of trading rounds will do*, where each round consists in trading claims contingently on a spot markets outcome, then clearing the spot markets. The technical achievement consists in verifying that an endowment point excluding multiple equilbria is bound to be reached in finitely many steps (one step in my example, where equilibrium is unique if and only if $(\omega_x^i - 1)(\omega_y^i - 1) \geq 0$. It is essential that agents trade on the spot markets without taking into account the perspective of future rounds, if my understanding is correct. Chichilnisky (1992) extends that result to *simultaneous clearing of the markets* (for contingent claims and for spot transactions) *of all (finitely many) rounds*. The sequential nature of the markets must here be understood and accepted by all agents, if my understanding is correct, and the same assumption of nonstrategic behavior should again be satisfied.

The notion of trading in claims contingent on the realization of a spots market equilibria may seem strange. On second thought, it is only natural, for market clearing prices emerge from trading, not from processing demand schedules. And trading is naturally sequential. Also, the transfers resulting in a unique equilibrium at E_c are reminiscent of the transfers implied by indexation of wages or house rentals. The dynamics of indexation are more complex, however, and the analogy remains purely suggestive at this stage.

---

[17] Chichilnisky (1992) refers to "two layers of uncertainty."

References

Allais, M., ed. 1953. *Fondements et Application de la Théorie du Risque en Econometrie*. Paris: CNRS.

Allen, B. 1987. General equilibrium with rational expectations. Chapter 1 in *Contributions to Mathematical Economics in Honor of Gérard Debreu*, ed. W. Hildenbrand and H. Sonnenschein. Amsterdam: North-Holland, pp. 1–23.

Arrow, K. J. 1953. Le rôle des valeurs boursières pour la répartition la meilleure des risques, *Econométrie*, 41–7. Paris: CNRS. Translated as The role of securities in the optimal allocation of risk-bearing. *Review of Economic Studies*, 31:91–6.

Arrow, K. J. 1971. The firm in general equilibrium theory. In *The Corporate Economy*, ed. R. Marris and A. Wood. London: Macmillan.

Arrow, K. J., and F. M. Hahn. 1971. *General Competitive Analysis*. San Francisco. Holden-Day.

Chichilnisky, G. 1992. Existence of a general equilibrium with price uncertainty. Mimeo, Columbia University, New York, this volume.

Chichilnisky, G. Dutta, and G. M. Heal. 1991. Price uncertainty and derivative securities in a general equilibrium model. Economic Theory Discussion Paper 178, University of Cambridge, Cambridge, UK.

Debreu, G. 1959. *Theory of Value*. New York: Wiley.

Drèze, J. H. 1971. Market allocation under uncertainty. *European Economic Review*, 2:133–65.

Drèze, J. H. ed. 1993. *Money and Uncertainty: Inflation, Interest, Indexation*. Rome: Elefante.

Drèze, J. H., and C. Gollier (forthcoming). Risk-sharing on the labour market and second-best wage rigidities. *European Economic Review*.

Geanakoplos, J. 1990. An introduction to general equilibrium with incomplete markets. *Journal of Mathematical Economics*, 19:1–38.

Grandmont, J. M. 1974. On the short-run equilibrium in monetary economy. In *Allocation under Uncertainty: Equilibrium and Optimality*, ed. J. H. Drèze. London: Macmillan.

Grandmont, J. M. 1977. Temporary general equilibrium theory. *Econometrica*, 45:535–72.

Grandmont, J. M. 1982. Temporary general equilibrium theory. In *Handbook of Mathematical Economics*, ed. K. J. Arrow and M. D. Intriligator. Amsterdam: North-Holland.

Grandmont, J. M., ed. 1988. *Temporary Equilibrium: Selected Readings*. San Diego: Academic Press.

Hahn, F. 1991. A remark on incomplete market equilibrium. Economic Theory Discussion Paper 179, University of Cambridge, Cambridge, UK.

Harrison, J. M., and D. Kreps. 1979. Martingale and arbitrage in multiperiod securities markets. *Journal of Economic Theory*, 20:381–408.

Hicks, J. R. 1931. The theory of uncertainty and profit. *Economica*, 11:170–89.

Jordan, J. S., and R. Radner. 1982. Rational expectations in microeconomic models: An overview. *Journal of Economic Theory*, 26:201–23.

Kreps, D. 1979. Three essays on capital markets. IMSSS Report 298, Stanford University, Stanford.

Kurz, M. 1974. The Kesten–Stigum model and the treatment of uncertainty in equilibrium theory. In *Essays on Economic Behavior under Uncertainty*, ed. M. S. Balch, P. L. McFadden, and S. Y. Wu. Amsterdam: North-Holland.

Kurz, M. 1993. General equilibrium with endogenous uncertainty. Mimeo, Stanford University, Stanford.

Magill, M., and W. Shafer 1991. Incomplete Markets. In *Handbook of Mathematical Economics*, ed. K. Arrow and M. Intriligator, Vol. 4, pp. 1523–614. Amsterdam: North Holland.

Marschak, J. 1938. Money and the theory of assets. *Econometrica*, 6:311–25.

Polemarchakis, H., and B. I. Ku. 1990. Options and equilibrium. *Journal of Mathematical Economics*, 19:107–12.

Radner, R. 1967. Equilibrie des marchés à terme et au comptant en cas d'incertitude. *Cahiers du Séminaire d'Econométrie*, 4:35–52.

Radner, R. 1968. Competitive equilibrium under uncertainty. *Econometrica*, 36:31–58.

Radner, R. 1972. Existence of equilibrium of plans, prices and price expectations in a sequence of markets. *Econometrica*, 40:289–303.

Radner, R. 1978. Rational expectations with differential information. Technical Report OW-12, Center for Research in Management Science, University of California, Berkeley.

Radner, R. 1979. Rational expectations equilibrium: Generic existence and the information revealed by prices. *Econometrica*, 47:655–78

Radner, R. 1982. Equilibrium under uncertainty. In *Handbook of Mathematical Economics*, ed. K. J. Arrow and M. D. Intriligator. Amsterdam: North-Holland.

Savage, L. J. 1953. Une axiomatisation du comportement raisonnable face à l'incertitude. Econométrie, Colloque International XL. Paris: CNRS.

Savage, L. J. 1954. *The Foundations of Statistics*. New York: Wiley.

Shafer, W., and H. Sonnenschein. 1975. Equilibrium in abstract economies without ordered preferences. *Journal of Mathematical Economics*, 2:345–8.

Shafer, W., and H. Sonnenschein. 1982. Market demand and excess demand functions. In *Handbook of Mathematical Economics*, ed. K. J. Arrow and M. D. Intriligator. Amsterdam: North-Holland.

Stigum, B. 1969. Competitive equilibria under uncertainty. *Quarterly Journal of Economics*, 83:533–61.

Svensson, L. E. O. 1976. Sequences of temporary equilibria, stationary point expectations and pareto efficiency. *Journal of Economic Theory*, 13:169–83.

Svensson, L. E. O. 1981. Efficiency and speculation in a model with price-contingent contracts. *Econometrica*, 49:131–51.

Tintner, G. 1941. The theory of choice under subjective risk and uncertainty. *Econometrica*, 9:298–304.

CHAPTER 4

A remark on incomplete market equilibrium

Frank Hahn

1   Introduction

Let S be the set of "Savage" states of nature. A state of nature describes the history of the environment which is independent of the action of agents – it is exogenous. Now consider a pure exchange economy with l goods which lasts for two periods. The consumption set C of agent h is a subset of $R_+^{l(S+1)}$ where S now stands for the cardinality of the Savage state space. Let there be Arrow securities which span S. Then by a famous theorem of Arrow (1953) the equilibria of this economy coincide with those of an Arrow–Debreu economy, that is, one which at the first date has a full set of contingent goods markets.

This result is at first sight counterintuitive since the economy with Arrow securities is a sequence economy whereas an Arrow–Debreu economy is not. But in a sequence economy agents in the first period must act on price expectations; in an Arrow–Debreu economy price expectations play no role. The mystery disappears when we notice that Arrow's theorem implicitly makes an assumption concerning price expectations: Agents are taken to have perfect foresight. That is, in the initial period agents know for sure the value of the price vector $p(s) \in R_+^l$ which in equilibrium is market clearing. Even so, there is the difficulty that second period equilibrium at s may not be unique. So the assumption is even stronger: Agents in some way have coordinated their expectations on one particular equilibrium. Let us partially drop this assumption: Agents know the set of second period equilibrium prices but do not know which will prevail.

This paper was presented at the Stanford Institute for Theoretical Economics in the summer of 1991.

2   Sunspots and multiple equilibria

Once we allow agents to be uncertain of second period equilibrium prices, we must add "endogenous uncertainty" to the exogenous uncertainty represented by Savage states. Kurz (1974) some time ago drew attention to price uncertainty as at least as significant as Savage-state uncertainty. Recently Chichilnisky (1992), Chichilnisky et al. (1991), and Chichilnisky and Wu (1991) have examined the equilibria of economies with endogenous uncertainty: My "remark" and their work overlap.

But the most relevant earlier discussion of the matter is to be found in the sunspot literature. In equilibrium sunspots can be taken as signals as to which of a number of equilibria will prevail. Agents' probability distribution over sunspots coincides, in equilibrium, with that over the set of price equilibria. Sunspots are thus a kind of coordinating device. However, should there be a full set of Arrow–Debreu markets conditioned on Savage states as well as on sunspots, no sunspot equilibrium is possible (Cass and Shell [1983]). I want now to make the connection between this result and the recent literature on incomplete securities markets. We shall see that a result analogous to "no sunspots are possible" has certain ramifications.

3   The model

Let there be B securities and let $a^h \in R^B$ be the portfolio of agent $h(h = 1, \ldots, H)$. Let $\hat{a}$ be the matrix of portfolios. A security j pays a return in numeraire and r_j is the vector of these over the states in which the security pays. I write R as the matrix formed by column r_j. Let

$$A = \left\{ \hat{a} \,\middle|\, \sum a^h = 0 \right\}$$

First we consider the second period economy once $\hat{a}$ has been chosen in the first period. Let $x^h(p.\hat{a}) \in R^{lS}$ be the second period excess demand vector of agent h given $p \in R^{lS}_+$ and $\hat{a}$. The agent's budget set is:

$$B_h\left(p, \hat{a}\right) = \left\{ x^h \,\middle|\, p(s)\square x^h(s) \le Ra^h \right\}$$

where $p(s)$ is a price vector in Savage state $s \in S$, $x^h(s)$ is an excess demand vector in this state, and $p(s)\square x^h(s)$ denotes the vector in R^S with components $p(s)\cdot x^h(s)$.

Let $E(\hat{a})$ denote the set of possible second period equilibrium prices and excess demand allocations given $\hat{a}$, that is, each element $\bar{p}, \{x^h(\bar{p}, \hat{a})\}_H$ in $E(\hat{a})$ satisfies

$$\sum_h x^h\left(\overline{p}, \hat{a}\right) = 0$$

and for each h, $x^h \in B^h(\overline{p}, \hat{a})$ implies $x_h^h \le x^h(\overline{p}, \hat{a})$.

In the second period some particular s is realized. So $E(\hat{a})$ is the set of possible second period outcomes as viewed from the first period when $\hat{a}$ has been chosen. In general $E(\hat{a})$ will have more than one member $(p, \{x^h(s)\}_s)$; there are multiple second period equilibria. I shall use

Assumption 1: *For all $\hat{a} \in A$ the second period economy is regular (it has countably many equilibria.)*

Let $n(\hat{a})$ be the number of second period equilibria given $\hat{a}$. Then I use

Assumption 2: *For all $\hat{a} \in A$, $n(\hat{a})$ is finite so that*

$$n = \max_a n\left(\hat{a}\right)$$

is well defined.

Now let $i = 1, \ldots, n$. Identify each of the numbers i with an auctioneer. Each "calls" some $p \in R_+^{lS}$ after $\hat{a}$ has been chosen, that is, at the end of the first period but before the Savage state of the second period has been realized. Some auctioneers may call the same price. Agents now face price uncertainty. It is therefore natural to enlarge the state space to

$$\Sigma = \left\{\sigma \,\middle|\, \sigma = (s, i),\ s \in S,\ i \in (1, n)\right\}$$

I am now interested in an economy whose securities are Σ-complete, that is, the security payoffs span Σ.

The formulation of the problem in terms of fictional auctioneers is a convenient way of introducing price uncertainty and does not appear to have any further implications. Thus $p(\sigma) = p(s, i)$ is the price expected (in the first period) to prevail in the second period in Savage state s if the ith auctioneer is "in charge" of setting prices. It could equally well be regarded as the ith element of price vectors for s which are in the support of the agents' first period beliefs.

4   The Σ-complete economy

The discussion in Section 3 motivates the following definition:

Definition 1: *An equilibrium for a Σ-complete economy is $\overline{p} \in R_+^{l(\Sigma+1)}$, $x^{-h} \in R^{l(\Sigma+1)}$, $h = 1, \ldots, H$, $a^{-h} \in R^\Sigma$, $h = 1, \ldots, H$, $\overline{q} \in R_+^\Sigma$ such that when*

$$B^{-h}(\overline{p}) = \left\{ x^h, a^h \middle| \overline{p}(0)x^h(0) = 0 \quad \text{and} \right.$$

$$\left. \overline{q}a^h = 0; \overline{p}(\sigma)\square x^h(\sigma) = Ra^h \right\}$$

one has $(x^h, p) \in B^{-h}(\overline{p})$ implies $x^h \le x^{-h}$ for all h and

$$\sum_H x^{-h} = 0 \quad \text{and} \quad \sum_H a^{-h} = 0$$

We now have

Proposition 1: *If an equilibrium exists for the Σ-complete economy, then $\overline{p}(s, i) = p(s)$ for all i. That is, second period market clearing prices depend only on s, are unique for each s.*

The proof of this proposition follows the same lines as that for the proposition that sunspot equilibria are impossible for a complete Arrow–Debreu economy. Since preferences are defined on $R^{l(S+1)}$ and are convex, it follows that if $x^h(s, i) \ne x^h(s, j)$ the agent would prefer the convex mixture. Since the securities are Σ-complete, the agent can indeed insure so he will have the same consumption at s whatever the prices, and he will do so. But then excess demands depend only on s and there can only be a rationally expected market clearing price. We are then back in the traditional model although there are Σ-s redundant securities.

The redundancy is special, however. Should it disappear while agents correctly calculate the set of second period equilibrium prices, the Σ would not be spanned and price uncertainty would again be present and no Σ-complete equilibrium exists.

We can make this more precise. Suppose the securities spanning Σ are all Arrow securities: Each pays at only σ (R is diagonal).

Then we have

Proposition 2: *If all securities are Arrow securities and agents only buy securities for which σ is in the support of their distribution of beliefs over Σ, then no Σ-complete rational expectations equilibrium exists, provided the economy with S securities has multiple second period equilibria.*

The proposition is a little counterintuitive. Agents realize the possibility of multiple equilibria and in the Σ-complete economy insure against price uncertainty. Once they have done that there can only be a unique equilibrium for each s. For rational expectations equilibrium all previous price equilibria for s must be given zero probability. But then, by my assumption, they will not insure.

5   Comment

The above I think gives a better understanding of "sunspots." So far, multiple equilibria have mainly played a role in the discussion of the existence of sunspot equilibria. Sunspots were equated with "extrinsic" uncertainty. But the possibility of multiple second period equilibria is an intrinsic feature of the market economy. To that extent sunspots reflect (are signals for) intrinsic uncertainty? Complete security markets imply that this uncertainty is included in the space to be spanned. If there is such complete spanning then the price uncertainty disappears as long as it is maintained.

A last remark. The device of a number of auctioneers allows one to treat each auctioneer as a state of nature. Thus, as far as existence for an economy with numeraire securities is concerned, no problems appear to arise.

References

Arrow, K. J. 1953. The role of securities in the optimal allocation of risk-bearing, in French. Econometrie: Proceedings of the Colloque sur les Fondements et Applications de la Théorie du Risque en Econométrie, Centre National de la Reserche Scientifique, Paris. English Translation: Review of Economic Studies (1964) 31:91–6.

Cass, D., and K. Shell. 1983. Do sunspots matter? *Journal of Political Economy* 91, 2:193–227.

Chichilnisky, G. 1992. Existence and optimality of a general equilibrium with endogenous uncertainty, this volume.

Chichilnisky, G., J. Dutta, and G. M. Heal. 1991. Options and price uncertainty. Working paper, Columbia University.

Chichilnisky, G., and H-M. Wu. 1991. Financial innovation and endogenous uncertainty in incomplete asset markets. Technical Report No. 50, Stanford Institute for Theoretical Economics, 1992.

Kurz, M. 1974. The Kesten–Stigum model and the treatment of uncertainty in equilibrium theory. In *Essay on Economic Behavior Under Uncertainty*, ed. M. C. Balch, D. McFadden, and S. Wu. Amsterdam: North-Holland.

Kurz, M. 1991. On the structure and diversity of rational beliefs. Technical Report No. 39, Stanford Institute for Theoretical Economics, November 1991.

CHAPTER 5

Existence and optimality of a general equilibrium with endogenous uncertainty

Graciela Chichilnisky

1   Introduction

Kenneth Arrow once said that uncertainty about prices may be the most important form of economic uncertainty. Yet the treatment of uncertainty in Arrow–Debreu markets reflects only nature's moves. It therefore neglects price uncertainty, because prices depend on human behavior.

This chapter attempts to close the gap. It defines a new concept of general equilibrium in markets where traders are uncertain about prices, and proves the existence of such an equilibrium. Traders do not know the possible equilibrium prices a priori. The state space which represents price uncertainty, and the financial instruments used to hedge this uncertainty, are all defined endogenously as part of a market equilibrium.

To motivate the problem, I show in Proposition 1 that trying to hedge price uncertainty within an Arrow–Debreu framework leads to paradoxical outcomes, which are connected with Russell's paradox in logics. Thus a new framework is needed.

The framework introduced here is similar to that of Arrow and Debreu in that there are several markets, several traders who act competitively, and all contracts are entered simultaneously. However, the treatment of uncertainty is different. It is given by "layers" of uncertainty, where each layer is logically conditional on the previous one.[1] Each layer

UNESCO Chair in Mathematics and Economics and Director, Program on Information and Resources, Columbia University. This essay was written with research support from the Universita di Siena and the Stanford Institute for Theoretical Economics during the summers of 1991 and 1992.

[1] This is similar to compound lotteries, which the Von Neumann axioms require should be equivalent to standard lotteries. However, the compound lotteries lead here to market structures different from standard lotteries because in the model introduced here

is a formalization of index-based securities markets which are widely traded today. They provide a conceptual explanation of the role of derivative securities and of their market organization. The states in the first layer represent all market clearing prices for commodities, the states in the second layer all market clearing prices for index-based securities, the states in the third layer are market clearing prices in markets which trade contingent on the prices of the indexes, and so forth.

The resulting economy expands the theory of markets to allow the states and the financial structure to be endogenously defined at an equilibrium, as a result of market forces. Each "layer" of uncertainty requires a constraint that is similar to a margin requirement. This is a realistic feature, and one that makes the economy quite different from that of Arrow and Debreu.

Theorem 1 establishes the existence of an equilibrium consisting of a "tree" of states representing uncertainty, the corresponding asset markets, and market clearing prices. The equilibrium allocation clears all markets, is fully insured, and is Pareto efficient.

1.1   Motivating endogenous uncertainty

Imagine an Arrow–Debreu economy facing several states of nature, with a complete set of asset markets to hedge nature's moves. For simplicity the economy has finitely many equilibria.[2] In a departure from the standard framework, the households anticipate that there may be several possible market clearing prices among which a random selection will be made. They do not know what these prices could be.

In addition to the states of nature, traders are now concerned about a new form of uncertainty, price uncertainty. This can be formalized by new "states" describing the possible market clearing prices.[3] These new states are endogenous to the functioning of the economy, whereas the states used in the Arrow–Debreu theory describe variables which are exogenous, such as the weather. If new assets are introduced to complete the market, the new augmented economy may have price uncertainty, because there may be several market clearing prices for the new assets themselves. This problem may reiterate, leading to a sequence of economies with an increasing number of asset markets, and gradually increasing state spaces. A first question is whether within an Arrow–Debreu framework traders can fully hedge all price risks. Proposition 1

there are several budget constraints akin to margin requirements, one for each "layer" of uncertainty.

[2] This is a generic property, Debreu (1970).

[3] See also Chichilnisky, Dutta, and Heal (1991).

shows that the Arrow–Debreu framework does not provide a satisfactory solution to the problem of price uncertainty. The Arrow–Debreu economy cannot hedge against its own price risks. One needs a new formalization for markets with price risks.

1.2   Expectations about prices

It seems useful to consider how price risks change traders' expectations and alter market behavior. Recall that in a standard Walrasian approach an auctioneer announces a vector of prices, and individuals choose asset holdings and consumption levels to maximize utility at those prices. Trade only occurs when demand equals supply, and all markets clear. This corresponds to individuals having *single valued* expectations about prices and leads to Pareto efficient allocations.

The problem is altered substantially when traders anticipate – or an auctioneer announces – that one of several possible market clearing prices will be chosen at random. Expectations about prices are now *multivalued* rather than *single valued*. The individuals' optimization problems are altered: Rather than choosing asset holdings to maximize utility at the equilibrium prices announced by the auctioneer, they choose so as to maximize expected utility, where the expectation is over *a set of several possible market clearing prices*. The old prices can no longer clear the markets, because the uncertainty faced now is different. The new market clearing prices reflect more complex behavior: The expected utility being maximized includes expectations about prices as well as about states of nature. The optimization problem solved by the traders is different, and therefore so are the solutions. This tallies with Proposition 1 below.[4]

2   Definitions

A pure exchange Arrow–Debreu E economy has l commodities, H traders indicated by h, and S "Savage states of nature." Each Savage state is a description of the environment arising from acts of nature and independent of the actions of the agents, a slight abuse of notation.[5] Let $R =$

---

[4] Hahn (1991) and Chichilnisky, Hahn, and Heal (1992) argue that correct anticipation of the Walrasian equilibrium prices is inconsistent with the new equilibrium when there are several equilibria prices. This tallies with the results of Chichilnisky, Dutta, and Heal (1991) and of Chichilnisky, Heal, Streufert, and Swinkels (1992) which argue, inter alia, that the correct anticipation of several market prices is inconsistent with an equilibrium having a price within this set.

[5] The most general interpretation of Savage states could incorporate price risks.

$\{r_1, \ldots, r_B\}$ denote an $S \times B$ matrix of returns on the economy's assets which pay contingent on the Savage states. There is a complete set of assets to hedge against the acts of nature so that rank $(R) = S$. The initial endowment for each household h is denoted w^h and the economy's endowment is $w = \Sigma_h w^h$. Trader h has a strictly quasiconcave, C^2 (twice continuously differentiable) monotonically increasing Von Neumann–Morgenstern utility function $V^h : R^l \to R$ with nonzero gradients, and satisfying standard boundary conditions which ensure that the aggregate excess demand vector of the economy increases beyond any bound when a price goes to zero. Let $p \in R^{l \times S}$ denote a price vector, $ED(p)$ denote the excess demand function of the economy, and define the set of equilibrium prices

$$E(w) = \left\{ p : ED(p) = 0 \right\}$$

Definition 1: *An economy has price uncertainty[6] when $E(w)$ has cardinality $N > 1$, and trader h maximizes expected utility*

$$W^h\left(\left(x^{hi} \right)_{i=1,\ldots,N} \right) = EV^h\left(\left(x^{hi} \right)_{i=1,\ldots,N} \right)$$

where $i = 1, \ldots, N$ are possible equilibrium prices and the expectation depends on a probability distribution over the set of prices $\{1, \ldots, N\}$ which is the same for all traders.[7]

Assumption 1: *The economy has a finite set of equilibria for any set of initial endowments.*

This is satisfied by many exchange economies. More precisely, a family of utility functions, of which a residual set gives finitely many equilibria for any endowment, is the family of C^∞ functions whose bordered Hessians are nonzero everywhere. See Debreu (1970) and extensions – references are in Chichilnisky, Dutta, and Heal (1991).

3   An Arrow–Debreu economy cannot hedge its price risks

Let E be an economy with price uncertainty. Can we obtain an optimal (Pareto efficient) allocation of risk bearing by adding as many assets as needed to hedge against price uncertainty? Within a sequence economy the answer was provided in Hahn (1991), and in an Arrow–Debreu context it was provided by Chichilnisky, Hahn, and Heal (1992), Lemma 1. In both cases the answer is negative. In the following I briefly recall

---

[6] In the following the terms *price uncertainty* and *price risks* are used interchangeably.
[7] This is not strictly necessary but simplifies notation.

their arguments. As in Section 2, the economy E faces N states of "price uncertainty" and S Savage states, making for a space $\Sigma = N \times S$ of states of both types. The initial economy has a complete set of Arrow–Debreu contingent markets for exogenous uncertainty, that is, one for each element of S, so it is equivalent to an economy without exogenous uncertainty. Traders are concerned only with price risks and attempt to maximize expected utility as specified in Section 2. However, as traders are aware of the price risks, and no instruments are available to hedge these risks, the economy is "incomplete," in the sense that it has risks for which no hedge exists. The question is whether the Arrow–Debreu framework can be used to hedge price risks optimally.

If so, then all that would be needed to hedge price risks fully would be to introduce Arrow–Debreu contingent markets, one for each of the N price risks; optimal hedging would then ensue. In our example, we would need to introduce N new contingent markets, or alternatively, as shown in Arrow (1953), N Arrow securities, since there are N "price" risks. The new economy obtained from augmenting the old one is called C. The procedure of adding Arrow securities, also called "completing the market," always leads to optimal allocation of risk bearing in the case of exogenous risks. The following result shows that it does not work with endogenous risks. In other words, the Arrow–Debreu framework does not work for hedging endogenous risks.

> **Proposition 1:** *An Arrow–Debreu economy with price risks cannot achieve optimal allocation of risk bearing by the introduction of Arrow–Debreu contingent markets or Arrow securities. No matter how many contingent markets or securities are introduced the augmented economy C has no Pareto efficient allocations, and therefore no competitive equilibrium.*

> *Proof:* First observe that at each of the states $s \in S$, for all $i \in N$, the total endowments of society are the same. By assumption all households attach the same probability to the event that one given equilibrium price will occur. Under these conditions, at a Pareto efficient allocation, each household must consume the same Savage state dependent allocation across all states in the set N, that is, $x^{hsi} = x^{hsj}$ for each household h and all Savage states s, for any two price states $i, j = i, \ldots, N$; for a proof see Chichilnisky, Hahn, and Heal (1992). Since for each $s \in S$, each household consumption across all states in the set N is the same, it follows that for each state $s \in S$ the price vectors dependent on the set of states N are all the same. But this implies that all

market clearing prices are equal, so that there is no price uncertainty in the model, a contradiction. Since the contradiction arises from assuming that all price uncertainty can be hedged by a complete set of Arrow–Debreu price contingent markets, the proof is complete.   QED.

4   Layers of uncertainty and the Russell paradox

We saw that an Arrow–Debreu economy cannot hedge price risks fully. Any attempt to complete the market by adding contingent markets or securities allocations fails. There are no Pareto efficient allocations. The failure can be viewed as the inability of the Arrow–Debreu economy to hedge against the price risks it generates.

A practical example will illustrate this failure and suggest an alternative market structure to hedge price risks. Consider a market in which oranges are traded forward. Assume that there are three possible market clearing prices for oranges, with the same probability each, and that this is common knowledge. In practice, to hedge against such price uncertainty, options on orange prices are introduced. This is how markets hedge against price uncertainty in concrete cases.

How are the market clearing prices determined? In an Arrow–Debreu economy all the market clearing prices are simultaneously determined for all states of nature by the auctioneer. When attempting to extend this procedure to our economy with price uncertainty a problem arises. An auctioneer cannot simultaneously determine the market clearing prices for oranges and for options on oranges.[8] This is because once the auctioneer announces any forward prices for oranges, there is no hedging role for the options on oranges. If, for example, the forward price for oranges announced by the auctioneer is \$2, then nobody will buy a call for oranges at a strike price \$$x$ if $x > 2$, and nobody will sell such a call if $x < 2$ unless paid at least the difference \$$2 - x$. At a strike price of \$2 the value of this option will be exactly zero. In other words: options on commodities do not have any role in allocation of price risks if they are traded simultaneously with forward commodity markets. Simultaneous trading across all states of uncertainty is of the essence in an Arrow–Debreu economy, so oranges at time t and their options are traded at once in such markets. This is the reason why an Arrow–Debreu economy cannot fully hedge price risks.

In practice, commodities at a given date are never traded at the same

---

[8] That is, the price of oranges at time t cannot be determined simultaneously with the price of options on oranges maturing at time t.

date as their options: The forward market for oranges is typically traded at a date posterior to that at which the option market closes, so that the price of oranges is still unknown when the option is traded. In other words, there is a natural "ordering" in the markets for assets to hedge price uncertainty which cannot be formulated within the Arrow–Debreu treatment of uncertainty, where all markets are simultaneous.

The ordering reflects the fact that the markets for those assets whose values depend on the prices of other assets will not improve risk allocation if the values of those underlying assets are revealed simultaneously. The uncertainty must be revealed in an orderly fashion for these markets to work together. There are "veils" of uncertainty which must be resolved in the proper order, and the time structure of trading takes care of this order. In our example, first the auctioneer must determine the price for the options *contingent on all the possible prices for oranges tomorrow*, and compute the corresponding aggregate demand for options. Only when market clearing prices have been found is the price for the underlying asset, forward oranges, realized. This argument leads to a nested sequence of ordered assets, and to orderly resolution of uncertainty. This is what we call here layers of price uncertainty, a treatment of uncertainty fundamentally different from that in the Arrow–Debreu economy.[9]

How then are assets to hedge price uncertainty to be traded? Rather than being contingent on several simultaneous states as in the Arrow–Debreu model, the assets are now defined in terms of nested risks, or layers of uncertainty. Each layer consists of *a set of states* which represent uncertainty of the same type, for example, uncertainty about all possible equilibrium prices for securities of a given type. All states within a layer are grouped together, and the uncertainty about a given layer is resolved by the assets of the following layer. I develop this concept formally in the next section.

To situate the problem within standard grounds and fix ideas, it is useful to draw an analogy between the problem of hedging endogenous uncertainty and the structure of the well-known Russell paradox. The solution to Russell's paradox led to the development of set theory as it is known today, see Halmos (1970). The paradox arises, for example, when we inquire whether a set is an element of itself, and can be illustrated as follows. A town has a barber who shaves all those who do not shave them-

---

[9] All uncertainty in the Arrow–Debreu economy derives from acts of nature, a type of uncertainty for which simultaneous contingent markets suffice to attain Pareto efficient allocations.

selves. The question is: Does the barber shave himself? There exists no answer to this question; yes leads to no, and no leads to yes.

The solution to the paradox is to structure the universe into appropriate layers or logical "classes." When this is done, the question of whether a set belongs to itself is shown to be ill defined, so that it cannot be answered. Some objects are points and others are sets: Only points can belong to sets, whereas sets can only belong to higher level objects, called classes. The question about the barber is ill posed because it refers to a set as belonging, or not, to itself. Our informal language allows us to pose ill-defined questions.

An analogy between this chapter's problem and the Russell paradox is as follows. Consider an Arrow–Debreu economy with price uncertainty as defined above, where traders have set valued expectations about the possible price equilibria. Introduce all markets needed to hedge all risks, thus obtaining a "complete" market E in the sense of Arrow–Debreu, one in which all commodities and all assets are simultaneously traded. Does E hedge all its price risks? If it did, then as seen in Proposition 1 above E has only one equilibrium price in the first place, contradicting the hypothesis that it has price risks. If it does not, then we may introduce a new market to hedge any remaining price risk, a market not already in E. This is also a contradiction because, as defined, E contains all needed markets for hedging its risks. In reality, there is no logical answer to the question of whether E hedges all its price risks. This is the same problem as with the Russell paradox.

When trying to hedge against price uncertainty within an Arrow–Debreu economy in which all markets are traded simultaneously, one is attempting to obtain from the markets of this economy a hedge against the price risks that these markets generate themselves. As we saw above there is no logical solution to this problem: Our economic language allows us to pose an ill-defined question. Developing further the analogy with the Russell paradox, a solution could be provided by structuring the problem in logical "classes" or layers. One must structure uncertainty into layers, each layer designed to resolve the uncertainty created by previous ones, without ever attempting to go outside the logical order and ask any one layer to hedge against its own price risks. The next section follows this course of action to its logical conclusion.

5   A new economy with endogenous uncertainty

This section formalizes an economy in which uncertainty takes the form of a compound lottery represented by a "tree," or layered sets of states.

This representation of uncertainty is novel, and it leads to several "margin" requirements, one for each layer.

Within this economy I prove the existence of a general equilibrium in which all markets clear, where individuals maximize expected utility within the corresponding budgets, and where at an equilibrium all individuals are fully insured against price risks (Theorem 1). The intention is to obtain, within one single economy with layers of uncertainty, a result similar to that which has been obtained recently for a sequence of different economies by Chichilnisky, Dutta, and Heal (1991). They construct a sequence of different economies by progressively adding more financial markets and modifying the endowments of the traders, and show that full price insurance is achieved at the end of finitely many steps.[10]

The results of Chichilnisky, Dutta, and Heal (1991) were obtained by building a sequence of economies, each an enlargement of the previous one. This section shows that it is possible to obtain similar results working within *one single economy where households face a set of possible prices for each state of each layer, and where each household solves a single optimization problem.* In other words, by changing the structure of the uncertainty, I obtain results similar to those of Chichilnisky, Dutta, and Heal within a single economy rather than in a sequence of economies.

A new economy L is defined now as follows. It has H households denoted $h = 1, \ldots, H$, and l commodities. There are S states of nature or "Savage states." Each household h has an initial endowment vector $w^h \in R^{l \times S}$ of commodities contingent on states of nature. For the Savage states we have a complete set of assets, as required in Section 2. As before, each trader h has a preference over commodities, $V^h : R \to R$. Commodities contingent on Savage states are indicated by vectors $x \in R^{l \times S}$; when it is clear from the context, I also refer to these vectors as commodities.

---

[10] To achieve this they start from a Walrasian economy with several equilibrium prices of this first economy. The corresponding Walrasian equilibrium allocations are used as the endowments of a second economy, the endowments consisting of price contingent goods traded in price contingent markets where agents may now hedge against the price uncertainty of the first economy. The second step is to inform agents that this second economy has in turn several price equilibria. Using the Walrasian allocation of the second economy as initial endowments of a third economy, the agents are then allowed to add new commodities, new endowment, and new financial instruments. The procedure continues until an economy is reached in which there is no price uncertainty, which means that an economy with a unique Walrasian equilibrium is achieved. Chichilnisky, Dutta, and Heal (1991) prove that, under regularity assumptions, such an economy can be reached in a finite number of steps. This result depends on the regularity assumptions made in Section 2.

The economy L is therefore defined by its l commodities, S Savage states of nature, H traders, and their endowments and utilities:

$$L = \left\{ X = R_+^l, s = 1, \ldots, S, w^h \in R^{l \times S}, V^h : X \to R, h = 1, \ldots, H \right\}$$

In addition to the Savage states there are states of price uncertainty in L. However, the actual market structure of L, namely what types of assets will be traded and how, is determined endogenously as part of the market equilibrium solution. The following determines the universe of "structures of uncertainty" in which the equilibrium structure of L will be pound.

5.1   The structure of uncertainty in L

A *structure of uncertainty* for L is defined by a finite set Y consisting of elements $y = 1, \ldots, Y$, each denoting a "layer" of uncertainty. For each layer y there is a set of states J^y, with J^y elements associated with and defined by the corresponding market clearing price for the market of the previous layer.

> **Example 1:** *In layer 1 there are J^1 states representing possible Arrow–Debreu market clearing prices for the $l \times S$ commodities; in level 2 there are J^2 possible prices for type 2 price indexes which pay contingent on the prices of the $l \times S$ commodities. Thus in the first two layers there are a total of $J^1 \times J^2$ possible equilibrium price combinations. The structure of uncertainty comes ordered into layers, and each state is contingent on the realization of previous states, thus describing an uncertainty "tree."*

The random variables describing uncertainty in L are paths through the uncertainty tree. A realization of random variable is called a *resolution of price uncertainty*. It is a vector consisting of Y states, one state from each of the Y layers. It is intended to represent a realization of one market clearing price for each of the Y layers. A resolution of price uncertainty is therefore a *realized path* of states and is represented by a Y dimensional vector $(j^1, \ldots, j^Y)$, where $\forall y = 1, \ldots, Y, j^y \in J^y$. The probability of the j^y state occurring within the set of states in the y-th layer is π_{j^y}, with $\sum_{z=1}^{j^y} \pi_{j^z} = 1$. The set Φ of resolutions of price uncertainty has therefore cardinality (denoted also Φ)

$$\Phi = \Pi_{z=1}^Y J^z \tag{5.1}$$

and each realized path $(j^1, \ldots, j^Y) \in \Phi$ occurs with a probability $\pi_{j^1 \ldots j^Y} = \pi_{j^1} \times \pi_{j^2} \times \ldots \times \pi_{j^Y}$. Figure 1 illustrates a tree and a realized path

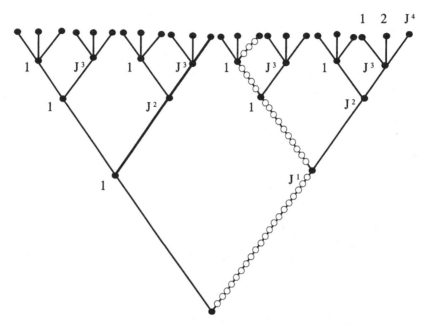

Figure 1. Four layers with two states in each of the first three layers and three states in layer 4 corresponding to the two equilibrium prices of the previous layer.

through the tree. There are four layers, and two possible equilibria in the markets defining each layer. At layer two, the four nodes of the tree correspond to the two equilibria in layer two markets, conditioned on each of the equilibria of the previous layer.

Summarizing all the above:

Definition 2: *A structure of uncertainty for the economy L is a list*

$$\left\{ Y, J^y, y = 1, \ldots, Y, \pi_{j^y} \text{ s.t.} \sum_{z=1}^{J^y} \pi_{j^z} = 1, j^y = 1, \ldots, J^y \right\}$$

where the finite set Y represents the layers of uncertainty, each finite set J^y represents the states in layer y, and π_{j^y} is the probability of state j^y within the yth layer. A resolution of price uncertainty is a vector $(j^1, \ldots, j^Y)$, where $j^y \in J^y$. The cardinality of the set of resolutions of price uncertainty is $\Phi = \Pi_{z=1}^{Y} J^z$.

5.2   *The financial markets of L*

Turning now to the financial structure of the economy L, define an elementary y-asset as an instrument which allows the transfer of wealth among the states of the yth layer of uncertainty. Formally:

> **Definition 3:**   *An elementary y-asset is a vector $(1, \ldots, k, \ldots, 0) \in R^{J^y}$ which pays k units of numeraire in state $j^y \in J^y$ in exchange for 1 unit of the numeraire in state $j^1 \in J^y$, and 0 in all other states. A portfolio of y-assets is a linear combination of y-assets, a vector $\theta^y = (\theta_1, \ldots, \theta_{J^y}) \in R^{J^y}$ representing a transfer of wealth among the J^y states of the yth layer of uncertainty.*

> **Assumption 2:**   *For each layer $y = 1, \ldots, Y$ there exists a complete set of y-assets, that is, there are $J^y - 1$ distinct elementary y-assets for all $y = 1, \ldots, Y$.*

In the example illustrated in Figure 1 the resolution of the price uncertainty path $(j^1, \ldots, j^Y)$ is marked with bubbles. The uncertainty structure is described as follows. There are four layers of uncertainty, $Y = 4$. The number of states in each of the layers is[11]

$$J^1 = 2, J^2 = 2, J^3 = 2, J^4 = 3$$

The resolution of price uncertainty illustrated is the path

$$\left(j^1, \ldots, j^Y\right) = \left(2, 1, 1, 3\right)$$

with probabilities

$$\pi_{j^1 \ldots j^Y} = \left(1/2\right) \cdot \left(1/2\right) \cdot \left(1/3\right) = 1/24$$

> **Assumption 3:**   *Assume that each trader $h = 1, \ldots, H$ owns initially no assets in any state of price uncertainty, so that $\forall h$, h's portfolio of y-assets θ^{hj^y}, satisfies*

$$\sum_{i=1}^{J^y} \theta_i^h = 0 \; \forall y = 1, \ldots, Y \tag{5.2}$$

> **Definition 4:**   *A portfolio θ is an ex ante hedging strategy for the entire price uncertainty of the economy. It has Y layers, $\theta =$*

---

[11] To simplify the illustration we assumed that there are two equilibria in each of the first three layers, even though regular economies satisfying our assumptions will typically have an odd number of equilibria.

$([\theta^1], \ldots, [\theta^Y])$, *each layer* $[\theta^y]$ *consisting of* J^y *different portfolios of* $(y - 1)$*-assets which hedge the price uncertainty of the previous layer,* $y - 1$:

$$\theta = \left(\left[\theta^1\right], \ldots, \left[\theta^Y\right]\right) \text{ s.t. } \forall y = 1, \ldots, Y,$$

$$\left[\theta^y\right] = \left(\theta^{j^1}, \ldots, \theta^{j^y}\right),$$

$$\text{with } \theta^{j^y} = \left(\theta_1^y, \ldots, \theta_{J^{y-1}}^y\right) \in R^{J^{y-1}} \; \forall j^y = 1, \ldots, J^y$$

$$\text{and for each } y, \; \sum_{i=1}^{J^{y-1}} \theta_i^y = 0 \tag{5.3}$$

The hedging role of the portfolio θ can be explained intuitively as follows. For each $y = 1, \ldots, Y$ the yth layer of the portfolio $[\theta^y]$ consists of one wealth transfer vector in $R^{J^{y-1}}$ for each of the J^y states in layer y, indicating that there are J^y ways of insuring against the J^{y-1} states of price uncertainty in layer $y - 1$, as defined above. Each J^{y-1}-dimensional vector θ^{j^y} defines a $(j^y - 1)$-asset, that is, a transfer of wealth across the J^{y-1} states of layer $y - 1$ uncertainty. This indicates that the uncertainty introduced by the $(y - 1)$th layer is not hedged at this layer of uncertainty but rather at the next layer; furthermore, this uncertainty is hedged in J^y different ways, indicating that the hedging of the $(y - 1)$th layer of uncertainty has introduced in turn a new layer of uncertainty. This new layer y has J^y new states, each representing the possible market clearing prices of the $(y - 1)$th level markets.

A portfolio θ provides an ex ante investment plan for all possible resolutions of uncertainty $(j^1, \ldots, j^Y) \in \Phi$. Therefore, at each realized path of price uncertainty $(j^1, \ldots, j^Y) \in \Phi$, θ defines a portfolio path indicated

$$\theta\left(j^1, \ldots, j^Y\right) = \left(\theta_{j^0}^{j^1}, \ldots, \theta_{j^{Y-1}}^{j^Y}\right) \in R^Y \tag{5.4}$$

where $\theta_{j^{y-1}}^{j^y} \in R$ is the realized value of the portfolio θ at the realized state j^y in layer y.

5.3   *The trader*

Turning now to the traders' behavior, a *plan* x^h for the h trader consists of an ex ante contract for each possible resolution of price uncertainty delivering an $l \times S$ vector at each state of each market layer. Therefore a trading plan is a vector $x \in R^{\Phi \times l \times S}$, where Φ is defined as in expression (5.1) above. For each resolution of price uncertainty $(j^1, \ldots, j^Y) \in \Phi$, the trading plan x^h of trader h defines *a path of Y net trade vectors in $R^{l \times S}$*, one vector in $R^{l \times S}$ for each state j^y in each layer y, denoted

$$x^h\left(j^1, \ldots, j^Y\right) = \left(x_{j^1}^h - w^h, x_{j^2}^h - x_{j^1}^h, \ldots, x_{j^Y}^h - x_{j^{Y-1}}^h\right) \in R^{\Phi \times l \times S}$$

to indicate the net additions to the initial endowment of the trader w^h along the realized path $(j^1, \ldots, j^Y)$. The trade at the 0 layer $(y = 0)$ is by definition $x_{j^0} = w^h$.

5.4   Prices

Corresponding to trading plans $x \in R^{\Phi \times l \times S}$, an ex ante price system for the economy L is a vector $p \in R^{\Phi \times l \times S}$, listing the set of all market equilibrium prices at each layer of uncertainty. For each resolution of price uncertainty $(j^1, \ldots, j^Y) \in \Phi$, p defines a *realized price path* $p(j^1, \ldots, j^Y)$ $= (p^{j^1}, \ldots, p^{j^Y}) \in R^{\Phi \times l \times S}$.

When price uncertainty is resolved a path $(j^1, \ldots, j^Y)$ is realized and all the net trades in that path $x^h(j^1, \ldots, j^Y)$ are realized. The total consumption vector of the household after each resolution of uncertainty is therefore the sum of the initial endowment w^h plus all the subsequent net trades in $x^h(j^1, \ldots, j^Y)$, adding up to a total consumption vector $x_{j^Y}^h$

$$x_{j^Y}^h = w^h + \sum_{z=0}^{Y}\left(x_{j^z}^h - x_{j^{z-1}}^h\right) \in R^{l \times S}$$

where $(x_{j^z}^h - x_{j^{z-1}}^h)$ is a net trade because $x_{j^{z-1}}^h$ is the endowment at layer z.

5.5   Utilities

Observe that the utility level trader h with plan x^h along the realized path $(j^1, \ldots, j^Y)$ is the utility of the sum of all the net trade vectors along it plus the initial endowment

$$V^h\left(x^h\left(j^1, \ldots, j^Y\right)\right) = V^h\left(w^h + \sum_{z=0}^{Y}\left(x_{j^z}^h - x_{j^{z-1}}^h\right)\right) = V^h\left(x_{j^Y}^h\right)$$

where the utility function V^h is as defined in Section 2. We may now define the utility functions of traders in the economy L over ex ante trading plans, which are the actions that traders take in this economy.

Definition 5:   *The utility derived by trader h from the ex ante trading plan x^h is the expected utility of consumption of x^h over all possible resolutions of uncertainty, namely over all paths $(j^1, \ldots, j^Y) \in \Phi$, each path considered with its probability, $\pi_{j^1 \ldots j^Y}$:*

$$U^h\left(x^h\right) = EV^h\left(x^h\left(j^1, \ldots, j^Y\right)\right) \tag{5.5}$$

5.6   Budgets and margins

Definition 6:   *For each price system p and portfolio θ^h, a budget set for the h trader is the set of all ex ante trading plans x^h which the trader can afford at all resolutions of price uncertainty:*

$$B\left(p, \theta^h\right) = \Big\{ x^h \; s.t. \; \forall\left(j^1, \ldots, j^Y\right) \in \Phi,$$

$$x^h\left(j^1, \ldots, j^Y\right) = \left(x_{j^1}^h - w^h, x_{j^2}^h - x_{j^1}^h, \ldots, x_{j^Y}^h - x_{j^{Y-1}}^h\right)$$

$$\text{satisfies } \sum_{j^1=1}^{J^1} p^{j^1} \cdot \left(x_{j^1}^h - w^h\right) = 0$$

$$\text{and } p^{j^y} \cdot \left(x_{j^y}^h - x_{j^{y-1}}^h\right) = \theta_{j^y}^{hj^{y+1}} \; \forall y = 1, \ldots, Y \Big\} \tag{5.6}$$

This means for at any resolution of price uncertainty $(j^1, \ldots, j^Y)$, trader h may add a net trade vector $(x_{j^y}^h - x_{j^{y-1}}^h) \in R^{I \times S}$ to her/his endowment at the realized state j^y, provided its value computed at j^y prices p^{jy} does not exceed that of the trader's portfolio at that state, $\theta_{j^{y-1}}^{hy}$. This is a natural extension of the notion of a budget set in Arrow–Debreu theory, adapted to the structure of uncertainty in this model. It contains several constraints that are akin to "margin" requirements, as they limit the amount of trading on a given market as a function of the holdings on lower layers.

5.7   An equilibrium of the economy L

The next step is to define an equilibrium of the economy L. Recall that in addition to the usual variables describing an equilibrium, namely prices and trading levels, our equilibrium concept includes an *endogenous determination of the structure of uncertainty*. The structure of price uncertainty is defined by Y layers of uncertainty with J^y states in each layer, and the corresponding set of yth assets for all layers $y = 1, \ldots, Y$. Together with the structure of uncertainty, an equilibrium of L consists of a price vector p^* and, for each trader h, a trading plan x^{h*}, and a portfolio θ^{h*}, such that the consumption plan x^{h*} maximizes the utility $U^h(x^h)$ over all consumption plans within the budget set $B(p^*, \theta^{h*})$, given the plans of the other traders, $x^{h'}$, $\forall h' \neq h$; all markets clear, and all traders are fully insured against price risks.

Full insurance for price risks is formally defined as follows.

Definition 7: *The traders $h = 1, \ldots, H$ are fully insured against price risks at their consumption plans $\{x^h\}$, $h = 1, \ldots, H$, when $\forall h$, their total consumption, and therefore their utility levels $U^h(x^h)$ are the same at any realization of the layers of price uncertainty, that is, $\forall (j^1, \ldots, j^Y), (j^{1'}, \ldots, j^{Y'}) \in \Phi$*

$$x_{j^Y}^{h*} = w^h + \sum_{z=1}^{Y} \left(x_{j^z}^* - x_{j^{z-1}}^* \right) = x_{j^y}^{h*}$$

$$= w^h + \sum_{z=1}^{Y} \left(x_{j^{z'}}^* - x_{j^{z-1'}}^* \right) \tag{5.7}$$

5.8   Institutional structure: An illustration

To fix ideas, I describe a possible institutional structure within which such an equilibrium may come about. This is to help the intuition and has no bearing on the formal definitions or the results. As in the Arrow–Debreu economy, one illustrates how an equilibrium emerges by imagining the actions of an auctioneer except that our auctioneer has a larger role than theirs.

The auctioneer announces here the structure of the price uncertainty in the second period, namely the number of layers of uncertainty Y, of states in each J^y, $y = 1, \ldots, Y$, and the probabilities π_{j^y} of each state j^y in J^y, with the corresponding financial markets.

For each such announcement, the auctioneer also provides an ex ante price system $p \in R^{\Phi \times I \times S}$ for the economy L. Using this information the traders, in turn, announce their portfolios θ^h and their ex ante plans $x^h \in R^{\Phi \times I \times S}$ within their budget sets $B(p, \theta^h)$. The auctioneer then reads the household plans; if an equilibrium obtains, trading is allowed. Otherwise the auctioneer tries again with another uncertainty structure, probabilities, and correspondingly new prices.

The auctioneer's role is to ensure that no trading takes place until all markets for commodities and for assets clear, and all households are fully insured against all price risks.

The existence of such an equilibrium seems like a tall order, but Theorem 1 below shows otherwise.

6   Existence of an equilibrium with full price insurance

Definition 8: *In the economy L defined above, the array $\{Y^*, J^{y*}, x^{h*}, \theta^{h*}, p^*$ for $y = 1, \ldots, Y^*$ and $h = 1, \ldots, H\}$ is an equilibrium with full insurance against price uncertainty if for each trader h, the consumption plan x^{h*} maximizes the expected utility*

$$U^h\left(x^h\right) \tag{6.1}$$

over the budget set $B(p^*, \theta^{h*})$ given the consumption plans $x^{h'}$ of all other traders $\forall h' \neq h$, each trader h is fully insured against price risks, at each resolution of price uncertainty $(j_1, \dots, j_Y) \in \Phi$ all asset markets to hedge price risks clear:

$$\sum_{h=1}^{H}\left(\theta^{h*}\right)^{j^y}_{j^{y-1}} = 0, \forall y = 1, \dots, Y, \text{ where } \left(\theta^{h*}\right)^1_0 = 0 \tag{6.2}$$

and all commodity markets clear at each state of every layer of uncertainty:

$$\sum_{h=1}^{H}\left(x^{h*}_{j^y} - x^{h*}_{j^{y-1}}\right) = 0, \forall y = 1, \dots, Y, \text{ where } x^{h*}_{j^0} = w^h \tag{6.3}$$

so that $\sum_{h=1}^{H} x^{h*}_{j^y} - w^h = 0$.

Theorem 1:   *The economy*

$$L = \left\{ X = R^l_+, s = 1, \dots, S, w^h \in R^{l \times S}, \right.$$
$$\left. V^h : X \to R, h = 1, \dots, H \right\}$$

as defined above has an equilibrium

$$\left\{ Y^*, J^{y*} =, x^{h*}, \theta^{h*}, p^* \text{ for } y = 1, \dots, Y^* h = 1, \dots, H \right\}$$

with full insurance against price risks, and yielding a Pareto efficient allocation.

Proof: The proof proceeds by constructing the equilibria of a sequence of auxiliary economies, which are then discarded. There is no need to know the equilibria ex ante. Consider first an Arrow–Debreu economy $\{w^h, U^h : X \to R, h = 1, \dots, H\}$ defined in Section 2, where the households are only concerned about the uncertainty defined by the Savage states $s = 1, \dots, S$. Call this economy E_1. The set of Walrasian equilibria of E_1 is denoted $J^{1*} = \{1, \dots, J^{1*}\}$; this set will define the first layer of price uncertainty of our economy $L, y = 1$. By definition, each of the J^{1*} equilibria of E_1 consists of a price vector $p^* \in R^{l \times S}$ and, for each h a consumption vector $x^{h*}_{j^1} \in R^{l \times S}$, for $j^1 = 1, \dots, J^{1*}$.

Define now a second economy E_2 having the same H households, l commodities, and S Savage states as E_1. Assign E_2 a different commodity space and, for each h, different endowments and different utilities. The commodity space of E_2 has J^{1*} new states of uncertainty and therefore the commodity space is $R^{l \times S \times J^{1*}}$. In E_2 household h's endowment is the vector defined by the J^{1*} equilibria of E_1 side by side, that is, by the vector $(x_1^{h*}, \ldots, x_{J^1}^{h*}) \in R^{l \times S \times J^{1*}}$, where $x_{J^1}^{h*} \in R^{l \times S}$. Trader h's utility of consumption in E_2 as in equation (5.1) is the expected utility of consumption over the J^{1*} states, $V^h : R^{l \times S \times J^{1*}} \to R$, all states evaluated with the same probability:

$$V^h(y_1, \ldots, y_{J^1}) = \sum_{i=1}^{J^{1*}} \left(1/J^{1*} \right) U^h(y_i)$$

Assume now that the second economy E_2 has J^{2*} Walrasian equilibria. Then each of the J^{2*} Walrasian equilibria of E_2 consists of a price vector $p_{j^2}^* \in R^{l \times S \times J^{1*}}$ and, for each h, a consumption vector $x_{j^2}^{h*} \in R^{l \times S \times J^{1*}}$ for $j^2 = 1, \ldots, J^{2*}$. The set $J^{2*} = \{1, \ldots, J^{2*}\}$ of Walrasian equilibria of the economy E_2 defines layer $y = 1$ of uncertainty of our economy L.

E_2 has new states of uncertainty over and above those of E_1, indeed J^{1*} of them, but it also has all instruments needed to hedge this uncertainty, because, by construction, in E_2 there are markets contingent on the J^{1*} states of price uncertainty. The financial instruments corresponding to these contingent trades correspond to the portfolios of l-assets defined above, namely vectors describing wealth transfers between the J^{1*} price uncertainty states of economy E_1, $(\theta_1, \ldots, \theta_{J^{1*}})$, with $\Sigma_{i=1}^{J1*} \theta_i = 0$. Since all assets needed to hedge the J^{1*} states of price uncertainty are available in E_2, at an equilibrium each trader h will achieve state independent consumption over the J^{1*} states. This is because in each of these J^{1*} states the total endowment $w = \Sigma_h w^h$ of the economy E_2 is the same, and every trader h has the same probability over the J^{1*} states.[12] Since each trader achieves state independent consumption over the J^{1*} states of price uncertainty, this means that at an equilibrium of E_2 the consumption vector $x_{j^2}^{h*} \in R^{l \times S \times J^{1*}}$ of the h trader consists of $S \times l$ coordinates repeated J^{1*} times. Clearly, this vector is then properly identified by $S \times l$ coordinates only, that is, $x_{j^2}^{h*} \in R^{l \times S}$. The corresponding prices are $p^{j^{2*}} \in R^{l \times S}$.

---

[12] This is the same point made in Proposition 1 above; the reader is referred to Chichilnisky, Dutta, and Heal (1991) for another proof.

Each trader in E_2 may shift wealth across the J^{1*} states to achieve the same consumption level at each, a shift represented by the vector with J^{1*} coordinates. At any market clearing equilibrium j^2 of E_2 this shift in wealth is, by definition, equal to a vector of differences between the value of the endowments evaluated at the equilibrium price $p_{j^2}^*$ in state j^2, namely $p_{j^2}^* . x_{j^2}^{h*}$, and the value of the equilibrium consumption at the same prices, namely, $p_{j^2}^* . x_{j^2}^{h*}$ for each $j^1 = 1, \ldots, J^{1*}$. By definition of an equilibrium, each trader's consumption must be within his/her budget constraint, so that $\forall h = 1, \ldots, H$,

$$p^{j^{2*}} . x_{j^2}^{h*} = \sum_{j^1=1}^{J^{1*}} \left(p^{2*} . x_{j^1}^{h*} \right) \text{ at each } j^2 = 1, \ldots, J^{2*}$$

and that $\forall j^2 = 1, \ldots, J^{2*}$

$$\sum_{j^1=1}^{J^{1*}} p^{2*} . \left(x_{j^2}^{h*} - x_{j^1}^{h*} \right) = 0 \tag{6.4}$$

Now define $[\theta^{h2}]$ as the following collection of J^{2*} vectors in $R^{J^{1*}}$:

$$\begin{aligned}
\left[\theta^{h2} \right] &= \left(\theta_1^{h*j^2}, \ldots, \theta_{J^1}^{h*j^2} \right) \\
&= \left(p^{2*} . \left(x_{j^2}^{h*} - x_1^{h*} \right), \ldots, p^{2*} . \left(x_{j^2}^{h*} - x_{j^1}^{h*} \right) \right) \in R^{J^{1*}}, \\
&\qquad \text{for } J^2 = 1, \ldots, J^{2*}
\end{aligned} \tag{6.5}$$

Then by equation (6.4), $[\theta^{h2}]$ defines a layer 2 portfolio of 1-assets, since for each $j^2 = 1, \ldots, J^{2*}$

$$\sum_{j^1=1}^{J^{1*}} \theta_i^{h*j^2} = 0$$

which is the condition required in the definition of a layer 2 portfolio, Section 5.

Recall that in the economy E_2 there are many different ways to achieve the equalization of consumption across the J^{1*} equilibria; there are precisely J^{2*} ways to do so, one for each of the equilibria of E_2. Corresponding to these are the J^{2*} portfolios of level 1 assets making the layer 2 portfolio $[\theta^{h2}]$ in equation (6.5). Since there are J^{2*} ways to achieve this equalization of consumption across all J^{1*} states of uncertainty, each yielding a different market clearing price or state in layer 2, E_2 introduces J^{2*} new states of price uncertainty which define our second layer

$y = 2$. To hedge these new states, consider a new economy E_3, which is defined exactly the same as E_2 but for its commodity space which is now equal to $R^{l \times S \times J^{2*}}$ to account for the fact that there are now J^{2*} new states of uncertainty. Repeating the same argument we build inductively a sequence of economies $\{E_y\}$, each economy E_y having the endowments provided by the set of J^{y-1*} equilibria of E_{y-1}, each economy E_y hedging the price risks of the former, E_{y-1}, and each trader h in E_y achieving state independent consumption over the states J^{y-1*}. This sequence of economies $\{E_y\}$ coincides with the sequence defined in Chichilnisky, Dutta, and Heal (1991).

To summarize: The economy E_y has a consumption set $R^{l \times S \times J^{y-1*}}$; trader h has as an initial endowment her/his allocation at the J^{y-1*} equilibria, namely the vector $(x_1^{h*}, \ldots, x_{J^{y-1*}}^{h*}) \in R^{l \times S \times J^{y-1*}}$, where $x_{J^{y-1*}}^{h*}$ is the state-independent j^{y-1}th equilibrium allocation of trader h at the economy E_{y-1}. Trader h's utility of consumption in E_y is the expected utility of consumption over the J^{y-1*} states, $V^h : R^{l \times S \times J^{y-1*}} \to R$, all states evaluated with the same probability:

$$V^h\left(y_1, \ldots, y_{J^{y-1}}\right) = \sum_{i=1}^{J^{y-1*}} \left(1/J^{y-1*}\right) U^h\left(y_i\right)$$

If the economy E_y has J^{y*} Walrasian equilibria, then each of the J^{y*} Walrasian equilibria of E_y consists of a price vector $p_{j^y}^* \in R^{l \times S \times J^{y-1*}}$ and, for each h, a consumption vector $x_{j^y}^{h*} \in R^{l \times S \times J^{y-1*}}$ for $j^y = 1, \ldots, J^{y*}$. The set $J^{y*} = \{1, \ldots, J^{y*}\}$ of Walrasian equilibria of the economy E_y defines the yth layer of uncertainty of our economy L. Since all assets needed to hedge the J^{y-1*} states of price uncertainty exist in E_y, households are fully insured against all the risk implicit in the J^{y-1*} states. This means that at an equilibrium of E_y the consumption vector $x_{j^y}^{h*} \in R^{l \times S \times J^{y-1*}}$ of the h trader consists of $S \times l$ coordinates repeated J^{y-1*} times. Clearly, this vector is then properly identified by $S \times l$ coordinates only, that is, $x_{j^y}^{h*} \in R^{l \times S}$ and the price $p^{j^y*} \in R^{l \times S}$.

Each trader in E_y shifts wealth across the J^{y-1*} states to achieve the same consumption level at each state, a shift represented by the vector with J^{y-1*} coordinates. At any market clearing equilibrium j^y of E_y this shift in wealth is, by definition, equal to a vector of differences between the value of the endowments evaluated at the equilibrium price $p_{j^y}^*$ in states j^y, namely $p_{j^y}^* . x_{j^y}^{h*}$. By definition of an equilibrium, each household's consumption must be within his/her budget constraint, so that $\forall h = 1, \ldots, H$, and

$$p^{y*} \cdot x_{j^y}^{h*} = \sum_{j^y=1}^{J^{y*}} \left(p^{y*} \cdot x_{j^{y-1}}^{h*} \right) = 0 \text{ at each } j^y = 1, \ldots, J^{y*}$$

(6.6)

Therefore $\forall j^y = 1, \ldots, J^{y*}$

$$\sum_{j^{y-1}=1}^{J^{y-1*}} p^{jy*} \cdot \left(x_{j^y}^{h*} - x_{j^{y-1}}^{h*} \right) = 0$$

(6.7)

Now define $[\theta^{hy}]$ as the following J^{y*} vectors in $R^{J^{y-1*}}$:

$$
\begin{aligned}
\left[\theta^{hy} \right] &= \left(\theta_1^{h*j^y}, \ldots, \theta_{J^1}^{h*j^y} \right) \\
&= \left(p^{jy*} \cdot \left(x_{j^y}^{h*} - x_1^{h*} \right), \ldots, \left(p^{jy*} \cdot \left(x_{j^y}^{h*} - x_{J^{y*}}^{h*} \right) \right) \in R^{J^{y-1*}}, \\
&\quad \text{for } j^y = 1, \ldots, J^{y*} \right)
\end{aligned}
$$

(6.8)

Then by equation (6.7) $[\theta^{hy}]$ defines a layer y portfolio of $(y - 1)$-assets, since for each $j^y = 1, \ldots, J^{y*}$

$$\sum_{i=1}^{J^{y-1*}} \theta_i^{h*j^y} = 0$$

(6.9)

which is the condition required in the definition of a layer y portfolio in Section 5.

Under the regularity assumption 2 of Chichilnisky, Dutta, and Heal (1991), which is also required here in Section 2, they proved that this process leads in a finite number of steps to an economy E_{Y*} having a unique, and Pareto efficient, Walrasian equilibrium.[13] In other words

---

[13] The result depends on the regularity of the economy, and the following fact: Any Pareto efficient allocation is the initial allocation of an Arrow–Debreu economy with a unique equilibrium, namely itself. Thus such economies have no price uncertainty. By regularity and the implicit function theorem, the number of equilibria is locally a continuous function of initial endowments. Therefore for all initial allocations in a neighborhood of a Pareto efficient allocation the economy has a unique equilibrium and thus no price uncertainty. The theorem in Chichilnisky, Dutta, and Heal (1991) shows that in a finite number of steps and by adding a finite number of assets, the initial endowment of the economy falls into the neighborhood of the Pareto frontier where the equilibrium is unique. Thus in a finite number of steps the process leads to an economy without price uncertainty. These, as shown in Proposition 1, are the only economies in which price uncertainty can be fully hedged within an Arrow–Debreu framework.

$$\exists Y^* \text{ such that } x_{j^y}^{h*} = x_{j',Y*}^{h*}, \forall j^{Y*}, j'^{Y*} = 1, \dots, J^{Y*}$$
$$(6.10)$$

The existence of an equilibrium for the economy L can now be established. The uncertainty structure is defined by Y^* layers indexed by $y = 1, \dots, Y^*$, with J^{Y*} states of uncertainty in each layer indicated $j^y = 1, \dots, J^y*$. For each j^y define the probability $\pi_{j^y} = 1/J^y*$. For $y = 1, \dots, Y^*$, consider $p^{j^y*} \in R^{I \times S}$ to be the j^y equilibrium price vector of the economy E_y, $j^y = 1, \dots, J^y*$. Define

$$p^* = \left(p^{j^1*}, \dots, p^{j^{Y*}} \right)_{j^1=1,\dots,J^Y,\dots,j^Y=1,\dots,J^{Y*}} \in R^{\Phi \times I \times S}$$
$$(6.11)$$

Finally let $[\theta^{hy}]$ be defined as in equation (6.8), and define household h's ex ante portfolio θ^{h*} in the economy L to be:

$$x^{h*} =$$
$$\left(\left(x_{j^1}^{h*} - w^h \right), \dots, \left(x_{j^{i+1}}^{h*} - x_{j^i}^{h*} \right) \right)_{j^1=1,\dots,J^Y,\dots,j^Y=1,\dots,J^{Y*}}$$
$$\in R^{\Phi \times I \times S}$$
$$(6.12)$$

It remains now to check that $\{Y^*, J^y*, p^*, x^{h*}, \theta^{h*}, h = 1, \dots, H, y = 1, \dots, Y^*\}$ is an equilibrium of L.

First check that $\forall h = 1, \dots, H, x^{h*}$ is in $B(p^*, \theta^{h*})$ as defined in equation (5.6). This follows from equations (6.4), (6.5), (6.7), (6.8), and (6.9).

Condition (6.3) for an equilibrium follows from the fact that for each $y = 1, \dots, Y^*$ each market contingent on the J^{y-1} states of uncertainty of the economy E_{y-1} must clear at each Walrasian equilibrium j^y of the economy E_y; condition (6.2) follows directly from (6.5). Finally we check that U^h is maximized at x^{h*} given $x^{h'*}, \forall h' \neq h$. For this, recall that $x_{j^y}^{h*} = x_{j^Y*}^{h*}, \forall j^Y*, j^{Y'} = 1, \dots, j^{Y*}$ by (6.5), so that traders are fully insured. Finally, note that the allocation $\{x_{j^Y}^{h*} \in R^{I \times S}, h = 1, \dots, H\}$ is Pareto efficient because it is the Walrasian equilibrium of the economy E_{Y*}. This completes the proof. QED.

7 The literature on endogenous uncertainty

The problem of price uncertainty in general equilibrium was introduced and analyzed in two independent and simultaneous essays, each offering a different solution and both quite different from what is presented here: Hahn (1991) and Chichilnisky, Dutta, and Heal (1991). The results were elaborated further in Chichilnisky, Hahn, and Heal (1992). Hahn (1991) defines a two-period economy with incomplete markets for price risks. The agents alter their behavior when they learn about the several possible equilibrium prices, but have no more assets to hedge this uncertainty, so the market remains incomplete. Chichilnisky, Hahn, and Heal (1992) price the existence of an equilibrium with incomplete markets for price risks. In a different approach to the same problem, Chichilnisky, Dutta, and Heal (1991) construct a sequence of different, progressively larger economies in which new derivative securities are introduced at each stage, and show that this process leads in a finite number of steps to a new economy, the original augmented by markets for derivative securities, which has unique market clearing prices, and hence no price risks. Their analysis differs from that provided here in a number of ways. The first difference is that they consider a sequence of Arrow–Debreu economies, each having different endowments and utilities from the previous one, and at each step contracting takes place before the next economy is known. By contrast, in this chapter there is only one economy, and all contracting takes place simultaneously. The economy in this chapter has one utility function and one endowment vector for each trader. The agents in Chichilnisky, Dutta, and Heal (1991) anticipate correctly at each stage all the possible Walrasian equilibrium prices, an assumption I do not make in our definition of the economy with endogenous uncertainty in Section 5, or in the proof of existence of a market equilibrium, Theorem 2. Moreover, the concept of a market clearing equilibrium proposed here is different from that of an Arrow–Debreu economy in that I require "margins," or covered trading on the newly introduced markets. Finally, in contrast to Hahn (1991), Chichilnisky, Dutta, and Heal (1991), and Chichilnisky, Hahn, and Heal (1992), the optimal behavior of the agents with respect to the introduction of new states of price uncertainty is that agents choose their trading strategies so as to maximize utility, taking as given the behavior of others in the newly introduced markets.

An unusual feature of the type of uncertainty contemplated here is that it depends on the behavior of the agents as well as on acts of nature. In this sense the economy has endogenous uncertainty. Kurz (1993) discussed endogenous uncertainty in the context of a comment on Kesten–Stigum's model, and recently proposed a model where price expectations follow "rational beliefs," a special form of temporary equilibrium model. Expectations alter prices and therefore induce a well-known form of endogenous uncertainty, typical of "temporary equilibrium" model. The concept of endogenous uncertainty was also discussed earlier in Hahn (1973) and in Dasgupta and Heal (1979). Within a three-period model, Henrotte (1992) has examined the role of options to hedge price uncertainty in securities markets. The first results on existence and characterization of markets with endogenous uncertainty in a general equilibrium framework were obtained in Chichilnisky and Wu (1991) and Chichilnisky, Dutta, and Heal (1991). Chichilnisky (1995) proves the existence of equilibrium in an economy where the state space varies with the production of the economy.

References

Arrow, K. J. 1953. The role of securities in the optimal allocation of risk-bearing (in French). *Econometrie: Proceedings of the Colloque sur les Fondements et Applications de la Théorie du Risque en Economomométrie*. Paris: Centre National de la Recherche Scientifique. English Translation: *Review of Economic Studies* (1964) 31:91–6.

Chichilnisky, G. 1998. The market as a public good. Working Paper, Program on Information and Resources, Columbia University, Invited address to the UNDP Workshop on Global Public Goods, 1998.

Chichilnisky, G. 1995. "Markets with Endogenous Uncertainty: Theory and Policy." *Theory and Decision*, 41:99–131, 1996.

Chichilnisky, G., J. Dutta, and G. M. Heal. 1991. Endogenous uncertainty and derivative securities in a general equilibrium model. Working paper, Columbia University, in *Markets with Endogenous Uncertainty* (eds. G. Chichilnisky and G. Heal), New York: Springer-Verlag to appear.

Chichilnisky, G., G. M. Heal, P. Streufert, and J. Swinkels. 1992. Believing in multiple equilibrium. Working paper, Stanford Institute for Theoretical Economics.

Chichilnisky, G., and H. M. Wu. 1991. Financial innovation and endogenous uncertainty in incomplete asset markets. Technical Report No. 50. Stanford Institute for Theoretical Economics, 1992.

Chichilnisky, G., F. Hahn, and G. M. Heal. 1992. Price uncertainty and incomplete markets, Working paper, Columbia University, in *Markets with Endogenous Uncertainty* (ed. G. Chichilnisky and G. Heal), New York: Springer-Verlag to appear.

Debreu, G. 1970. Economics with a finite set of equilibria. *Econometrica* 38:387–92.

Dasgupta, P., and G. M. Heal. 1979. *Economic Theory of Exhaustible Resources*, Cambridge University Press.

Hahn, F. 1992. Making general equilibrium theory more plausible. The Second Annual Arrow Lecture Series, Department of Economics, Stanford University, May 5 and 6.

Hahn, F. 1991. A remark on incomplete market equilibrium. Working paper, Cambridge University and University of Siena; this volume.

Hahn, F. 1973. *The Concept of Equilibrium in Economics*. Inaugural lecture, Chair in Economics, at Churchill College, Cambridge University, Cambridge UK.

Halmos, P. 1970. *Naive Set Theory*. New York-Heidelberg-Berlin: Springer-Verlag.

Henrotte, P. 1992. An example of general equilibrium with derivative securities: The binomial case. Working paper, Stanford University.

Kurz, M. 1993. General equilibrium with endogenous uncertainty. Working paper, Stanford University.

Kurz, M. 1991. On the structure and diversity of rational beliefs. Technical Report No. 39, Stanford Institute for Theoretical Economics (November).

Kurz, M. 1974. The Kesten–Stigum model and the treatment of uncertainty in equilibrium theory. In *Essays in Economic Behavior under Uncertainty* (ed. M. C. Balch, D. McFadden, and S. Wu), Amsterdam: North Holland.

Milnor, J. 1965. *Topology from a differentiable viewpoint*. Charlottesville: The University Press of Virginia.

CHAPTER 6

Market equilibrium with endogenous price uncertainty and options

Peter H. Huang and Ho-Mou Wu

1   Introduction

Arrow's (1953) classic two-period general competitive equilibrium
model introduced the canonical theoretical setting for the study of
market behavior under uncertainty. The types of randomness described
by Arrow's formalization are those factors external to human influence,
such as hurricanes, earthquakes, droughts, and floods, that affect production capabilities or consumer tastes. In one bold stroke, Arrow (1953)
and Debreu (1959), with the introduction of a complete set of contingent commodity markets, reinterpret the static Arrow and Debreu (1954)
model of certainty in terms of a sequential model of uncertainty. This
reinterpretation allowed their results about existence and Pareto
optimality of static competitive equilibria to carry over completely to a
dynamic and uncertain world. Arrow's (1953) model also provided what
has become the standard role for securities, namely hedging against
exogenous risks by shifting income across exogenous states. As Duffie
(1991) noted, Arrow (1953) and Arrow and Debreu (1954) provided
financial economists with benchmarks for market behavior that had been
missing until then.

In Arrow's paradigm, uncertainty means not knowing which of several
possible states will prevail. Agents are assumed to know all the conceivable states that can arise. These states are assumed to form a mutually
exclusive and exhaustive description of the future. Arrow's conceptual-
ization of states of nature is related to, but differs from Savage's (1954)

It is our pleasure to contribute this essay to honor our mutual advisor and teacher, Ken
Arrow, from whose work, generosity, and scholarly example we have learned much. We
thank Ken Arrow, Don Brown, Graciela Chichilnisky, Frank Hahn, Geoff Heal, Philippe
Henrotte, Mordecai Kurz, Chris Shannon, Jan Werner, three anonymous referees, and the
audiences of seminars at Columbia, Duke, and Stanford for helpful discussions.

97

definition of personal states of the world for subjective probabilities in statistical decision theory because the state space must be agreed on by everybody in Arrow's framework in order to have markets for either contingent commodities or securities. A crucial assumption of the Arrow paradigm is that traders know the mapping from states into equilibrium prices, $p(s)$. Any uncertainty about market prices disappears once the true state is known. In other words, individuals possess perfect foresight about prices, conditional on knowledge of the realized state.[1]

Criticisms of Arrow's (1953) notion of rational expectation as conditional perfect foresight focus on either the restriction that the equilibrium mapping $p(s)$ is a function with a unique p for each s or on the incredible computational abilities economic agents must have to compute the function $p(s)$. In this chapter, we explore the possible extensions that economic theory can now offer to address both these criticisms. First, we consider a departure from Arrow's paradigm which examines the implications when mapping of $p(s)$ is not a function, but a correspondence instead. In other words, people know that several equilibrium prices exist. We review the leading work by Chichilnisky (1992; 1994), Chichilnisky, Dutta, and Heal (1991), and Chichilnisky and Wu (1992). Although it is difficult to ensure uniqueness of equilibria, local finiteness of equilibria is easily ensured. Debreu (1970) proved that a typical (or technically regular) economy has a finite number of equilibria. However, even this mild form of nonuniqueness of equilibria creates difficulties for the usual notion of rationality of expectations in general equilibrium theory. It raises four questions: If the agents know that several equilibrium prices exist, what optimization problems do individuals face when they are uncertain as to which of several possible equilibrium prices will prevail; what is a sensible notion of general equilibrium with price uncertainty; can such an equilibrium be shown to exist; and what is the role of options in such an equilibrium with price uncertainty?

The first part of this chapter examines these questions when agents are assumed to possess, as in Arrow (1953), structural knowledge of the economy. The second part studies the notion of price uncertainty when

---

[1] Since then, Arrow's position on the rational expectations doctrine has evolved somewhat. Arrow (1978) explained how differential information alters the policy neutrality propositons regarding macroeconomic fluctuations of the "rational expectations" school of thought. Arrow (1982) suggested that experimental evidence from cognitive psychology can explain such observed failures of the rational anticipations hypothesis in financial markets as analogous to Shiller's (1981) findings about excess volatility in bond and stock markets. Arrow (1986) discussed the implications of bounded rationality for formulating a concept of equilibrium.

agents do not possess structural knowledge of the economy and form expectations on this. Kurz (1974; 1996), Kurz and Wu (1996), and others pursue this line of research. It is conceivable that before equilibrium prices are realized, investors may not have enough information to select a correct set of possible equilibrium prices. This means that prior beliefs may have as their support a much larger space than the set of realized equilibrium prices. Ex post market prices are observable and posterior beliefs place probability one on the equilibrium price actually realized. Our notion of rationality of beliefs drops the restriction, due to Hicks (1946), that beliefs have to be time invariant.[2] Such a time dependence of beliefs is natural in light of the multiplicity of equilibria and the irreversible nature of a sequential economy. The diffuse nature of these priors can be due to uncertainty about other households' endowments and utility functions, the lack of time or ability to compute equilibrium prices, complexity reasons, or some unforeseen contingencies.

In Section 2, we discuss further the meaning of price uncertainty and review the related literature about endogenous uncertainty. In Section 3, we discuss the role of options and price-contingent securities in the allocation of endogenous risk. Section 4 describes an economy in which agents face price uncertainty. We suggest that investors can hedge against spot price uncertainty by trading European options when they know the equilibrium price correspondence $p(s)$. We also study the properties of equilibria when there are complete or incomplete options markets. In Section 5, we examine the notion of equilibrium when economic agents do not have enough computational ability to identify the equilibrium correspondence $p(s)$. Section 6 offers concluding thoughts.

2   The meaning of price uncertainty

As Arrow (1991) noted, uncertainty is clearly unavoidable in (economic) life. How to deal with uncertainty for both economic theorists and practitioners is the problem. Before Arrow's (1953) tour de force essay, economists represented uncertainty by probability distributions over exogenous and endogenous randomness. Since Arrow's seminal formulation of uncertainty in terms of exogenously given states of nature, economic theory in general and general equilibrium theory in particular

---

[2] The idea of decoupling the set of date 1 spot prices that households expect are possible into those they expect at date 0 versus those they expect at date 1 is inspired by Arrow. He observed that what is crucial in his 1953 equivalence result between complete contingent commodity markets and complete security markets is the assumption that households not only have single-valued price expectations at date 0, but also that households maintain those same beliefs at date 1.

have been expressed primarily in terms of such "states of nature."[3] Two facts must be true of these states if markets for state-contingent commodities or assets with payoffs indexed by states to exist. First, states must be agreed on and commonly observable by economic actors. Second, states can only capture uncertainty not influenced by human action. If either property fails to hold for the concept of states, the well-known problems of moral hazard and/or adverse selection can lead to the nonexistence of markets or nonexistence of equilibria when competitive markets do exist.

The comprehensive nature of these states is such that once the true state is known, no residual uncertainty remains. In particular, this means that on learning the actual state s, agents know the values of market prices $p(s)$. In other words, $p(s)$ is assumed to be a common knowledge single-valued function. This informational assumption is restrictive in several ways. First, agents might not be able to solve for the function $p(s)$. This is the approach taken by Kurz (1994a, 1994b, 1996) and Kurz and Wu (1996) in a model of endogenous uncertainty and rational beliefs, where agents do not know the structure of the economy and possess heterogeneous beliefs about the values of endogenous variables in their economy. Second, if agents have structural knowledge of their economy, they might realize that generically $p(s)$ is a correspondence. This is what Chichilnisky, Dutta, and Heal (1991), Chichilnisky (1992, 1994), and Chichilnisky and Wu (1992) assume. The difference between these works concerns the agents' knowledge of their economy. Kurz (1994a, 1994b, 1996) and Kurz and Wu (1996) postulate that agents do not know the structural equations describing their economy and so does Chichilnisky (1992, 1994). Chichilnisky, Dutta, and Heal (1991) assume that agents know the "reduced form" of their economy, namely the correspondence $p(s)$. Finally, agents may not even be aware of all the possible states. This more realistic and less understood setting is that of unforeseen contingencies. Kreps (1992) and Huang (1993) offer the beginnings of such a theory.

---

[3] A notable exception to Arrow's legacy is game theory which by its very nature is an interactive multiperson decision-making theory. The fundamental problem of game theory (for players and game theorists alike) is to predict how players will behave. Thus players face uncertainty over the endogenous decisions of other players. Incomplete information games are converted into complete, but imperfect information games by introducing the notion of players' types. Thus, strategic uncertainty over endogenously chosen decisions can often be replaced by structural uncertainty over exogenously fixed parameters describing a game. Aumann and Brandenburger (1991) recently introduced the notion of an interactive belief system to deal simultaneously with strategic and structural uncertainty.

The recently growing literature about price uncertainty has its roots in the study of endogenous uncertainty discussed by Kurz (1974). Kurz pointed out that the dominant form of uncertainty economic agents face is not exogenous uncertainty, but a qualitatively different type of uncertainty he termed endogenous uncertainty. The difference between exogenous and endogenous uncertainty is that the former results from events determined by nature whereas the latter is determined by the decisions of economic agents themselves. Kurz made an important observation about the crucial nature of endogenous uncertainty, especially in modern economies. Undoubtedly, the driving source of uncertainty behind macroeconomic and financial time series does not come from natural disasters, important and tragic as they may be. Instead, the volatility in financial markets and of national incomes is primarily due to endogenous uncertainty. In particular, economic agents are uncertain about the values of endogenous economic variables, such as prices, quantities, and qualities. But, as Arrow (1994) pointed out, the concept of endogenous uncertainty has many possible interpretations that require unpacking or unbundling.

Svensson (1981) considered uncertainty about prices in a temporary general equilibrium model involving a complete set of Arrow–Debreu commodity markets contingent on any relative price vector in the unit simplex. He applied the infinite dimensional commodity space model of Bewley (1972) to show the existence of competitive equilibria. Kurz (1994a, 1994b) introduced a theory of rational beliefs which allows for heterogeneous beliefs about prices due to agents not knowing the structural equations of the economy they inhabit. Kurz and Wu (1996) analyzed the equilibrium and welfare properties of competitive equilibrium when trading endogenous uncertainty is accomplished by using price-contingent contracts rather than the Arrow–Debreu state-contingent contracts. They introduce rationality restrictions on beliefs and construct a "price state space" which requires the expansion of the exogenous state space to include the "state of beliefs." Kurz (1996) reviewed the recent work on endogenous uncertainty with rationality restrictions on beliefs.

A different interpretation and formalization of endogenous uncertainty, as in Chichilnisky, Dutta, and Heal (1991), is based on the multiplicity of equilibria, which they assume economic actors have the computational power to calculate. Chichilnisky, Dutta, and Heal (1991) proved that finitely many successive levels of price-contingent Arrow–Debreu futures markets are sufficient to ensure fully against price uncertainty. Hahn (1992, 1994) argued that a set of complete Arrow securities contingent on exogenous states and endogenous prices leads to the nonexistence of a rational expectations equilibrium if there are multiple spot market equilibrium prices. Chichilnisky (1992) investigated general equilibrium in a model with nested layers of endogenous uncertainty. She drew a parallel between Russell's famous paradox in formal logic and the problem of hedging endogenous uncertainty. Chichilnisky, Heal, and Tsomocos (1994) model endogenous uncertainty over whether options will be exercised. Chichilnisky (1994) considered the theory and policy applications of endogenous uncertainty induced by production activities in an economy. In yet another framework not involving multiplicity of equilibria, Chichilnisky and Wu (1992) analyzed individual and collective risk (as studied by Cas, Chichilnisky, and Wu [1996]) in a general equilibrium model of default. Their model demonstrated that endogenous uncertainty can be due to financial innovation and that it depends crucially on the endogenous pattern of trade.

3   The role of options

Arrow's (1953) model provided what has become the standard role for securities, namely hedging against risks by shifting income across *exogenous* states. He demonstrated that a complete set of (what have since then become known as Arrow) security markets can replace the larger number of complete contingent commodity markets in achieving a Pareto efficient allocation of risk over exogenous uncertainty. Financial economists have since then focused on what is the span, in the space of income across states, of a set of assets. Ross (1976) showed that (sufficiently many) options can be used to complete state-contingent asset markets and provide insurance against exogenous uncertainty. Other state-contingent assets can achieve the same goal of completing state-contingent markets. Ross cited the relative easiness or cost advantages of writing options as the main reason for trading options.

We reexamine here the role that price-contingent securities or options play in insuring against *endogenous* price uncertainty. To complete markets in a world with exogenous uncertainty one can also use other state-contingent assets instead of options. Then options may or may not offer any "comparative advantage" in completing asset markets. This presents us with a puzzle: Why are options traded so actively in real world economies? The answer becomes clear when we consider endogenous uncertainty: because endogenous price uncertainty is so prevalent in real world economies and price-contingent securities, such as options, are uniquely suited to handle those price-related risks. Options therefore play the same important role for handling endogenous price uncertainty that state-contingent assets do for handling exogenous state uncertainty in Arrow (1953). This role of options cannot be replaced by any other kinds of assets which are not price-contingent.

In the case of complete state-contingent markets for exogenous uncertainty, options are "redundant" in terms of their payoffs and can be priced by arbitrage (see Hakansson (1978)). In spite of this, we show that options also serve the indispensable role of protecting investors from disequilibrium expectations about endogenous price uncertainty. The fact that option payoffs can be replicated by portfolios of existing primary assets does not mean that option markets have no role to play in the optimal allocation of risk concerning price uncertainty. Just the opposite is true. Our viewpoint turns out to be analogous to that of Mas-Colell (1992) regarding asset redundancy and sunspots.

In our model, as discussed in the next section, option markets play two additional roles. First, a set of option markets changes not only the number of, but also the actual set of, equilibrium spot prices and commodity allocations. Thus, the financial sector (consisting of commodity option markets) in our economy fundamentally affects the real sector. Second, complete option markets select a particular spot market equilibrium as being focal. Option premia facilitate the coordination of households' beliefs on a particular vector of commodity prices by the no-arbitrage condition on equilibrium option premia. Notice that we do not claim option premia are unique. Different equilibrium option premia correspond to different spot prices via the no-arbitrage condition on equilibrium option premia.

4   Price uncertainty with structural knowledge

It is helpful to view this section as investigating the logical implications of two axioms:

A1   An economy is regular (this ensures finiteness of equilibria).
A2   Investors have knowledge of the mapping $p(s)$, whether it be a function or a correspondence.

We also evaluate two properties of equilibria:

P1   Multiple price equilibria exist.
P2   Price-contingent option markets efficiently allocate risk about endogenous uncertainty.

In the following section, we describe an economy satisfying A1, A2, and P1 and we introduce price-contingent option markets. We then investigate the compatibility of P1 with A1 and A2 when there are complete option markets. The question of what role price-contingent securities play in the allocation of endogenous risk is what P2 addresses. This question is analogous to Arrow's (1953) concern over the role of securities in the optimal allocation of exogenous risk. In the case of complete option markets, P2 is true. In fact, complete option markets completely eliminate any price uncertainty in the spot market. In the case of incomplete option markets, obviously a first-best allocation of risk from price uncertainty is too much to ask for. So P2 fails; but it can be shown that P1 is generically true with incomplete option markets.

4.1   The economy with price uncertainty

Consider a pure exchange economy with G goods, two dates 0 and 1, and N exogenous states of nature at date 1. There are complete asset markets with respect to these exogenous states. In what follows, we concentrate on the study of price uncertainty. To simplify our notation, we set $N = 1$ for the rest of the chapter. There are G spot commodity markets at date 1, while no consumption occurs at date 0. It might be helpful to think of date 1 as when this economy actually takes place, whereas date 0 is an instant just before then, as in Arrow (1953). The raison d'être for date 0 is to allow households to trade in assets written on spot commodity prices at date 1. There are H households, each with a (column) vector of initial commodity endowments, $e^h (\varepsilon) R^G$. Let $e = (e^1, \ldots, e^H) \in R^{GH}$. We denote the consumption of commodities by household h as a (column) vector $X^h \varepsilon R^G$. We denote the (row) vector of spot commodity prices by $p \in S = \{p \in R_{++}{}^G \mid \Sigma_{j=1}^G p_j = 1\}$.

We assume that at date 0, households possess common probability beliefs over a common (finite) set of possible date 1 equilibrium spot market prices, $C = \{p^1, \ldots, p^n\}$, that is a subset of S. If C is a nonsingleton set, then households do not have single-valued expectations about equilibrium prices. Let $\pi = (\pi(p^1), \ldots, \pi(p^n))$ denote the shared vector of date 0 subjective probability beliefs over C. At date 1, households also possess common probability beliefs over a common set of possible date 1 equilibrium spot market prices, D, which is a subset of S.

We require as part of the definition of equilibrium that all households' beliefs at both dates be correct in the sense that C is a (possibly, proper) subset of the actual set of equilibrium date 1 spot prices that are possible from the perspective of date 0 and that D is another (possibly, proper and possibly, different) subset of the actual set of equilibrium date 1 spot prices that are possible from the perspective of date 1. We write $B = (C, D)$. Notice that C and D are endogenous in two senses: They are chosen endogenously by households and endogenously constrained in equilibrium to be correct in the sense that the support of shared beliefs cannot include any spot prices known not to be possible equilibria (at the date of those beliefs). In many interesting cases, D is a subset of C. Notice also that nothing rules out the possibility that C is not equal to D, but clearly, unless there is a reason for changing or updating beliefs, C will equal D. In that case, we let $I = C = D$ denote the time-invariant set of (rationally) expected possible equilibrium date 1 prices.

Households have strictly monotone and strictly convex preferences representable by differentiable utility functions, u^h, satisfying the assumption of Debreu's (1970) regular economy approach. For expositional purposes, we first consider the absence of any options trading at date 0. In such a no-asset economy, households formulate date 0 plans regarding date 1 consumption.

Definition 1: *A consumption plan for household h, $x^h(p)_{p \in C} = (x^h(p^1), \ldots, x^h(p^n))$ is feasible if it satisfies a set of n budget constraints:*

$$px^h(p) = pe^h \text{ for each } p \in C \tag{4.1}$$

Note that equation (1) represents multiple budget constraints, one for each member of C; only a single budget constraint realizes from the set of conceivable ones because only a single p in C realizes. Household h with (e^h, u^h) chooses a consumption plan to maximize expected utility $EU^h = \Sigma_{i=1}^n \pi^h(p^i)u^h(x^h(p^i))$ among feasible consumption plans. Without assets or any other decisions to be made at date 0, expected utility reduces to utility. Nonetheless, households must choose a plan that consists of consumption vectors x^h for each member of C that might realize.

Definition 2: *A consumption allocation is given by $x(p)_{p \in C} = (x^1(p)_{p \in C}, \ldots, x^H(p)_{p \in C})$. A consumption allocation is feasible if all its component consumption plans $x^h(p)_{p \in C}$ are feasible.*

Definition 3: *An SME (spot market equilibrium) $(I,(p)_{p \in I}, x(p)_{p \in I})$ is a time-invariant set (commonly held across households) of expected equilibrium spot prices I, commodity spot market prices $p \in I$, and an allocation $x(p)_{p \in I}$ such that for all h, $x^h(p)_{p \in I}$ maximizes $EU^h = \Sigma_{i=1}^n \pi(p^i)u^h(x^h(p^i))$ subject to budget constraints (1) and*

$$\sum_h x^h(p) = \sum_h e^h \text{ for all } p \in I \qquad (4.2)$$

$$\left(commodity\ market\ clearing \right)$$

We reiterate that this is a no-asset economy and households are unable to shift across different possible equilibrium spot prices the income realized from the sale of price-independent endowments. Although there are n budget constraints, one for each price vector in I, at date 1 only a single p is realized and only one of the n budget constraints actually obtains. A complete set of price-contingent markets would mean that all n budget constraints have to be satisfied at date 0 with no spot markets necessary at date 1. The latter scenario involves nG markets at date 0, while an SME involves only G markets at date 1. An immediate question that arises is whether an equilibrium can be shown to exist. We can answer this question in the affirmative in the case of regular economies.

Proposition 1: *For a regular economy, an SME exists.*

Proof: Notice that our no-asset economy differs from a static pure exchange Arrow–Debreu (1954) economy without uncertainty in only two ways: our economy takes place over two dates and involves the maximization of expected utility instead of utility. Because households do not have to make consumption decisions until date 1 occurs, however, expected utility reduces to certain utility. Thus, we have an Arrow–Debreu economy, for which existence of an equilibrium is well known (see, for example, Debreu [1959]). Because our economy is regular, we know (see, for example, Debreu [1970]) that there is a finite number of equilibria. Thus, I is finite.   QED.

Next, we suppose that households can trade options to hedge against price uncertainty. Since there are only two dates, American options are equivalent to European options, which expire on the second date. The asset structure of this economy consists of European call and put options, which pay off in a numeraire commodity (such as gold). The payoff amounts are assumed to depend on the date 1 spot price of the first good. Our model can be generalized to include options written on commodity futures contracts or an index of spot prices. The available European commodity options are characterized by their strike prices, k, that lie in a set P. Each k is measured in prices normalized by $\Sigma_{j=1}^G p_j = 1$. Thus, P can be used to represent the asset structure and is a subset of $[0,1]$. For now, we assume that P is countable and is given exogenously. Option payoffs are defined as follows:

Definition 4: *The European option payoff $V_E(p,k) = Max [0,p_1-k]$ if $E = c$ for a call option and $V_E(p,k) = Max [0,k-p_1]$ if $E = p$ for a put option.*

We represent option premia by $q_E(k)$, $E = c$, p, and the vector of option premia by q. We denote a household's option portfolio by $\theta_E(k)_{k \in P} = (\theta_E^1(k)_{k \in P}, \dots, \theta_E^H(k)_{k \in P})$ with the vector of option holding by $\theta_E^h(k)_{k \in P}$.

Definition 5: *A general equilibrium with price uncertainty (GEPU) is a set (commonly held across households) of expected equilibrium spot prices $B = (C,D)$, a price system $(q,(p)_{p \in C},(p)_{p \in D})$, and an allocation $(\theta(k)_{k \in p}, x(p)_{p \in C}, x(p)_{p \in D})$ such that, for all h, $(\theta^h(k)_{k \in p}, x^h(p)_{p \in C})$ maximizes $EU^h(x^h(p)_{p \in C})$ subject to:*

$$\sum_{k \in P} \sum_E q_E\left(k\right)\theta_E^h\left(k\right) = 0 \tag{4.3}$$
$$\left(option\ budget\ constraint\right)$$

$$px^h\left(p\right) = \sum_{k \in P} \sum_E V_E\left(p, k\right)\theta_E^h\left(k\right) + pe^h \tag{4.4}$$
for each $p \in C$, $\left(ex\ ante\ budget\ constraint\right)$

and

$$\sum_h \theta_E^h\left(k\right) = 0\ for\ E = c,\ p\ and\ all\ k \in P, \tag{4.5}$$
$$\left(option\ market\ clearing\right)$$

$$\sum_h x^h\left(p\right) = \sum_h e^h\ for\ all\ p \in C \tag{4.6}$$
$$\left(ex\ ante\ commodity\ market\ clearing\right)$$

Furthermore, $x^h(p)$ maximizes $u^h(x^h(p))$ subject to:

$$px^h\left(p\right) = \sum_{k \in P} \sum_E V_E\left(p, k\right)\theta_E^h\left(k\right) + pe^h \tag{4.7}$$
for each $p \in D$, $\left(ex\ post\ budget\ constraint\right)$

and

$$\sum_{h} x^{h}(p) = \sum_{h} e^{h} \ for \ all \ p \in D \qquad (4.8)$$
$$(ex \ post \ commodity \ market \ clearing)$$

As before, an immediate question arises: How do we know whether a GEPU exists? We can answer this question in the affirmative when $C = D = I$ is a singleton. Notice that this does not necessarily require there be a unique equilibrium, only that economic agents somehow coordinate on one of the multiple equilibria, if there are several.

Proposition 2: *For a regular economy, if $C = D = I$ is a singleton, then a GEPU exists.*

Proof: Notice that if C is a singleton, there will be no activity in options markets because there is no price uncertainty. But the zero volume of trade in options means this economy is a regular no-asset economy, for which the existence of an SME (x^*,p^*) has already been proved in Proposition 1. That SME with $\theta_E^h(k) = 0$ for all h and k, $q = 0$, and $C = D = \{p^*\}$ is a GEPU (with the obvious modification that a free option can be in excess demand). QED.

The question remains: What about existence when C or D is not a singleton? We answer this question by separately considering the case of complete and incomplete option markets.

4.2   Price uncertainty with complete option markets

By complete option markets, we mean that all options, characterized by $k \in P$, are available for trading. For example, P can be a dense set in [0,1]. Complete option markets result in an ex ante Pareto efficient consumption allocation. We can thus show that an equilibrium allocation exists and must be invariant across which member of C realizes. This is due to the strict convexity of preferences and because the economy-wide endowment is independent of spot prices. Such price independence of equilibrium consumption plans means that price uncertainty is no longer payoff-relevant for households. Thus, in equilibrium, households are fully insured against price uncertainty and can achieve an ex ante Pareto optimum allocation. But any point on the expected utility possibility frontier maximizes a weighted sum of households' expected utilities. This characterization of the equilibrium allocation as the solution to a concave maximization problem over a compact set guarantees the existence of an equilibrium allocation, x^*. This method of proof, due to Negishi (1960), is used later to show the existence of GEPU. For an equilibrium allocation, the corresponding unique shadow price vector forms an equilibrium spot market commodity price vector, p^*. Thus, an active set of complete option markets has allowed households to coordinate on a particular spot market price vector. In our notation, $(C,D) = (E^*,p^*)$, where E^* is the finite set of equilibria of this regular economy without full insurance.

Proposition 3: *With complete option markets, the GEPU allocation x^* is invariant with respect to which element of C realizes.*

Proof: This result is the consequence of the strict convexity of preferences and endowments being independent of price. If a GEPU allocation x^* varies with $p \in C$, then by strict convexity of preferences, household h strictly prefers the allocation Ex^{*h} $= \Sigma_{p \in C} \pi(p)x^{*h}(p)$, formed by the expected value of x^* over $p \in$ C, to the allocation, x^{*h}. That is to say, for all h, $u^h(Ex^{*h}) >$ $Eu^h(x^{*h})$ if $x^{*h}(p)$ varies over $p \in C$. Because π is a probability vector over $P \varepsilon C$, $\Sigma_{p \in C}\pi(p) = 1$, and $\Sigma_h Ex^{*h} = \Sigma_h \Sigma_{p \in C} \pi(p)x^{*h}(p)$ $= \Sigma_h x^{*h}(p) = \Sigma_h e^h$. We have thus constructed a feasible allocation, Ex^*, that is Pareto superior to x^*, which contradicts the assumption that x^* is a GEPU with complete options. Thus, any GEPU allocation x^* must be independent of which $p \in C$ realizes because households trade options to smooth out consumption independently of which price from C realizes.   QED.

This result implies that a GEPU allocation, x^* reaches full insurance against price uncertainty. Any GEPU allocation lies on the expected utility possibility frontier, or maximizes a social welfare function that is a weighted sum of households' expected utilities.

At this point, it might seem that Proposition 2 should apply. But, it does not for two reasons. First, $C \neq D$. Second, there is no reason that option premia at date 0 are unique. They will typically not be. Different option premia and portfolio trades correspond to different (x^*,p^*) by no-arbitrage and the above construction. In a sense, complete option markets have allowed households to shift the multiplicity from date 1 equilibrium spot prices to date 0 equilibrium option premia. This might seem to be merely an intertemporal transfer of equilibrium price multiplicity, but such a reallocation of multiplicity over time has real consequences because there is a genuine difference between uncertainty about which equilibrium spot market price will prevail at date 1 and uncertainty about which one of several equilibria option premia q could have been realized at date 0. In terms of the formal model, this is because there is no date (-1) before date 0.

In this model we do not assume that households worry about forecasting at some prior date which q would occur at date 0. To embark on this scenario is to become quickly embroiled in an infinite regress as considered in Chichilnisky, Dutta, and Heal (1991). Although that approach is logically satisfying, options on options are uncommon and higher than second-order options are even less common. Alternatively, Hahn's (1992) point is that complete option markets eliminate their own raison d'être by eliminating price uncertainty so effectively. But if option markets are not utilized because traders believe there will be no price uncertainty, then price uncertainty will in fact occur. This reasoning leads to the view that a rational expectations equilibrium cannot exist. In order to resolve this apparent paradox, we note that arguing that options are not required once they have already been traded is analogous to saying that after buying full insurance, there is no further demand for any insurance. Our approach separates the set C from the set D and stops going back in time from date 1 to date 0 after trading options at date 0.

A complementary viewpoint is that we assume households are sophisticated enough to understand that if nobody trades in options there will be multiplicity in spot prices. The usual argument is that any individual household's option portfolio is insignificant (of measure zero if there were a continuum of households) and so everybody will try to free-ride on the options trading of others to eliminate spot price multiplicity. We hold the view that households also realize the possibility that spot price multiplicity will occur if there is no (or not enough) activity in the options market.[4] They trade in options not out of any sense of public service, but because they want to guard against the off-the-equilibrium possibility that not enough other households trade in options to eliminate spot price uncertainty. Formally, at date 0, households believe C will prevail; but at date 1, households believe D will prevail. Households possess rational expectations at both dates. A complete set of option markets changes not only the cardinality of, but also the actual set of, equilibria for our economy. Next we outline the proof that there exists a general equilibrium with price uncertainty.

---

[4] This phenomenon is analogous to the trembling-hand reasoning in game theory. Players can revise beliefs about strategies in an extensive form game on reaching a node that has zero probability given their prior beliefs. However, in our framework, D is required to be a subset of C.

Proposition 4: *A GEPU exists, consisting of a fully insured unique allocation x* and a spot price vector, p*, supporting the full insurance allocation.*

Proof: Following Negishi's (1960) approach to proving the existence of an Arrow–Debreu competitive equilibrium, we note that any fully insured allocation must lie on the frontier of the expected utility set. An ex ante Pareto efficient allocation maximizes, for some weights, λ^h, a weighted sum of expected utilities, $\Sigma^h \lambda^h E u^h(x^h(p)_{p\in C})$, over the set of feasible expected utility allocations. Such an optimization problem involving the maximization of a concave objective function over a compact set is known to have a solution, x^*. By the second fundamental theorem of welfare economics, which applies to SME of this regular convex economy, there exists a unique spot price vector, p^*, that supports x^*. In other words, (p^*,x^*) is an Arrow–Debreu competitive equilibrium for the date 1 economy. With asset prices and portfolios (q,θ) derived by the no-arbitrage condition, it forms a GEPU.   QED.

We have now provided some answers to the four questions posed in Section 1. With complete options, market equilibrium exists and is efficient (P2 is true), but the spot equilibrium price is unique (P1 fails). We observe that in the unique complete market GEPU, options look like "redundant" assets. This redundancy is consistent with such existing financial theories as the Black–Scholes option pricing model. But options are required to guard against off-equilibrium expectations. In this sense, option markets substitute for the coordination of expectations. Options are uniquely required for accomplishing such a task and therefore cannot be replaced by other nonprice-contingent assets. This finding is stronger than Ross's (1976) result because in our model options are the only assets capable of providing insurance against multiple price equilibria, whereas in Ross's model options are sufficient, but certainly not necessary, to span asset markets.

4.3   Price uncertainty with incomplete option markets

By incomplete option markets, we mean that the number of possible equilibrium spot prices exceeds the number of available options in P. Recall that so far, P has been exogenously specified. However, if P remains exogenously specified, then a GEPU can fail to exist and, even when it exists, may not be efficient.

With exogenous uncertainty and incomplete options markets, it is well known that market equilibria are generically constrained suboptimal (see Geanakoplos and Polemarchakis [1986]). A similar reasoning can be applied to the case of endogenous price uncertainty to establish the suboptimality of GEPU if it exists. In other words, a central planner restricted to utilizing existing incomplete options markets can, in principle, construct a reallocation of commodities and assets that is a Pareto improvement over the market equilibrium. Hence P2 fails and the equilibrium allocation does not entail full insurance against price uncertainty. In addition, we cannot use the method of Propositon 4 to establish the existence of GEPU with incomplete options markets.

In the context of exogenous uncertainty, a robust counterexample to generic existence of an equilibrium was constructed by Polemarchakis and Ku (1990). Generic existence fails to hold because a neighborhood exists in the parameter space of initial endowments and the strike prices for which the European call or put option pays out zero in all states. The subspace spanned by the columns of the asset matrix drops rank, which leads to aggregate excess demand being a discontinuous function of spot prices. This, in turn, causes problems for the existence of an equilibrium. The same reasoning applies to the case with price uncertainty. But, following Huang and Wu (1994; 1996), one can consider a model with endogenously chosen options contracts, which can be used to show generic existence of a GEPU.

In Huang and Wu (1996) options are set by an exchange to be at-the-money. This assumption means that the strike price is the date 0 equilibrium price of the underlying commodity futures contract. By the no-arbitrage condition on equilibrium asset prices, the date 0 equilibrium price of the underlying commodity futures contract is a weighted average of the possible equilibrium liquidation values of that futures contract. These weights form what is known as an equivalent martingale measure. There are multiple date 1 equilibrium liquidation values of the underlying futures contract which do not all coincide. In particular, there is a highest and lowest possible date 1 equilibrium value of the underlying futures contract. An at-the-money strike price lies inside the interval formed by the highest and lowest possible liquidation values of the underlying futures contract. This property ensures that generically options do not all pay off zero and therefore that the asset payoff matrix will not drop rank for different equilibrium spot prices.

We note that similar reasoning in the context of price uncertainty can be used to show that a GEPU exists generically for the above described economy with incomplete option markets. With price uncertainty, the no-arbitrage condition still implies a martingale characterization of strike prices, which enables us to prove the generic existence of a GEPU in a way analogous to the method by which Huang and Wu (1996) prove that a GEI (general equilibrium with incomplete markets) with exogenous state uncertainty generically exists. With incomplete options markets, there may exist multiple price equilibria (P1 is true), which was not possible with complete options (Proposition 4). The equilibrium allocation, if it exists, may not be efficient (P2 fails). Options still play the role of providing insurance against price uncertainty, but they cannot eliminate all price risk and D is not a singleton.

5   Price uncertainty without structural knowledge

In this section, we consider the formulation of an economic model where the agents do not have structural knowledge. Given the assumptions of Debreu's (1970) regular economy approach, there are finitely many spot market equilibria for almost all initial endowments. Nonetheless, the set of market equilibria will change when security markets are introduced. This is only natural in a general equilibrium setting, but it means that households may not know at date 0 which are the finitely many equilibrium spot prices that can occur with positive probability at date 1. The agents' date 0 beliefs are not based on structural knowledge of equilibrium prices at date 1. Moreover, actual security markets are not indexed by finitely many possible equilibrium prices. Instead, the most famous example of a price-contingent security, an option, has a payoff that is a continuous function of all underlying prices, not just finitely many equilibrium prices. This motivates the two types of security markets that we discuss below as well as our treatment of probability beliefs over underlying prices. In particular, we do not restrict date 0 beliefs to coincide with date 1 beliefs and date 0 beliefs may or may not have a finite support.

First, we consider the case of infinitely many expected prices. We assume that at date 0, households possess prior probability beliefs with the set C of infinitely many or a continuum of prices as the support. An infinite price state space arises natually when households do not have structural knowledge and cannot rule out any price as impossible, that is, $C = S$. Denote by π^h household h's date 0 subjective probability distribution over S. At date 1, households possess common posterior beliefs over date 1 equilibrium spot prices; they place probability one on the price p^* that is observed. Since $p^* \in s$, their beliefs at date 0 are not contradicted by the data at date 1. This updating of beliefs in light of publicly observable spot market commodity prices becoming available goes to the heart of what price uncertainty means. At date 0, households do not have the necessary information to determine which proper, finite subsets of the unit simplex are possible spot market equilibria. At date 1, all households know the date 1 price. But, they cannot go back in time from date 1 to date 0. This obvious point means that, formally, at date 0, households believe that at date 1 some member of C will prevail, and indeed at date 1, an element of C does realize, namely p^*, which all households can publicly observe. Households in our model are cognizant of this metamorphosis in the sense of holding different rational beliefs at dates 0 and 1. Finally, there are complexity reasons to believe that households at date 0 will not be able to compute the spot equilibrium price vector p^* at date 1. Instead, they merely observe it when date 1 arrives.

Household h selects a consumption plan, $x^h : C \to R$ where, for each $p \in C$, $x^h(p)$ is the quantity of commodities that household h plans to buy if spot price vector p realizes. Let $x = (x^1, \dots, x^H) \in R^{GH}$ denote a consumption plan allocation, so that $x : C \to R^{GH}$. If $C = S$, commodity plans are members of the function space, $Lp(C)$. Commodity prices p are in the topological dual, $Lq(C)$, where $1/p + 1/q = 1$. The asset structure includes options written on the spot price of the first commodity. The set of possible strike prices, P, is a subset of $[0,1]$. Let P be specified exogenously to be countable and dense in $[0,1]$. For example, the set of strike prices can include all rational numbers between 0 and 1.

Each household h also chooses a portfolio $\theta_E^h : P \to R$, for $E = C$ or P. Security portfolios are members of the space $Lp(C)$. As before, $\theta_E = (\theta_E^1, \dots, \theta_E^H)$ and $\theta = (\theta_C, \theta_P)$. Security prices q are in the topological dual. In order to rule out arbitrage opportunities, we require that security prices be arbitrage-free. This means that no household can find a sequential arbitrage opportunity as defined in Brown and Werner (1994). Our definition of GEPU can be modified when the agents believe that any price in the simplex S is possible ($C = S$).

> **Definition 6:** *A general equilibrium with price uncertainty (GEPU), given a continuum of expected prices, is a set (commonly held across households) of expected equilibrium spot prices $B = (S,p^*)$, a commodity spot market price vector p^*, a consumption plan allocation $x(p)$, a security price vector q, and a portfolio allocation θ such that q is a no-arbitrage security price, and:*
> *For all h,*

$$\left(x^h(p), \theta^h(k)\right) \text{ maximizes } Eu^h\left(x^h(p)\right)$$
$$= \int_s u^h\left(x^h\right)\pi^h(p)dp$$

subject to the budget constraints:

$$\sum_{k\in P}\sum_E q_E(k)\theta_E^h(k) = 0 \;\left(\text{option budget constraint}\right)$$
$$(5.1)$$

$$px^h(p) = \sum_{k\in P}\sum_E V_E(p, k)\theta_E^h(k) + pe^h \text{ for each } p \in S$$
$$\left(\text{ex ante budget constraint}\right)$$

and

$$\sum_h \theta_E^h(K) = 0 \text{ for } E = C, \, P \text{ and all } K \in P \qquad (5.2)$$
$$\left(\text{option market clearing}\right)$$

$$\sum_h x^h(p) = \sum_h e^h \text{ for each } p \in S \qquad\qquad (5.3)$$
$$\left(\text{ex ante commodity market clearing}\right)$$

$$\sum_h \theta_E^h(K) = 0 \;\left(\text{option market clearing}\right) \qquad (5.4)$$

Furthermore, $x^h(p^*)$ maximizes $u^h(x^h(p^*))$ subject to:

$$p*x^h(p) = p*e^h + \sum_{k\in P}\sum_E V_E(p^*, k)\theta_E^h(k) \qquad (5.5)$$
$$\left(\text{ex post budget constraint}\right)$$

and

$$\sum_h x^h(p^*) = \sum_h e^h \qquad\qquad (5.6)$$
$$\left(\text{ex post commodity market clearing}\right)$$

There is a limited amount of work about asset market equilibria when the state space is infinite. Brown and Ross (1991) show how the Ross (1976) result can be extended to an infinite state space. Aliprantis and Brown (1994) answer the question of what asset market in completeness means when there is a continuum of states. If options complete markets in the sense of Aliprantis and Brown (1994), then existence of market equilibrium follows by applying the standard infinite dimensional space results. By applying Aliprantis and Brown (1994), one may show that a GEPU exists if the set of marketed assets M is the Lp-closure of the space of European call options.

Our model differs from Svensson's (1981) model of Arrow–Debreu markets for commodities contingent on any price in the simplex because the possibility of short sales of securities in our model implies that households face a commodity space that may not be bounded below. Svensson's results are not applicable to financial markets. Our model also differs from Henrotte's (1992) analysis because he studies a three-period model in which there are infinitely many derivative securities traded in period 1, finitely many primitive securities traded in period 2, and consumption occurs in period 3. Henrotte's results are based on a closedness condition utilized by Mas-Colell (1986) and Aliprantis, Brown, and Burkinshaw (1989). This means that the utility possibility set is a closed subset of R^H, which also awaits verification in a framework of incomplete options. Whether proof of existence can be shown for a continuum of fixed possible endogenous price states is unclear, because there are several well-known unsolved problems with incomplete security markets for infinite dimensional spaces, as discussed in Mas-Colell and Zame (1991).

Next consider the case of finitely many expected prices. When the support of agents' date 0 beliefs is a proper subset C of the price simplex S, there is no guarantee that the realized price actually belongs to C. The agent's beliefs can therefore be contradicted with observed data. This is especially true when there are only finitely many expected prices. Kurz and Wu (1996) work with the case of a finite support of beliefs and show that these beliefs with some rationality restrictions can be made compatible with the observed data.

When agents do not posess structural knowledge, the temporary equilibrium approach taken by Svensson (1981) and Henrotte (1992) does not use any rationality conditions and has to deal with a space of the order of a continuum. As discussed before, it entails some technical complexities. On the other hand, the rational expectations approach covered in the last section endows the agents with an unrealistically high capability of computing economic equilibria. The approach by Kurz and Wu (1996) formulates an equilibrium model with rational beliefs to account for endogenous price uncertainty and to establish the existence and efficiency of market equilibrium when there is a complete set of options markets. They also construct a finite "price state space" which includes exogenous states and the states of diffuse beliefs. However, the case with incomplete options markets remains unresolved as yet.

6   Conclusion

We have demonstrated how to extend the traditional Arrow–Debreu general equilibrium analysis of an economy with exogenous state uncertainty to deal with endogenous price uncertainty. In his Nobel lecture, Arrow (1974) stated that he viewed the model of general equilibrium with uncertainty not only as a normative ideal for public policy to strive for, but also as a description of existing reality. As Shiller (1993) pointed out, the focus of economic theory should be on an economy's largest risks, namely fluctuations in aggregate income and prices. Such important fluctuations in the economy cannot be solely attributed to exogenous shocks.

It has been two decades since Kurz's (1974) call to model endogenous uncertainty. Kurz himself and others have recently made progress in that endeavor, but much remains to be done. The contribution of this essay is to provide a particular and natural formulation of a type of endogenous uncertainty, namely, price uncertainty and indicate the subtle issues in showing existence of an equilibrium and establishing its properties in the face of endogenous price uncertainty. We also examine the role of options in dealing with endogenous price uncertainty. The attempt to understand the full implications of endogenous uncertainty presents a very interesting challenge for economic theory (and theorists) for decades to come.

References

Aliprantis, C. D., and D. J. Brown. 1994. Existence of competitive equilibria in markets for derivative securities. Working paper, Stanford University.

Aliprantis, C. D., D. J. Brown, and O. Burkinshaw. 1989. Existence and optimality of competitive equilibria. New York: Springer-Verlag.

Arrow, K. J. 1953. The role of securities in the optimal allocation of risk-bearing. *Econometrie*. Translated and reprinted in *Review of Economic Studies* (1964)31:91–6.

Arrow, K. J. 1974. General economic equilibrium: Purpose, analytic techniques, collective choice. *American Economic Review*, 61:253–72.

Arrow, K. J. 1978. The future and the present in economic life. *Economic Inquiry*, 16:157–70.

Arrow, K. J. 1982. Risk perception in psychology and economics. *Economic Inquiry*, 20:1–9.

Arrow, K. J. 1986. Rationality of self and others in an economic system. *Journal of Business*, 59:S385–99.

Arrow, K. J. 1991. Economic forecasting. In *New Technologies and the Future of Food and Nutrition*, ed. G. E. Gaull. New York: Wiley.

Arrow, K. J. 1994. General equilibrium under uncertainty: Survey and problems. Presented at SITE (Stanford Institute of Theoretical Economics).

Arrow, K. J., and G. Debreu. 1954. Existence of equilibrium for a competitive economy. *Econometrica*, 22:265–90.

Aumann, R. J., and A. Brandenburger. 1991. Epistemic conditions for Nash equilibrium. Working Paper No. 91-042, Harvard Business School.

Bewley, T. 1972. Existence of equilibrium in economies with infinitely many commodities. *Journal of Economic Theory*, 4:514–40.

Brown, D., and S. A. Ross. 1991. Spanning, valuation and options. *Economic Theory*, 1:3–12.

Brown, D. J., and J. Werner. 1995. Arbitrage and existence of equilibrium in infinite asset markets. *Review of Economic Studies*, 62:101–14.

Cass, D., G. Chichilnisky, and H. M. Wu. 1966. Individual risk and mutual insurance. *Econometrica*, 64:333–41.

Chichilnisky, G. 1992. General equilibrium with endogenous uncertainty. Working paper, Columbia University; this volume.

Chichilnisky, G. 1994. Markets with endogenous uncertainty: Theory and policy. Presented at SITE, Stanford University, August, *Theory and Decision*, 41: 99–131, 1996.

Chichilnisky, G., J. Dutta, and G. M. Heal. 1991. Price uncertainty and incomplete markets. Columbia Business School working paper.

Chichilnisky, G., G. M. Heal, and D. P. Tsomocos. 1995. Option values and endogenous uncertainty in ESOPs, MBOs, and asset-backed securities. *Economics Letters*, 48(3–4):379–88.

Chichilnisky, G., and H. M. Wu. 1992. Financial innovation and endogenous uncertainty in incomplete asset markets. Working paper; SITE Technical Report No. 50, Stanford.

Debreu, G. 1959. *Theory of Value*. New Haven: Yale University Press.

Debreu, G. 1970. Economies with a finite set of equilibria. *Econometrica*, 38:387–92.

Duffie, D. 1991. The theory of value in security markets. In *Handbook of Mathematical Economics*, Vol. 4, ed. W. Hildenbrand and H. Sonnenschein. Amsterdam: North-Holland, pp. 1614–82.

Hahn, F. 1992. On Arrow securities. Working paper, Cambridge University.

Hahn, F. 1994. A remark on incomplete market equilibrium. Working paper, Cambridge University; this volume.

Harkasson, N. H. 1978. Welfare of options and supershares. *Journal of Finance*, 33:759–76.

Henrotte, P. 1992. Existence and optimality of equilibria in markets with tradeable derivative securities. SITE Technical Report No. 48, Stanford University.

Hicks, J. 1946. *Value and Capital*. Oxford: Clarendon Press.

Huang, C. 1993. Time and uncertainty. Presented at the General Equilibrium Theory 40th Anniversary Conference at CORE, Louvain-la-Neuve, Belgium, June.

Huang, P. H., and H. M. Wu. 1994. Competitive equilibrium of incomplete markets for securities with smooth payoffs. *Journal of Mathematical Economics*, 23:219–34.

Huang, P. H., and H. M. Wu. 1996. General equilibrium with incomplete markets of European options. Working paper, National Taiwan University.

Geanakoplos, J., and H. Polemarchakis. 1996. Existence, regularity, and constrained suboptimality of competitive allocations when markets are incomplete, in *Uncertainty, Information, and Communication: Essays in Honor
of Kenneth Arrow*, Vol. 3, ed. W. P. Heller, R. M. Ross, and D. A. Starrett.
Cambridge: Cambridge University Press.

Kreps, D. 1992. Static choice in the presence of unforeseen contingencies. In
*Economic Analysis of Markets and Games: Essays in Honor of Frank
Hahn*, ed. P. Dasgupta, D. Gale, O. Hart, and E. Maskin. Cambridge, MA:
MIT Press, pp. 258–81.

Kurz, M. 1974. The Kesten–Stigum model and treatment of uncertainty in equilibrium theory. In *Essays on Economic Behavior Under Uncertainty*, ed. M.
S. Balch, D. L. McFadden, and S. Y. Wu. Amsterdam: North-Holland, pp.
389–99.

Kurz, M. 1994a. On the structure and diversity of rational beliefs. *Economic
Theory*, 4:877–900.

Kurz, M. 1994b. On rational belief equilibrium. *Economic Theory*, 4:859–76.

Kurz, M. 1996. Rational beliefs and endogenous uncertainty: Introduction.
Economic Theory, 8:383–97.

Kurz, M., and H. M. Wu. 1996. Endogenous uncertainty in a general equilibrium
model with price-contingent contracts. *Economic Theory*, 8:461–88.

Mas-Colell, A. 1986. The price equilibrium existence problem in topological
vector lattices. *Econometrica*, 54:1039–53.

Mas-Colell, A. 1992. Three observations on sunspots and asset redundancy. In
*Economic Analysis of Markets and Games, Essays in Honor of Frank
Hahn*, ed. P. Dasgupta, D. Gale, O. Hart, and E. Maskin. Cambridge, MA:
MIT Press, pp. 465–74.

Mas-Colell, A., and W. R. Zame. 1991. Equilibrium theory in infinite dimensional
spaces. In *Handbook of Mathematical Economics*, Vol. 4, ed. W.
Hildenbrand and H. Sonnenschein. Amsterdam: North-Holland, pp.
1835–98.

Negishi, T. 1960. Welfare economics and existence of an equilibrium for a competitive economy. *Metroeconomica*, 12:92–7.

Polemarchakis, H. M., and B. Ku. 1990. Options and equilibrium. *Journal of
Mathematical Economics*, 19:107–12.

Ross, S. 1976. Options and efficiency. *Quarterly Journal of Economics*, 90:85–9.

Savage, L. 1954. *The Foundations of Statistics*. New York: Wiley.

Shiller, R. J. 1981. Do stock prices move too much to be justified by subsequent
changes in dividends? *American Economic Review*, 71:421–36.

Shiller, R. J. 1993. *Macro Markets: Creating Institutions for Managing Society's
Largest Economic Risks*. Oxford: Oxford University Press.

Svensson, L. E. O. 1981. Efficiency and speculation in a model with price-
contingent contracts. *Econometrica*, 49:131–51.

CHAPTER 7

Catastrophe futures: Financial markets for unknown risks

Graciela Chichilnisky and Geoffrey Heal

1   Introduction

New risks seem to be unavoidable in a period of rapid change. The last few decades have brought us the risks of global warming, nuclear melt-down, ozone depletion, failure of satellite launcher rockets, collision of supertankers, AIDS, and Ebola.[1] A key feature of a new risk, as opposed to an old and familiar one, is that one knows little about it. In particu-lar, one knows little about the chances or the costs of its occurrence. This makes it hard to manage these risks. Existing paradigms for the rational management of risks require that we associate frequencies to various levels of losses. This poses particular challenges for the insurance indus-try, which is at the leading edge of risk management. Misestimation of new risks has led to several bankruptcies in the insurance and reinsur-ance businesses.[2] In this chapter we propose a novel framework for pro-viding insurance cover against risks whose parameters are unknown. In fact many of the risks at issue may not be just unknown but also unknow-able. It is difficult to imagine repetition of the events leading to global warming or ozone depletion, and therefore difficult to devise a relative frequency associated with repeated experiments.

A systematic and rational way of hedging unknown risks is proposed here, one which involves the use of securities markets as well as the more traditional insurance techniques. This model is consistent with the

We are grateful to Peter Bernstein, David Cass, and Frank Hahn for valuable comments on an earlier version of this chapter.
[1] A deadly viral disease.
[2] Many were associated with hurricane Andrew which at $18 billion in losses was the most expensive catastrophe ever recorded. Some of the problems which beset Lloyds of London arose from underestimating environmental risks.

120

current evolution of the insurance and reinsurance industries, which are beginning to explore the securitization of some aspects of insurance contracts via Act of God bonds, contingent drawing facilities, catastrophe futures, and similar innovations. Our model provides a formal framework within which such moves can be evaluated. An earlier version of this framework was presented in Chichilnisky and Heal (1993). Chichilnisky (1996) gives a more industry-oriented analysis.

This merging of insurance and the securities market is not surprising: Economists have traditionally recognized two ways of managing risks. One is risk pooling, or insurance, invoking the law of large numbers for independent and identically distributed (IID) events to ensure that the insurer's loss rate is proportional to the population loss rate. This will not work if the population loss rate is unknown. The second approach is the use of securities markets, and of negatively correlated events. This does not require knowledge of the population loss rate, and so can be applied to risks which are unknown or not independent. Securities markets alone could provide a mechanism for hedging unknown risks by the appropriate definition of states, but as we shall see this approach requires an unreasonable proliferation of markets. Using a mix of the two approaches can economize greatly on the number of markets needed and on the complexity of the institutional framework. In the process of showing this, we also show that under certain conditions the market equilibrium is anonymous in the sense that it depends only on the distribution of individuals across possible states, and not on who is in which state.

The reason for using two types of instruments is simple. Agents face two types of uncertainty: uncertainty about the overall incidence of a peril, that is, how many people overall will be affected by a disease, and then, given an overall distribution of the peril, uncertainty about whether they will be one of those affected. Securities contingent on the distribution of the peril hedge the former type of uncertainty; contingent insurance contracts hedge the latter.

Our analysis implies that insurance companies should issue insurance contracts which depend on the frequency of the peril, or statistical state. The insurance companies should offer individuals an array of insurance contracts, one valid in each possible statistical state. Insurance contracts are therefore contingent on statistical states. Within each statistical state probabilities are known, and companies are writing insurance only on known risks, something which is actuarially manageable. Individuals then buy the insurance they want between different statistical states via the markets for securities that are contingent on statistical states. The following is an illustration for purchasing insurance against AIDS, if the actuarial risks of the disease are unknown. One would buy insurance against AIDS by (1) purchasing a set of AIDS insurance contracts each of which pays off only for a specified incidence of AIDS in the population as a whole, and (2) making bets via statistical securities on the incidence of AIDS in the population. Similarly, one would obtain cover against an effect of climate change by (1) buying insurance policies specific to the risks faced at particular levels of climate change, and (2) making bets on the level of climate change, again using statistical securities. The opportunity to place such bets is provided in a limited way by catastrophe futures markets which pay an amount depending on the incidence of hurricane damage.

This chapter draws on recent findings of Chichilnisky and Wu (1991) and Cass, Chichilnisky, and Wu (1996), both of which study resource allocation with individual risks. Each of these essays develops further Malinvaud's (1972, 1973) original formulation of general equilibrium with individual risks, and Arrow's (1953) formulation of the role of securities in the optimal allocation of risk bearing. Our results are valid for large but finite economies with agents who face unknown risks and who have diverse opinions about these risks. In contrast, Malinvaud's results are asymptotic, valid for a limiting economy with an infinite population, and deal only with a known distribution of risks. The results presented here use the formulation of incomplete asset markets for individual risks used to study default in Chichilnisky and Wu (1991), Section 5.c. The risks considered here are unknown and possibly unknowable, and each individual has potentially a different opinion about these risks, whereas Chichilnisky and Wu (1991) and Cass, Chichilnisky, and Wu (1991) assume that all risk is known.

2   Notation and definitions

Denote the set of possible states for an individual by S, indexed by $s = 1, 2, \ldots, S$. Let there be H individuals, indexed by $h = 1, 2, \ldots, H$. All households have the same state-dependent endowments. Endowments depend solely on the household's individual state s, and this dependence is the same for all households. The probability of any agent being in any state is unknown, and the distribution of states over the population as a whole is also unknown. A complete description of the state of the economy, called a *social state*, is a list of the states of each agent. A social state is denoted σ: it is an H – vector. The set of possible social states is denoted Ω and has S^H elements. A statistical description of the economy, called a *statistical state*, is a statement of the fraction of the population in each state. It is an S – vector. As shown by Malinvaud (1973) there are $\begin{pmatrix} H + S - 1 \\ S - 1 \end{pmatrix}$ statistical states. Clearly many social states map into a given statistical state. For example, if in one social state you are well and I am sick and in another, I am well and you are sick, then these two social states give rise to the same statistical state. Intuitively, we would not expect the equilibrium prices of the economy to differ in these two social states. One of our results shows that under certain conditions, the characteristics of the equilibrium are dependent only on the statistical state.

How does the distinction between social and statistical states contribute to risk management? Using the traditional approach, we could in principle trade securities contingent on each of the S^H social states. This would require a large number of markets, a number which grows rapidly with the number of agents. However, the institutional requirements can be greatly simplified. When the characteristics of the equilibrium depend only on the statistical state, one can trade securities which are contingent on statistical states, that is, contingent on the distribution of individual states within the population, and still attain efficient allocations. This means that we trade securities contingent on whether 4% or 8% of the population are in state 5, but not on which people are in this state. Such securities, which we call *statistical securities*, plus mutual insurance contracts also contingent on the statistical state, lead (under the appropriate conditions) to an efficient allocation of risks. A mutual insurance contract contingent on a statistical state pays an individual a certain amount in a given individual state if and only if the economy as a whole is in a given statistical state.

Let $z_{jh\sigma}$ denote the quantity of good j consumed by household h in social state σ: $z_{h\sigma}$ is an N dimensional vector of *all* goods consumed by h in social state σ, $z_{h\sigma} = z_{jh\sigma}, j = 1, \ldots, N$, and z_h is an NS^H dimensional vector of *all goods consumed in all social states* by h, $z_h = z_{h\sigma}, \sigma \in \Omega$.[3]

Let $s(h, \sigma)$ be the state of individual h in the social state σ, and $r_s(\sigma)$ the proportion of all households for whom $s(h, \sigma) = s$. Let $r(\sigma) = r_1(\sigma)$, $\ldots, r_s(\sigma)$ be the distribution of households among individual states within the social state σ, that is, the proportion of all individuals in state s for each s. $r(\sigma)$ is a statistical state. Let R be the set of statistical states, that is, of vectors $r(\sigma)$ when σ runs over Ω. R is contained in the S-dimensional simplex and has $\begin{pmatrix} H + S - 1 \\ S - 1 \end{pmatrix}$ elements, see Malinvaud (1973) p. 385.

---

[3] Consumption vectors are assumed to be nonnegative.

Π^h is household h's probability distribution over the set of social states Ω, and Π^h_σ denotes the probability of state σ. Although we take social states as the primitive concept, we in fact work largely with statistical states. We therefore relate preferences, beliefs, and endowments to statistical states. This is done in the next section. Any distribution over social states implies a distribution over statistical states.

The following *anonymity assumption* is required:

$$r(\sigma) = r(\sigma') \to \Pi^h_\sigma = \Pi^h_{\sigma'}.$$

This means that two overall distributions σ and σ' which have the same statistical characteristics are equally likely. Then Π^h_σ defines a probability distribution Π^h_r on the space of statistical states R. Π^h_r can be interpreted, as remarked above, as h's distribution over possible distributions of impacts in the population as a whole. The probability that a statistical state r obtains and that simultaneously, for a given household h, a particular state s also obtains, Π^h_{sr}, is[4]

$$\Pi^h_{sr} = \Pi^h_r r_s \text{ with } \sum_s \Pi^h_{sr} = \Pi^h_r \tag{2.1}$$

The probability Π^h_s that, for a given h, a particular individual state s obtains is therefore given by

$$\Pi^h_s = \sum_{r \in R} \Pi^h_r r_s$$

where r_s is the proportion of people in individual state s in statistical state r. Note that we denote by $\Pi^h_{s|r}$ the conditional probability of household h being in individual state s, conditional on the economy being in statistical state r. Clearly $\Sigma_s \Pi^h_{s|r} = 1$. Anonymity implies that

$$\Pi^h_{s|r} = r_s$$

that is, that the probability of anyone being in individual state s contingent on the economy being in statistical state r is the relative frequency of state s contingent on statistical state r.

3   The behavior of households

Let e^h_s be the endowment of household h when the individual state is s. We assume that household h always has the same endowment in the indi-

---

[4] See Malinvaud (1973), p. 387, para. 1.

vidual state s, whatever the social state. We also assume that all households have the same endowment if they are in the same individual state. Endowments differ, therefore, only because of differences in individual states. This describes the risks faced by individuals.

Individuals have von Neumann–Morgenstern utilities:

$$W^h\left(z_h\right) = \sum_\sigma \Pi_\sigma^h U^h\left(z_{h\sigma}\right)$$

This definition indicates that household h has preferences on consumption which may be represented by a "state separable" utility function defined from elementary state-independent utility functions.

We assume like Malinvaud (1972) that *preferences are separable over statistical states*. This means that the utility of household h depends on σ only through the statistical state $r(\sigma)$. If we assume further that in state σ household h takes into account only its individual consumption, and what overall frequency distribution $r(\sigma)$ appears, and nothing else, then its consumption plan can be expressed as $z\sigma^h = z_{hsr}$: Its consumption depends only on its individual state s and the statistical state r. Summation with respect to social states σ in the expected utility function can now be made first within each statistical state. Hence we can express individuals' utility functions as:

$$W^h\left(z_{h\sigma}\right) = \sum_{r,s} \Pi_{sr}^h U^h\left(z_{hsr}\right) \tag{3.1}$$

which expresses the utility of a household in terms of its consumption at individual state s within a statistical state r, summed over statistical states. This expression is important in the following results, because it allows us to represent the utility of consumption across social states σ as a function of statistical states r and individual states s only. The functions U_s^h are assumed to be C^2, strictly increasing, strictly quasiconcave, and the closure of the indifference surfaces $\{U_s^h\}^{-1}(x) \subset int\ (R^{N+})$ for all $x \in R^+$. The probabilities Π_σ^h are in principle different over households.

4   Efficient allocations

Let p^* be a competitive equilibrium[5] price vector of the Arrow–Debreu economy E with markets contingent on all social states and let z^* be the associated allocation. We will as usual say that z^* is *Pareto efficient* if it is impossible to find an alternative feasible allocation which is preferred

---

[5] Defined formally below.

by at least one agent and to which no agent prefers z^*. Let $p\sigma^*$ and $z\sigma^*$ be the components of p^* and z^* respectively which refer to goods contingent on state σ.

We now define an Arrow–Debreu economy E, where markets exist contingent on an exhaustive description of all states in the economy, that is, for all social states $\sigma \in \Omega$. We therefore have NS^H contingent markets. An *Arrow–Debreu equilibrium* is a price vector $p^* = (p_\sigma) \in R^{N \times \Omega}$, for each $\sigma\, p_\sigma \in R^{N+}$, $\sigma \in \Omega$, and an allocation z^* consisting of vectors $z_h^* = (z_{h\sigma}^*) \in R^{N \times \Omega}$, $z_{h\sigma}^* \in R^{N+}$, $\sigma \in \Omega$, $h = 1, \ldots, H$ such that for all h, z_h^* maximizes

$$W^h\left(z_h^*\right) = \sum_\sigma \Pi_\sigma^h U^h\left(z_{h\sigma}^*\right) \tag{4.1}$$

subject to a budget constraint

$$p\left(z_h^* - e_h\right) = 0 \tag{4.2}$$

and all markets clear:

$$\sum_h \left(z_h^* - e_h\right) = 0 \tag{4.3}$$

Proposition 1 considers the case when households agree on the probability distribution over social states,[6] this common probability is denoted Π. It follows that they agree on the distribution over statistical states. In this case, the competitive equilibrium prices p^* and allocations z^* are the same across all social states σ, leading to the same statistical state r.[7]

> **Proposition 1:** *When agents have common probabilities, (see footnote 6) i.e., $\Pi^h = \Pi^j \forall h, j$, then equilibrium prices depend only on statistical states. Consider an Arrow–Debreu equilibrium of the economy E, $p^* = (p_\sigma^*)$, $z^* = (z_\sigma^*)$, $\sigma \in \Omega$. For every state σ leading to a given statistical state r, that is, such that $r(\sigma) = r$, equilibrium prices and consumption allocations are the same, that is, there exists a price rector p_r^* and an allocation z_r^* such that $\forall \sigma$: $r(\sigma) = r$, $p_\sigma^* = p_r^*$, and $z_\sigma^* = z_r^*$, where $p_r^* \in R^{N+}$ and $z_r^* \in R^{NI}$ depend solely on r.*

[6] In a recent article, Klimper and Requate (1997) show that Proposition 1's proof holds also for households that do not agree on a common probability distribution over social states.

[7] Related propositions were established by Malinvaud in a simpler economy where all agents are identical, and risks are known.

Proof: In the Appendix.   QED.

Definition: *An economy E is regular if at all equilibrium prices in E the Jacobian matrix of first partial derivatives of its excess demand function has full rank. Regularity is a generic property (Debreu (1970), Dierker (1982)).*

We now consider the general case, which allows for $\Pi^h \neq \Pi^j$ if $h \neq j$. Proposition 2 states that if the economy is regular, if all households have the same preferences and if there are two individual states, there is always one equilibrium at which prices are the same at all social states leading to the same statistical state. This confirms the intuition that the characteristics of an equilibrium should not be changed by a permutation of individuals: If I am changed to your state, and you to mine, everyone else remaining constant, then provided you and I have the same preferences, the equilibrium will not change.

Proposition 2: *Assume $\Pi^h \neq \Pi^k$ for some households h, k. When E is a regular economy, all agents have the same utilities,[8] and there are two individual states, then one of the equilibrium prices p^* must satisfy $p^*_{\sigma 1} = p^*_{\sigma 2}$ for all σ_1, σ_2 with $r(\sigma_1) = r(\sigma_2)$.*

Proof: In the Appendix.   QED.

5   Equilibrium in incomplete markets for unknown risks

Consider first the case where *there are no assets to hedge against risk*, so that the economy has incomplete asset markets. Individuals cannot transfer income to the unfavorable states. Examples are cases where individuals are not able to purchase hurricane insurance, as in some parts of the southeastern United States and in the Caribbean. Market allocations are typically inefficient in this case, since individuals cannot transfer income from one state to another to equalize welfare across states. Which households will be in each individual state is unknown. Each individual has a certain probability distribution over all possible social states σ, Π^h. In each social state σ each individual is constrained in the value of her/his expenditures by her/his endowment [which depends on the individual state s (h,σ) in that social state]. In this context, a *general equilibrium of*

---

[8] The condition that all agents have the same preferences is not needed for this result. However, it simplifies that notation and the argument considerably. The general case is treated in the working papers from which this article derives.

the economy with incomplete markets E_I consists of a price vector p^* with NS^H components and H consumption plans z_h^* with NS^H components each, such that z_h^* maximizes $W^h(z_h)$:

$$W^h(z_h) = \sum_\sigma \Pi_\sigma^h U^h(z_{h\sigma}) \tag{5.1}$$

subject to

$$p_\sigma(z_{h\sigma} - e_{h\sigma}) = 0 \text{ for each } \sigma \in \Omega \tag{5.2}$$

and

$$\sum_{h=1}^H (z_h - e_h) = 0 \tag{5.3}$$

The above economy E_I is an extreme version of an economy with incomplete asset markets (see, for example, Geanakoplos 1990) because there are no markets to hedge against risks. There are S^H budget constraints in equation (5.2).

6   Efficient allocations, mutual insurance, and securities

In this section we study the possibility of supporting Arrow–Debreu equilibria by combinations of statistical securities and insurance contracts, rather than by using state contingent contracts. As already observed, this leads to a very significant roduction in the number of markets needed. In an economy with no asset markets at all, such as E_I, the difficulty in supporting an Arrow–Debreu equilibrium arises because income cannot be transferred between states. On the basis of Propositions 1 and 2, we show that households can use securities defined on statistical states to transfer into each such state an amount of income equal to the expected difference between the value of Arrow–Debreu equilibrium consumption and the value of endowments in that state. The expectation here is over individual states conditional on being in a given statistical state. The difference between the actual consumption-income gap given a particular individual state and its expected value is then covered by insurance contracts. In the following, A denotes the combinatorial number $A = \begin{pmatrix} H + S - 1 \\ S - 1 \end{pmatrix}$.

Theorem 1: *Assume that all households in E have the same probability Π over the distribution of risks in the population.*

Then any Arrow–Debreu equilibrium allocation (p^*, z^*) of E (and therefore any Pareto optimum) can be achieved within the general equilibrium economy with incomplete markets E_I by introducing a total of A mutual insurance contracts to hedge against individual risk, and A statistical securities to hedge against social risk. In a regular economy with two individual states and identical preferences, even if agents have different probabilities, there is always an Arrow–Debreu equilibrium (p^*, z^*) in E which is achievable within the incomplete economy E_I with the introduction of I.A mutual insurance contracts and A statistical securities.

Proof: In the Appendix. QED.

6.1 *Market complexity*

We can now formalize a statement made before about the efficiency of the institutional structure proposed in Theorem 1 by comparison with the standard Arrow–Debreu structure of a complete set of state-contingent markets. We use complexity theory, and in particular the concept of *NP completeness*. The key consideration in this approach to studying problem complexity is how fast the number of operations required to solve a problem increases with the size of the problem.

> **Definition:** *If the number of operations required to solve a problem must increase exponentially for any possible way of solving the problem, then the problem is called "intractable" or more formally, NP-complete. If instead this number increases polynomially, the problem is "tractable."*[9]

The motivation for this defiuition is that if the number of operations needed to solve the problem increases exponentially with some measure of the size of the problem, there will be examples of the problem that no computer can or ever could solve. Hence there is no possibility of ever designing a general efficient algorithm for solving these problems. However, if the number of operations rises only polynomially then it is in principle possible to devise a general and efficient algorithm for the problem.

Theorem 2 investigates the complexity of the resource allocation problem in the Arrow–Debreu framework and compares this with the

---

[9] Further definitions are in Garey and Johnson (1979).

framework of Theorem 1. We focus on how the problem changes as the economy grows in the sense that the number of households increases, and consider a very simple aspect of the allocation problem, described as follows. Suppose that the excess demand of the economy $Z(p)$ is known. A particular price vector p^* is proposed as a market clearing price. We wish to check whether or not it is a market clearing price. This involves computing each of the coordinates of $Z(p)$ and then comparing with zero. This involves a number of operations proportional to the number of components of $Z(p)$; we therefore take the rate at which the dimension of $Z(p)$ increases with the number of agents to be a measure of the complexity of the resource allocation problem. In summary: we ask how the difficulty of verifying market clearing increases as the number of households in the economy rises. We show that in the Arrow–Debreu framework this difficulty rises exponentially, whereas in the framework of Theorem 1 it rises only polynomially.

Theorem 2: *Verifying market clearing is an intractable problem in an Arrow–Debreu economy, that is, the number of operations required to check if a proposed price is market clearing increases exponentially with the number of households H. However, under the assumptions of Theorem 1, in the economy E_I supplemented by I.A mutual insurance contracts and A statistical securities, verifying market clearing is a tractable problem, that is, the number of operations needed to check for market clearing increases only polynomially with the number of households.*

Proof: The number of operations required to check that a price is market clearing is proportional to the number of market clearing conditions. In E we have NS^H markets. Hence the number of operations needed to check if a proposed price is market clearing must rise exponentially with the number of households H. Consider now the case of E_I supplemented by I.A mutual insurance contracts and A securities. Under the assumptions of Theorem 1, by Propositions 1 and 2, we need only check for market clearing in one social state associated with any statistical state, because if markets clear in one social state leading to a certain statistical state they will clear in all social states leading to the same statistical state. Hence we need to check a number of goods markets equal to $N.A$, plus markets for mutual insurance contracts and securities. Now

$$A = \binom{H + S + 1}{S - 1} = \Phi\left(H, S\right)$$

where Φ (H,S) is a polynomial in H of order $(S - 1)$. Hence A itself is a polynomial in H whose highest order term depends on H^{S-1}, completing the proof.   QED.

7   Catastrophe futures and bundles

We mentioned in the introduction that securities contingent on statistical states are already traded as "catastrophe futures" on the Chicago Board of Trade, where they were introduced in 1994. (The concept was introduced and developed in Chichilnisky and Heal (1993).) Catastrophe futures are securities which pay an amount that depends on the value of an index (PCS) of insurance claims paid during a year. One such index measures the value of hurricane damage claims; others measure claims stemming from different types of natural disasters. The value of hurricane damage claims depends on the overall incidence of hurricane damage in the population, but is not affected by whether any particular individual is harmed. It therefore depends, in our terminology, on the statistical state, on the distribution of damage in the population, not on the social state. Catastrophe futures are thus financial instruments whose payoffs are conditional on the statistical state of the economy. They are statistical securities. According to our theory, a summary version of which appeared in Chichilnisky and Heal (1993), they are a crucial prerequisite to the efficient allocation of unknown risks. As the incidence and extent of natural disaster claims in the United States has increased greatly in recent years, risks such as property casualty due to hurricane risks are in effect unknown risks. Insurers are concerned that the incidence of storms may be related to trends in the composition of the atmosphere and incipient greenhouse warming. However, catastrophe futures are not on their own sufficient for this; they do not complete the market. Mutual or contingent insurance contracts, as described above, are also needed. These provide insurance conditional on the value of the catastrophe index. The two can be combined into "catastrophe bundles". See Chichilnisky (1996).

8   Conclusions

We have defined an economy with unknown individual risks and established that a combination of statistical securities and mutual or contingent insurance contracts can be used to obtain an efficient allocation of risk bearing. Furthermore, we have shown that this institutional structure is efficient in the sense that it requires exponentially fewer markets than the standard approach via state-contingent commodities. In fact, the state-contingent problem is "intractable" with individual risks (formally, NP-complete) in the language of computational complexity, whereas our approach gives a formulation that is polynomially complex. This greatly increases the economy's ability to achieve efficient allocations. Another interesting feature of this institutional structure is the interplay of insurance and securities markets involved. Its simplicity leads to successful hedging of unknown risks and predicts a convergence between the insurance and securities industries.

9   Appendix

Proposition 1: *When agents have common probabilities, that is, $\Pi^h = \Pi^j \forall h, j$, then equilibrium prices depend only on statistical states. Consider an Arrow–Debreu equilibrium of the economy E, $p^* = (p_\sigma{}^*)$, $z^* = (z_\sigma{}^*)$, $\sigma \in \Omega$. For every state σ leading to a given statistical state r, that is, such that $r(\sigma) = r$, equilibrium prices and consumption allocations are the same, that is, there exists a price vector p_r^* and an allocation z_r^* such that $\forall \sigma: r(\sigma) = r$, $p_\sigma{}^* = p_r^*$, and $z_\sigma{}^* = z_r^*$, where $p_r^* \in R^{N+}$ and $z_r^* \in R^{NI}$ depend solely on r.*

Proof: Consider σ_1 and σ_2 with $r(\sigma_1) = r(\sigma_2) = r$. Note that the total endowments of the economy are the same in σ_1 and σ_2, both equal to $s_r = Hr_s e_{hs}$ (recall that $e_{hs} = e_s$ as endowments depend only on individual states and not on household identities). Also, by the anonymity assumption, $\Pi_{\sigma_1} = \Pi_{\sigma_2} = \Pi_r$, where Π_r is the common probability of any social state in the statistical state r. Let $\Pi_{\sigma|r}$ be the probability of being in social state σ given statistical state r. By the anonymity assumption on probabilities this is just $1/\#\Omega_r$. We now show that for every household h, $z_{h\sigma_1}^* = z_{h\sigma_2}^*$, due to the Pareto efficiency of Arrow–Debreu equilibria. Let $\Omega_r = \{\sigma : r(\sigma) = \sigma\}$. Let $z^* = (z_{h\sigma}^*)$, and assume in contradiction to the proposition that there are σ_1 and $\sigma_2 \in \Omega_r$ such that $z_{h\sigma_1}^* \neq z_{h\sigma_2}^*$ for some h. Define $Ez_{hr} = \Sigma_{\sigma \in \Omega_r} z_{h\sigma}^* \Pi_{\sigma|r} = (1/\#\Omega_r) \Sigma_{\sigma \in \Omega_r} z_{h\sigma}^*$. This is the expected value of $(z_{h\sigma}^*)$ given that the economy is in the statistical state r. Now

$$\sum_h Ez_{hr} = \sum_h \frac{1}{\#\Omega_r} \sum_{\sigma \in \Omega_r} z_{h\sigma}^* = \sum_h z_{h\sigma}^*$$

so that $Ez_{h\sigma}$ is a feasible consumption vector for each h in the statistical state r. Next we show that by strict concavity, moving for each h and each σ from $z_{h\sigma}^*$ (which depends on σ) to Ez_{hr} (which is the same for all $\sigma \in \Omega$) is a strict Pareto improvement. This is because

$$W^h\left(z_{h\sigma}^*\right) = \sum_\sigma \Pi_\sigma U^h\left(z_{h\sigma}^*\right) = \sum_r \Pi_r \sum_{\sigma\in\Omega} \Pi_{\sigma|r} U^h\left(z_{h\sigma}^*\right)$$

By strict concavity of preferences,

$$\sum_r \Pi_r \sum_{\sigma\in\Omega_r} \Pi_{\sigma|r} U^h\left(z_{h\sigma}^*\right) <$$

$$\sum_r \Pi_r \sum_{\sigma\in\Omega_r} U^h\left(\sum_{\sigma\in\Omega} z_{h\sigma}^* \Pi_{\sigma|r}\right) = \sum_r \Pi_r \sum_{\sigma\in\Omega} U^h\left(Ez_{h\sigma}\right)$$

Since $Ez_{h\sigma}$ is Pareto superior to z^* with $z_{h\sigma_1}^* \neq z_{h\sigma_2}^*$, such a z^* cannot be an equilibrium allocation. Hence $z_{h\sigma_1}^* = z_{h\sigma_2}^* = z_{hr}^*$ for all $h = 1, \dots, H$. Note that this implies that in an equilibrium, household h consumes the same allocation z_{hr}^* across all individual states s, that is, it achieves full insurance. Since p^* supports the equilibrium allocation z^*, and $z_{h\sigma_1}^* = z_{h\sigma_2}^*$ it follows that $p_{\sigma_1}^* = p_{\sigma_2}^*$ when $r(\sigma_1) = r(\sigma_2)$, because utilities are assumed to be C^2 and, in particular, to have a unique gradient at each point which, by optimality, must be collinear both with $p_{\sigma_1}^*$ and with $p_{\sigma_2}^*$, that is, $p_{\sigma_1}^* = p_{\sigma_2}^* = p_r^*$. This implies that at an equilibrium, household h faces the same prices p_r^* at any σ with $r(\sigma) = r$. QED.

Proposition 2: *Assume $\Pi^h \neq \Pi^k$ for some households h, k. When E is a regular economy, all agents have the same utilities,[10] and there are two individual states, one of the equilibrium prices p^* must satisfy $p_{\sigma_1}^* = p_{\sigma_2}^*$ for all σ_1, σ_2 with $r(\sigma_1) = r(\sigma_2)$.*

Proof:

Assume that E is regular, that all agents have the same preferences, and that $S = 2$. Consider two social states σ_1 and σ_2 with $r(\sigma_1) = r(\sigma_2)$, and such that σ_1 differs from σ_2 only on the individual states of the two households h_1 and h_2 which are permuted, that is, $s(h_1,\sigma_1) = s(h_2,\sigma_2)$ and $s(h_2,\sigma_1) = s(h_1,\sigma_2)$. Assume

---

[10] The condition that all agents have the same preferences is not needed for this result, but simplifies the notation and the proof considerably. In the working papers from which this article derives, the general case was covered. See also footnote 6 for the case where agents have different probabilities.

that there exists an equilibrium price for $E, p^* \in R^{NSH}$, such that its components in states σ_1 and σ_2 are different, that is, $p_{\sigma_1}^* \neq p_{\sigma_2}^*$. Define now a new price $p_c^* \in R^{NSH}$, called a "conjugate" of p^*, which differs from p^* only in its coordinates in states σ_1 and σ_2, which are permuted as follows: $\forall \sigma \neq \sigma_1, \sigma_2, \overline{p}\sigma^* = p_\sigma^*, \overline{p}_{\sigma_1}^* = p_{\sigma_2}^*$, and $\overline{p}_{\sigma_2}^* = p_{\sigma_1}^*$. We now show that $\overline{p}^*$ is also an equilibrium price for the economy E. At $\overline{p}^*$, household h_1 has the same endowments and faces the same prices in states σ_1 and σ_2 as it did at states σ_2 and σ_1 respectively at price p^*; at all other states $\sigma \in \Omega$, h_1 faces the same prices and has the same endowments facing p^* and facing $\overline{p}^*$. The same is true of household h_2. Furthermore h_1 and h_2 have the same utilities and probabilities at σ_1 and σ_2 because $r(\sigma_1) = r(\sigma_2)$ and probabilities are anonymous. Therefore the excess demand vectors of h_1 in states σ_1 and σ_2 at prices p^* equal the excess demand vectors of h_2 in σ_2 and σ_1 respectively at prices $\overline{p}^*$, and at all other states $\sigma \in \Omega$ the excess demand vectors of h_1 are the same at prices p^* and $\overline{p}^*$. Reciprocally, the excess demand vectors of h_2 in σ_1 and σ_2 at prices p^* equal the excess demand vectors of h_1 in σ_2 and σ_1 respectively at prices $\overline{p}^*$, and in all other states σ, the excess demand vectors of h_2 are the same as they are with prices p^*. Formally:

$$z_{h_1\sigma_1}\left(\overline{p}^*\right) = z_{h_2\sigma_2}\left(p^*\right), \; z_{h_1\sigma_2}\left(\overline{p}^*\right) = z_{h_2\sigma_1}\left(p^*\right)$$
$$z_{h_2\sigma_1}\left(\overline{p}^*\right) = z_{h_1\sigma_2}\left(p^*\right), \; z_{h_2\sigma_2}\left(\overline{p}^*\right) = z_{h_1\sigma_1}\left(p^*\right)$$

and $\forall \sigma \in \Omega, \sigma \neq \sigma_1, \sigma_2$:

$$z_{h_1\sigma}\left(p^*\right) = z_{h_1\sigma}\left(\overline{p}^*\right), \; z_{h_2\sigma}\left(p^*\right) = z_{h_2\sigma}\left(\overline{p}^*\right)$$

The excess demand vectors of all other households $h \neq h_1, h_2$ are the same for p^* and $\overline{p}^*$. Therefore at $\overline{p}^*$ the aggregate excess demand vector of the economy is zero, so that $\overline{p}^*$ is an equilibrium. The same argument shows that permuting the two components $p_{\sigma_1}^*, p_{\sigma_2}^*$ of a price p^* at any two social states σ_1, σ_2 leading to the same statistical state $r(\sigma_1)$ leads from an equilibrium price p^* to another equilibrium price $\overline{p}^*$. This is because if two social states σ_1 and σ_2 lead to the same statistical state and there are two individual states s_1 and s_2 then there is a number $k > 0$ such that k households who are in s_1 in σ_1 are in s_2 in σ_2 and another k households who were in s_1 in σ_2 are in s_2 in σ_1, while remaining in the same individual states otherwise. These two sets of k households can be paired. For every pair of households, the above argument applies. Hence it applies to the sum of the demands, so that the new price $\bar{p}^*$ is an equilibrium.

Now consider any regular economy E with a finite number of equilibrium prices denoted $p_1^*, \ldots, p_k^*$. We shall show that there exists a $j \leq k$ s.t. p_j^* assigns the same price vector to all social states σ_1, σ_2 with $r(\sigma_1) = r(\sigma_2)$. Start with p_1^*; if p_1^* does not have this property, consider the first two social states σ_1, σ_2 with $r(\sigma_1) = r(\sigma_2)$ and $p_{1\sigma_1}^* \neq p_{1\sigma_2}^*$. Define $\bar{p}_1^*$ as the conjugate of p_1^* constructed by permuting the prices of the social states σ_1 and σ_2. If $\forall j > 1$, $p_j^* = \bar{p}_1^*$, then there are two price equilibria, that is, $k = 2$; since, however, the number of price equilibria must be odd,[11] there must exist $p_{j_1}^*$ with $j_1 > 1$ and $p_{j_1}^* \neq \bar{p}_1^*$. Consider now the conjugate of $p_{j_1}^*$ with respect to the first two social states σ_1, σ_2 which correspond to the same statistical state and have different components in $p_{j_1}^*$, and denote this conjugate $\bar{p}_{j_1}^*$. Repeat the procedure until all equilibria are exhausted. In each step of this procedure, two different price equilibria are found. Since the number of equilibria must be odd, it follows that there must exist a $j \leq k$ for which all conjugates of p_j^* equal p_j^*. This is the required equilibrium which assigns the same equilibrium prices $p_{\sigma_1}^* = p_{\sigma_2}^*$ to all σ_1, σ_2 with $r(\sigma_1) = r(\sigma_2)$, completing the proof.   QED.

Theorem 1: *Assume that all households in E have the same probability Π over the distribution of risks in the population. Then any Arrow–Debreu equilibrium allocation (p^*, z^*) of E (and therefore any Pareto optimum) can be achieved within the general equilibrium economy with incomplete markets E_I by introducing a total of A mutual insurance contracts to hedge against individual risk, and A statistical securities to hedge against social risk. In a regular economy with two individual states and identical preferences, even if agents have different probabilities, there is always an Arrow–Debreu equilibrium (p^*, z^*) in E which is achievable within the incomplete economy E_I with the introduction of A mutual insurance contracts and A statistical securities.*

---

[11] This follows from Dierker (1982), p. 807, noting that his condition D is implied by our assumption that preferences are strictly increasing (see Dierker's remark following the statement of property D on p. 799).

Proof: Consider first the case where all households have the same probabilities, that is, $\Pi^h = \Pi^j = \Pi$. By Proposition 1, an Arrow–Debreu equilibrium of E has the same prices $p_\sigma^* = p_r^*$ and the same consumption vectors $z_{h\sigma}^* = z_{hr}^*$ for each h, at each social state σ with $r(\sigma) = r$. Define $\Omega(r)$ as the set of social states mapping to a given statistical state r, that is, $\Omega(r) = \{\sigma \in \Omega : r(\sigma) = r\}$. The budget constraint equation is

$$p^*\left(z_h^* - e_h\right) = \sum_\sigma p_\sigma^*\left(z_{h,\sigma}^* - e_{h\sigma}\right)$$
$$= \sum_r p_r^* \sum_{\sigma \in \Omega(r)} \left(z_{h\sigma}^* - e_{h\sigma}\right) = 0$$

Individual endowments depend on individual states and not on social states, so that $e_{h\sigma} = e_{hs(\sigma)} = e_{hs}$. Furthermore, by Proposition 1 equilibrium prices depend on r and not on σ, so that for each r the equilibrium consumption vector $z_{h\sigma}$ can be written as z_{hs}. The individual budget constraint is therefore $\Sigma_r p_r^* \Sigma_{s(r)}(z_{hs} - e_{hs})$, where summation over $s(r)$ indicates summation over all individual states s that occur in any social state leading to r, that is, that are in the set $\Omega(r)$. Let $\#\Omega(r)$ be the number of social states in $\Omega(r)$. As $\Pi_{s|r} = r_s$ is the proportion of households in state s within the statistical state r, we can finally rewrite the budget constraint equation (4.2) of the household h as:

$$\#\Omega(r)\sum_r p_r^* \sum_s \#\Omega(r)\Pi_{s|r}\left(z_{hs} - e_{hs}\right) = 0 \qquad (A.1)$$

Using equation (3.1), the household's maximization problem can therefore be expressed as:

$$\max_{s,r} \sum \Pi_{sr} U^h\left(z_{hsr}\right) \text{ subject to } (A.1)$$

and the equilibrium allocation z_h^* by definition solves this problem. Similarly, we may rewrite the market clearing condition (4.5) as follows:

$$\sum_h \left(z_h^* - e_h\right) = \sum_h \left(z_{h\sigma}^* - e_{hs(\sigma)}\right) = 0, \quad \forall \sigma \in \Omega$$

Rewriting the market clearing condition (4.3) in terms of statistical states r, and within each r, individual states s, we obtain

$$\sum_s r_s H\left(z_{hr}^* - e_{sr}^h\right) = 0, \quad \forall r \in R \tag{A.2}$$

or equivalently

$$\sum_s \Pi_{s|r} H\left(z_{hr}^* - e_{sr}^h\right) = 0, \quad \forall r \in R$$

Using these relations, we now show that any Arrow–Debreu equilibrium allocation $z^* = (z_{hr}^*)$ is within the budget constraints (5.2) of the economy E_I for each $\sigma \in \Omega$, *provided that* for each $\sigma \in \Omega$ we add the income derived from a statistical security $A_r, r = r(\sigma)$, and, given $r(\sigma)$, the income derived from mutual or contingent insurance contracts $m_{sr}^h = m_{s(\sigma)r(\sigma)}^h$, $s = 1, \ldots, S$. We introduce A statistical securities and $I.A$ mutual insurance contracts in the general equilibrium economy with incomplete markets E_I. The quantity of the security A_r purchased by household h in statistical state r, when equilibrium prices are p^*, is

$$a_r^{h*} = \sum_s \Pi_{s|r}\, p_r^*\left(z_{hr}^* - e_{hs}\right) \tag{A.3}$$

The quantity a_r^{h*} has a very intuitive interpretation. It is the expected amount by which the value of equilibrium consumption exceeds the value of endowments, conditional on being in statistical state r. So *where the law of large numbers applies*, the statistical securities purchased deliver enough to balance a household's budget in each statistical state. Otherwise, differences between the average and each individual state are taken care of by the mutual insurance contracts. Note that equation (A.2) implies that the total amount of each security supplied is zero, that is, $\Sigma_h a_r^{h*} = 0$ for all r, so that this corresponds to the initial endowments of the incomplete economy E_I. Furthermore, $\Sigma_r a_r^{h*} = 0$ by (A.1), so that each household h is within her/his budget in E_I.

We now introduce a mutual insurance contract as follows. The transfer made by individual h in statistical state r and individual state s, when prices are p_r^*, is

$$m_{sr}^{h*} = p_r^*\left(z_{hr}^* - e_{hr}\right) - a_r^{h*} \tag{A.4}$$

Note that, as remarked above, m_{sr}^{h*} is just the difference between the actual income-expenditure gap, given that individual state s is realized, and the expected income-expenditure gap a_r^{h*} in statistical state r, which is covered by statistical securities. In each statistical state r, the sum over all h and s of all transfers m_{sr}^{h*} equals zero, that is, the insurance premia match exactly the payments. For any given r,

$$\sum_{h,s} H\Pi_{s|r} m_{sr}^{h*} = \sum_{h,s} H\Pi_{s|r} p_r^*\left(z_{hr}^* - e_{hs}\right) - \sum_h Ha_r^{h*}\sum_s \Pi_{s|r} = 0$$
(A.5)

because $\Sigma_s\Pi_{s|r} = 1$. Therefore, the $\{m_{sr}^{h*}\}$ meet the definition of mutual insurance contracts. Finally, note that with N spot markets, A statistical securities $\{a_r\}$ and mutual insurance contracts $\{m_{sr}^h\}$

$$p_r^*\left(z_{hr}^* - e_s^h\right) = m_{sr}^{h*} + a_r^{h*},$$
$$\forall\sigma\in\Omega \text{ with } r(\sigma) = r, s = s(\sigma)$$
(A.6)

so that equation (5.2) is satisfied for each $\sigma \in \Omega$. This establishes that when all households have the same probabilities over social states, all Arrow–Debreu equilibrium allocation z^* of E can be achieved within the incomplete markets economy E_I when A securities and A mutual insurance contracts are introduced into E_I, and completes the proof of the first part of the proposition dealing with common probabilites.

Consider now the case where the economy E is regular, different households in E have different probabilities over social states but have the same preferences, and $S = 2$. By Proposition 2, we know that within the set of equilibrium prices there is one p^* in which at all social states $\sigma \in \Omega(r)$ for a given r, the equilibrium prices are the same, that is, $p_\sigma^* = p_r^*$. In particular, if E has a unique equilibrium (p^*,z^*), it must have this property. It follows from the above arguments that the equilibrium (p^*,z^*) must maximize (3.1) subject to (A.1). Note, however, that now for the same r, z_{hsr}^* may be different from $z_{hs'r}^*$ when $s \neq s'$. Now define the quantity of the security A_r purchased by a household in the statistical state r by

$$a_r^{h*} = \sum_s \Pi_{s|r}^h p_r^*\left(z_{hsr}^* - e_s^h\right)$$
(A.7)

and the mutual insurance transfer made by a household in statistical state r and individual state s, by

$$m_{sr}^{h*} = p_r^*\left(z_{hsr}^* - e_s^h\right) - a_r^{h*}$$
(A.8)

As before, $\Sigma_r a_r^{h^*} = 0$ and for any given r, $\Sigma_{h,s} \Pi_{s|r}^h H m_{sr}^{h^*} = \Sigma_{h,s} r_s H m_{sr}^{h^*}$
$= 0$, so that the securities purchased correspond to the initial
endowments of the economy E_I and at any statistical state the
sum of the premia and the sum of the payments of the mutual
insurance contracts match, completing the proof.   QED.

References

Arrow, K. J. 1953. The role of securities in an optimal allocation of risk-bearing. *Econometrie, Proceedings of the Colloque sur les Fondements et Applications de la Theorie du Risque en Econometrie, Centre National de la Recherche Scientifique*, Paris. English translation in *Review of Economic Studies*, 1964, 31:91–6.

Arrow, K. J., and R. C. Lind. 1970. Uncertainty and the evaluation of public investments. *American Economic Review*, 364–78.

Cass, D., G. Chichilnisky, and H. M. Wu. 1991. Individual risks and mutual insurance. CARESS Working Paper #91-27, Department of Economics, University of Pennsylvania, *Econometrica*, Vol 64, No 2, March 1996, 333–41.

Chichilnisky, G. 1996. Catastrophe Bundles. *Bests' Review*, March.

Chichilnisky, G., and G. M. Heal. 1993. Global environmental risks. *Journal of Economics Perspectives*, Fall, pp. 65–86.

Chichilnisky, G., and H. M. Wu. 1991. Individual risk and endogenous uncertainty in incomplete asset markets. Working paper, Columbia University and Technical Report No. 50, Stanford Institute for Theoretical Economics, 1992.

Chichilnisky, G., J. Dutta, and G. M. Heal. 1991. Price uncertainty and derivative securities in general equilibrium. Working paper, Columbia Business School.

Chichilnisky, G., G. M. Heal, P. Streufert, and J. Swinkels. 1992. Believing in multiple equilibria. Working paper, Columbia Business School.

Debreu, G. 1959. *The Theory of Value*. New York: Wiley.

Debreu, G. 1970. Economies with a finite set of equilibria. *Econometrica*, 38:387–92.

Dierker, E. 1982. Regular economies. In *Handbook of Mathematical Economics, Volume II*, ed., K. J. Arrow and M. D. Intrilligator. North Holland.

Gary, M. R., and D. S. Johnson. 1979. *Computers and Intractability: A Guide to NP-Completeness*. New York: W. H. Freeman and Company.

Geanakoplos, J. 1990. An introduction to general equilibrium with incomplete asset markets. *Journal of Mathematical Economics*, 19:1–38.

Heal, G. M. 1992. Risk management and global change. Paper presented at the *First Nordic Conference on the Greenhouse Effect*, Copenhagen, 1992.

Klimper, S. and T. Requate 1997. Financial Markets for Unknown Risks: A Generalization. Working Paper No. 245, Interdisciplinary Institute of Environmental Economics, University of Heidelberg, Grabengasse 14, 69117 Heidelberg, Germany.

Malinvaud, E. 1972. The allocation of individual risk in large markets. *Journal of Economic Theory*, 4:312–28.
Malinvaud, E. 1973. Markets for an exchange economy with individual risk. *Econometrica*, 3:383–409.

Market externalities and justice

CHAPTER 8

Moral hazard and independent income in a modern intertemporal-equilibrium model of involuntary unemployment and mandatory retirement

Edmund S. Phelps

It is a special pleasure to participate in this *Festschrift* celebrating the contributions of Kenneth Arrow to economics. Almost uniquely in our profession, Arrow bestrides two worlds in economic theory – the Old World of neoclassical theory and the New World of modern theory, as I like to call it.

Arrow made significant contributions to the final expression of neo-classical theory with his work in the 1950s and subsequent years, some of it in collaboration with Gerard Debreu. Their work on the existence and uniqueness of general equilibrium and its extension to stochastic and intertemporal settings is well known. This is the theory of the equilibrium of a competitive economy operating under perfect information.

The "Arrow" to which I (and most in my age group and younger) have been drawn, however, is the pioneer in models exhibiting imperfect information. By that term, now widely used if inadequate, I refer to economic settings in which not every one is able or willing (because of costliness) to become perfectly informed about the state of the world and each participant's actions. Some information may be inherently private, hence concealable and unverifiable.[1] His best remembered contribution, to my mind, is his rather informal yet trenchant analysis of market fail-

This chapter was drafted in 1994 while the author was a visiting scholar at the Russell Sage Foundation and revised when he was visiting Universita "Tor Vergata," Rome, in the same year. Discussions with Oliver Blanchard, Alessandra Casella, and Graciela Chichilnisky are gratefully acknowledged.
[1] An acquaintance of mine said of his homeland that it was a place where if one were to speak the truth no one would believe it.

143

ure in the provision of insurance (Arrow (1953)). That essay, with its emphasis on asymmetric information, seems to have heralded the direction of the modern economic models emerging in subsequent years. Moral hazard and adverse selection both make their appearance in that essay. I am not suggesting that this was the first modern work on economics – both Hume and Marx, for example, understood something of the problems arising from imperfect information – but it may be the first systematic investigation of information problems, and the first to be conscious of its departure from the antecedent neoclassical tradition.

The article did not at once precipitate a torrent of work in the new vein. A few years went by before everyday transactions in the marketplace began to be viewed from the new modern perspective. It took time, apparently, to see the wide applicability of this way of thinking to the working of labor, product, and credit markets.

My article on labor-market equilibrium is one of the 1960s works in this modern vein (Phelps (1968)). The avowed message of that article was clearly contrary to neoclassical thinking. In a thoroughly neoclassical setting, market clearing is necessary for a market to be in equilibrium – where equilibrium, as in Marshall, Hayek, Myrdal, and sometimes Hicks, means an outcome or path in which expectations are borne out, absent unforeseeable shocks.[2] [The gist of the argument is that if there are participants in a market either placing orders based on a certain price expectation that cannot be satisfied (excess demand) or making offers based on a certain price expectation that cannot be satisfied (excess supply), the actual price will immediately respond and hence not be found at the level expected. For expectations to be correct – for an equilibrium path following any shock – the actual and expected prices must already have jumped in anticipation of whatever level is necessary to preclude nonclearing and thus an unexpected price adjustment.] In the setting of this chapter, however, firms cope with a personnel problem – the imperfectly foreseeable decision of many or all employees in whom the firm has "invested" sooner or later to quit – by driving wages *above* the market clearing level as a stratagem aimed at reducing the quit rate and thus reducing training/hiring costs. The only possible equilibrium (if such exists) is one of *non*clearing. The equilibrium rate of unemployment created by this job rationing is generally positive, being just large enough that each firm is no longer bent on paying more than other firms. Thus market clearing is not, in general, necessary for labor-market equilib-

[2] Most regrettably, by the 1950s some theorists had come to *define* equilibrium as clearing!

rium[3] (see Salop (1979) and Hoon and Phelps (1992) for more recent exposition and further development).

It is unclear, what the modern sand in the neoclassical machine is. (Moreover, an ill-advised desire to insist from the start on worker heterogeneity, to help smooth recruitment, and to generate a positive vacancy rate alongside the unemployment rate obscured its unemployment-generating mechanism.) In one sense, there is no "asymmetric information" in the setting since the employee does not know any better than the employer at what point, if any, he or she will feel the impulse to move on to another locale or industry; if there is a decision to quit, both parties may learn about it virtually at the same moment. (Only later was a parallel model of shirking introduced – by Calvo, Bowles, and Solow – that visibly *did* have such an asymmetric information feature; see below.) Further, since all workers are alike, it would not help if every worker had a meter protruding from his or her head indicating a propensity to quit, since every firm already knows the universal hazard rate and how it would be improved if the firm sweetened its wage scale.

It was a few years before I realized that the anti-neoclassical element buried deep in the machine was the nonexistence (in most cases, at any rate) of a trustworthy, hence incentive-compatible, contract that would indemnify the firm for an employee's decision to quit, through agreement that the employee either forfeit a deposit made when he joined the firm or forfeit the "gold watch" the employer promised on completion of a full term of service. There is an analogy to the moral hazard in insurance contracts in that the *employer*, if protected in this way against the contingency of a quit, might be motivated not to take good care of the employee, even possibly to goad him into quitting in order to lay claim to the deposit or reclaim the pledge of the watch. Thus there turns out to be a link after all between my model and Arrow's fundamental work on insurance.

This chapter discusses an extension of this *kind* of model of equilibrium unemployment, an extension well beyond my imagination when groping toward a rudimentary understanding of the model decades ago. The objective is a simple utility-theoretic model of intertemporal equilibrium along modern lines. The model is at least in the spirit of my 1968 model, and in stripping away the inessential moneyness of the economy

---

[3] In a sense, the message of my "island parable" a couple of years later was that market clearing is not *sufficient* for equilibrium either. Again, however, the setting is non-neoclassical, since there is no unified market but, instead, markets operating without instant and complete communication with one another.

it is even closer to the spirit of my recent essay with Hian Teck Hoon (Hoon and Phelps (1992)). In working toward this model, however, I have found it simpler to draw on the sister models based on the personnel problem of *shirking* rather than quitting. I comment in the concluding section on some of the complications arising in a similar intertemporal model of quitting.

1   An intertemporal equilibrium model of the shirking type

The model describes a closed economy in which the problem at enterprises is motivating employees not to shirk and the social problem is the unemployment to which that personnel problem gives rise. (For a shirking model of unemployment, see Calvo (1979).) Much of the social interest in unemployment, though by no means all, is put aside in supposing that all persons are equally capable of potential productivity and, in the same circumstances and at the same stage of life, equally able to be motivated to conduct themselves productively.

For both simplicity and familiarity, the Blanchard–Yaari demographics are used in which an individual is born into the labor force and is thereafter subject to a constant instantaneous force of mortality, μ (>0). Thus the old are blessed with the same expectation of remaining life as the young, though nothing of apparent importance appears to turn on that convenient feature. Further, the inflow of new workers into the society, entering with zero wealth, is equal to the outflow through mortality. Hence the population and age distribution are constant over time. Finally, what a person saves is, in effect, turned over to an insurance pool in return for an annuity, so that the income from wealth – the "independent income" of the chapter title – includes an *actuarial dividend* in addition to pure interest. (This income may also be called unearned income, although that term of accountants, if I am not mistaken, is broader, as it includes all nonlabor income.) Symmetrically, nonsavers also enter into an insurance pool, paying an *actuarial premium* on top of the interest on their debt to offset the losses from their mortality. So borrowing and lending is between pools.

In the model, everyone prefers having a job to unemployment or retirement – even if utility-maximizing conduct does not permit any shirking from its continuous duties. (Following custom, shirking means any unauthorized leisure taken on the job.) Preferences are identical with regard to lifetime consumption, leisure when jobless, and shirking, or on-the-job leisure. These are represented by the standard lifetime utility function (or functional). The decision problem of the individual is to choose a consumption policy (in the sense of Bellman), which is generally a contingency plan, and when employed, to choose a shirking policy to maximize the expected value of lifetime utility. In the present model, there are no changes in taste (such as quitting models have) and none is expected at any time.

It will be supposed until notice to the contrary that there is no technical change, anticipated or unanticipated. The technology is described by constant returns: Output at any enterprise and in the economy as a whole is proportional to weighted employment, where the weight given a worker's employment is the fraction of time the worker gives to the task of his job. That is, the weight of an employed worker is the rate at which he is not shirking. All nonshirking (or equally shirking) employees are equally productive; there is no fall-off of a person's productivity with age or experience. Hence these latter factors never operate to erode an employee's wages, no matter how many decades he might work, and they are not responsible for the retirement phenomenon found in the model.

In this setting, an enterprise does not represent an accumulation of customers or of employees having firm-specific training or experience. The enterprise here is considered a *firm*, in the familiar sense of the term, only in that it offers *continuing* employment to every current employee if he is not caught shirking, subject to some provisos concerning retirement and downsizing. Why, therefore, would a person not do as well working for himself as for a firm? No one then would ever be unemployed. Self-employment would always be an option as good as employment in an enterprise. The answer is that each enterprise here is to be interpreted as a *team* of workers, and no enterprise would be profitable if its workforce did not constitute the necessary team. Hence the unemployed do not have the option of working in a self-employed mode as productively as those employed in enterprises, and if some unemployed persons banded together into the requisite team they would encounter the same problems of shirking and monitoring as existing enterprises.

There is no tangible capital stock, as is implicit in the description of the technology just given. Neither do firms accumulate assets of possible value in the form of customers or employees possessing firm-specific training or experience. What, then, can a worker accumulate, if anything? I am content to suppose that the only assets an employed worker might save for the future, especially for retirement, are consumer loans sought by the unemployed. It is hoped that, for all its eccentricity, this model offers an improvement over the assumption in a rather important predecessor model that nothing is saved or dissaved at any time (Shapiro and Stiglitz (1984)). It would not be a large step to insert physical capital into the simple story told here, but doing so would not eliminate the consumer loans, so it is just as well to put them in from the start, regardless of the risk of overemphasizing them.

We may apply to this setting the familiar arguments of incentive-wage theory: We can imagine an equilibrium in which each enterprise offers employment only on condition that the worker pay a deposit which would be forfeited to the employer if the enterprise detects the worker in an act of shirking. Such an employment contract, however, would be open to abuse by an unscrupulous enterprise willing to defraud the worker of the deposit by giving false testimony about his conduct. A worker may accept a contract offering an employer protection against misconduct demonstrable to others, but not a contract giving the employer the right to make a claim without the burden of proof.[4] Hence each enterprise will be driven to the nonclassical solution of raising wages to achieve a wage premium over other enterprises. In the last analysis the only general equilibrium possible is one at a positive unemployment rate – one so large that shirking is sufficiently dampened that each firm is content to pay the same wages as the others (labor-market equilibrium) and wages low enough that enterprises are not forced to contract employment further (product-market equilibrium).

The goal, from a technical standpoint, is to uncover an equilibrium path of the rate of interest, wage rates, shirking rates, labor force participation – in this model equivalent to determining retirement or the active-age population – and unemployment. My more limited objective is to investigate the properties of any *stationary* equilibrium (if such exists) in this model. (Experience with certain other models suggests that if there is a *unique* stationary equilibrium, there is no other equilibrium, stationary or nonstationary.) Matters of existence and uniqueness will not be treated rigorously, however, or even explicitly. (An article on another modern intertemporal model illustrative of an approach to these matters is Calvo and Phelps (1983).)

---

[4] This is possibly the intuition behind the postulate in Gary Becker's (1961) model of wage profiles that a worker is willing to pay for his general training but *not* for any *firm-specific* training: He is afraid the firm will not keep any promise to pay a higher wage later as a reward for his investment. (If so, it is ironic since it is ultimately argued in the same analysis that the *firm* will be willing pay for firm-specific training and thus induce the employee not to quit or at least not to quit so readily. The firm protects its investment by a policy of paying a lower wage in the initial years to finance its training outlay, and restoring the wage after the outlay has been repaid. It is not clear to me why the worker contemplating the initial wage reduction and promised restoration later would regard this promise as any more reliable than the promise of higher wages later if the worker lays out his own money for the firm-specific training.)

My main interest, however, is to show how the accumulation of wealth by employed workers leads inevitably to mandatory retirement of the rich and the involuntary unemployment of the poor. Another interest of mine is the robustness of the peculiar device used by Shapiro and Stiglitz (1984) in their model of shirking equilibrium: Linearizing the utility from shirking, they postulate that at a given unemployment rate there will exist a corresponding wage just high enough to prevent shirking, whereas any lower wage would cause shirking by everyone. An obvious liability of such a description is that no shirking is just as unrealistic a characterization of equilibrium as no quitting would be in a quitting story of incentive wages. Another drawback is that in a richer model in which workers exhibit differences in circumstances or temperament, the wage just sufficient to deter one worker's shirking would be too low to deter another's (Phelps (1994)).[5] In the present model, however, the latter complication is not so much a difficulty as a source of some interesting implications. Those who would need a higher wage since their circumstances make them readier to shirk do not get it – instead they are let go! I argue that the greater accumulated wealth of older workers leads to their mandatory retirement at a certain trigger level of wealth.

1.1   Specifying the firms' and the worker-consumers' possibilities and preferences

It is not possible to discuss the decision problems of the worker-consumer (hereafter the worker) without reference to the firm, and vice versa. First, a few remarks on firms.

Just as competition on the buying side of the market ensures that two farmers will receive the same price for identical output, no matter that one of them had superior land, and two workers will command the same wage for an identical service, no matter that one dislikes (or likes) one more than the other, the competition of firms in the economy modeled here ensures that all employed workers, from those far from shirking to those close to shirking (all day long), receive the same wage.

In the spirit of Ricardo's extensive margin, therefore, we may interpret the firms' required wage as the wage required to deter shirking by the *marginal* employed worker, the oldest and thus (in steady state) the wealthiest employees. Given the distribution of the accumulated financial wealth of workers uninterruptedly employed once hired, and given the length of the unemployment queue to which an employee

---

[5] Hence, in that book I work only with models exhibiting positive quitting and shirking in (and out of) equilibrium.

would be sent if caught shirking, there will be a corresponding schedule showing the required wage (as determined by the marginal worker) rising with total employment – thus rising with the wealth of the marginal employee. Clearly this schedule shifts up with a reduction of the unemployment queue or a general increase of wealth. But for equilibrium, this required wage at the margin cannot exceed the wage that firms can afford to pay for the services of nonshirking workers. Given the wealth of the marginal employee, the unemployment queue must be just long enough that all employed workers with lesser wealth are deterred from shirking whereas workers with greater wealth would shirk continuously: The required wage is just equal to the wage determined by the zero-profit condition. (Not surprisingly, since wealth rises with age, this equilibrium condition can be viewed as determining the mandatory retirement age as an increasing function of the steady-state volume of unemployment, both because of the discipline exerted by the length of the queue and because higher unemployment means poorer employees.)

Most of the work of this chapter involves structuring the worker's opportunities and preferences in such a way that there may exist an equilibrium displaying a queue of unemployed youth and a rising age profile of wealth during employment that triggers mandatory retirement. We therefore next consider the workers.

Workers must decide, at each moment in their lifetime, their current rate of consumption, $c(t)$, and (when employed) their rate of shirking, $s(t)$, both of which give utility. We assume the worker makes these decisions so as to maximize the expected value of lifetime utility, which is represented by the integral of the discounted instantaneous rates of utility. The exponential rate of utility discount is $\mu + \varrho$, where ϱ is the rate of pure time preference and μ, to repeat, is the death rate. Optimal decisions depend on the individual's current personal situation, described by his wealth, $w(t)$, or (equivalently, given the constant rate of interest, r) his income from wealth, $y^w(t)$, and by his employment status.

At a given moment a worker must either be unemployed, designated status 0, or employed, status 1, or retired, status 2. A worker in the employed status has an implicit (or for that matter explicit) contract protecting him against replacement by another employee as long as he is not caught shirking and does not meet the conditions for mandatory retirement.[6] If an employee chooses to shirk continuously over

---

[6] This protection of the employee serves, at no cost to the employer, to strengthen the penalty the employee would pay if caught shirking. But there will be a clause protecting the firm's right to terminate in the event the firm wants to shed labor and, as argued below, there is a provision for mandatory retirement.

some time interval and happens to be caught by his employer, the employee passes to unemployment status. Provided there is a positive pool of unemployed workers, a worker in the unemployed status has to wait (on the average at any rate) to gain or regain employment. That happens when his number comes up in a random drawing or, in an alternative model that is conceptually less problematic, when his turn comes.

The penalty paid for shirking (continuously over some interval of time) is that with some probability this nonperformance will be detected. An enterprise is assumed to find it cost-effective to observe a worker's performance or non-performance only when there is some other reason for dealing with that worker, so the discovery of shirking comes as a free by-product. The fraction of a group of continuously shirking workers not caught would thus decline exponentially at the instantaneous rate π. This may be called the detection rate or, loosely, the probability of detection.

The penalty paid for consuming is the shrinkage of wealth that results, which costs the worker some future consumption possibilities. The gross rate of interest on wealth is $r + \mu$, taking into account the actuarial dividend.

Rather generally, we may view the worker as solving a problem of dynamic programming consisting of a system of three functional equations in the (unknown) functions giving the utility of wealth in status 0, status 1, and status 2. The utility of wealth in a given status is equal to the expected value of lifetime utility, discounted back to the current time (rather than to date of entry into the labor force), when an optimal policy is followed, given the net financial wealth on hand at the current moment. Further, in this system, the utility of the wealth of the person when unemployed at present, w_0, consists of the expected utility during unemployment plus the expected utility after passage (not necessarily for the first time) into employment.

Formulation of the time spent waiting in the unemployment pool to a reader steeped in the customary modeling of intertemporal choice is probabilistic. I back away from this formulation. Employers draw randomly from the unemployment pool so all unemployed persons have equal chances of escaping that status. Making a few provisional assumptions to which we must eventually return, the corresponding functional equations take account of the probability of moving from one status to another – from unemployment to a job and from employment either to retirement or back into the unemployment pool. We may take the system of equations to be the following, letting Δ denote a small interval of time following the initial moment. The utility of wealth w belonging to a person when unemployed satisfies

$$
\begin{aligned}
u(w_0; 0) = \max_{c_0} \Big\{ & U(c_0)\Delta + \gamma\Delta + (1 - \mu\Delta)(1 - \varrho\Delta) \\
& \times \big[(1 - a\Delta)u(w_0 + (dw_0/dt)\Delta; 0) \\
& + a\Delta\, u(w_0 + (dw_0/dt)\Delta, x; 1)\big]\Big\}
\end{aligned}
\tag{1.1}
$$

Here γ denotes the rate of utility from full leisure, whether enjoyed while unemployed or taken while on the job through full shirking; a denotes the rate at which a given cohort of unemployed persons are accepted into employment; and the second u function is the utility of wealth in the event of acceptance into employment. If employed, an individual with x_1 length of time until retirement has a utility of wealth satisfying

$$
\begin{aligned}
u(w_1; x_1; 1) = \max_{c_1, s} \Big\{ & U(c_1)\Delta + \gamma s\Delta + (1 - \mu\Delta)(1 - \varrho\Delta) \\
& \times \big[(1 - \pi s\Delta)u(w_1 + (dw_1/dt)\Delta, x_1 + (dx_1/dt)\Delta; 1) \\
& + \pi s\Delta\, u(w_1 + (dw_1/dt)\Delta; 0)\big]\Big\}
\end{aligned}
\tag{1.2}
$$

If the worker is ever retired, the utility of wealth satisfies

$$
\begin{aligned}
u(w_2; 2) = \max_{c_2} \Big\{ & U(c_2)\Delta + \gamma + \\
& (1 - \mu\Delta)(1 - \varrho\Delta)u(w_2 + (dw_2/dt)\Delta; 2)\Big\}
\end{aligned}
\tag{1.3}
$$

In these equations the time derivatives of x and w appear. If *age* is what triggers retirement and is the same across workers and through time, then an employed person who does not shirk for a small period of time is assured of being that much closer to retirement at the end of that time. Then,

$$
dx_1/dt = -1
\tag{1.4}
$$

I am interested in endogenizing mandatory retirement, however, not parameterizing it. If, as I have suggested, it is employees' *wealth* that triggers their retirement, x_1 becomes a function of current financial wealth, w_1, given the trigger level of wealth. Thus a decision by the individual to accumulate wealth more slowly would delay his retirement. In this formulation,

$$
dx_1/dt = -\big(dw_1(t)/dt\big)/\big(dw_1(t + x_1)/dx_1\big)
\tag{1.4'}
$$

Here -1 is multiplied by the ratio of the pace of current wealth accumulation to that at the moment before retirement. Exactly how much extra wage-earning time a higher present consumption rate would buy thus depends on how fast wealth is accumulated at the end.

The algebraic accumulation of wealth in these equations is given by

$$\mathrm{d}w_i/\mathrm{d}t = \left(r + \mu\right)w_i + v_i - c_i, v_0 = 0 = v_2 \qquad v_1 = v \qquad (1.5)$$

Here v is the economywide real wage. As the notation suggests, the wage and the other prices are taken to be constant over time, since we are looking for a stationary equilibrium in an economy that is stagnant, that is, stationary in the everyday sense of the term. Further, the wage is taken to be constant across persons at any moment of time, hence not varying with the wealth, age, or any other attribute of the employee. A sketch of the argument, subtleties aside, is this: Owing to the linearity of utility in the shirking rate, an employee shirks either to the hilt over any small interval of time or else not at all. A firm would not employ a worker who shirks all the time. Hence all employees are equally nonshirking. Since the input capabilities of all workers are the same, so that employees are equally productive, the law of one price holds. Hence all employed persons are paid the same wage.

The probabilistic formulation in (1.1) of the time spent in the unemployment pool raises some conceptual problems. (They could be addressed in some buttressed version of the model, but it is far from clear that such a model would be convenient for understanding the phenomena of principal interest.) One problem is that, assuming our stationary equilibrium will exhibit a pool of unemployed persons, it is possible that a person joining the pool might, especially if starting as a new entrant with zero net worth, see his net worth go so far into the negative range that the mathematical expectation of the present discounted value of his earnings (which, even if he got a job at once and never retired or shirked, would only amount to $v/(r + \mu)$) would be insufficient, even if he were to stop consuming forever, to service his debt (equal to $-w$). A person might obtain insurance against this contingency, but there would be the moral hazard that he would then be less motivated to register as unemployed and to monitor the random drawings. A safety net or a network of kin and nonkin would have to be modeled.

It would seem attractive as a solution to suppose that firms would hire only those with the largest net indebtedness. Then there would be no catastrophic cases, as everyone would be called to a job at the same (negative) net worth level. It would not seem to cost the individual firm anything to follow that rule; the person keeping track of the unemployed people's social security numbers (for the continuous random drawing) would keep track of their net debt to the banks instead. However, such a priority rule for employing the jobless would have a disincentive effect. It would motivate an unemployed person to increase his consumption rate to hasten the time when his debt reached the communitywide maximum, and thus become employed sooner. The result would be higher consumption during unemployment and lower consumption during employment, a sort of indebtedness competition. (Further, the waiting time in unemployment would be shorter, I conjecture, since the reduced net worth of employed workers would moderate their willingness to shirk, so a smaller pool of unemployment would be required to deter their shirking.) A further unattractive consequence of the convention would arise *if* the solution involves no retirement, only the endless servicing by employed workers of the debt incurred when unemployed at the start of life. Anyone caught shirking could thus expect to qualify immediately under the rule for a new job, since his perpetual debt is forever at the qualifying level.

An alternative solution is for firms to adopt the convention of hiring those who have been unemployed the longest in their current spell. This has the advantage over the previous solution in that it would not invite an indebtedness competition. It also has the advantage of familiarity. Adopting this solution, we replace (1.1) with

$$u(w_0; x_0; 0) = \max_{c_0}\{U(c_0)\Delta + \gamma\Delta + (1 - \mu\Delta)(1 - \varrho\Delta)$$
$$\times u(w_0 + (dw_0/dt)\Delta, x_0 - \Delta; 0)\} \quad (1.1')$$

where x_0 denotes the unemployed person's remaining waiting time in the pool. Equation (15.2) must also be replaced since the penalty for being caught shirking is now deterministic, being simply the wages lost in present-value terms during the fixed wait in the unemployment pool. First, however, we consider another problem.

The other conceptual decision to be made concerns the modeling of retirement. It would be good to endogenize it, since doing so might illuminate the determination of the point of retirement in real life. An idea stimulating this chapter is the intuition that, under a variety of underlying specifications, the intertemporal equilibrium path of the economy (in the present discussion a stationary-state path) will induce employed workers to go on amassing wealth until they are so comfortable that, despite the threat of unemployment, they have insufficient incentive not to shirk (at the wage firms can afford to pay) and employers are forced to retire them. To implement this idea I assume that the firms can monitor or estimate rather well the wealth accumulation of their employees and the firms' optimal policy is to retire employees when their wealth is so large that the prevailing wait (in deterministic or expected-value terms) is insufficient to deter them from shirking. If laws are passed forbidding firms from demanding data on employees' wealth, such monitoring is blocked, but the employer can still ask himself how much wealth he would have accumulated had he been a specific employee – and come up with the right answer, since preferences and opportunities are the same for all in the economy modeled.[7]

The question now becomes whether wealth will head toward a target level sufficiently high to trigger the mandatory retirement of workers sufficiently old (and thus sufficiently far out on the age-wealth profile). One might conjecture that in a stationary economy like the one modeled here, the equilibrium would be one making it optimal for each worker to adopt a *flat* consumption profile over time, dissaving when unemployed through borrowing from insurance intermediaries, and, when employed, consuming just enough to *service but never work off* the debt contracted during the wait in the unemployment pool. Employed workers would not save enough to precipitate their retirement by becoming too wealthy to refrain from shirking. From (1.2) we may calculate that, with no retirement in prospect, the flat consumption profile and the flat aggregate net worth (financial wealth plus the present value of future wages) would mean that the gross rate of interest, $r + \mu$, was equal to the gross rate of utility discount, $\mu + \varrho$, hence that the interest rate was equal to the rate of pure time preference. I argue that this conjecture is false. To evaluate it, however, we need to consider the worker's wealth accumulation program when mandatory retirement is triggered by excessive wealth.

Proceeding with this way of modeling retirement, we settle on the variable x_1 formulation in (1.4′) and replace (1.2) with the deterministic formulation of the penalty for being caught shirking in which the initial waiting time to get out, x_0, is known:

$$
\begin{aligned}
u(w_1; x_1; 1) = \max_{c_1, s} \Big\{ & U(c_1)\Delta + \gamma s\Delta + (1 - \mu\Delta)(1 - \varrho\Delta) \\
& \times \Big[(1 - \pi s\Delta)u\big(w_1 + (dw_1/dt)\Delta, x + (dx_1/dt)\Delta; 1\big) \\
& + \pi s\Delta\, u\big(w_1 + (dw_1/dt)\Delta, x_0 - \Delta; 0\big)\Big]\Big\}
\end{aligned}
\tag{1.2′}
$$

where x_0 is the initial waiting time in the unemployment pool.

---

[7] Incidentally, the notion that privacy is a long-established right seems to be unfounded. In the United States, for example, the Constitution does not envisage any right to privacy, teachers at many state universities have their salaries published, and some loan applications ask for data on income and wealth.

Finally, for (15.3) we may substitute the solution for the utility of wealth,

$$u(w_2; 2) = U((r + \mu)w)/(\mu + \varrho) \tag{1.3'}$$

If, as we have sometimes assumed, mandatory retirement awaits an employee whose wealth reaches some critical level, because the prevailing unemployment pool (and its waiting time) is insufficient to deter a switch from no shirking to full shirking once the worker has amassed sufficient income from wealth, the question arises: What does the profile of the worker's consumption look like in the neighborhood of that retirement point? A clue is offered by equation (1.2'). Once this is no longer employed, there is no longer a reason to hold down saving in order to delay retirement and thus delay the end of the wage stream. The standard manipulation of (1.2') gives the following equation in the limit as Δ goes to zero:

$$
\begin{aligned}
(\mu + \varrho)&u(w_1, x_1; 1) + u_x(w_1, x_1; 1) \\
&= \max\{U(c_1) + \gamma s \\
&\quad - \pi s[(u(w_1, x_1); 1) - u(w_0, x_0; 0)] \\
&\quad + [u_w(w_1, x_1; 1) - (dw_1(t + x_1)/dx)^{-1} \\
&\quad u_x(w_1, x_1; 1)](dw_1/dt)\}
\end{aligned}
\tag{1.6}
$$

An increase in the present rate of wealth accumulation clearly gets less "credit" since saving has an effect weighted by the marginal utility of employment time remaining that must be subtracted from the (familiar) effect that is weighted by the marginal utility of wealth of the conventional sort. From this consideration, there is apparently a drag on wealth accumulation. With retirement, the consumption path is no longer weighed down by this factor. (Since the marginal utility of consumption must be continuous in the absence of any unforeseen shock, there is no break in the consumption path at retirement.)

The determination of the optimal rate of shirking has already been anticipated in previous remarks. Owing to the linearity of the maximand, it is optimal for a worker to shirk to the hilt over a given small interval or else not shirk at all. We take it that the firm knows whether conditions do or do not deter workers of a given wealth level. Only a deviance from the norm could and probably would go undetected for a while.

Hence the equilibrium path has the property that no employed persons actually shirk.

1.2   Some aspects of general equilibrium

I argue on two levels independently that the steady-state equilibrium rate of interest is greater than the rate of pure time preference. First, very informally, it may be argued that there cannot exist a stationary equilibrium in which r is equal to ϱ. In that assumed equilibrium, the employed workers would not owe their debts to anyone but other employed workers older than themselves, and as each of them would consume his total net income, employed workers would consume in the aggregate exactly the aggregate wage bill. (If young employed workers were consuming only their wage *minus* their debt service, the older employed workers to whom the debt service must be paid would be consuming their wage *plus* that debt service less the service on their own original debts. This latter debt service is consumed by still older employed workers receiving payments, and so forth.) Hence there would be nothing for the young unemployed workers to consume. That contradicts the assumption that the consumption profile is flat over life. In addition, it is not utility maximizing to go without consumption for any time. The stationary equilibrium, assuming such exists, exhibits a higher rate of interest, tilting the consumption profile upward, lowering consumption in the early years (relative to the flat-profile reference path) in order to have higher consumption later on. The young employed workers, in consuming *less* than their wages net of the interest on their debt – less, therefore, than their net income – are contributing the saving needed to counterbalance the dissaving that the unemployed want to do. Further, the only way that the employed workers can go on having rising consumption is by continuing to save in order to have continuing growth of their net income. As a result, an employed worker's wealth must grow to a level at which he is ready (at the market wage given by the average/marginal product of labor) to switch from full effort to full shirking, at which point he is retired from the firm and becomes unemployable. Stationary equilibrium is thus possible only at an interest rate sufficient to induce an upward tilt to the consumption profile, and such an equilibrium precipitates the phenomenon of mandatory retirement.[8]

---

[8] In Blanchard's (1985) model of saving and interest determination the rate of interest also exceeds the rate of pure time preference by an amount involving the mortality rate. In that model, though, the extra term in the interest rate formula arises because the divergence between the two rates is needed to induce households to accumulate the capital

At the algebraic level there is the following argument. Its sole limitation, so far as I can see, is that it abstracts from the complication that during employment the worker slows his wealth accumulation to prolong his period of employment. The first relation needed is the consumer-good supply equation. It simply equates the sum, adding over cohorts of the population, of the aggregate consumption of each cohort of working-age people to the corresponding sum of the aggregate output produced by those cohorts in employment. In the case of the logarithmic utility function, the surviving individual's consumption is growing at rate $r - \varrho$ while every cohort is shrinking at rate μ. Hence, expressing the left-hand side in terms of the individual's age-zero consumption level, $c(0)$, and writing a for the age of employment and $a + n$ for the age of retirement, we have

$$c(0)\big/\big[\mu - (r - \varrho)\big] = \exp\{-\mu a\}\big[1 - \exp\{-\mu n\}\big]v/\mu \qquad (1.7)$$

where the wage, v, has been substituted for labor's average and marginal product. Clearly consumption cannot start off at the level of the wage, not only because of the desire to leave room for its growth rate but also because the population obtains positions from which to produce the consumer good only after a delay of length a, when people are unemployed, and symmetrically because employment may not be of indefinite duration, as people are forced into retirement. Note finally that, with the cohort normalized to be one in size, $c(0)$ is the individual's initial consumption as well as the cohort's initial consumption.

The second relation is the consumer demand equation. In the above notation, it gives another condition on the individual's initial consumption level,

$$c(0)\big/\big[r + \mu - (r - \varrho)\big]$$
$$= \exp\{-(r + \mu)a\}\big[1 - \exp\{-(r + \mu)n\}\big]v\big/(r + \mu) \qquad (1.8)$$

where the denominator on the left-hand side reduces to the same propensity to consume out of total net worth, financial and human, as that found by Blanchard (1985) in his models. Consumption demand is also reduced by the delay in obtaining earnings and by retirement, both of which decrease lifetime discounted wage income (to which discounted lifetime consumption is equal).

stock and/or the public debt. Here the rate of interest must be high enough to generate positive saving by the employed to permit dissaving by the unemployed. As a result, consumption is ever increasing, implying ever-rising wealth and leading thus to mandatory retirement.

Readers may now solve for $c(0)$ in each of these equations and plot the two solutions as a function of r. In the practice exercise in which a is held at zero and n goes to infinity, the two curves intersect twice, once at $r = \varrho$ and again at $r = 0$, corresponding to the two roots in the implied equation for r. The former has the saddlepath flavor that in its neighborhood excess consumption demand is increasing in r. In any case, it will be taken to be the only applicable solution. In the neighborhood of this solution, the introduction of the delay, a, decreases consumption demand more than it decreases consumption supply, since r is an addition to the discount rate in the demand equation. Since consumption demand shows the smaller absolute interest elasticity of the two, it follows that the interest rate is pushed up above the previous level of ϱ. The reduction in discounted earnings caused by the truncation of employment at $a + n$ is also greater the larger is the discount rate, and the r makes it larger in the demand equation; consumption demand is thus again reduced more than is consumption supply. Thus r is driven above ϱ by both of the two factors, a and n.

The model's novel feature that retirement is the result of the high propensity of employees to shirk after long wealth accumulation is strengthened if sustained technological progress or sustained population increase is introduced. Then the employed must consume still less than in the stationary-state equilibrium since the young in the unemployment pool will exhibit greater consumer demand than before: Either they look forward to a higher wage than the current level (because of the anticipation of technical progress) and hence each wants to consume more (at the same rate of interest as before) or they are more numerous than the previous generation of young unemployed workers.

The above analysis leaves us still some distance from a simultaneous determination of all the variables in general equilibrium. A possible way to reach a simultaneous determination is as follows. The deterrent effects of unemployment on shirking provide one relationship between n, the length of time in employment, and a, the length of time in unemployment. (An increase of a, in starting employees out in a worse net worth position and in deterring shirking, serves to increase the equilibrium level of n.) The next step is to derive the homogeneous workers' family of indifference curves in the (n, a) plane. The point of tangency with the aforementioned opportunity locus would determine the general equilibrium. A proper analysis is left for the future.

I am more interested now in the qualitative features of a possible equilibrium unemployment among the young and mandatory retirement. A basic point in this connection is that there would not exist any unemployment among those young workers not yet employed – the virgin workers – if any formerly employed persons caught shirking suffered a visible stigma (spontaneously, in the classical fashion, or through the high-minded efforts of the victimized employer to put a stamp on the miscreant). Then shirking could be punished by casting the worker into an unemployment pool especially designated for shirkers. If, further, a lengthy stay in that pool according to some socially determined rule could be enforced somehow, the threat of being cast into that pool would constitute a deterrent to shirking. This specification is rejected on the ground that other firms would not be sufficiently motivated to spend the time and resources to check the credentials of each person in the unemployment pool to see whether he or she is, indeed, to continue the simile, a virgin worker rather than damaged goods. Further, the offended firm, though having reason enough to replace the worker caught shirking, since doing so serves as an object lesson to the other employees does not have the incentive to go to the inconvenience of circulating the expelled employee's social security number among firms. In addition, merely placing the number in some public register where other firms could find it might cause trouble, since the worker might then bring suit against the employer on various grounds (the grounds for dismissal were bogus, making public his case had other motives, and so forth).

Nevertheless it is a puzzle that those most prone to fall into the shirking mode are not the regular occupants of the unemployment pool, only the young are, who (besides being utterly innocent) are the least prone to shirk, having no wealth. The resolution of this puzzle, I believe, is to imagine that, in an economywide gesture, the firms hire everyone, leaving no one in unemployment or in retirement. If, because the rate of interest has long exceeded the pure time preference rate, the older workers have been lending to the younger ones, who have higher wage expectations for their careers as a whole, it will be the older ones who shirk. Naturally the firms will fire them, not the younger ones. But if, as assumed above, the firms have no cost-effective way of keeping that unemployment pool separate from the others, the new entrants into the labor force will join that pool, taking their place at the end of the queue. As the older workers die off, the unemployment pool will come to consist more and more of the new entrants to the labor force. To eliminate youth unemployment, firms need a convention of hiring only the penniless upon their entry into the labor force, thus discriminating against former shirkers or the still wealthy should they present themselves in the unemployment pool. My postulate, to repeat, is that firms retire employees when they become shirkers but cannot be relied on to discriminate (with appreciable success) against former shirkers or (as an indirect device) against those who have done some saving, reduced their debts, and so forth (as any former shirker would have done).

Perhaps a case of sorts could be made for the existence of another equilibrium in the present setting: There is no unemployment and no wealth – no saving at all, not by anyone. If there is technical progress, not population growth, each new entrant would become employed at once, and continuously consume all his growing wage income, wishing that he could borrow in order to consume at a higher rate in view of his rising wage expectations. If there is population growth, again employment is immediate upon entry, with consumption always equal to wage income. There are two objections, however. First, if there were just a little bit of land or gold or capital or any of a wide range of other assets (even human capital, financed by borrowing from the old), that equilibrium without wealth and retirement comes apart. It is not robust. In contrast, unless the analysis here has made a basic mistake, the equilibrium outlined here would not collapse with the introduction of a small amount of a supplementary asset. The omission of other kinds of capital was made to simplify the analysis, not to prop up an artificial kind of equilibrium that would not emerge from settings with other kinds of assets. Second, although accumulating wealth is necessary for the endogenous retirement phenomenon studied here, wealth accumulation is not necessary for shirking. There must, under the social arrangements envisaged here at any rate, be positive unemployment in order to check shirking – as well as quitting and other counterproductive activities that employees may engage in. The main question here was the incidence of unemployment – who bears it. (In a quite different setting, with an advantaged-worker-disadvantaged-worker dimension rather than a time-age dimension, unemployment could be argued to concentrate among the least advantaged workers.)

A final comment on the behavior of firms. A reader coming to this setting for the first time might conjecture that firms will set lower wage rates for workers having lower levels of wealth. For every worker of a given wealth level, w, there exists a wage that is cost-effective in the sense that, up to that wage level, the increased wage more than pays for itself through its incentive effects, in this case, the deterrence of shirking in a zero-one way. But since every employed worker is understood to be nonshirking, there is an opportunity for a pure profit if any category of worker was available at a wage less than the average and marginal product of labor, a constant in the present model.

2   Concluding remarks with some attention to models of the quitting type

This chapter has sought to explore the possibility of producing *intergenerational* extensions of incentive-wage models. Doing so is not notably easy, at least not in the experience here. It is apparent that some technical details, particularly having to do with the consumption profile, create some inconveniences. I have been mainly interested, however, in the many conceptual issues that come up in such extensions.

It may be that the notion of a loan market in which the young can borrow, backed by their future wages, is unacceptable from some points of view. I suggest that this essay should not be taken literally on this point. If there is considerable borrowing by young unemployed persons from parents or grandparents (even if it is only an implicit contract calling for the former to supplement the retirement income of the latter), that is evidence that the mechanism here has some counterpart in reality. And there is such evidence. In Italy, at least, where the young, many of them unemployed or underemployed, have no other way, short of crime or charity, to obtain economic support.

The thrust of the chapter, however, is in other directions orthogonal to the matter of consumer loans. Accumulating wealth by employees constitutes a neglected reason for mandatory retirement. The unemployment that has to exist if the workers are to do any actual work, in the social settings envisaged here at any rate, is concentrated among the young. Once a person is hired, his implicit contract promises him continuing employment if (so far as can be detected) he does not shirk; only those who have not landed a contract suffer unemployment. Employed persons are exposed to the risk of it, however, which is in a sense its function.

This purely exploratory article has left at least two loose ends. Is it not possible that employees slow down their wealth accumulation enough to avoid crossing the wealth boundary that causes employers to retire them? Undoubtedly. But it has been my assumption in this chapter that, at a sufficiently low rate of utility discount, workers will gain by liberating themselves from the wealth bound that firms impose. Is it not possible that workers once fired will prefer to rejoin the unemployment queue to have another spell of earnings rather than accept joblessness? My assumption has been that, under a sufficiently low utility discount rate, the worker would prefer to break out of that pattern, in which her wealth remains bounded by her firm's retirement policy, in favor of unbounded wealth accumulation – bounded only by death. These questions warrant careful analysis.

Let me offer a few impressions about the differences presented by a parallel intergenerational treatment of the quitting story. The present shirking model has some unusual features that would not be present in a model of incentive wages founded on the quitting problem rather than on the shirking problem. In a quitting model we portray the young as having stronger reasons to quit from time to time than have older employees. Another difference is that the law of one price – here, one wage – would not hold. Two workers with different wealth levels are two quite different properties. The richer one cannot offer the expectation of staying with as high a probability as the other; hence their net lifetime productivity does not appear to be the same. There is also room in such a model for the famed "gold watch" as a device to dampen the propensity to quit. Yet the optimal wage profile may not be everywhere rising with seniority, since firms know that older workers are less willing than younger ones to strike out in a new industry or region. Further, as long as owners and managers of firms are self-interested and not always above dishonesty, and especially if the rate of interest continues to be positive or firms continue to disappear, backloading of wage payments will have its limitations as a device against quitting.

I hope this chapter, its eccentricities notwithstanding, indicates that research into the intergenerational dimensions of labor markets – and the dimension of worker heterogeneity with respect to wage-earning power – will substantially deepen our understanding of how the equilibrium volume of unemployment is determined.

References

Arrow, K. J. 1953. Uncertainty and the welfare economics of medical care. *American Economic Review,* 53(December):941–73.

Becker, G. 1961. *Human Capital.* Chicago: University of Chicago Press.

Blanchard, O. J. 1985. Debts, deficits and finite horizons. *Journal of Political Economy,* 93(April):223–47.

Calvo, G. 1979. Quasi-Walrasian models of unemployment. *American Economic Review,* 69(May):102–8.

Calvo, G., and E. S. Phelps. 1983. "A model of nonWalrasian general equilibrium. In *Macroeconomics, Prices and Quantities: Essays in Memory of Arthur M. Okun,* ed., James Tobin, Washington, D.C.: Brookings Institution, pp. 135–57.

Hoon, H. T., and E. S. Phelps. 1992. Macroeconomic shocks in a dynamized model of the natural rate of unemployment. *American Economic Review,* 82 (September):889–900.

Phelps, E. S. 1968. Money-wage dynamics and labor-market equilibrium. *Journal of Political Economy,* 76(August): Part 2, 678–711.

Phelps, E. S. 1994. *Structural Slumps: The Modern Equilibrium Theory of Employment, Interest and Assets.* Cambridge, MA: Harvard University Press.

Salop, S. C. 1979. A model of the natural rate of unemployment. *American Economic Review*, 69 (March):117–25.

Shapiro, C., and J. E. Stiglitz. 1984. Equilibrium unemployment as a discipline device. *American Economic Review*, 74 (June):433–44.

CHAPTER 9

On the optimal schedule for introducing a new technology, when there is learning by doing

P. B. Linhart and Roy Radner

Abstract

A known, time-dependent output stream can be produced by either of two technologies. We ask: What mixture of these technologies should be used to minimize the discounted present value of the cost of production? Each technology is characterized by a unit cost function that declines with experience. Typically one of these functions (the "new technology") starts out higher, but has a lower final asymptote than the other (the "old technology").

We show that there exists an optimal policy that never uses both technologies at once. We also show that if the two cost functions cross at most once, then there exists an optimal policy that switches at most once.

We also explore two examples. In the first example, output is constant, but the cost of the "new" technology declines exogenously while we are waiting to use it. In the second example, demand jumps abruptly from a lower to a higher constant value. A variety of optimal policies, depending on parameter values, is displayed.

Finally, we discuss what changes in assumptions might lead to optimal policies that are mixed, rather than extreme.

1   Introduction

This chapter is concerned with decisions by a firm, or a manager within the firm, as to whether, and when, and how rapidly to replace an old pro-

The authors did most of the research on which this chapter is based when they were at AT&T Bell Laboratories. The views expressed are those of the authors and do not necessarily reflect the views of AT&T Bell Laboratories.

165

ductive technology with a new one, where both technologies display the phenomenon of "learning by doing." Thus we are in different territory (although there are formal similarities) from that of Arrow (1962) in his essay "The Economic Implications of Learning by Doing," which deals with the effects of learning by doing on the evolution of an economy. In our much narrower problem, we assume that learning (which we shall interpret as cost reduction) occurs as a function of cumulative output, rather than cumulative gross investment, as in Arrow; such learning can be expected to saturate. That is, as the problems associated with the technology are overcome, declining cost will approach a positive asymptote.

These problems come in many flavors; only the simplest is discussed here. We assume that the learning curves of the old and new technologies are certain, and are known by the decision maker. A treatment of uncertainty in learning curves can be found in Majumdar and Radner (1993). We also assume that the future path of output is known; a treatment of price-dependent output is more difficult. There exists a literature on oligopolistic competition by means of technical innovation, but without learning; in the present chapter, since output is given and price is not discussed, competitive issues do not arise. Finally, we do not treat the possibility that learning achieved at a low level of output (say a pilot project) can be transferred to the larger productive process.

In this section, we lay out the problem in detail. In Section 2 we reformulate it in mathematical terms. In Sections 3 and 4 we show that there always exists an optimal policy that is "extreme" in that we need never mix the old and new technologies. In Section 5 we show that, under a "single-crossing" condition, we need never switch technologies more than once. In Sections 6 and 7, we develop two examples. The first example assumes a constant level of output, but allows exogenous improvement of the new technology before we adopt it. We find (among other results) that the total (present worth of) cost, as a function of switching time, may have several local minima. Thus if the optimal switching time is missed by too much, it may be conditionally optimal to wait a while for the next local minimum. The second example deals with a sudden jump upward in the level of output. We find (among other results) that if it is desirable to switch at all, one should do so somewhat before – never after – the jump in output. Finally, in Section 8, we discuss changed assumptions that might lead to optimal policies involving mixed technology.

Starting at some initial date, $t = 0$, a firm (or a manager) has a choice of implementing production by either of two technologies, for example, two programming languages. We shall call these, for convenience, the "old" and the "new" technologies, although formally they are on an equal footing. Both technologies have the property that the more they are used the more profitable they become; this is called "learning from experience," or "learning by doing." Typically, the new technology is characterized by a lower initial, but a higher final, profitability. We allow that the two technologies may be mixed; for example, the new technology may be "phased in."

The firm's objective is to maximize the present worth of future profits generated by this production activity. (Thus we have assumed away any possible relationship between this activity and the profitability of the firm's other activities.) The question is: *What is the optimal mix, over time, of the two technologies?* In some cases, this simplifies to the question: *According to what schedule should the new technology be introduced, if at all?*

Estimation of the profit stream generated by either technology involves many factors, including at least level of productivity after a given amount of experience, possible exogenous improvement *before* adoption (for example, use by the firm's competitors), and the level of output over time. The level of output, in turn, depends on the exogenous growth in demand, the firm's pricing policy, and the pricing and technological strategies of its competitors.

We divide the problem into two parts. The first part is to estimate the profit stream *as a function* of price and technology, a task for experts on costs and markets. We do not address this part of the problem here, only remarking that:

1 Profits should be estimated for the smallest organizational unit that includes all effects of the change, and for which financial data exist.
2 The costs considered should include the costs of capital and retraining.

The second part of the problem is to calculate how to mix the two technologies, given the profit function. This is the problem we deal with here but in a considerably simplified version. Our first major simplification is to assume that both price and total output, and hence the revenue stream, are given as functions of time. In so doing, we have effectively assumed away any considerations of industry structure.[1] In this case, maximization of profit is equivalent to minimization of total costs. In this chapter we concentrate on this latter objective. Thus the

---

[1] A discussion of the relationship between learning by doing and industry structure can be found in Dasgupta and Stiglitz (1988). See also Fudenberg and Tirole (1983).

learning curves or experience curves describe reduction in unit costs.[2]
We assume that there are no economies of scale aside from those implied
by learning from experience itself, so that total cost is output times unit
cost. The decision maker seeks to minimize the present value of total
costs; his discount rate, ϱ, is given. For mathematical convenience, we do
the calculations in continuous time.

We also assume, to begin with, complete information. Both costs and
output, as functions of experience, are known with certainty in advance
to the decision maker.

Most of our attention is given to the question of whether the two technologies should be used simultaneously and to the *timing* of technical
change.

An earlier treatment of this problem, containing a more detailed discussion of the first example, was given in Linhart, Radner, and VanZandt
(1990). (This class of problem was originally suggested to us by
L. Bernstein, who has also made several helpful suggestions.)

2   A more formal statement of the problem

A specified (nonnegative) output stream is to be produced by a combination of two processes, operating simultaneously and independently. We
denote these two processes by 0 and 1.

Let $q(t)$ be the required instantaneous rate of output:

$$q(t) \geq 0 \qquad \text{for all} \qquad t \in [0, T]$$

(Here and in what follows, the time horizon T may be finite or infinite;
we shall nonetheless, for convenience, refer to the time domain as $[0, T]$.)

Let $y_i(t)$ be the rate of output of process i ($i = 0, 1$):

$$y_i(t) \geq 0 \qquad \text{for all} \qquad t \in [0, T]$$

The functions y_i are measurable, and

$$y_0(t) + y_1(t) = q(t) \qquad \text{for all} \qquad t$$

Let

$$Y_i(t) \equiv \int_0^t y_i(s)\,ds$$

---

[2] Unit costs may, on the other hand, increase with the rapidity of investment; see Peles
(1991). We do not consider this effect in this essay.

be the cumulative output of process i; we call $Y_i(t)$ the *experience* with process i at time t.

Learning is expressed by the decline of unit costs with experience. Let the instantaneous unit cost of process i at time t be

$$c_i\big[Y_i(t)\big]$$

measured in dollars per minute per unit of output.

We take the functions c_0 and c_1 to be nonnegative and nonincreasing, and hence measurable. Thus the instantaneous *total* cost for process i at time t is

$$c_i\big[Y_i(t)\big]y_i(t)$$

in dollars per minute. The discounted total cost for both processes is

$$W \equiv \int_0^T e^{-\varrho t}\sum_{i=0}^{1} c_i\big[Y_i(t)\big]y_i(t)dt \tag{2.1}$$

in dollars. The discount rate ϱ is nonnegative, and we assume that the present worth of output exists:

$$\int_0^T e^{-\varrho t}q(t)dt < \infty$$

Notice that the effect of learning from experience somewhat resembles a scale economy: The greater the (accumulated) output, the lower the unit cost. But aside from this effect, we assume there are no scale economies in the usual sense.

> **Problem:** *Given the functions q, c_0, and c_1, and the numbers ϱ and T, characterize the function y_0 (and hence y_1) that minimizes W, subject to:*
>
> $$y_0(t) \geq 0 \qquad y_1(t) \geq 0$$
> $$y_0(t) + y_1(t) = q(t) \tag{2.2}$$
>
> *for all $t \in [0, T]$.*

3   A lemma

Let K be the set of Lebesgue-measurable functions y on $[0, T]$ satisfying

$$0 \leq y(t) \leq q(t) \tag{3.1}$$

where q is nonnegative and, as above,

$$\int_0^T e^{-\varrho t} q(t) dt < \infty \tag{3.2}$$

and ϱ is some (nonnegative) discount rate. Notice that, with respect to the usual vector space operations on functions, the set K is convex. Let c be a nonnegative, nonincreasing function on $[0, +\infty)$, and for each (function) y define

$$C(y) = \int_0^T e^{-\varrho t} c[Y(t)] y(t) dt \tag{3.3}$$

where

$$Y(t) = \int_0^t y(s) ds \tag{3.4}$$

We find the following Lemma useful:

Lemma 1: *C is concave on K, and strictly concave if c is strictly decreasing.*

Proof: Let x and y be functions in K, and let λ be a number in $[0, 1]$. We want to show that, for $z \equiv \lambda x + (1 - \lambda) y$,

$$C(z) \geq \lambda C(x) + (1 - \lambda) C(y) \tag{3.5}$$

For this it is sufficient to show that, considered as a function of λ, $C(z)$ is concave in λ; that is, $dC/d\lambda$ is decreasing in λ.

Define, analogously to Y in equation (3.4)

$$X(t) = \int_0^t x(s) ds, \; Z(t) = \int_0^t z(s) ds \tag{3.6}$$

and finally, define v by

$$v(t) = \int_0^{Z(t)} c(u) du \tag{3.7}$$

Note that

$$\frac{dv(t)}{dt} \equiv v'(t) = c[Z(t)] z(t)$$

Thus

$$C(z) = \int_0^T e^{-\varrho t} v'(t) dt \tag{3.8}$$

Integrating by parts, and noting that $Z(0) = v(0) = 0$, we can rewrite (3.8) as

$$C(z) = e^{-\varrho T}v(T) + \varrho\int_0^T e^{-\varrho t}v(t)dt \tag{3.9}$$

Differentiating (3.7) and (3.9) with respect to λ, we find

$$\frac{dv(t)}{d\lambda} = c\big[Z(t)\big]\big[X(t) - Y(t)\big] \tag{3.10}$$

and

$$\frac{dC(z)}{d\lambda} = e^{-\varrho T}c\big[Z(T)\big]\big[X(T) - Y(T)\big]$$
$$+ \varrho\int_0^T e^{-\varrho t}c\big[Z(t)\big]\big[X(t) - Y(t)\big]dt \tag{3.11}$$

Notice that $Z(t)$ is nondecreasing or nonincreasing in λ according as $X(t) - Y(t)$ is nonnegative or nonpositive. Hence $c[Z(t)][X(t) - Y(t)]$ is nonincreasing in λ and is strictly decreasing in λ if c is strictly decreasing and $X(t) \neq Y(t)$. Thus $dC(z)/d\lambda$ is nonincreasing in λ and is strictly decreasing if c is strictly decreasing and $X(t) \neq Y(t)$ on a set of positive measure. (If $X(t) = Y(t)$ for all t, (3.5) is trivially true.) This completes the proof of the lemma.   QED.

4 Optimal policies and extreme policies

We call a policy y_i extreme if, for almost all t in $[0, T]$, either $y_i(t) = 0$ or $y_i(t) = q(t)$. y_0 is extreme if and only if y_1 (as defined in (2.2)) is.
    In this section we show that

1 There is an optimal policy, and among the optimal policies there is one that is extreme.
2 If either c_0 or c_1 is strictly decreasing, then every optimal policy is extreme.[3]

Let L_1 denote the linear space of all measurable functions y on $[0, T]$ such that

$$\int_0^T e^{-\varrho t}\big|y(t)\big|dt < \infty$$

---

[3] Notice that, although it is sufficient for either c_0 or c_1 to be strictly decreasing, in order for every optimal policy to be extreme, it may not be necessary; we leave this point open.

and let L_∞ denote the linear space of all essentially bounded[4] measurable functions on $[0, T]$. Endow L_1 with the weak (or L_∞) topology, that is, a sequence $\{y_n\}$ converging to y in L_1 means that, for every x in L_∞,

$$\int_0^T e^{-\varrho t} y_n(t) x(t) dt \to \int_0^T e^{-\varrho t} y(t) x(t) dt$$

It is straightforward to show that the set K of Section 3 is closed in this topology.[5] Furthermore, since every function y in K is majorized in absolute value by the integrable function q, the set K is uniformly integrable (Neveu [1965], Prop. II.5.1, p. 50), and hence compact in the weak topology (Neveu [1965], Prop. IV.2.3, p. 118).

Proposition 1:   *There exists an optimal policy that is extreme.*

Proof: We noted above that the set K is convex and is weakly compact (that is, compact in the weak topology); we also note that what we have called the "extreme" functions in K do indeed constitute the set of extreme points of K.

Under these circumstances, a theorem of H. Bauer (Choquet [1969], vol. 2, p. 102, Th. 25.9) states that any concave and (weakly) continuous function on K attains its minimum value at an extreme point of K. It follows from the lemma of Section 3 that the cost-functional W in (2.1) is concave in y_1 (with $y_0 = q - y_1$ and y_1 in K; see the constraints (2.2)). Hence it suffices to show that W is weakly continuous in y_1, and for this in turn it suffices to show that the functional C of (3.3) is continuous.

Recall that for y in L_1,

$$C(y) = \int_0^T e^{-\varrho t} c[Y(t)] y(t) dt \qquad (4.1)$$

---

[4] That is, bounded except on a set of measure zero.

[5] For example, suppose that $\{y_n\}$ in L_1 are nonnegative, that $y_n \to y$, but that $y < 0$ on some set A of positive measure. Let x be the indicator function of A, that is, $x(t) = 1$ or 0 according as t is or is not in A. Then:

$$\int e^{-\varrho t} y_n(t) x(t) \geq 0$$

but

$$\int e^{-\varrho t} y(t) x(t) < 0$$

a contradiction. A similar argument deals with the constraint $y(t) \leq q(t)$.

$$Y(t) = \int_0^t y(s)ds \qquad (4.2)$$

Suppose that $y_n \to y$, and let Y_n correspond to y_n as in (4.2). Let x_t be the indicator function of the interval $[0, t]$, with $t < \infty$, and note that the function f defined by

$$f(s) = x_t(s)e^{\varrho s}$$

is in L_∞. We have

$$\begin{aligned}
Y_n(t) &= \int_0^T y_n(s)x_t(s)ds \\
&= \int_0^T e^{-\varrho s} y_n(s)x_t(s)e^{\varrho s} ds \\
&\to \int_0^T e^{-\varrho s} y(s)x_t(s)e^{\varrho s} ds \\
&= \int_0^t y(s)ds = Y(t) \qquad (4.3)
\end{aligned}$$

From (3.9) we have

$$C(y_n) = e^{-\varrho T} v_n(T) + \varrho \int_0^T e^{-\varrho t} v_n(t)dt \qquad (4.4)$$

where

$$v_n(t) \equiv \int_0^{Y_n(t)} c(u)du$$

From (4.3),

$$v_n(t) \to v(t) \equiv \int_0^{Y(t)} c(u)du \qquad (4.5)$$

Also, $c(t)$ is bounded, that is, for some γ,

$$|c(t)| \le \gamma$$

so that

$$0 \le v_n(t) \le \gamma Y_n(t) \le \gamma Q(t)$$

We have assumed that

$$\int_0^T e^{-\varrho t} q(t)dt < \infty$$

from which it follows by integration by parts that

$$\int_0^T e^{-\varrho t} Q(t) dt < \infty \tag{4.6}$$

Hence, by the Lebesgue Dominated Convergence Theorem,

$$\int_0^T e^{-\varrho t} v_n(t) dt \to \int_0^T e^{-\varrho t} v(t) dt \tag{4.7}$$

If $T < \infty$, then by (4.5),

$$e^{-\varrho T} v_n(T) \to e^{-\varrho T} v(T) \tag{4.8}$$

If $T = \infty$, then by (4.6),

$$\lim_{t \to \infty} e^{-\varrho t} Q(t) = 0$$

so that

$$\lim_{t \to \infty} e^{-\varrho t} v_n(t) = \lim_{t \to \infty} e^{-\varrho t} v(t) = 0 \tag{4.9}$$

By integrations (4.4) and (4.7)–(4.9), we have

$$C(y_n) \to C(y)$$

which completes the proof of the proposition.   QED.

5   Under the "single-crossing condition," an optimal policy switches at most once

We say there is a *single crossing from* c_0 *to* c_1 if there is a $Q^*, 0 \le Q^* \le \infty$, such that

$$c_1(Q) - c_0(Q) \begin{cases} \ge 0 & \text{for} \quad Q \le Q^* \\ \le 0 & \text{for} \quad Q \ge Q^* \end{cases} \tag{5.1}$$

Proposition 2: *If the single-crossing condition is satisfied, then there is an optimal policy y_0 and a time $\hat{T}$, such that $0 \le \hat{T} \le \infty$, and*

$$\hat{y}_0(t) = \begin{cases} q(t) < & \text{for} \quad t < \hat{T}, \\ 0 & \text{for} \quad t \ge T \end{cases} \tag{5.2}$$

In other words, it is never optimal to switch "back" from c_1 to c_0. (We are now thinking of c_0 as the unit cost of the "old" technology, and c_1 as the unit cost of the "new" technology, which is initially higher but, with experience, eventually becomes lower than c_0.)

Proof: Let $M \equiv$ the set of all policies satisfying (2.2).
Let $E \equiv$ the set of all extreme policies (see Section 4).
Let $F \equiv$ the set of all policies for which there is a partition (I_k) of $[0, T]$ into a finite number of intervals such that, for each k, either $y_1(t) = 0$ for all t in I_k, or $y_1(t) = q(t)$ for all t in I_k.
Finally, let $H_1 \equiv$ the set of those policies in F for which there is at most one switch, and that is from $y_1 = 0$ to $y_1 = 1$.
In Section 4 it was shown that

$$\hat{W} = \min_M W = \min_E W$$

One can show (see Appendix) that

$$\hat{W} = \inf_F W$$

We now wish to go beyond this, and show that:

$$\hat{W} = \min_{H_1} W \qquad \qquad \text{QED.} \qquad (5.3)$$

The idea of the proof is as follows: Consider an extreme policy in F that switches at some time from technology 1 to technology 0. We show that there is another policy in F that is at least as good and has no such switch. From this it will follow that it is sufficient to consider policies in H_1, and in this class of policy a minimum of W is in fact attained.

Suppose a policy in F switches from 1 to 0, and let t_1 $(0 < t_1 < \infty)$ be the time of the last such switch. Let the previous interval of using 1 start at time t_0 $(0 \le t_0 < t_1)$, and let the next switch from 0 to 1 (if any) occur at time t_2 $(t_1 < t_2 \le \infty)$.

We first note that if, at any time t,

$$c_1\big[Y_1(t)\big] \le c_0\big[Y_0(t)\big]$$

then it is optimal to use only technology 1 from time t on. Hence, for the policy in question,

$$c_1\big[Y_1(t_0)\big] > c_0\big[Y_0(t_0)\big] \qquad (5.4)$$

Otherwise the policy could be improved by eliminating the switch at t_1.
There are two cases:

Case I:

$$c_1\big[Y_1(t_1)\big] \le c_0\big[Y_0(t_0)\big] = c_0\big[Y_0(t_1)\big] \tag{5.5}$$

In this case, by the above observation, the best thing to do at t_1 would be to stay with technology 1 from then on.

Case II:

$$c_1\big[Y_1(t_1)\big] > c_0\big[Y_0(t_0)\big] \tag{5.6}$$

In this case,

$$c_1\big[Y_1(t)\big] > c_0\big[Y_0(t_0)\big]$$

for all t in $[t_0, t_1]$, and so it would have been better to stay with technology 0 throughout the interval.

Hence, for every policy in F that at some time has a switch from 1 to 0, there is another policy that has no such switch and that is as good. A policy of this latter type has at most one switch, and that is from 0 to 1, say at time $s(0 \le s \le T)$. Thus

$$\hat{W} = \inf_{H_1} W \tag{5.7}$$

But for a policy in H_1, W is continuous in s, so its minimum is actually attained in H_1 (possibly with $s = 0$ or ∞).

6   First example: Constant output

The case in which $q(t) = 1$ for all t was explored in some detail in an essay by Linhart et al. (1990). In this case, $Q(t) = t$; also, experience with a technology equals the length of time it has been used.

In this earlier treatment, policies were assumed to be extreme; we now know that this assumption does not limit the class of optimal policies (Proposition 1, above). It was also assumed that an optimal policy switches at most once; we now know that this can only be assured if the single-crossing condition of Section 5 is satisfied. Thus we can regard the previous study as finding optimum policies *among the class of policies that switch at most once*, or alternatively, as applying only when the single-crossing condition is satisfied.

The simplicity introduced by the assumption $q(t) \equiv 1$ enabled us, in the previous article, to consider the case in which the "new" technology improves (that is, its unit cost is lowered) while we are waiting to adopt it. (The distinction between, on the one hand, an improvement in an old technology, and, on the other hand, the invention of a new technology, is somewhat arbitrary.[6]) Before introducing this consideration, we first summarize briefly the results for constant output and no exogenous improvement in technology.

Consider then an extreme policy that switches at most once, say at s, as above, and let the horizon be infinite ($T = \infty$). If $s = 0$ or $s = \infty$, then there is no switch. Without loss of generality, let the switch, if any, be from technology 0 to technology 1. Under these circumstances, and with $q(t) \equiv 1$, Equation (2.1) may be written

$$W(s) = \int_0^s e^{-\varrho t} c_0(t)\,dt + \int_{t=s}^{\infty} e^{-\varrho t} c_1(t - s)\,dt \tag{6.1}$$

Equivalently,

$$W(s) = \int_0^s e^{-\varrho t} c_0(t)\,dt + e^{-\varrho s} C_1 \tag{6.2}$$

Here C_1 denotes the present worth, from its inception to infinity, of the unit cost of technology 1:

$$C_1 \equiv \int_0^{\infty} e^{-\varrho t} c_1(t)\,dt$$

Thus we see that only the present worth of technology 1's cost curve matters, not its shape. This result depends on our choice of an infinite time-horizon.

It is useful to consider the derivative of Equation (6.2):

$$W'(s) = e^{-\varrho s}\left[c_0(s) - \varrho C_1\right] \tag{6.3}$$

From this expression we readily obtain:

---

[6] The relation between invention (as of the new technology) and learning by doing is discussed in Young (1991).

Proposition 3: *Under the circumstances detailed above (constant demand, at most one switch, no exogenous improvement in technology), either technology 0 or technology 1 should be used throughout.*

Proof: If $c_0(s)$ is by assumption nondecreasing. If $c_0(s) \geq \varrho C_1$ for all s, then $W'(s)$ is everywhere positive, so $W(s)$ is minimized at $s = 0$. If $c_0(s) \leq \varrho C_1$ for all s, then $W'(s)$ is everywhere negative, so $W(s)$ is minimized at $s = \infty$. If $c_0(s)$ crosses ϱC_1 it only does so once; at this point $W'(s)$ is decreasing, so $W(s)$ has an internal extremum that is a *maximum*. In this last case the minimum is $W(0)$ or $W(\infty)$, whichever is smaller. There are no other possibilities.   QED.

We now introduce exogenous improvement in technology 1 by assuming that if any amount of this technology, however small, is first used at time s, then its cost at time $t \geq s$ is

$$c_1(t) = e^{-\phi s} h_1\big(Y_1(t)\big) \tag{6.4}$$

where

$$Y_1(t) \equiv \int_0^t y_1(t)dt$$

as in Section 4. That is, the unit cost *curve* (not, the unit cost) of technology 1 is frozen at the instant of its first use. (This is the *vintage* of technology.) It is easy to see, as follows, that Proposition 1 still applies:

Proposition 4: *With exogenous technology improvement, as defined by Equation (6.4), there exists an optimal policy that is extreme.*

Proof: During the interval $[0, s)$, which may consist of a single point, $y_1(t) = 0$, by definition. Thereafter, $c_1(t)$, as defined by Equation (6.4), is no different in principle from any other nonincreasing, nonnegative, measurable unit cost function. Therefore there exists an optimal policy for $t \geq s$ that is extreme. Optimizing over s then yields an optimal policy on $[0, \infty)$.
                                                QED.

We can now, as above, either assume the single-crossing property or optimize among those policies with at most one switch. In either case, there will be no switching back from technology 1 to technology 0, and we may write

$$c_1(t) = e^{-\phi s} h_1(t - s) \qquad (6.5)$$

Equation (6.2) must now be replaced by

$$W(s) = \int_0^s e^{-\varrho t} c_0(t) dt + e^{-(\varrho + \phi)s} H_1 \qquad (6.6)$$

Here

$$H_1 \equiv \int_0^\infty e^{-\varrho t} h_1(t) dt$$

Correspondingly, (6.3) is now replaced by

$$W'(s) = e^{-\varrho s} \left[c_0(s) - (\varrho + \phi) e^{-\phi s} H_1 \right]$$

The situation is now more complicated, since the two declining functions

$$c_0(s) \qquad \text{and} \qquad (\varrho + \phi) e^{-\phi s} H_1$$

may well cross more than once.

For the purpose of working out numerical examples, we choose a particular family of forms for $c_0(\cdot)$:

$$c_0(t) = \delta - \gamma \left[1 - e^{-\alpha Y_0(t)} \right]^n \qquad (6.7)$$

Where

δ	is the initial value of the unit cost,
$\delta - \gamma$	is its final (asymptotic) value,
α	measures the speed of its decline,
n	characterizes the abruptness of this decline.

We envisioned that the four parameters would be chosen to fit data, that is, to fit numerical point estimates of unit cost. Equation (6.4) describes a family of declining "S-shaped" curves, ranging from exponential for $n = 1$ to square as $n \to \infty$.

Note that (6.7) is not the usual form in the learning by doing literature. One usually encounters some variant of

$$c_0(t) = a \left[Y_0(t) \right]^{-b} \qquad b > 0 \qquad (6.8)$$

with perhaps an additive term to bound the asymptotic unit cost away from zero. Examples may be found in Argote and Epple (1990) and

Teplitz (1991). The form (6.7) is easier to handle analytically; we believe that in cases of managerial decisions, such as we are discussing here, the data will generally be insufficient to distinguish between (6.7) and (6.8).

With such functions, $W'(s)$ can have as many as three zeros.

Figures 1 to 4 show the behavior of $W(s)$ for the special case

$$c_0(t) = 2 - \left(1 - e^{-t}\right)^2 \tag{6.9}$$

(Note that an arbitrary choice of units is available to us for both time and cost.)

We also take

$$\varrho = 0.1$$

$$\phi = 0.03$$

Proceeding from Figure 1 to Figure 4, the new technology becomes increasingly attractive, that is, H_1 decreases from 20 to 1. In each of these figures, the optimal switch time, which we call $\hat{s}$, is indicated. As H_1 decreases, $\hat{s}$ decreases to zero, where it remains. The dependence of $\hat{s}$ on H_1 is shown explicitly in Figure 5, and the dependence of the minimum cost, $W(\hat{s})$, on H_1 is shown in Figure 6.

We make several observations:

1   We have chosen functional forms such that $c_0(t)$ approaches unity as $t \to \infty$ (Equation (6.9)), while $c_1(t)$ approaches zero (Equation (6.5)). Hence, whatever the value of H_1, there is

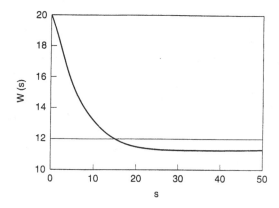

Figure 1. $H_1 = 20$, $\hat{s} = 31.85$.

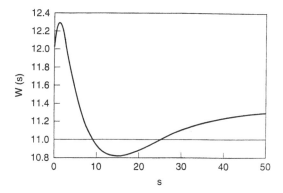

Figure 2. $H_1 = 12, \hat{s} = 14.82$.

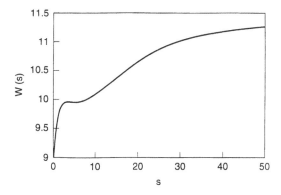

Figure 3. $H_1 = 9, \hat{s} = 0$.

always a time after which we should switch to the new technology.

2 As in Figure 2, $W(s)$ can have an internal maximum. Hence a locally optimal time to switch may be followed by an undesirable period before the next "window" opens.

3 We see from Figure 5 that $\hat{s}$, as a function of H_1 (or other parameters), can jump discontinuously, as an internal minimum moves lower than $W(0)$. However, as in Figure 6, $W(\hat{s})$, as a function of H_1, is not discontinuous at such a point.

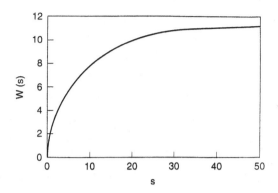

Figure 4. $H_1 = 1, \hat{s} = 0.$

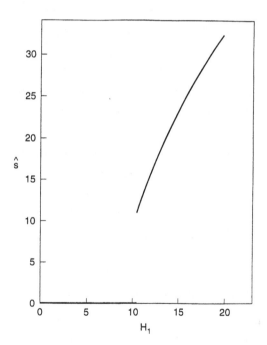

Figure 5. Optimal switch time, as a function of H_1.

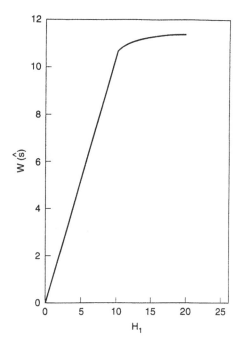

Figure 6. $W(\hat{s})$ as a function of H_1.

7   Second example: Abrupt increase in output

We now discuss the case

$$q(t) = \begin{cases} a, & t < t^* \\ b, & t \geq t^* \end{cases} \quad \text{with} \quad b \geq a \tag{7.1}$$

This case has been studied in some detail by Anna Berns (1991).

Let us choose unit cost curves that satisfy the single-crossing condition, for instance, exponentials (drawn from the class (6.7)):

$$c_0(Y_0) = 2 + e^{-Y_0}$$
$$c_1(Y_1) = 1 + 3e^{-Y_1} \tag{7.2}$$

By Proposition 1 there exists an optimal policy that is extreme; by Proposition 2 there is at most one switch, and if there is a switch it is from technology 0 to technology 1.

As usual, let s denote the moment of the switch from technology 0 to technology 1. This can occur (in principle) either before or after the required output increases from a to b, at time t^*. In these two cases, we can write Equation (2.1) as follows: For $s \leq t^*$,

$$W(s) = a\int_0^s e^{-\varrho t} c_0(at)dt + a\int_s^{t^*} e^{-\varrho t} c_1[a(t-s)]dt$$

$$+ b\int_{t^*}^{\infty} e^{-\varrho t} c_1[a(t^* - s) + b(t - t^*)]dt \qquad (7.3)$$

For $s \geq t^*$,

$$W(s) = a\int_0^{t^*} e^{-\varrho t} c_0(at)dt + b\int_{t^*}^{s} e^{-\varrho t} c_0[at^* + b(t - t^*)]dt$$

$$+ b\int_s^{\infty} e^{-\varrho t} c_1[b(t - s)]dt \qquad (7.4)$$

We have explored numerically the dependence of the optimal switching time, s, on a, b, and t^*. We note the following trade-off: If we switch from technology 0 to technology 1 at some time s before t^*, our unit cost will at first increase; however this increased unit cost will be applied to the small output a. When the time for increased output b comes along, we will have acquired experience – and hence lowered unit cost – with technology 1. This lowered unit cost will be applied to the large output b.

Figure 7 shows $\hat{s}$ as a function of t^* for the particular values $a = 0.01$, $b = 0.5$. It appears that for t^* less than about 15, the initial savings of using technology 0 are not justified by its application to such a small output for such a short time. For t^* greater than about 15 it is optimal to switch to technology 1 shortly before the (perfectly anticipated) increase in demand, and this interval grows shorter as t^* increases.

To explore the dependence of $\hat{s}$ on a and b, we fix t^*. In the example illustrated in Figure 8, t^* is fixed at 15. We notice first that for $a = b = k$, we are in a situation of constant demand, similar to that of the preceding section. Optimal behavior, therefore, is to switch at either zero or infinity, that is, to use only one technology throughout. But since our cost functions depend on time rather than experience, the choice of technology depends on the magnitude of k. There is a critical value of k, equal in the present example to about 0.18305. For $a = b < 0.18305$, we should use only technology 0; otherwise, only technology 1. If both a and b are

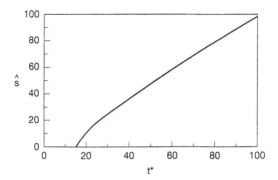

Figure 7. $\hat{s}$ vs. t^* for $a = 0.01, b = 0.5$.

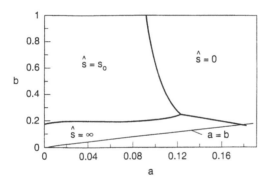

Figure 8. $\hat{s}$ boundaries: $t^* = 15$.

above or below the critical value, the same results occur. Thus there will be no internal minimum of $W(s)$ unless $a < 0.18305 < b$.

Figure 8 (resembling a phase diagram) shows the ab-plane divided into three regions, according as $\hat{s} = 0$, $\hat{s} = \infty$, or $\hat{s} = s_0$. $(0 < s_0 < \infty; s_0$ is a shorthand for an internal minimum, at whatever value it occurs.) The triple point occurs at $a = b = 0.18305$. The shapes of the regions are derived from a mixture of analysis and numerical experimentation; we do not go into detail here. Figure 9 superimposes on Figure 8 typical curves $W(s)$, so that the manner in which the minimum is obtained in the three regions can be seen.

Note that in the cases shown it is optimal to switch either before t^*, or not at all. We can easily prove this property for a slightly different case, namely, instead of (7.2) we assume that the old technology is

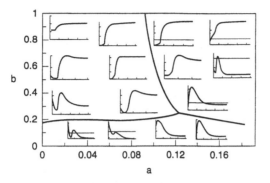

Figure 9. $\hat{s}$ boundaries: $t^* = 15$. Typical curves $W(s)$ are shown.

mature, that is, $c_0(\cdot) = \text{constant} = c_0$; about $c_1(\cdot)$ we only assume that it is strictly decreasing.

Proposition 5: *For the problem just described, one of the following is always true:*

$$
\begin{aligned}
&\hat{s} = 0 \\
&\hat{s} = \infty \\
&0 < \hat{s} < t^*
\end{aligned}
\tag{7.5}
$$

Proof: We know that there exists an optimal policy that is "extreme," that is, we need never mix the two technologies. Moreover, since c_0 is constant, the cost curves cross only once, and hence there exists an optimal policy that switches technologies at most once. As before, let $\hat{s}$ be the optimal switching time; that is, $\hat{s}$ minimizes

$$
W(s) = c_0 \int_0^s e^{-\varrho t} q(t)\,dt + \int_s^\infty e^{-\varrho t} c_1\big(Q(t) - Q(s)\big) q(t)\,dt
\tag{7.6}
$$

We want to characterize the optimal switching-time, $\hat{s}$. To this end we examine the derivative $W'(s)$:

$$
\begin{aligned}
W'(s) = {}& e^{-\varrho s} c_0 q(s) - e^{-\varrho s} c_1(0) q(s) \\
& - \int_s^\infty e^{-\varrho t} c_1'\big(Q(t) - Q(s)\big) q(t) q(s)\,dt
\end{aligned}
\tag{7.7}
$$

Let

$$F(s) \equiv \frac{e^{\varrho s} W'(s)}{q(s)}$$

$F(s)$ has throughout the same signs as $W'(s)$. From (7.7)

$$F(s) = c_0 - c_1(0) - \int_0^\infty e^{-\varrho t} c_1'\big(Q(t+s) - Q(s)\big) q(t+s) dt$$

(7.8)

or

$$F(s) = c_0 - c_1(0) - \int_0^\infty e^{-\varrho t} dc_1\big(Q(t+s) - Q(s)\big)$$ (7.9)

Integrating by parts,

$$F(s) = c_0 - \varrho \int_0^\infty e^{-\varrho t} c_1\big[Q(t+s) - Q(s)\big] dt$$ (7.10)

If the new technology were not worth using even at the higher constant level b for all time, then it is certainly not worth using in the present case, and we would have $\hat{s} = \infty$. Otherwise,

$$\frac{c_0}{\varrho} > \int_0^\infty e^{-\varrho t} c_1(bt) dt$$ (7.11)

Let us now assume that (7.11) obtains. If it were worth switching to the new technology at any finite $t > t^*$, it would be worth doing so at $t = t^*$. Therefore we need only consider

$$\hat{s} \leq t^*$$ (7.12)

To show that $\hat{s} < t^*$, it will suffice to show that $W(\cdot)$ is increasing at t^*, that is, $F(t^*) > 0$. From (7.1)

$$Q(t) = \begin{cases} at, & t \leq t^* \\ at^* + b(t - t^*), & t \geq t^* \end{cases}$$ (7.13)

Thus, from (7.10),

$$F(s) = c_0 - \varrho \left\{ \int_0^{t^*-s} e^{-\varrho t} c_1 \left[a(t+s) - as \right] dt \right.$$

$$\left. + \int_{t^*-s}^{\infty} e^{-\varrho t} c_1 \left[at^* + b(t+s-t^*) - as \right] dt \right\} \quad (7.14)$$

In particular,

$$F(t^*) = c_0 - \varrho \int_0^{\infty} e^{-\varrho t} c_1(bt) dt \quad (7.15)$$

We see at once that (7.11) is the condition for

$$F(t^*) > 0 \quad (7.16)$$

Hence either $\hat{s} = 0$ or $0 < \hat{s} < t^*$.   QED.

8   Beyond extreme policies

If the conclusion (Proposition 1), that there is always an extreme policy that is optimal, were true in reality, then one would expect extreme policies to be used often, for simplicity, since there would be no superior mixed policy. Sometimes extreme policies are used; for example, it is plausible to shift an entire programming group from the language C to $C++$ at the same time.

Often, however, mixed policies are used. For example, an examination of the history of telephone switching would show simultaneous use of as many as three or four very distinct kinds of switching machines that had been developed at successive epochs. Indeed, new examples of older technologies continued to be *installed* long after newer technologies were in use.

What features would we have to incorporate in our model in order to explain this phenomenon? We note first that the older technology may, at a certain date, have been the economic choice for certain applications – for example, for smaller switching centers. The optimum choice for such applications may have shifted to the new technology only after the cost of the latter had come down.

Another consideration is the following: We have expressed unit costs only as a function of experience, that is, of accumulated *output*. But suppose cost reduction can be achieved by experience defined a little differently, as accumulated *time* at a relatively low level of output? This is surely often the case, to some degree, and would clearly lead to optimal mixed policies – one reason for the existence of pilot projects.

At a more fundamental level, we have assumed that the decision maker has complete information, about the required future output and about both experience curves (in reality there might be more than two). But what if he does not? Suppose he is learning, by use, about the shapes of the experience curves; might he hedge his bets by going along for a while with both technologies? This is a version, somewhat more complicated than the usual one, of a problem that arises in clinical trials (it is also known as the two-armed bandit problem).[7] This problem is treated in Majumdar and Radner (1993).

Appendix

We show (in the proof of Proposition 1) that W is weakly continuous in y_1. Thus to show that

$$\hat{W} = \inf_F W \tag{A.1}$$

it will suffice to show that, for every extreme y in E, there is a sequence y_n in F that converges weakly to y.

Let y in E be extreme, and let

$$A \equiv \left\{ t : y(t) = q(t) > 0 \right\} \tag{A.2}$$

Suppose first that A is Borel; then there exists a monotone decreasing sequence of sets J_n such that:

1   $A = \bigcap_n J_n$.

2   Each J_n is the union of a finite number of disjoint intervals.

Define y_n by

$$y_n(t) = \begin{cases} q(t) & \text{for } t \text{ in } J_n \\ 0 & \text{otherwise} \end{cases} \tag{A.3}$$

Then, for every t, $y_n(t) \to y(t)$.

If A is Lebesgue measurable but not Borel, let A' be a Borel set that

---

[7] For a discussion of the two-armed bandit problem in continuous time (but without learning from experience) see Presman (1991).

differs from A by a set of Lebesgue measure zero; then construct the sequence y_n as above, but with A replaced by A'. In this case,

$$y_n(t) \to y(t) \quad \text{a.e} \tag{A.4}$$

Note that each y_n is in H_1, which completes the proof. To see that $y_n \to y$ weakly, let x be essentially bounded, with $|x(t)| \leq \zeta$, a.s.: then

$$\left| \int_0^T e^{-\varrho t} y_n(t) x(t) dt - \int_0^T e^{-\varrho t} y(t) x(t) dt \right| \leq \xi \int_0^T e^{-\varrho t} |y_n(t) - y(t)| dt \tag{A.5}$$

Note that $|y_n(t) - y(t)| \leq q(t)$, and recall that

$$\int_0^T e^{-\varrho t} q(t) dt < \infty \tag{A.6}$$

Hence, by the Lebesgue Dominated Convergence Theorem, the right-hand side of (A.6) converges to zero.

References

Argote, L., and D. Epple. 1990. Learning curves in manufacturing. *Science*, 247:920–4.

Arrow, K. J. 1962. The economic implications of learning by doing. *Review of Economic Studies*, 29:155–73.

Berns, A. 1991. An example in optimal timing of the introduction of new technology. AT&T Bell Laboratories, unpublished, August.

Choquet, G. 1969. *Lectures on Analysis*, Vol. 2. Reading, MA: W. A. Benjamin.

Dasgupta, P., and J. Stiglitz. 1988. Learning-by-doing, market structure and industrial and trade policies. *Oxford Economic Papers*, 40:246–68.

Fudenberg, D., and J. Tirole. 1983. Learning by doing and market performance. *Bell Journal of Economics*, 14:522–30.

Linhart, P., R. Radner, and T. VanZandt. 1990. On optimal timing of the introduction of new technology. AT&T Bell Laboratories, unpublished, July.

Majumdar, M., and R. Radner. 1993. When to switch to a new technology: Learning about the learning curve. AT&T Bell Laboratories, unpublished, March.

Neveu, J. 1965. *Foundations of the Calculus of Probability*. San Francisco: Holden-Day.

Peles, Y. C. 1991. On deviations from learning curves. *Journal of Accounting Auditing and Finance*, 6:349–59.

Presman, E. L. 1991. Poisson version of the two-armed bandit problem with discounting. *Theoretic Probability and Applications*, 35, No. 2:307–17.

Teplitz, C. J. 1991. *The Learning Curve Deskbook*. New York: Quorum Books.

Young, A. 1991. Invention and bounded learning by doing. National Bureau of Economic Research working paper No. 3712, May.

CHAPTER 10

Price and market share dynamics in network industries

Geoffrey Heal

1   Introduction

This chapter addresses the economics of certain types of value-added networks (VANs) that are common in the financial sector and are becoming widespread in other sectors. It investigates the effect of different pricing regimes on allocative efficiency, and studies the nature of competition between vendors of these services. It emerges that there is a very strong tendency toward monopoly in VAN industries. VANs appear to be a classic case of natural monopoly, although this is not dependent on increasing returns in their technologies. The main cause is externalities between users. which lead to a "critical mass" phenomenon. A VAN is only economically viable after a certain critical mass of users is achieved. Standard prescriptions for achieving efficiency in such situations, such as marginal cost pricing and interconnection, are of limited value.

The classic example of a VAN in the financial sector is the Reuters FX monitor, a network system very widely used in trading foreign currencies by all major foreign exchange dealers. SWIFT,[1] the international interbank communications network, is another very important example. Reuters and SWIFT provide the infrastructure on which international capital markets run: They process transactions totaling tens of billions of dollars daily. They are to financial markets what roads and bridges are

The first draft of this essay was presented at the Summer Research Workshop of the Jerome Levy Economics Institute in June 1989. I am grateful to Peter Albin, Graciela Chichilnisky, Robert Mundell, and participants in the microeconomics seminars at Columbia and Washington Universities for valuable comments. The research for this paper was funded by a grant from the Faculty Research Fund of the Graduate School of Business, Columbia University.
[1] Society for Worldwide Interbank Financial Telecommunications.

191

to transportation systems. Electronic mail systems, facsimile transmission networks, securities settlement networks, and electronic data interchange (EDI) networks provide further examples. VANs are also important in the travel industry. Airline reservation systems are VANs, whose strategic importance is already widely recognized in the travel business.

Economically, all such systems are characterized by large fixed costs and relatively low variable costs, and by externalities between users so that to a potential user the value of joining the network depends on which others also join. These are examples of the network externalities discussed in the literature by Littlechild (1975), Oren and Smith (1981), Katz and Shapiro (1985), Farrell and Saloner (1985, 1986), Chichilnisky (1990, 1995), and others. The idea of "critical mass" looms large in industry discussions of these products.[2] It is recognized that such a product will succeed only if it can succeed in attracting a "critical mass" of major users, thus providing strong incentives to other potential users to join. Such incentives are at the root of the "bandwagon effects" studied by Farrell and Saloner (1985).

Given the importance of VANs, certain questions naturally arise. How can we characterize the socially optimal provision of these networks? Can we give substance to the critical mass concepts mentioned above? Can we characterize the noncooperative equilibrium patterns of use of the network that result from individual choices and competitive entry? Is there a role for regulation in this industry and if so what is it?

There are two strands of literature related to this chapter, one on network externalities and the other on standardization. The two key phenomena studies by these literatures are critical masses and bandwagon effects. Rohfls (1974), Katz and Shapiro (1985, 1986) and Chichilnisky (1990, 1995) identify critical mass and the multiplicity of equilibria as key to understanding the dynamics of network adoption. Farrell and Saloner (1985) identify bandwagon effects as a key phenomenon in understanding the adoption of standards. The models of network adoption and standard adoption have obvious structural similarities arising from the pervasiveness of reinforcing externalities in both cases. The model that follows has some of the characteristics of both, and provides a unified framework within which both issues can be addressed. Sections 3 to 6 analyze various critical mass concepts in a network and their dependence on pricing systems. This generalizes and provides an alternative perspective on the critical mass results of Rohfls (1974). Sections 7 to 10 analyze various Nash equilibria, and establish results some of which have

---

[2] For a discussion of critical mass issues, see Rohfls (1974), Oren and Smith (1981), and Chichilnisky (1990, 1995).

some similarity to results in Katz and Shapiro (1985, 1986) and Farrell and Saloner (1985). The framework is very different, as it deals with customer choice among competing networks that are perfect substitutes, but results emerge that are clear analogs to those in Farrell and Saloner and Katz and Shapiro. Unique about this chapter are

1 An emphasis on pricing policies and strategies, which is missing from the earlier literature (for example, Farrell and Saloner [1985] consider the adoption of standards without any discussion of the pricing of the alternative standards or how pricing can be a tool in the adoption of a standard)
2 The integration of critical mass and bandwagon effects into a single framework permitting the analysis of their sensitivity to pricing policies
3 An analysis of market share dynamics under a reasonable model of customer choice between networks
4 The beginnings of a model of optimal intertemporal networks pricing, given the constraints that prices must initially be below average cost to encourage adoption, reach a critical mass, and start a bandwagon, and that this loss must eventually be recouped from pricing above average cost

A literature with results analytically similar to those here on natural monopoly concerns mode selection and economies of adoption. This literature studies, for example, why the QWERTY keyboard layout became the equilibrium mode from the set of possible layouts.[3] Reinforcing positive externalities between new and existing users of a given mode are crucial in determining that only one mode survives.[4]

2   Basic assumptions

I work with a model in which there are consumers who can spend income on consumption of "other goods" and on the network product. The utility to them of consuming the network product depends only on the number of other users of this product. The costs of providing the network product have both a fixed and a variable element.

Let the total cost $TC(n)$ of providing network-based services to n users be

[3] See, for example, David (1985).
[4] See, for example, Arthur (1989), Chichilnisky (1990, 1995).

$$TC(n) = F + f(n) \quad \text{where} \quad F \geq 0 \quad \text{and} \quad f'(n) \geq 0$$

Define $AC(n) = \dfrac{F + f(n)}{n}$. We assume $f(n)$ to be concave so that $\dfrac{\partial AC(n)}{\partial n} < 0$.

Individual utility is given by either $u(c, n)$ for a network user or $u(c,0)$ for a nonuser, where c represents consumption of other goods. The utility of a network user thus depends on the total number of users of the network; u is increasing in both c and n and is strictly concave. The dependence of u on n and thus on choices made by others introduces a fundamental externality into the analysis. Even with convex technologies this introduces an effective nonconvexity into the problem through a "critical mass" phenomenon.

The assumption that utility is given by $u(c,0)$ for nonusers of the network amounts to a normalization. I assume that $u(c,1) > u(c,0)$ so that a user gets positive benefits from the network even if there are no other users. We might motivate this by assuming a user to be an organization rather than an individual, so that the firm might use the network to connect its branches even if there are no other users. A fax network or an electronic mail network has this property.

Let $t_{nu}(n)$ and $t_u(n)$ be the tariffs levied on nonusers and on users of the network respectively when the total number of users is n. For average cost pricing $t_{nu}(n)$ will typically be zero, whereas it may be positive for marginal cost pricing. We refer to a rule for determining the pair $(t_u(n), t_{nu}(n))$ as a *pricing system*.

Let y be the income level of a user (all assumed to be identical) and p the price of the other consumption goods. The price of the consumption good p will be taken to equal one from now on. The total number of potential users is N, of whom n are actual users. Total social welfare is given by the sum of individual utilities W.

Individuals face the following budget constraint:

$$y = c + t_j(n) \quad \text{where} \quad j = u \quad \text{or} \quad nu$$

so that utility levels are given by

$$u = u\big(y - t_u(n), n\big) \quad \text{or} \quad u = u\big(y - t_{nu}, 0\big)$$

We can now define the *private critical mass* PCM and *social critical mass* SCM corresponding to a given pricing system.

D1. *The private critical mass (PCM) n* corresponding to a* *pricing system $(t_u(n), t_{nu}(n))$ is the smallest number of users to satisfy the equation*

$$u\left(y - t_u\left(n\right), n\right) = u\left(y - t_{nu}\left(n\right), 0\right)$$

In words, the PCM is the smallest number of users such that a user and a nonuser are equally well off.

D2. *The social critical mass (SCM) ñ corresponding to a pricing system $(t_u(n), t_{nu}(n))$ is the smallest number of users to satisfy the equation*

$$Nu\left(y, 0\right) = nu\left(y - t_u\left(n\right), n\right) + \left(N - n\right)u\left(y - t_{nu}\left(n\right), 0\right)$$

In words, the SCM is the smallest number of users such that society is as well off in terms of total utility with the network as it is without the network.

3   Average cost pricing

We next develop an analysis of the average cost pricing case. The users share equally the total cost of the network. The typical user's budget constraint is

$$y = c + \frac{\left\{F + f\left(n\right)\right\}}{n} \tag{3.1}$$

and so utility is given by

$$u\left(y - \frac{F + f\left(n\right)}{n}, n\right) \tag{3.2}$$

Note that the total derivative of this with respect to the number of users n is

$$\frac{du}{dn} = -\frac{\partial u}{\partial c}\frac{\partial c}{\partial n} + \frac{\partial u}{\partial n} \tag{3.3}$$

As $\dfrac{\partial AC}{\partial n} < 0$ and $\dfrac{\partial u}{\partial n} > 0$ we have $\dfrac{du}{dn} > 0$.

For nonusers, we have just $u(c,0)$ and $y = c$. Total social welfare, W, is given by the sum of individual utilities so that

$$W = nu\left(y - AC\left(n\right), n\right) + \left[N - n\right]u\left(y, 0\right) \tag{3.4}$$

as all individuals are the same except insofar as they do or do not use the network. Rearranging equation (3.4) gives

$$W = Nu(y, 0) + n\{u(y - AC(n), n) - u(y, 0)\} \qquad (3.5)$$

so that

$$\frac{\partial W}{\partial y} = u(y - AC(n), n) - u(y, 0) + n\frac{\partial u}{\partial n} \qquad (3.6)$$

In equation (3.6) the expression $\partial u/\partial n$ is positive: We assume that

$$u(y - AC(1), 1) < u(y, 0) \qquad \text{and} \qquad u(y - AC(N), N) > u(y, 0) \qquad (3.7)$$

so that for a single network user the costs of supporting the network exceed the gains from its use, whereas when everyone uses the network the gains from its use clearly exceed its costs.

These assumptions imply that for small values of the number of users n, $\partial W/\partial n$ will be negative, whereas for large values of n it is positive. Define n_1 as

$$\partial W/\partial n \qquad \text{is negative for all values of} \qquad n \le n_1 \qquad (3.8)$$

n_1 is defined by equation (3.8): n^* is the SCM defined by the condition that

$$W(n^*) = W(0) \qquad (3.9)$$

so that the social critical mass n^* is the first positive value of n at which total social welfare reaches the value it has when there are no network users and no one pays any network support costs. Equation (3.9) implies, by equation (3.5), that

$$Nu(y, 0) = Nu(y, 0) + n\{u(y - AC, n^*) - u(y, 0)\} \qquad (3.10)$$

that is,

$$u(y - AC, n^*) = u(y, 0) \qquad (3.11)$$

so that the SCM n^* is also characterized as the first level of network use n at which a network user is as well off as a nonuser, that is, n^* is also the PCM. It is now possible to state formally:

> **Proposition 1:** *Under average cost pricing, SCM = PCM = $n^* > 0$. The existence of $n^* > 0$ does not depend on the existence of fixed costs in the provision of the network service. This proposition holds even if in the cost function (1) the fixed cost $F = 0$ and the variable cost $f(n)$ is linear so that the network service is*

provided under conditions of constant returns and costs. A socially optimal pattern of use of the network will involve either that all potential users use the network, or that none do so. No intermediate outcomes can be optimal.

Proof: $n^* > 0$ does not depend on fixed costs. It depends only on the boundary conditions (3.7) and in particular on the assumption that for a single network user the gains from supporting the network outweigh the benefits. This condition guarantees that $\partial W/\partial n$ will be negative at zero, which in turn ensures that $n^* > 0$. The remainder of the proposition is proven above.

QED.

4   Marginal cost pricing

With this pricing rule, each user pays the marginal cost of supporting an extra user. If this does not cover the total costs of operating the network, then the deficit is covered by a general tax on all individuals regardless of whether or not they are users. Denoting by $f'(n)$ the marginal cost, this implies that the budgets are

$$y = c + f'(n) + T \qquad \text{and} \qquad y = c + T$$
$$\text{for users and nonusers respectively}$$

where T is chosen to cover the shortfall between selling at marginal cost and the total cost:

$$TN = F + f(n) - nf'(n)$$

Social welfare is given by

$$W(n) = Nu(y - T, 0) + n\left[u\left(y - f'(\tilde{n}) - T, \tilde{n}\right) - u(y - T, 0)\right]$$

(4.1)

and the social critical mass SCM $\tilde{n}$ must satisfy

$$Nu(y, 0) = W(\tilde{n})$$

(4.2)

This can be rewritten as

$$N\left[u(y, 0) - u(y - T, 0)\right] = n\left[u\left(y - f'(\tilde{n}) - T, \tilde{n}\right) - u(y - T, 0)\right]$$

(4.3)

In (4.3) the LHS is positive. Therefore at $\tilde{n}$ the RHS of (4.3) is also positive, implying that

$$u\left(y - f'\left(n\right) - T, n\right) > u\left(y - T, 0\right)$$

so that at the SCM a user of the network is better off than a nonuser. It is easily verified that the utility of a user is increasing in n: For concave variable cost functions $f(n)$, however, the utility of a nonuser is nonincreasing in n. Hence at the private critical mass PCM n^* where the utilities of users and nonusers are equal, we must have $n^* < \tilde{n}$.

> **Proposition 2:** *With marginal cost pricing and concave variable cost functions the private critical mass n^* is less than the social critical mass $\tilde{n}$. As N tends to ∞, n^* tends to $\tilde{n}$.*

> *Proof:* All that remains to be proven is the convergence of n^* and $\tilde{n}$ as N tends to ∞. To see this note that as N increases then T tends to zero. Hence the LHS of (4.3) tends to zero, and the result follows immediately.   QED.

There is a simple intuition behind this result. Marginal cost pricing offloads some of the cost of the network onto nonusers of the network, reducing the financial burden on network users at any n. Users can be expected to reach utility levels comparable to nonusers before the level of usage is sufficient to justify the network from a social point of view.[5]

5   Comparison of pricing regimes

The previous three sections have characterized the private and social critical masses for the pricing regimes of marginal cost pricing, average cost pricing, and two part tariffs. The latter two were shown to have identical solutions. In this section I compare the solutions for average and marginal cost pricing, and establish that the private critical mass for mar-

---

[5] An alternative approach to pricing, in some respects a compromise between average and marginal cost pricing, is to use a system of two-part tariffs with a variable charge equal to marginal cost and an entry fee to the market calculated to cover any shortfall between the revenues from marginal cost pricing and total costs. This is the marginal cost pricing rule of the previous section with taxes levied only on users, so that the costs of the network are borne fully by its users. A simple extension of the arguments above leads to the following proposition:

> **Proposition 3:** *Consider a system of two part tariffs with the variable charge equal to marginal cost and the fixed part uniform across users and calculated to ensure breakeven. This leads to an outcome identical to that with average cost pricing.*

ginal cost pricing is always less than that for average cost pricing. The
social critical mass for marginal cost pricing is less than for average cost
pricing for large values of N, the total population of potential users. For
other values of N the social critical masses may have either order. For
average cost pricing equation (3.11) characterizes the private critical
mass:

$$u\big(y - AC, n\big) = u\big(y, 0\big)$$

For marginal cost pricing the equivalent equation is

$$u\big(y - f'(n) - T, n\big) = u\big(y - T, 0\big) \tag{5.1}$$

Figure 1 compares equations (3.11) and (5.1) graphically. Clearly
$u(y - T,0) < u(y,0)$ so the RHS of (5.1) is less than that of (3.11). Also
note that

$$\big\{f'(n) + T\big\}n + T\big(N - n\big) = TC = ACn$$

Average cost times the number of network users equals total cost.
Marginal cost plus tax times the number of users plus tax times the
number of nonusers also equals total cost. So $f'(n) + T < AC$, and for
any given n the first argument of $u(\bullet,\bullet)$ in the LHS of (5.1) is greater
than that in the LHS of (3.11). This confirms the relative positions of the
curves in Figure 1. The PCM for marginal cost pricing is the horizontal
component of the intersection of the line $u(y - T,0)$ with the curve $u(y - f'(n) - T, n)$, and the PCM for average cost pricing is the horizontal
component of the intersection of the line $u(y,0)$ with the curve $u(y - AC, n)$. *The private critical mass for marginal cost pricing is thus below
that for average cost pricing.*
    For the social critical masses, note that the appropriate equations are
(3.11) for the average cost pricing case again and (4.3) for the marginal
cost case:

$$N\big[u\big(y, 0\big) - u\big(y - T, 0\big)\big] = n\big[u\big(y - f'(\tilde{n}) - T, \tilde{n}\big) - u\big(y - T, 0\big)\big] \tag{4.3}$$

Note that $T = \dfrac{f(n) + F - f'(n)n}{N}$ so that for any fixed n as $N \to \infty$, $T \to 0$. Hence (4.3) becomes for very large N

$$u\big(y - f'(\tilde{n}), \tilde{n}\big) = u\big(y, 0\big) \tag{5.1'}$$

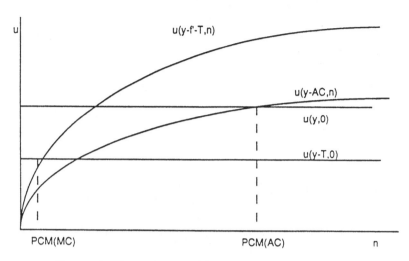

Figure 1. The private critical mass for marginal cost pricing ($PCM(MC)$) is less than for average cost pricing ($PCM(AC)$).

A comparison of (5.1') with (3.11) shows that because $u(y - f'(\tilde{n}),\tilde{n}) = u(y,0)$, and because marginal cost is less than average cost, the LHS of (5.1') is larger for any given n than the LHS of (3.11). So the n that solves (5.1') is less than the solution to (3.11). *So for large populations, the social critical mass under marginal cost pricing is less than that under average cost pricing.* It is not possible to order these two critical masses except for large values of N. In summary, we have proven:

Proposition 4:   *The ordering of the critical masses is as follows: MC and AC in parentheses denote that the value refers to marginal or average cost pricing respectively.*

$$PCM\big(MC\big) < PCM\big(AC\big):$$
$$SCM\big(MC\big) < SCM\big(AC\big) \text{ for large } N:$$
$$PCM\big(MC\big) < SCM\big(AC\big):$$
$$PCM\big(MC\big) < SCM\big(MC\big): PCM\big(AC\big) = SCM\big(AC\big)$$

6   More general pricing policies

Consider a private firm that is the single supplier of a network and that charges only users, so that $t_{nu}(n) = 0$. The private critical mass depends

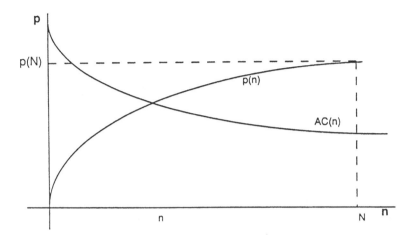

Figure 2. The price $p(n)$ at which n is a critical mass of users and the average cost per user $AC(n)$.

on $t_u(n)$. We shall define $p(n)$ as that price at which n is a private critical mass. Formally,

D3. $p(n)$ *is the solution to* $u(y - p(n),n) = u(y,0)$

$p(n)$ is the price this firm has to charge to make network use as attractive as nonuse. The following results are immediate:

$$\frac{\partial p(n)}{\partial n} > 0 \qquad \frac{\partial^2 p(n)}{\partial n^2} < 0, \quad p(0) = 0$$

Figure 2 plots $p(n)$ and $AC(n)$. $\hat{n}$ is the number of users at which $p(n)$ equals average cost. Clearly for a number of users less than $\hat{n}$, the firm has to make a loss (set price less than average cost) to attract users to the network, whereas for $n > \hat{n}$, it is possible to make a profit (price above average cost) and attract users to the network. Not surprisingly, $\hat{n}$ is an important number in our discussion of dynamic pricing policies in Section 8 below. Note that $p(N)$, the price at which the entire population forms a critical mass, is the monopoly price, that is, the price that a single seller will charge once all users are on the network.

The results of this and the previous two sections generalize those of Rohfls on critical mass for the case of uniform calling patterns. Rohfls considers additive utilities and does not focus at all on pricing systems. He also reviews "equilibrium user sets," a concept closest to the Nash equilibria of the next section.

7   Nash equilibrium usage patterns

Clearly if there are no users of the network, then no one has an incentive to join it. For the first to join, costs exceed benefits, and there is no gain from joining. Equally, if all but one of the population are users, then for the remaining one the best choice is to join. Costs will be low and benefits high, leading to a net gain. The moral of these simple observations is that not joining the network is any potential user's best choice, given the assumption that no one else joins. Similarly joining is his or her best choice if the assumption is that all others are joining. So there are at least two Nash equilibrium patterns of use: no one a user and everyone a user. Furthermore, it is intuitively clear that each of these is locally stable. If there are few users, then no one else has an incentive to join and the existing members have an incentive to leave. Conversely, if most of the population are members, then the remainder have an interest in joining and current members have no interest in leaving. These Nash equilibria correspond to Rohfls' "equilibrium user sets" and to the "fulfilled expectations Cournot equilibria" of Katz and Shapiro (1985).

In the rest of this section I formalize these observations, and extend them to the case of several competing sellers. We see that if there are M competing sellers of the network service, then there are $M + 1$ locally stable Nash equilibrium patterns of use, with M of these socially optimal. In studying the dynamics of the system, we note that there is a very fundamental case of natural monopoly in the VAN industry. M of the $M + 1$ locally stable equilibria involve all users buying from only one provider, and the other locally stable equilibrium involves no user of any network. In terms of the model of adoption of standards used by Farrell and Saloner (1985), we could interpret each network as an alternative standard without doing undue violence to the intuition behind the model, and then see that the equilibria involve the dominance of a single standard. Which standard dominates will depend on the initial conditions of the model, according to the the dynamics of Section 8 below.

This natural monopoly may have regulatory implications. In Section 9, therefore, I investigate the effect of compulsory interconnection between competing networks. This implies that a user of any network can access a user of any competing network, thus greatly increasing the value of network membership.[6] In the United States, competing telephone systems (long distance and cellular) are required to interconnect, and have always met identical technical standards, making the interconnection feasible. In the field of data networks based on the X.25 protocol, the development of the X.400 protocol will greatly increase the ease of interconnection. Competing vendors using X.25 systems to provide electronic mail and related services have recently voluntarily interconnected their networks.

7.1   A single vendor

I now formalize the above discussion for a single vendor of a VAN service. We are studying a noncooperative game where the players are the actual or potential network users, of whom there are N, and where each has a strategy space consisting of the two choices of joining or not joining the network. Formally:

S_i is i's strategy space, $S_i = \{J, NJ\}$, where J is joining

the network and NJ is not joining

A player's choice of strategy is denoted by $s_i \in S_i$. We let $S = \{s_1, \ldots, s_N\}$, a vector of strategy choices for each player, and $S_{-i} = \{s_1, \ldots s_{i-1}, s_{i+1}, \ldots, s_N\}$ be a vector of choices for all players other than i. All players move simultaneously without knowing the choices made by the others. Payoffs are the utility levels associated with the vector of strategies chosen by all players, according to the definitions of the previous sections. This completes a formal definition of the game. A Nash equilibrium is as usual a vector $S = \{s_1, \ldots, s_N\}$ of strategy choices such that for all players $s_i \in S_i$ is i's best response to $S_{-i} = \{s_1, \ldots s_{i-1}, s_{i+1}, \ldots, s_N\}$. It is clear that if $S_{-i} = \{NJ, \ldots, NJ\}$ then $s_i = NJ$ is i's best response. This confirms that $S = \{NJ, \ldots, NJ\}$ is a Nash equilibrium. An identical argument confirms that $S = \{J, \ldots, J\}$ is also a Nash equilibrium. Hence we have

> **Proposition 5:** *Assume that for all three pricing systems discussed above, the PCM is less than $N - 1$. Then for average or marginal cost pricing or two part tariffs with variable charges equal to marginal cost, and for the game defined above, played between potential network users whose strategy spaces are to join or not join the network, there are at least two Nash equilibria. One has no one using the network. The other has everyone using it.*

---

[6] For this to be feasible, it is in general necessary that all networks use identical technical standards. On the emergence of common standards, see David and Greenstein (1990), Katz and Shapiro (1985, 1986).

7.2   *Multiple vendors*

Now assume there are M vendors of an identical network product all having the same cost structures and indexed by $j = 1, 2, \ldots M$. A user can join any one of the M competing networks or join none: We assume that it is never interesting to join more than one network and exclude this possibility from the strategy spaces. Hence i's strategy space is now $S_i = \{J_1, J_2, J_3, \ldots \ldots J_M, NJ\}$. In all other respects the game and the equilibrium concept are as before. We can now establish

> **Proposition 6:**   *Assume that for the three pricing systems discussed above, the PCM is less than $N - 1$. Then for average or marginal cost pricing or two part tariffs with variable charges equal to marginal cost, and for the game defined above, played between potential network users whose strategy spaces are to join or not join one of the M identical networks, there are at least $M + 1$ Nash equilibria. These are given by the $M + 1$ strategy vectors*
>
> $$S_{NJ} = \{NJ, NJ, \ldots NJ\}, S_{Ji} = \{J_i, J_i, J_i, \ldots J_i\}, \quad i = 1 \text{ to } M$$
>
> *One equilibrium involves no users of any network. The other M involve everyone using one of the networks, with no users of the others.*
>
> **Remark:**   *Proposition 6 provides a part of the basis for the earlier statement that there is a natural monopoly tendency in markets for VANs. We show below that all locally stable Nash equilibria with positive usage levels involve the use of only one network and therefore a 100% market share for one vendor.*
>
> *Proof:* This follows immediately from equation (3.7) and the assumption that PCM $< N - 1$.   QED.

Proposition 6 is an analog of results about standards in Farrell and Saloner (1985). In particular, the fact that all equilibria involve all consumers making the same choices is an example of their bandwagon effects. It would be a straightforward matter to reformulate the choice of a network by consumers as a sequential game in which one potential user makes a choice in each period. In this case, we would have a result analogous to Farrell and Saloner's (1985) Proposition 4 to the effect that each of the equilibria of Proposition 6 above is a perfect equilibrium of the sequential game.

8   Price and market share dynamics

In this section we review the dynamics of market share under the assumption that the number of users selecting a particular strategy j adjusts from any initial value according to the difference between the utility from strategy j and the utility yielded by the best alternative. If the utility from j exceeds that from the best alternative then the number selecting j increases, and vice versa. We consider the case of two competing vendors, as this can easily be analyzed graphically. Very similar results are available for larger numbers, but have to be obtained by more abstract analysis. Only the case of average cost pricing will be considered. Again similar results hold for the other pricing systems examined above. The assumption of average cost pricing implies that throughout the adjustment process toward equilibrium, each firm has to break even at every point in time. Possible alternatives to this will be reviewed at the end of this section.

The fundamental adjustment process to be considered is as follows:

$$\frac{dn_1}{dt} = a_1\left\{\bar{u}_{n_1} - \max\left[\bar{u}, \bar{u}_{n_2}\right]\right\} \qquad \text{for} \qquad n_1 > 0 \qquad \text{or}$$

$$n_1 = 0 \qquad \text{and} \qquad \bar{u}_{n_1} > \max\left[\bar{u}, \bar{u}_{n_2}\right]$$

$$\frac{dn_1}{dt} = 0 \text{ otherwise}$$

$$\frac{dn_2}{dt} = a_2\left\{\bar{u}_{n_2} - \max\left[\bar{u}, \bar{u}_{n_1}\right]\right\} \qquad \text{for} \qquad n_2 > 0 \qquad \text{or}$$

$$n_2 = 0 \qquad \text{and} \qquad \bar{u}_{n_2} > \max\left[\bar{u}, \bar{u}_{n_1}\right]$$

$$\frac{dn_2}{dt} = 0 \text{ otherwise}$$

where

$$\bar{u} = u\left(y, 0\right), \qquad \bar{u}_{n_1} = u\left(y - AC(n_1), n_1\right), \qquad \bar{u}_{n_2} = u\left(y - AC(n_2), n_1\right)$$

Here $\bar{u} = u(y, 0)$ is the utility from not joining either network, $\bar{u}_{n_1} = u(y - AC(n_1), n_1)$ is that from joining network one, and $\bar{u}_{n_2} = u(y - AC(n_2), n_1)$ is that from joining network two. So the first equation says that the number of users of network one rises if the utility from using that network exceeds the greater of the utilities from joining no network or the other network, and vice versa. This formalizes the idea that for each vendor the number of users increases if it can provide a utility level greater than that of the best alternative (either joining the other network or joining no network), and otherwise decreases. The intuition behind this is clear: A vendor's market share depends on how competitive it is relative to other choices. Technical complications arise because we have to ensure that these adjustment processes cannot decrease variables whose values are already zero. The "otherwise" case in each equation ensures this.[7] The basic adjustment rule is applied to the number of users on network one only if this is positive, or if the application of this rule will make it so. Otherwise, which in particular means that n_l is zero, there is no change.

Figure 3 gives a graphical analysis of this system. We plot n_1 and n_2 on the axes. The point $(N,0)$ represents all users using network one and $(0,N)$ represents all using network two. Anywhere on the line joining these two points all users are members of one or other of the networks. For each network, n^* is the PCM, the same for both as they are assumed identical. When both n_1 and n_2 are less than n^*, both vendors offer utility levels less than those obtained by joining neither network. So both lose members and both n_1 and n_2 decline toward zero. Otherwise, at least one vendor offers a utility level in excess of that of not joining either. If both n_1 and n_2 exceed n^* then both networks are more attractive than not joining either, and to the right of the 45 degree line network one is more attractive than network two, and vice versa.

From these considerations it is clear that $(0,0)$, $(0,N)$ and $(N,0)$ are three locally stable limits of the adjustment processes defined above. Obviously these correspond to the three Nash equilibria which Proposition 5 establishes for the case of two vendors. Note that besides the three equilibria that occur on the boundaries $\{(0,0), (0,N), (N,0)\}$, there are equilibria at $(0, n^*), (n^*, 0), (n^*, n^*)$, and $(N/2, N/2)$. At all these points both n_1 and n_2 are constant. However, these are unstable equilibria. In fact all are Nash equilibria of the game defined in the previous section in addition to the Nash equilibria described in Proposition 6.

Finally, a comment on the adjustment process of this section is in order. The most restrictive aspect of it is the condition that at all times each firm must break even. This condition has the implication that the industry will never be established at a positive level unless the initial conditions are such that at least one firm has a critical mass of users. In practice, VAN industries do arise from zero, so that there must be a path from the origin to one of the other equilibria. Key in establishing such a possibility is giving each firm the ability to price at less than average cost,

[7] These equations are discontinuous on the boundaries of the state space. The first discussion of systems of this type, as far as I know, is in Arrow and Hurwicz (1958). Champsaur, Drèze, and Henry (1973) establish the existence of a solution. Their results are used by Heal (1983) in a way which could be applied here to ensure the existence of a solution.

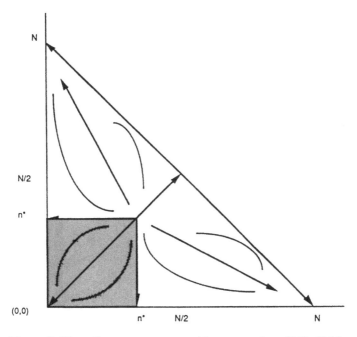

Figure 3. The adjustment process with two vendors. (0,0), (0,*N*), and (*N*,0) are locally stable equilibria. (0,*n**), (*n**,0), (*n**,*n**), and (*N*/2,*N*/2) are unstable equilibria. The set of initial points from which the system converges to the origin is shaded. From initial points outside of this shaded region it converges to either (0,*N*) or (*N*,0).

and so run a loss, in the early stages of its growth. The critical mass shown in Figure 4 is derived on the assumption that price equals average cost. For a lower price, the critical mass would be lower, as shown in Figure 2. Hence the attracting region of the equilibria at the origin, the shaded area in Figure 4 would be correspondingly smaller. By allowing arbitrarily low prices, this region can be made as small as we wish. However, the loss-making pricing policies that allow us to reduce the attracting region of the origin are feasible for the firms only if they can price above average cost at the eventual equilibrium, making profits, and if they are able in the early stages of their existence to borrow against these expected eventual profits. There is thus a crucial role for capital markets in establishing industries based on VANs.

We can begin to formalize a price dynamic based on these ideas as follows. Consider a single firm entering the market for a network product. Initially it has no users, but wishes to build up the market over

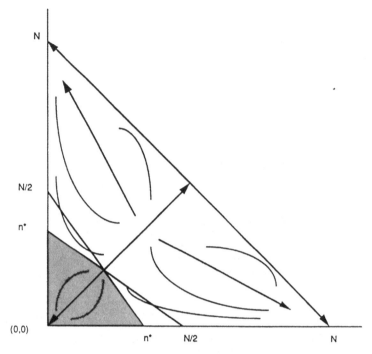

Figure 4. The adjustment process with two vendors and interconnection of their networks. (0,0), (0,N), and (N,0) are locally stable equilibria. There is no qualitative change in the pattern of stable equilibria
from the case without interconnection. However, the rates of convergence to the stable equilibria are likely to be lower in this case, and the
region of convergence to one of the socially optimal locally stable equilibria is larger. This region is the unshaded area in the triangle (0,0),
(0,N), (N,0). The shaded area is the set of initial points from which the
origin is approached.

time. What price path should it follow over time? Assume that it can
attract users at a rate given by the adjustment process

$$\frac{dn}{dt} = \alpha\{\bar{u}_n - \bar{u}\} \quad \text{for} \quad n > 0 \quad \text{or} \quad n = 0 \quad \text{and} \quad \bar{u}_{n_1} > \bar{u}$$

$$\frac{dn}{dt} = 0 \text{ otherwise}$$

where

$$\bar{u} = u(y, 0), \qquad \bar{u}_n = u(y - p(n), n)$$

which is just a specialization of the adjustment process used earlier in this section to the case of a single firm. Here $p(n)$ is as defined in **D3** of Section 6: It is the price at which n is a private critical mass. Let T be the first time at which $n = N$, that is, the first time at which all potential users are on the network. It seems reasonable that the firm's optimal price path should go through the following three phases:

1 At $t = 0, p < 0$.

2 For all t with $0 < t \le T$, $\dfrac{\partial p}{\partial t} > 0$ and $p(t) < p(n(t))$.

3 For some Δt, the firm set $p = p(N)$ for all $t > T + \Delta t$. Here $p(N)$ is the monopoly price as defined in Section 6 above.

In intuitive terms, such a strategy involves first paying users to join the network, in order to move away from zero users and start the number of users increasing. It then involves raising the price as the number of users and therefore their willingness to pay rises, but always keeping the price below the level at which the current number of users is a critical mass. This ensures that number of users is always increasing. Finally, when all users are on the network, price is set at the monopoly price. Clearly such a strategy involves losses at least until $n = \hat{n}$, where $\hat{n}$ is defined in Figure 2 and is the number of users at which average cost equals the $p(n)$, the price at which n is a critical mass. I conjecture that an optimal pricing policy for the single firm will go through the three phases described above, though a complete characterization of the growth of price in the intermediate phase is not yet available. This pricing strategy formalizes and generalizes one of the approaches to the network startup problem discussed by Rohlfs (1974, Section 5).

9   Interconnection and regulatory issues

As mentioned in the introduction, a frequent regulatory response to the economic conditions described above is to require interconnection between competing services, and in particular between any dominant service provider and incoming competitors. Thus in the United States AT&T was required to allow MCI and Sprint to interconnect, as was British Telecomm with respect to Mercury in the United Kingdom. The CCITT is also beginning to promote interconnectivity between services based on packet switch technology via its X.400 protocols. The general move toward common software standards for network applications is a response to pressure for interconnection by end users.

The intuition behind the drive toward interconnectivity is that it will improve the competitive position of smaller vendors by giving their users access to all the members of larger and more established networks. For example, MCI's competitive position with respect to AT&T would clearly be very poor if MCI users could communicate only with other MCI users. Such a restriction would hardly have weakened AT&T's position, particularly in the early days of the entry of new long distance carriers. Hence, it is argued, interconnection makes it easier for the MCIs to enter and compete.

We shall see from the analysis that follows that this intuition is spurious. Even with full interconnectivity there is still a clear tendency to domination of the market by a single vendor. Imposing interconnectivity does not alter in any way the set of locally stable Nash equilibria, which still consist of the concentration of all users on one network or of no use of any network.

Interconnectivity does offer one important advantage from a policy point of view. In the model analyzed in the previous sections, the socially efficient allocation is that all potential users actually use one network, and one network only. From the point of view of social efficiency it does not matter which network they use, so the locally stable Nash equilibria with positive usage levels are all socially efficient. Viewed in this context, the beneficial effect of interconnection can be defined as follows. It increases the set of initial conditions from which the system will converge to an efficient allocation, and decreases the set from which it converges to the socially inefficient locally stable outcome involving no network use. Intuitively, this occurs because interconnectivity makes it easier for any given vendor to attain critical mass, because its users have access to the users of competitors. It therefore has to recruit fewer users to attain its PCM. Hence it is easier to attain the initial conditions exceeding the PCMs and from which the system moves to equilibria with positive usage levels. This point is formalized below. Suppose that there are two competing network vendors, 1 and 2. Then under average cost pricing the utility of a user of 1 is given by $u(y - AC(n_1), n_1 + n_2)$. Here costs depend only on the number of users of network one, n_1, but benefits depend on the total number of users of both networks, $n_1 + n_2$, as any user of either can access all other users of both. The PCM of network 1 is therefore defined by

$$u\left(y - AC\left(n_1\right), n_1 + n_2\right) = u\left(y, 0\right)$$

Rather than defining a unique value of n_1, as before, this PCM defines a relationship between n_1 and n_2. On the graph of this relationship, network 1 reaches its PCM. Obviously, for $n_2 = 0$, this gives n_1* the PCM of network 1 without interconnection. As n_2 increases, the value of n_1 needed to reach PCM falls. In general it does not seem possible to say that the graph of the relationship between n_1 and n_2 is concave or convex. Because the problem is fully symmetric, the graph showing the PCM of network 1 as a function of n_2 will be identical, up to a permutation of coordinates, with that which shows the PCM of network 2 as a function of n_1. In the $n_1 - n_2$ plane, these two curves will therefore cross on the line $n_1 = n_2$.

These considerations are reflected in Figure 4, which is a revision of Figure 3 to incorporate the changes in PCMs and the impact of this on the system's dynamics. The only qualitative change is that the region from which the origin is approached is now smaller. It is the shaded area bounded above by the PCM curves for the two networks. This replaces the area bounded above by $(0,n^*)$ and $(n^*,0)$ in Figure 3. The other difference worth mentioning is that now all networks offer their users the same benefits but differ in the costs of membership. Because of this, the differences in utility levels between networks at any point in the plane are now less than without interconnection. This may be reflected in lower velocities and therefore lower rates of convergence than in the earlier case.

10   Diverse users

So far we have assumed all users of the network to be identical. Interesting issues arise if this assumption is dropped. In particular, two types of equilibria arise, which we call separating and pooling equilibria by analogy with results in the area of contract theory. Separating equilibria are those at which only certain types of users join a network; pooling equilibria are those at which all agents join.

The obvious difference between agents is a difference in preferences and therefore in willingness to pay for use of the network. In a simple way, such differences can be captured by the assumption that each user faces a fixed one-time cost in joining the network, over and above the charges that may be levied by the network. Think of this as the cost of buying a telephone, or, more substantially, the cost to a bank of writing the software and purchasing the communications hardware needed to connect to SWIFT or any of the interbank networks. For major users of important networks, such costs can be millions of dollars. Clearly they vary from user to user, depending on the initial state of their hardware and software.

Let c_i be the cost to user i of joining the network. Then the budget equation of an agent becomes

$$y = c + t_j(n) - c_i$$

and utility levels are given by

$$u = u\Big(y - t_u\big(n\big) - c_i, n\Big) \qquad \text{or} \qquad u = u\Big(y - t_{nu}, 0\Big)$$

for users and nonusers respectively. The social critical mass can now be defined as before without ambiguity, but the private critical mass will vary from person to person. For each individual i there will be a number PCM_i that is the smallest number of users needed to make i indifferent between joining and not joining. Clearly this will be lower for individuals with lower joining costs.

Suppose now that the population consists of two types, those with low joining costs C_L and those with high joining costs C_H. Within each group all are identical. Across groups the only differences are in the joining costs. There are now two private critical masses, PCM_L and PCM_H, with $PCM_L < PCM_H$. There are N_L agents with low joining costs and N_H with high costs, where $N_L + N_H = N$.

The introduction of two types of agents with different critical masses alters substantially the structure and dynamics of Nash equilibria, discussed in Sections 7 and 8. Consider first the structure of Nash equilibria in the case where $N_L < PCM_H$. In this case, once the number of users of a network exceeds PCM_L, then all low-cost users have an incentive to join. There is Nash equilibrium at which all low-cost users join, and only low-cost users join. The numbers of users resulting from this – N_L – is below the critical mass for high-cost users PCM_H, that is, $PCM_H > N_L$, so that no high-cost user has an incentive to join. If instead $PCM_H < N_L$, then the attainment of a critical mass for low-cost users would lead to them all joining the network, at which point the number of users would exceed the critical mass for high-cost agents and all agents would join, leading to an equilibrium with all agents as network users. In this case there is no equilibrium at which only one type of user joins. Depending, therefore, on the numbers of agents of different types and their joining costs, we may or may not have Nash equilibrium at which different user types are separated out. This is reminiscent of the separating and pooling equilibria arising under imperfect information, though the causes are entirely different.

Consider next the dynamics of equilibria with two competing vendors. Figure 5 shows the dynamics of Section 8 modified for the case of two agent types with $N_L < PCM_H$. This is the case in which there exists a separating equilibrium at which only low-cost agents join the network. Now there are two locally stable equilibria at which the low-cost agents all join either network 1 or network 2. There is also a saddle-point equilibrium at which half the low-cost agents join each vendor. There are still locally stable equilibria with all agents using one or the other of the networks.

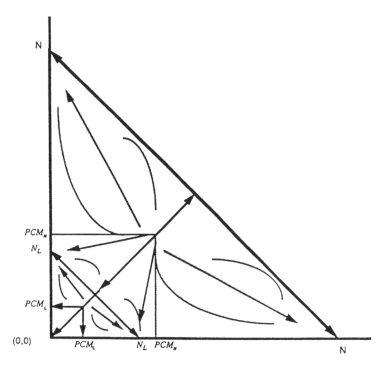

Figure 5. The adjustment process with two vendors and two user types. $(0, N), (N, 0), (0, 0), (N_L/2, N_L/2)$ is the saddle-point (provided that $N_L/2 > PCM_L$). $(PCM_L, 0), (0, PCM_L), (0, PCM_H)$, and $(PCM_H, 0)$ are unstable equilibria. The set of initial points from which the systems converge to the origin is shaded, as is the set from which it converges to either $(0, N)$ or $(N, 0)$.

In the alternative case of $PCM_H > N_L$, there are no separating equilibria and the set of locally stable equilibria is identical with that in Section 8 where all agents have the same joining costs.

11   Conclusions

A key feature of VANs is a tendency toward monopoly, coupled with a critical mass effect, which means that unless the industry grows beyond a certain minimum scale it will not survive at all. The industry either takes off, and is likely to be monopolized, or does not grow at all. Interconnection, which requires the adoption of common standards, makes quantitative but not qualitative changes to the picture. Without the evolution or imposition of common standards, interconnection is not an option.[8] In the model analyzed here, there is no resource allocation loss from average rather than marginal cost pricing. An average cost pricing solution supports the socially optimal use pattern, which is that everyone uses the network.

There is a simple intuitive reason for this. When everyone is using the network, then in an average cost pricing regime, the total cost of the network is divided equally among all. In a marginal cost pricing regime, with everyone using the network, the total costs of the network are covered by the fixed and variable charges imposed on everyone. Each person's network use costs are the same in either case. As their incomes are the same by assumption in the two cases, their consumption of the other good is also the same. So both pricing systems – average and marginal cost pricing – support the optimal resource allocation in this model.[9]

From a dynamic perspective, marginal cost pricing is preferable, as the private critical mass is lowest in this case. Thus the attainment of the efficient outcome where everyone uses the network is "more likely" with marginal cost pricing than with average cost pricing. Marginal cost pricing makes the cost of using the network less at any given number of users, lowering the number of other users needed to make joining attractive and so making it easier to get a critical mass. A number of private network vendors have clearly noticed this phenomenon, and have subsidized their networks heavily until a critical mass has been attained. Marginal cost pricing is then preferable as a way of *getting to* an optimum, though not as a way of supporting it. The best regime for getting to an optimum is marginal cost pricing plus interconnection, which gives the greatest possible set of initial conditions from which a full-use equilibrium is approached.

References

Arrow, K. J., and L. Hurwicz. 1958. Gradient methods for concave programming, 1, local results. In *Studies in Linear and Nonlinear Programming*, ed. K. J. Arrow, L. Hurwicz, and H. Uzawa. Stanford University Press.

Arthur, W. B. 1989. Competing technologies, increasing returns, and lock-in by historical events. *Economic Journal*, 99:116–31.

Berg, S. V. 1989. The production of compatibility: Technical standards as collective goods. *Kyklos*, 42, Facs. 3:361–83.

[8] On the evolution of common standards, see David and Greenstein (1990), Katz and Shapiro (1985, 1986).

[9] For another case when average cost pricing can support a first-best allocation of resources, see Brown and Heal (1985).

Brown, D. J., and G. M. Heal. 1985. The optimality of regulated prices. In *Advances in Equilibrium Theory*, ed. C. D. Aliprantis, O. Burkinshaw, and N. J. Rothman. Springer-Verlag, Lecture Notes in Economic and Mathematical Systems.

Carlton, D. W., and J. M. Klamer. 1983. The need for coordination among firms, with special reference to network industries. *University of Chicago Law Review*, 50:446–65.

Champsaur, P., J. Dreze, and C. Henry. 1973. Dynamic processes in economic theory. Center for Operations Research and Econometrics Discussion Paper No. 7417. Louvain-la-Verve, Belgium.

Chichilnisky, G. 1990. International financial networks: Externalities and increasing returns. Discussion Paper, Department of Economics, Columbia University, published as The Evolution of a Global Network: A Game of Coalition Formation. *Journal of International and Comparative Economics*. 4:179–97, 1995.

Chichilnisky, G. 1995. "Network Evolution and Coalition Formation" in *Private Networks Public Objectives* (Eli M. Noam and Aine Ni Shuilleabhain) Amsterdam: Elsevier, pp. 177–235.

David, P. A. 1985. Clio and the economics of QWERTY. *American Economic Review*, 75(2,May):332–6.

David, P. A., and S. Greenstein. 1990. The economics of compatibility standards: An introduction to recent research. Center for Economic Policy Research, publication number 207, Stanford University, June.

Dybvig, P. H., and S. S. Spatt. 1983. Adoption externalities as a public good. *Journal of Public Economics*, 20:231–47.

Farrell, J., and G. Saloner. 1985. Standardization, compatibility, and innovation. *Rand Journal of Economics*, Vol. 16, 1(Spring 1985):70–83.

Farrell, J., and G. Saloner. 1986. Standardization and variety. *Economics Letters*, 20:71–74.

Farrell, J., and G. Saloner. 1988. Coordination through committees and markets. *Rand Journal of Economics*, Vol. 19, 2(Summer 1988):235–52.

Heal, G. M. 1983. Stable disequilibrium prices. Discussion Paper, Columbia Business School.

Katz, M., and C. Shapiro. 1985. Network externalities, competition and compatibility. *American Economic Review*, 75:424–40.

Katz, M., and C. Shapiro. 1986. Technology and adoption in the presence of network externalities. *Journal of Political Economy*, 94:822–41.

Kindleberger, C. 1983. Standards as public, collective and private goods. *Kyklos*, 36:377–96.

Littlechild, S. C. 1975. Two-part tariffs and consumption externalities. *Bell Journal of Economics and Management Science*, Vol. 6, 2(Autumn 1975):661–70.

Oren, S. S., and S. A. Smith. 1981. Critical mass and tariff structure in electronic communications markets. *Bell Journal of Economics and Management Science*, 12 (Autumn):467–86.

Rohlfs, J. 1974. A theory of interdependent demand for a communication service. *Bell Journal of Economics and Management Science*, Vol. 5, 1(Spring 1974):16–37.

CHAPTER 11

Exchange in a network of trading posts

Ross M. Starr and Maxwell B. Stinchcombe

Foreword

I first met Kenneth Arrow in 1965, half a lifetime ago. As an under-graduate at Stanford University, I took Ken's graduate advanced mathematical economics course. It was a view into another world, where the precision of mathematics had a compass limited only by imagination. The focus of the course was mathematical general equilibrium theory, presented in part from the working manuscript of Arrow and Hahn's *General Competitive Analysis* (as Ken lectured from the manuscript the ink on some pages was still wet). As the quarter progressed, I discussed the course's required term paper with Ken (then "Prof. Arrow") and expressed annoyance with the convexity assumption on preferences in *Theory of Value*. Ken referred me to a well chosen bibliography including Aumann's measure theoretic work (in working paper form), Shapley and Shubik on approximate cores, and the geometric discussions of J. Rothenberg. He did not suggest that the project under discussion was too ambitious. The term paper became an early draft of my first published work "Quasi-equilibria in markets with non-convex preferences." The final version benefited from detailed critical correspondence from Robert Aumann and the mathematical innovations of Lloyd Shapley and John Folkman communicated by Shapley. From that beginning there was no turning back. Pure mathematical economic theory seemed the most intellectually challenging and rewarding pursuit one could undertake.

At Stanford University in the mid-1960s the mathematical economics and econometrics faculty and graduate students had offices in Serra House, an amiably rundown former official residence of the president of the university on the fringes of the campus's classroom and office area. There was a strong esprit de corps in the group there. We were joined occasionally by my parrot, Samson, a green-feathered Mexican redhead about the size of a pigeon, with habits both noisy and dirty. Celebrations

216

included weekly wine and cheese parties during the summer that significantly reduced the productivity of Friday afternoons.

In 1968, when Ken moved to Harvard, he was followed by a devoted group of graduate students and colleagues; on the faculty were David Starrett and Masahiko Aoki, trailing graduate students were Louis Gevers, Walter P. Heller, and myself. Visiting at Harvard that year were Amartya Sen and Leonid Hurwicz, making the move even more interesting. I cherish the memory of a lunch at the faculty club with Ken, Leo Hurwicz, and Mike Rothschild. Mike and I were overwhelmed into comparative silence by a conversation that moved in minutes from Jewish jokes to Banach spaces to deciphering linear B.

My dissertation, submitted to Stanford with Ken as advisor, included the following passage:

A unique common medium of exchange against which all other goods trade [implies that] the number of markets in which goods trade against one another is drastically reduced. If there are N goods, the reduction is from $\frac{1}{2}N(N - 1)$ to N. This reduction is thought to correspond to the cost of running the markets. The argument assumes some nonconvexity in the costs of operating the markets so that many small markets are more costly than a few large markets. . . .

After a hiatus of two decades, the present assay is intended to fulfill the research agenda implied in these remarks.

All of Ken's students owe him a debt that can never fully be repaid. He has shared with us his brilliance and insight, and communicated his enthusiasm. We are permanently richer for having the opportunity to study with and to know him.

Ross M. Starr

1 Introduction

We consider the problem of organizing bilateral trade for given equilibrium prices. In particular we wish to establish reasonably sufficient conditions on the structure of transaction costs so that monetary trade is the low cost method of conducting transactions. Walras suggests that we think of trade taking place at a family of trading posts, one for each pair of goods:

In order to fix our ideas, we shall imagine that the place which serves as a market for the exchange of all the commodities $(A), (B), (C), (D) \ldots$ for one another is divided into as many sectors as there are pairs of commodities exchanged. We should then have $\dfrac{m(m - 1)}{2}$ special markets each identified by a signboard indicating the names of the two commodities exchanged there as well as their prices or rates of exchange. (1954)

Thus for each good i and each good j, there may be a trading post for the trade of i and j for one another. This leads to an array, as Walras notes, of approximately $\frac{1}{2}n^2$ trading posts where n is the number of commodities. In most economies we see far fewer pairs of goods in active trade. Most trade takes place between the n goods and a single good differentiated as money. The number of moneys is small, typically unity, in a single economy (though this raises the tricky question of what the boundaries of an economy are). A monetary trade structure reduces the number of active trading posts from approximately $\frac{1}{2}n^2$ to approximately n. Is this reduction the distinguishing feature of a monetary economy? What motivates the collapse of the full array of trading posts? Professor Tobin suggests that the use of a single money is in the nature of a public good, perhaps reflecting a scale economy at the level of the economy as a whole.

Social institutions like money are public goods. Models of . . . competitive markets and individual optimizing agents . . . are not well adapted to explaining the existence and quantity of public goods. . . . Both [money and language] are means of communication. The use of a particular language or a particular money by one individual increases its value to other actual or potential users. Increasing returns to scale, in this sense, limits the number of languages or moneys in a society and indeed explains the tendency for one basic language or money to monopolize the field. (1980)

In this article we will formalize the view expressed above (without implicating Tobin) by characterizing the use of a unique money as the result of an optimizing (cost minimizing) decision on the array of active trading posts in the model posited by Walras. In particular, we will develop sufficient conditions to allow us to derive the self-confirming public good character of the choice of the monetary instrument.

The character of the cost structure in this model is formally very similar to the cost structure in Hendricks, Piccione, and Tan (1992) and Starr and Stinchcombe (1992). In Starr and Stinchcombe (1992) we analyzed the cost minimizing structure of airline route systems. There are n cities to be linked by airline routes. Direct flights between each city pair implies $\frac{1}{2}n(n-1)$ air routes. A hub-and-spoke network uses only $n-1$, at the cost, however, of causing some passengers to travel redundant mileage and to incur the delays of changes of plane. The saving in routes is efficient if there are strong set-up costs on each route and if the costs of extra mileage are correspondingly low. A transportation cost function displaying sufficient scale economy causes the route structure of the airlines to minimize costs for a given level of service with a hub-and-spoke network. All travel passes through the hub to take advantage of scale economies (declining average cost per passenger) at the level of a single flight.

In the present study of trading structure, we will find similarly that for suitable transaction cost structures, transaction cost minimization implies that all trade pass through a unique (but arbitrary) money to take advantage of scale economies (declining average cost per unit transaction) at the level of the trading post. If we depict the structure of trading relations as a graph, direct trade of each good for each other good would look like the map of an airline route system with direct links among all n cities (n commodities). The graph of a monetary trade system will look like a hub-and-spoke system with the monetary commodity at the hub. This observation gave rise to an examination question at the University of California at San Diego: "Why is money like Chicago's O'Hare airport?"

Most models of money as a medium of exchange, following Jevons (1875) (see also Ostroy and Starr [1974], and the models discussed in Ostroy and Starr [1990]) focus on trade as an interaction between individual agents in the economy – the primitive unit is the pair of traders. The present study, following Walras's discussion above, treats the primitive unit as pairs of commodities in which active trade takes place. In this it follows the approach of Rogawski and Shubik (1986), and of Shubik (1973; 1993).

The pairs of goods in active trade for one another will be described by a binary relation on the set of goods. A trading relation in which most goods are traded for one another will be nonmonetary; a trading relation in which there is a distinguished good for which most goods are traded but where most goods are not traded directly for one another is monetary with the distinguished good acting as money. The trading relation will be determined endogenously as a cost minimizer subject to fulfillment of demands and supplies. We seek to establish the observation that "money buys goods and goods buy money but goods do not buy goods" Clower (1967), as the result of optimization rather than as an assumption.

2   Initial conditions

Let there be n goods, denoted $i = 1, 2, 3, \ldots, n$, constituting the set N. Prices will be denoted by $p \in P$, the unit simplex in $\mathbb{R}^n_+$. Let the typical trading household be denoted h, an element of the (finite) set of households $\mathcal{H}$, $\#\mathcal{H} \geq 2$. For each $h \in \mathcal{H}$, $z^h \in \mathbb{R}^n$ is h's excess demand vector. We assume that z^h fulfills household h's budget constraint (2.1) and that market excess demands at p clear (2.2). Hence we assume:

$$p \cdot z^h = 0 \tag{2.1}$$

and

$$\sum_{h \in \mathcal{H}} z^h = 0 \tag{2.2}$$

Let $\tilde{Z} \equiv [z^h]_{h \in \mathcal{H}}$ where $[\cdot]_{h \in \mathcal{H}}$ denotes the $\#\mathcal{H} \times n$ matrix. We maintain the following nontriviality assumptions on the problem of organizing trade:

All goods are traded, that is, $\tilde{Z}$ has no column of 0's, and $\#\mathcal{H} + n < \#\mathcal{H} \cdot n$.

We describe an array of trading posts as a relation R on N following Haller (1989a; 1989b). The intended interpretation is that iRj if there is a trading post for trade of i and j. The notation $\neg iRj$ denotes "it is not the case that iRj."[1] By convention, there is no trading post for trade of i with i, that is, $\neg iRi$ for all $i \in N$. Viewing R as a subset of $N \times N$, this can be rewritten as $\Delta \cap R = \emptyset$, where Δ is the diagonal in $N \times N$. When convenient, we also regard any relation S on N as a correspondence by defining $S(i) = \{j: iRj\}$. Thus, for a trading post structure R, $R(i)$ is the set of j that can be acquired with i by direct trade.

For arbitrary relations S on N we will use the following notation:

i   For $m \in \mathbb{N}$, define the relation S^m by iS^mj if there are m commodities $i = i_1, i_2, \ldots, i_{m-1}, i_m = j$, such that i_jRi_{j+1} for $j = 1, 2, \ldots, m - 1$. For a trading post structure R, $R^m(i)$ is the set of goods j that can be acquired by trade starting with i in exactly m successive trades.

ii For $m \in \mathbb{N}$, let $\overline{S}^m$ denote $\cup_{m' \leq m} S^{m'}$. For a trading post structure R, $i\overline{R}^mj$ if it is possible to trade i for j in m or fewer successive trades. $\overline{S}^n = \overline{S}$ is the transitive closure of S.

iii For $i \in N$, $S_-(i)$ denotes the set $\{j \in N: jSi\}$. For a trading post structure R, $R_-(i)$ is the set of goods for which i can be acquired by a single direct trade, $\overline{R}^m_-(i)$ is the set of goods for which i can be acquired in m or fewer trades, and $R^m_-(i)$ denotes the set of goods for which i can be acquired in exactly m trades.

We will restrict attention to trading post structures R, connected in the sense that it is possible to trade each good i for any other j in a succession of trades using the trading posts available. Formally, this is the requirement that

$$\overline{R}^n = N \times N \tag{2.3}$$

---

[1] Stinchcombe (1968) also contains a variety of network models of social phenomena.

or equivalently, $E \subset \bar{R}^n$, where $E = \{N \times N\} \backslash \Delta$ is the relation iEj for all $i \neq j$.

Finally we require

$$R \text{ is a symmetric binary relation on } N \times N \qquad (2.4)$$

That is, we suppose that the trading post where i can be traded for j is the trading post where j can be traded for i.

As an aid to intuition, it is often convenient to have a matrix representation of trading post structures. For this purpose we use adjacency matrices (Lawler [1976], p. 22). For example, if R is the cyclical trading post structure $1 \rightarrow 2, 2 \rightarrow 3, 3 \rightarrow 4$, and $4 \rightarrow 1$, then the following four matrices represent R, R^2, R^3, $\bar{R}^3$, and $\bar{R}^4$.

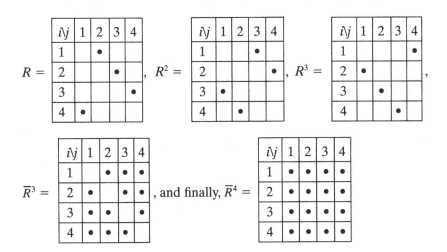

$R =$

i\j	1	2	3	4
1		•		
2			•	
3				•
4	•			

$R^2 =$

i\j	1	2	3	4
1			•	
2				•
3	•			
4		•		

$R^3 =$

i\j	1	2	3	4
1				•
2	•			
3		•		
4			•	

$\bar{R}^3 =$

i\j	1	2	3	4
1		•	•	•
2	•		•	•
3	•	•		•
4	•	•	•	

and finally, $\bar{R}^4 =$

i\j	1	2	3	4
1	•	•	•	•
2	•	•	•	•
3	•	•	•	•
4	•	•	•	•

In this case, $\bar{R}^3$ is equal to E, the trading post structure where every good is connected by a direct trade to every other good.

In a similar fashion, if R is the monetary trading post structure with the money $k = 1$, the corresponding graphs are

$R =$

i\j	1	2	3	4
1		•	•	•
2	•			
3	•			
4	•			

and $R^2 =$

i\j	1	2	3	4
1	•	•	•	•
2	•	•	•	•
3	•	•	•	•
4	•	•	•	•

> **Definition 1:** *A trading post structure R is connected if it is possible to trade from each good i to any other good j using the trades available in the trading post structure. Formally, R is connected if $\overline{R}^n = N \times N$ or, equivalently, $E \subset \overline{R}^n$.*

We seek now to describe the array of active trading posts as an optimizing decision.

3   Trade plans

Household h's trading plan is characterized by the $n \times n$ matrix $V^h = (v^h_{ij})$. The intended interpretation is that v^h_{ij} is h's net receipt of i in exchange for j: $v^h_{ij} < 0$ is a delivery of i in exchange for j; $v^h_{ij} > 0$ is a receipt of i in return for j. We expect each good traded to be paid for at the trading post by opposite delivery of the other good traded at the post.

$$p_i v^h_{ij} = -p_j v^h_{ji} \tag{3.1}$$

Further, the trading plans should seek fully to implement h's demands z^h.

$$\sum_j v^h_{ij} = z^h_i \tag{3.2}$$

However, h's trading plans should be consistent with the array of trading posts in active operation according to the relation R. Thus

$$v^h_{ij} \neq 0 \qquad \text{only if} \qquad iRj \qquad \text{or} \qquad jRi \tag{3.3}$$

It is convenient to be able to distinguish h's planned receipts ($v^h_{ij} > 0$) from his planned deliveries ($v^h_{ij} < 0$). To this end, let

$$v^{h+}_{ij} = \begin{cases} v^h_{ij} & \text{if} \quad v^h_{ij} \geq 0 \\ 0 & \text{if} \quad v^h_{ij} < 0 \end{cases} \tag{3.4}$$

and let

$$v^{h-}_{ij} = \begin{cases} 0 & \text{if} \quad v^h_{ij} \geq 0 \\ -v^h_{ij} & \text{if} \quad v^h_{ij} < 0 \end{cases} \tag{3.5}$$

so that h's planned receipts are v^{h+}_{ij}, planned deliveries are v^{h-}_{ij}, and $v^h_{ij} = v^{h+}_{ij} - v^{h-}_{ij}$. We discuss below the endogenous determination of the v^h_{ij}.

To illustrate how R, the array of active trading posts, affects the pattern of trade, consider three very different cases:

- E (the universal array) where there are $\frac{1}{2}n(n-1)$ trading posts and all goods can trade against each other,

- A linear array with $n - 1$ trading posts and only prescribed pairs of goods trade against one another, each good trading against two other goods only, $i_1 \leftrightarrow i_2 \leftrightarrow \ldots \leftrightarrow i_n$, and
- Monetary exchange, where there are $n - 1$ trading posts only but a single good, "money," is one of the goods traded in each pair.

When E is the trading array, all goods trade directly for one another. There are $\frac{1}{2}n(n - 1)$ trading posts in use. Each agent goes to the trading posts dealing in the combination of goods ij where i is one of his excess demands and j is one of his excess supplies. His dollar (unit of account) volume of trade is precisely equal to the value of his excess supplies plus the value of his excess demands, that is, each excess supply is traded once for an excess demand.

In the linear array, there are $n - 1$ trading posts in use. There will typically be only two trading posts available where j, of which the trader has an excess supply, is traded. She chooses the one that will lead eventually to a post trading i for which she has an excess demand. The trader goes to the first chosen trading post to deliver her excess supply and withdraw an equal value of the other good traded at the post. She retrades this good at the adjacent post for a third good, and then to an adjacent post for a fourth good, . . . , eventually arriving with a suitable supply at a post dealing in her desired excess demand for which she then trades. Trading volumes in this setting may be many times the value of excess demands, since each good may be retraded several times as a carrier of value between trading posts.

In the monetary array, there are $n - 1$ trading posts in use. The trader goes to each trading post dealing in a (nonmoney) good for which he has an excess supply and exchanges it for the money good. He then goes to the trading post where one of his demanded goods is traded and exchanges the money for the demanded good. The volume of trade is approximately two times the value of excess supplies plus excess demands (since each of these is traded once for an equal value of money). The number of active trading posts is the same as in the linear array, but the volume of trade is much smaller. The number of trading posts is $\frac{2}{n}$ths the number in the universal array and the gross volume of trade is twice as high.

There are a few other distinctions of the monetary trading array to note. The classical explanation for the use of money is the absence of a double coincidence of wants (Jevons [1875]), that is, absence of a condition where for each agent with an excess supply of i and an excess demand for j, there is a corresponding agent with the opposite demands and supplies. In the present model, the rationale for monetary trade does not depend on the absence of a double coincidence of wants. It is rather a scale economy at the level of the trading arrangements of the economy as a whole. If households' demands and supplies are sufficiently diverse (so that nonmonetary trade would use a large variety of trading posts even with double coincidence) then monetary trade is the low cost trading arrangement when the fixed cost of a trading post is high and marginal costs of trade are low, even in the (rare) case of double coincidence of wants.

Nonmonetary trade in the trading post model, even ignoring transaction costs, has a distinct problem that monetary trade can solve, market clearing at the trading post. Though markets clear for all goods (2.2), there is no guarantee that the flows at any single trading post will clear, that is, that $\Sigma_{h \in \mathcal{H}} v_{ij}^h = 0$. This implies that there is an untreated issue of interpost trade in the nonmonetary model. However, monetary trade resolves this issue. All trade for good i in a monetary trading array is at the trading post for i and money. Hence, in monetary trade (2.1) implies that purchases equal sales at the trading post. This follows simply because monetary trade is exchange of excess demands and supplies for money and (16.1) guarantees that the excess demands and supplies clear.

4   The central problem of efficient exchange

How should an economy arrange its bilateral trade? Some arrays of trading posts may be more costly than others to arrange, sustain, and use for trade.

In particular, if a choice of R (like the linear array) meant that most trades had to go through a circuitous trading sequence, or an alternative choice (like E) meant that many redundant trading posts were kept open, then these might represent excessively costly, nonoptimal choices of trading array. Is it efficient or desirable to organize trade as monetary trade? Given $p \in P$, z^h fulfilling equations (2.1), (2.2), then an optimal choice of R would minimize the cost of V, R subject to equations (3.1)–(3.3).

For all $i,j \in N$ pairs with $i \neq j$, let α_{ij} be a fixed cost of running the trading post for the pair of goods ij. Because we assume that the trading post where i is traded for j is the same as the trading post where j is traded for i, it is natural to assume that $\alpha_{ij} = \alpha_{ji}$. For $i \in N$, let β_i be the marginal cost of flows of good i. Let $\tilde{\alpha}$ and $\tilde{\beta}$ be the vectors of α's and β's. We study cost functions of the form

$$C\left(R, \tilde{Z}; \tilde{\alpha}, \tilde{\beta}\right) = \sum_{\substack{i>j \\ iRj}} \alpha_{ij} + \sum_{i>j} \beta_i \left(m_{ij}^+\left(R, \tilde{Z}, \tilde{\beta}\right) + m_{ij}^-\left(R, \tilde{Z}, \tilde{\beta}\right)\right)$$

$$(4.1)$$

where $m_{ij}^+(R, \tilde{Z}, \tilde{\beta})$ denotes quantity of i delivered to households from the market with j, and $m_{ij}^-(R, \tilde{Z}, \tilde{\beta})$ denotes quantity of i sent by households to the market with j. That is, $m_{ij}^+(R, \tilde{Z}, \tilde{\beta}) = \Sigma_{h \in \mathcal{H}} v_{ij}^{h+}$ and $m_{ij}^-(R, \tilde{Z}, \tilde{\beta})$ $= \Sigma_{h \in \mathcal{H}} v_{ij}^{h-}$ where households choose their planned trades, V^h, in response to R, $\tilde{Z}$, and (potentially) to $\tilde{\beta}$. Specifically, we assume that household h chooses their trading pattern, V^h to be consistent with (3.1)–(3.3), and to minimize

$$\sum_{i>j} \beta_i^h \left(v_{ij}^{h+} + v_{ij}^{h-}\right)$$

$$(4.2)$$

where each $\beta_i^h > 0$. A final piece of notation: At various points in the analysis it becomes convenient to talk about phenomena that are true for "small" vectors $\mathbf{x} \in \mathbb{R}^\ell$, $\ell \in \mathbb{N}$. To this end, we use the notation "$\mathbf{x} \simeq$ $\mathbf{0}$," which is read as "$\mathbf{x}$ is small," or "$\mathbf{x}$ is negligible." Thus, the statement "if $\mathbf{x} \simeq \mathbf{0}$ then $S(\mathbf{x})$ is true" means "if $\mathbf{x}^n$ is a sequence with $\|\mathbf{x}^n\| \to 0$, then for all sufficiently large n, $S(\mathbf{x}^n)$ is true," or equivalently, "there is a neighborhood of $\mathbf{0}$ in which $S(\mathbf{x})$ is true." Thus, negligible vectors or numbers represent the behavior of small numbers and vectors where the exact size of "small" can vary by context. Note that the finite sum of negligible vectors or numbers is again negligible. The notation "$\mathbf{y} \simeq \mathbf{x}$ " is shorthand for "$\mathbf{y} - \mathbf{x} \simeq \mathbf{0}$."

5   Small fixed costs

In this section we consider cost functions for which the marginal costs of trade flows dominate, and the fixed costs are negligible. Section 6 considers the opposite case of negligible marginal costs.

Here, total costs are virtually linear in the quantity of goods traded. The cost minimizing trading post structure is, for generic $\tilde{Z}$, $E(\tilde{Z})$, the array of trading posts containing all pairs of goods which at least one household would like to trade,

$$E\left(\tilde{Z}\right) = \left\{(i, j): \quad \text{for some} \quad h \in \mathcal{H}, \text{sgn}\left(z_i^h\right) \neq \text{sgn}\left(z_j^h\right)\right\} \quad (5.1)$$

In other words, $E(\tilde{Z})$ is the universal relation E minus all those pairs of goods that no household might want to trade.

Genericity enters as follows. Suppose it were possible to partition N into two disjoint sets of goods, N_1 and N_2, with the property that for all $h \in \mathcal{H}$,

$$\sum_{i \in N_1} p_i z_i^h = 0 \quad \text{and} \quad \sum_{i \in N_2} p_i z_i^h = 0 \tag{5.2}$$

In this case, there would be no need to have any trading links between the sets N_1 and N_2 because the households could separately fulfill their desired net trades within the N_1 goods and within the N_2 goods. For any given vector of prices p, it is a generic property of $\tilde{Z}$ that no such partition of N is possible, and it is this genericity that we use. In particular, it implies that any trading structure that allows the households to complete all their desired net trades must be connected. This genericity also implies that if a household might want to trade goods i and j, then they must in fact trade them in order to exactly fulfill their desired net trades.

The trading post array $E(\tilde{Z})$ is the solution in this case because with any other system, some trader(s) would be obliged to trade indirectly, increasing the volume of trade flows and hence increasing costs by a non-negligible amount. In particular, a system of monetary trade with all flows through a single good k cannot be optimal, except in the extreme (and nongeneric) case that all households either have an excess supply of only one good and that single good is k, or they have excess demand for only one good and that single good is k.

We wish to describe the efficient trading post arrays, R, as cost minimizing solutions for the following problem,

$$\left[\text{Symmetric}(m) \right]$$

$$\min_R C\left(R, \tilde{Z}\right) \quad \text{s.t.} \quad E \subseteq \overline{R}^m \quad \text{and} \quad R \quad \text{symmetric}$$
$$\tag{5.3}$$

Here m is a positive integer indicating the maximum number of trading posts at which the household may need to trade successively in order to exchange good i for good j. In other words, the constraints are that R be symmetric and connected in m or fewer steps. Note that when $m \geq n$, $\overline{R}^m = \overline{R}^n = \overline{R}$, so that the problem Symmetric(n) has no restrictions beyond symmetry and connectedness. We will use the restriction implied by m only once in Theorem 2 of Section 6. There we intend it as a proxy for the costs of many successive trades. In this section, the cost of many successive trades is the object of analysis.

Theorem 1:   *If $\tilde{\alpha} > 0$ and $\tilde{\alpha} \simeq 0$ and $\tilde{\beta} > 0$, then for generic $\tilde{Z}$, $E(\tilde{Z})$ is the unique solution to the problem Symmetric(n).*

Proof: We present the proof in two parts. First we argue at the level of the household that direct trade is optimal. Second, we show that the same result holds at the level of the economy. The essential intuition in both cases is that any pattern of trade other than the most direct increases indirect flows and this increases cost.

Consider first household h's decision to choose the trading pattern v_{ij}^h. By assumption, they are trying to minimize a function which can be rewritten as $\frac{1}{2}\Sigma_{i,j}(\beta_i^h + \beta_j^h) \cdot (v_{ij}^{h+} + v_{ij}^{h-})$. Suppose it is possible to reroute a quantity of trade δ between goods 1 and 2 through good 3. This leads to a change of $\frac{1}{2}$ times $(-\beta_1^h + \beta_2^h)\delta + (\beta_1^h + \beta_3^h)\delta + (\beta_2^h + \beta_3^h)\delta = \beta_2^h\delta$ in the objective function. Thus, for any proposed route structure, moving in a direction of more direct trade, $\delta < 0$, lowers the function to be minimized. Thus, household h will choose direct trade if possible.

Turning now to the economywide problem, substituting β_i and β_j for β_i^h and β_j^h in the above argument shows that the most direct possible trade also solves the problem of minimizing the total cost of flows. Because $\tilde{\alpha} \simeq \mathbf{0}$, the cost of any given trading post that some household might want to pay is negligible in comparison to the saving to be had by including it in the trading post array. Finally, because $\tilde{\alpha} > 0$, we save by omitting unused trading posts, and the result is $E(\check{Z})$. QED.

The following demonstrates some of the range of trading post arrays that may arise as solutions in Theorem 1.

Example 1: *Suppose that the matrix of excess demands is given by*

$h\backslash i$	1	2	3	4
1	+1	−1	0	0
2	0	+1	−1	0
3	0	0	+1	−1
4	−1	0	0	+1

so that $E(\check{Z})$ is the symmetric, cyclical trading post structure satisfying 1R2, 2R3, 3R4, and 4R1.

6   Small marginal costs and monetary trade

We now examine the implications of negligible marginal costs, a situation where the fixed costs of trading posts dominate, formally, $\tilde{\beta} \simeq \mathbf{0}$ and

$\tilde{\alpha} > 0$. In this case, the minimal total cost is achieved by establishing the minimal number of trading posts consistent with $E \subset \bar{R}^m$, that is, connecting all commodities with the minimal number of trading posts. This is $(n - 1)$. The trading posts could then be in the form of a line, $i_1 \leftrightarrow i_2 \leftrightarrow \ldots \leftrightarrow i_n$, a hub-and-spoke array (monetary trade), or a variety of alternative configurations.

Line structures of trading post arrays have an obvious drawback from the point of view of the traders; a single exchange of one good for another in a line array might involve as many as $n - 1$ distinct transactions as an excess supply was traded for each of a succession of intervening goods with active trading posts, eventually achieving the good in excess demand. In a cycle this trade might require $\frac{1}{2}(n - 1)$ transactions. Our proxy for this cost is the restriction that traders need make no more than m distinct transactions in order to complete a two good (one supply, one demand) trade. If $m = 1$, then the only connected trading post structure is a system of trading posts for every commodity pair, E. The case $m = 2$ corresponds to retrading more than once being prohibitively expensive. In this context, with low variable costs and fixed costs approximately uniform, we are led to monetary trade networks with a single money, Theorem 2. Example 2 below shows that the assumption of approximately uniform fixed costs cannot be loosened and gives some sense of the range of possible cost minimizing trading arrays.

By contrast, when the fixed costs are not uniform and m is unrestricted, we are led to multi-money systems, Theorem 3 below. In Example 3 below, multiple currencies ($ and £) arise as efficient allocations where the cost structure favors concentrating trade in US goods on $ and UK goods on £ allowing trade between US and UK goods to require three steps. Here, $m = 3$ corresponds to US goods to $, $ to £, £ to UK goods, rather than the $m = 2$ of a monetary trading array with a single money.

It seems then that the emergence of a single money is unlikely. However, Corollary 4 gives sufficient conditions for a good to be a "natural" money under the conditions of Theorem 3. This leads us to a brief discussion of the rate-of-return dominance puzzle and its relation to this work.

6.1   The emergence of a single money

We begin with our definition of a money.

> **Definition 2:** *A monetary trade system with a single money $k \in N$ is a relation R such that iRk and kRi for all $i \neq k$, and $\neg iRj$ if neither i nor j is equal to k.*

Note that monetary trade systems with a single money are connected. Indeed, $\bar{R}^2 = N \times N$. Further, they have $(n - 1)$ trading posts in them.

Theorem 2: *If $\#N \geq 3$, $\tilde{\beta} \simeq 0$, $\tilde{\alpha} \simeq \alpha \cdot \tilde{\mathbf{1}}$, $\alpha > 0$, then the only solutions to Symmetric(2) are monetary trade systems with a single money.*

Proof: Because $\tilde{\beta} \simeq 0$ and $\tilde{\alpha} \simeq \alpha \tilde{\mathbf{1}}$, it is sufficient to show that monetary trade systems with one money are the only solutions to the problem

$$\min_R \#R \quad \text{s.t.} \quad E \subset \bar{R}^2, \quad R \text{ symmetric} \quad (6.1)$$

Monetary trade systems with a single money satisfy the constraint and have $(n - 1)$ trading posts in them. Hence, if R is a solution to (6.1), then $\#R \leq 2(n - 1)$.

Let $\underline{m}$ denote $\min_{i \in N} \#R(i)$. Because R is connected, we know that $\underline{m} > 0$. If $\underline{m} \geq 2$, then $\#R \geq 2n$, a contradiction. Hence $\underline{m} = 1$. Let $\bar{m} = \max_{i \in N} \#R(i)$. As an intermediate step in the proof, we will show that if $n = \#N \geq 4$, then $\bar{m} = n - 1$.

Let i' be a point in N such that $\#R(i') = 1$. If $\bar{m} \leq n - 3$, then it is impossible to get from i' to some point $j \in N$ in 2 or fewer trades, violating the constraint. Hence, either $\bar{m} = n - 2$ or $\bar{m} = n - 1$.

Suppose that $\bar{m} = n - 2$ and let k be a point (commodity) in N with $\#R(k) = n - 2$. Because $\#R \leq 2(n - 1)$ and $\underline{m} = 1$, there is at most 1 point $j \in N\backslash\{k\}$ such that $\#R(j) = 2$. Because N has at least 4 points in it, $\#R(i') = \#R(i'') = 1$ for some pair $i' \neq i''$ in N. But because $\bar{m} = n - 2$, from either i' or i'' (or both), it is impossible to reach some point $j \in N$. This violates the constraint, hence $\bar{m} = n - 1$.

To finish the proof, let k be that point in N such that $\#R(k) = n - 1$ (there clearly cannot be two k with this property). Because $\bar{m} = n - 1$, $\underline{m} = 1$, and $\#R \leq 2(n - 1)$, we know that for all $i \neq k$, $\#R(i) = 1$. If for some $i \neq k$, $R(i) \neq \{k\}$, then there is some $j \in N$ that cannot be reached from i in two steps, violating the constraint. Hence S is a monetary trade system with money k.
QED.

If $\tilde{\alpha} \neq \alpha\tilde{\mathbf{1}}$, the conclusions of Theorem 2 can fail quite conclusively.

Example 2 (Yes we have no money) *Let $\#N = 4$, $\tilde{\beta}, \tilde{\gamma} \simeq 0$. Suppose that $\alpha_{ij} = \alpha_{ji}$, $\alpha_{12} = \alpha_{23} = \alpha_{34} = \alpha_{41} = 1$ whereas $\alpha_{13} =$*

$\alpha_{24} = x$. *Let S denote a monetary trade system with money being any point in N. The cost of S is* $4 + 2x$ *plus a finite sum of negligibles. Let R denote the symmetric trading post structure connecting all pairs except* $\{1,3\}$ *and* $\{2,4\}$. *The cost of R is 8 plus a finite sum of negligibles. It is easy to check that* $\overline{R}^2 = E$. *For* $x >$ *2, R is strictly better than S.*

6.2   The emergence of multiple moneys

To state our next result, it is convenient to use some concepts from graph theory.

Definition 3:   *A graph G on N is a pair* (N,A) *where N is a finite set and A is a collection of unordered pairs, arcs, of elements of N. A path from i to j in a graph G is an ordered sequence of nodes in N,* $i = i_1,i_2,\ldots,i_{K-1},i_K = j$, *where each arc* (i_k,i_{k+1}), $k = 1,\ldots,$ $K - 1$ *is in A. G is connected if there is a path from each i to each j in N. For* $h \geq 2$, *an h-cycle is a path from i to i containing h arcs in which no node except i is repeated. If G is connected and contains no h-cycles,* $h \geq 3$, *it is called a tree.*

We relate this to our trading post arrays by

Definition 4:   *For a symmetric binary relation R, the graph associated with R is* (N,A) *where A is the set of unordered pairs* (i,j) *such that* iRj.

Note that $\#R = 2 \cdot \#A$ when (N,A) is the graph associated with R.

Unlike Theorem 2, the following result puts no restriction on the number of trading posts a household may need to visit in order to fulfill their desired net trades.

Theorem 3:   *If* $\tilde{\beta} \simeq 0$ *and* $\tilde{\alpha} > 0$, *then the graph associated with any solution, R, to Symmetric(n) is a tree. In particular,* $\#R = 2(n - 1)$.

Proof: Let R be a solution to Symmetric(n) and let G be the graph associated with R. If R has an h-cycle, $h \geq 3$, removing one of the arcs reduces cost by a nonnegligible amount because $\tilde{\alpha} > 0$, increases costs by a negligible amount because $\tilde{\beta} \simeq 0$, and it leaves R connected. Therefore, R has no h-cycles, $h \geq 3$, and is a tree. But this is equivalent to G being connected and having $n - 1$ arcs (Lawler [1976], Prop. 5.2).   QED.

The monetary trade systems that arise in Theorem 2 are trees where only one good, the money, is directly connected to many other commodities. The following two-money example indicates some of the range of tree structures that may arise as solutions under the conditions of Theorem 3.

Example 3 (An International Perspective) *Suppose that $n = n_1 + n_2$, and that n_1 of the commodities in N are in the United States and n_2 in the United Kingdom. Pick a distinguished node in the United States and call it $US, pick a distinguished node in the United Kingdom and call it £ Sterling. Consider the symmetric relation connecting all of the United States (respectively United Kingdom) commodities to $ US (respectively £ Sterling), as well as connecting $ US and £ Sterling. This symmetric relation is connected, $\overline{R}^3 = N \times N$, and its graph is a tree so that $\#R = 2(n - 1)$.*

In Example 3, the relation was a pair of monetary trade systems, each with a single money, joined together with an arc between the distinguished nodes $ US and £Sterling. This is a special case of a more general construction. The restrictions $E \subset \overline{R}^n$ and $\#R = 2(n - 1)$ are always satisfied by such trading post structures that are built by connecting smaller monetary trade systems, each with a single money: Begin with a distinguished point, i_0; connect it to $n(i_0) \geq 1$ other points using a monetary trade system with money i_0. For each point i_1 in the resulting system, connect it to $n(i_1) \geq 0$ other points using a monetary trade system with money i_1. Such a process can be continued indefinitely. Having $n(i_t)$ large gives a very "bushy" trading post structure with a small number of very heavily used moneys; having $n(i_t)$ small gives a "sprawling" trading post structure with many moneys.

Note that monetary trading structures arise without any distinctive designation of the properties of "money" in the cost function; it is the cost structure of trade rather than a low cost of trading money that generates the concentration on common trading medium. Intuitively, it is clear that adding such complications to the cost structure would tend to concentrate the solution on a smaller number of moneys. We investigate two factors that might lead to such concentration. The first is the existence of a "natural" money, the second is a formalization of Professor Tobin's (1980) observation that the use of "a particular money by one individual increases its value to other actual or potential users." This last observation turns out to be intimately related (in our framework) to the rate-of-return dominance puzzle.

6.3   A natural money

As noted, the trading arrays that arise in Theorem 3 may have many moneys. Let K be the set of "moneys" in a tree, $K = \{k: \#R(k) \geq 2\}$. The cost of such an array is, ignoring marginal costs,

$$\sum_{k \in K} \sum_{i \in R(k)} \alpha_{ki} \tag{6.2}$$

Now, a good k is a natural money if most or all of the α_{ki} are relatively small. Thus, an immediate sufficient condition for k to be a "natural" money is that the α_{ki} be small relative to the other α's.

> **Corollary 4:** *Assume that $\tilde{\beta} \simeq 0$. Suppose further that for some $k \in N$ and for all $i \neq k$, $\alpha_{ki} \simeq 0$ while $\alpha_{ij} \geq \alpha$ for some $\alpha > 0$ for all ij pairs not containing k. Then the unique solution to Symmetric(n) is a monetary trade system with the single money k.*

> *Proof:* As indicated.   QED.

6.4   Rate-of-return dominance

One of the classic issues of microeconomic monetary theory is rate-of-return dominance according to Hicks: "What has to be explained is the decision to hold assets in the form of barren money, rather than of interest- or profit-yielding securities." This model suggests the question "Are there solutions to Symmetric(m) that are dominated?" The answer is "no." Symmetric(m) asks for a global minimum, and a global minimum will be a minimum globally. Alternatively, is the choice of a monetary trading array self-enforcing locally even if it is dominated globally?

Professor Tobin suggests that the answer is "yes."

Why are some assets selected by a society as generally acceptable media of exchange while others are not? This is not an easy question because the answer is self-justifying. . . . The principal reason . . . that Treasury bills are not media of exchange is that they are not generally acceptable. This unsatisfactory circular conclusion underlines the essential point, that general acceptability in exchange is one of those phenomena – like language, rules of the road, fashion in dress – where the fact of social consensus is much more important and more predictable than the content. (1980)

Let us first consider incremental moves from one monetary trading array to another under the conditions of Theorem 2, specifically, $m = 2$, that all goods can be traded in two or fewer steps. For example, suppose that Treasury bills are a superior money in the sense of Corollary 4 but that society presently uses the single money, $ US. Changing the trading post between good i and $ US and to a trading post between good i and Treasury Bills lowers total costs, but it violates the condition that all goods be connected in two steps. The restriction $m = 2$ in solving the problem Symmetric(2) secures the choice of a single monetary instrument against small perturbations in the trading array, even in the presence of a potentially superior monetary instrument.

This argument breaks down when m is unrestricted as in Theorem 3. Suppose also that R is any monetary trading array that includes Treasury bills but for which Treasury bills are not the single money. Open any trading post between a good i and Treasury bills and close any of the trading posts between i and some other good j. This results in a lower cost connected trading array that may require more steps. Thus, provided m is unrestricted, small changes toward the best money in *any* alternative arrangement lead to improvements. Any money other than the best one is unstable to small changes in this sense.

This instability depends on there being no advantages to concentration per se. Suppose that instead of the a_{ij}'s being fixed independent of R and the v_{ij}^h's, they depend on the volume of trade through the nodes. Specifically, suppose that the cost of trade through the good k is an increasing and concave function of the total volume of trade through k. A natural money in this context would be one for which the concave function is uniformly lower than it is for any other good. With concavity, an inferior money may well prove to be stable to small changes. All that is needed is that the first small increases in trading volume with the superior money cost more than they cost when they were the last units traded with the inferior money.

Once the trading post array is monetary with a single money, there is a strong incentive for additional trading posts to use that money as well. There is a small scale economy built into the specification of the problem by the fixed cost a_{ij} (or the concave cost function) at each trading post. The interaction across posts through the implementation of the array of agents' excess demands turns this small scale economy into a large systemic scale economy.

References

Clower, R. W. 1967. "A Reconsideration of the Microfoundations of Monetary Theory," *Western Economic Journal*, 6:1–8.
Freeman, S. 1989. "Fiat Money as a Medium of Exchange," *International Economic Review*, 30:137–51.

Granot, F., and A. F. Veinott, Jr. 1985. Substitutes, complements and ripples in network flows. *Mathematics of Operations Research*, (10)3:471–97.

Haller, H. 1989a. Topologies as trade infrastructures. Virginia Polytechnic Institute and State University, Department of Economics, Working Paper, November.

Haller, H. 1989b. Large random graphs in pseudo-metric spaces. Virginia Polytechnic Institute and State University, Department of Economics, Working Paper, November.

Hendricks, K., M. Piccione, and G. Tan. 1995. The economics of hubs: The case of monopoly. *Review of Economic Studies*, 62:83–99.

Jevons, W. S. 1875. *Money and the Mechanism of Exchange*. London: H. S. King.

Lawler, E. 1976. *Combinatorial Optimization, Networks and Matroids*. New York: Holt, Rinehart, and Winston.

Ostroy, J. M., and R. M. Starr. 1974. Money and the decentralization of exchange. *Econometrica*, 42:1093–113.

Ostroy, J. M., and R. M. Starr. 1990. The transactions role of money. In *Handbook of Monetary Economics*, ed. B. Friedman and F. H. Hahn. Amsterdam: North Holland.

Rogawski, J., and M. Shubik. 1986. A strategic market game with transaction costs. *Mathematical Social Sciences*, 11(2):139–60.

Shubik, M. 1973. Commodity money, oligopoly, credit and bankruptcy in a general equilibrium model. *Western Economic Journal*, 11(March):24–38.

Shubik, M. 1993. *The Theory of Money and Financial Institutions*. Cambridge: MIT Press.

Starr, R. M., and M. B. Stinchcombe. 1992. Efficient transportation routing and natural monopoly in the airline industry: An economic analysis of hub-spoke and related systems. University of California, San Diego, Working Paper, May.

Stinchcombe, A. L. 1968. *Constructing Social Theories*. New York: Harcourt, Brace, and World.

Tobin, J. 1959. *The Tobin Manuscript*. Mimeograph. New Haven: Yale University.

Tobin, J. 1980. Discussion. In *Models of Monetary Economies*, ed. J. Kareken and N. Wallace. Minneapolis: Federal Reserve Bank of Minneapolis.

Tobin, J., and S. Golub. 1998. *Money, Credit, and Capital*. Boston: Irwin/McGraw-Hill.

Walras, L. 1954. *Elements of Pure Economics*. Jaffe translation. Homewood, IL: Irwin.

CHAPTER 12

Equilibrium market formation causes missing markets

Walter P. Heller

1   How markets emerge

Kenneth Arrow (1969) was perhaps the first to point out that markets are not a fixture of the economy, but are the results of decisions made by private economic agents and government agencies. Private agents will establish a market in a particular good only if the costs of doing so are more than met by gains. Such markets are *open*. Gains are the expected markup over the price paid to owners or producers of the good. Setup costs may be present because there are costs of organization which are independent of scale. These include administration, exclusion, information gathering, and dissemination.

A market for a particular commodity will fail to exist when private calculations show that there is no profit in its existence. No price is quoted and no transactions can take place. Such markets are *closed*. Market failure arises when private calculations dictate a closed market, but a social calculation shows that a gain is possible through exchange. Government action can make profitable the establishment of a market when there is market failure.

Externality is a case in point: Exclusion is either too costly under existing modes of organization or impossible because property rights have not been established. See Arrow (1969). An auction market in pollution rights could be farmed out to an entrepreneur, if property rights were established, and monitoring mechanisms were sufficiently cheap.

Thus, in the case of externalities, exclusion is impossible unless there is government action. Exclusion may be possible at low cost, but infor-

Thanks go to participants at CORE, the Workshop on General Equilibrium at Zinal, the SPES Conference on Markets as Games, Stanford, UC Davis, and USC. Particular thanks to Kenneth Arrow, Don Brown, Graciela Chichilnisky, Birgit Grodal, Heracles Polemarchakis, Martine Quinzii, and an anonymous referee for useful comments.

mation is decentralized and market prices are the only channels of communication. A market will open and a price will be quoted if there is a prospect of profit, since such actions are costly. It may not be profitable for one market to open if the market in some complementary commodity is closed. This latter market is not profitable if the first market is closed. Closed, and therefore missing, markets could be a noncooperative equilibrium. There could also be equilibrium if both markets are open, but only in this instance is the equilibrium Pareto efficient. This situation is classic coordination failure.

The nonexistence of markets is mutually reinforcing when there are pecuniary externalities (Rosenstein-Rodan [1943]; Scitovsky [1954]). This classic example assumes that there are two firms, both having setup cost technologies. Thus, an electric power plant would be profitable only if a bauxite refinery were buying electric power, and conversely, the bauxite refinery would be profitable only if there were plentiful electricity. There is a coordination failure. As Arrow pointed out in Scitovsky (1954, fn. 16), a futures market in electricity would provide the proper signals.

Coordination failure in models of market (or product) innovation has been formally analyzed by Durlauf (1992), Hart (1980), Makowski (1980), and Makowski and Ostroy (1995).[1] Models of innovation in securities markets include Allen and Gale (1988; 1990; 1994), Bisin (1992; 1994), Duffie and Rahi (1995), and Pesendorfer (1995). In this type of economy, one finds Pareto inefficiency, but not coordination failure.

2   Open, inactive, and closed markets

A market is *open* if a price is quoted to all participants and transactions can take place freely. Otherwise, the market is *closed*. A market could be open, but with no transactions taking place at the quoted price because the supply curve is always above the demand curve. Such a market is *inactive*.

An interesting question is why an Arrow futures market is not open in Scitovsky's example. Heller and Starrett (1976) suggested it might be because

the demand for future contracts is low because they are perceived as risky. (One may not wish to make a long-term commitment to a particular grade of aluminum when technological change may make that grade obsolete.) Then, the inactivity on the futures markets may be explained by the nonexistence of a complementary market, in this case an insurance market for these technological risks.

[1] See also the informal remarks of Hahn (1990).

The insurance marketmaker fails to open operations because he perceives no current demand from the inactive futures market.

Thus, if either market opened, it would be profitable to open the other one, and there would be a gain in economic efficiency. The implication is clear: Missing markets can occur endogenously.[2]

I show there can be multiple, Pareto-rankable equilibria in the market formation model as well.[3] Here, the coordination failure occurs in competition, because of the informational differences for the decentralized agents. If either the power plant agent or the bauxite agent had the same information about technologies as their counterpart, a Pareto efficient equilibrium would be possible. The following example[4] illustrates the problem.

Suppose that each marketmaker correctly perceives demand on his market as a function of his own price. But demand in a market is also affected by the quantities transacted on other markets. However, the marketmaker has informational myopia about other markets: He does not recognize that new markets may open in response to his opening first.

In Figure 1, with constant marginal costs of providing services (futures or insurance) above the demand curve in each case, both markets will be closed. This noncooperative equilibrium will be Pareto inefficient by comparison with a complete markets competitive equilibrium. This is illustrated in Figure 2. Each market can run at a profit under any imperfectly competitive pricing rule if the other market operates.

3   Market formation

These examples suggest an equilibrium model of market formation. A particular *market* spectrum σ of open and closed markets is hypothesized. The vector σ consists of 0's and 1's, denoting closed and open markets, respectively. Each household is assumed to maximize its utility subject to its budget constraint and a transaction constraint requiring purchases and sales in closed markets is assumed to be zero. The household budget constraint is defined only over open markets. Each producer maximizes profits subject to the usual constraints and the additional restriction that transactions occur only on open markets. There are also agents in the economy, called *marketmakers*, who specialize in the operation of markets. Marketmakers behave like firms in that they max-

---

[2] See the analysis of Figures 1 and 2 below.
[3] See Heller (1986) for an analysis of coordination failure when markets are already open.
[4] See Heller and Starrett (1976).

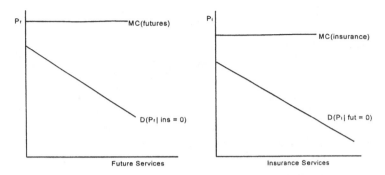

Figure 1. Before futures and insurance markets are introduced.

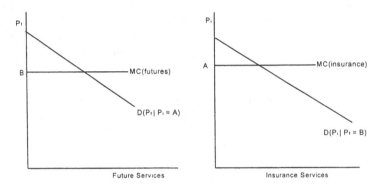

Figure 2. After one of the markets is introduced.

imize profits subject to technological constraints. As postulated in Foley (1970) or Hahn (1971), some marketmakers earn profits by buying wholesale and selling retail. However, marketmakers in this model differ from those of Foley and Hahn in that they may face the decision of price or quantity setting in markets that can have no quoted price in their absence. In addition, each marketmaker can operate in at most one market. This is one way of capturing the notion of decentralized agents who possess local information only about a particular product or service.

One reason for assuming partial equilibrium knowledge by market-makers is to capture the notion that information about a market is private to that market. This maintains the spirit of myopic information in the competitive model. Nevertheless, it is possible that agents, through a familiarity with recent history of open markets, have knowledge of the effects of their actions on open markets, but not on closed markets. They do not realize that opening their market might make profitable another market that is now closed, but they do recognize the general equilibrium interdependencies between their market and any open market. This is the general equilibrium information structure of Hart (1980), Makowski (1980), and Makowski and Ostroy (1995).

I consider a more restrictive information set for the marketmaker: A competitive marketmaker takes as given other closed markets, prices, and incomes. The marketmaker is assumed to know the *partial* equilibrium demand and supply functions for this product that would obtain *ceteris paribus*. In other words, the marketmaker does partial equilibrium market research. He then chooses whether to open his market and, if so, at what volume to operate. This kind of myopia seems quite realistic when the markets are widely separated by location, commodity characteristics, or time of delivery. It also makes possible the following question: When is general equilibrium forecasting necessary for Pareto efficiency? See Heal's Chapter in this volume for more on this.

I consider two cases that are polar opposites: perfect competition and monopolistic competition. In the former case, if the market in a particular commodity is already open with buying and selling prices specified, any marketmaker will enter that market if it is profitable to do so. Thus, a potential marketmaker might be ex ante a monopolist, but ex post a perfect competitor. With monopolistic competition, there is no free entry, and all marketmakers are Nashlike monopolists. This case would arise when setup costs are large relative to the size of the market.

I will say that a *Market Formation Equilibrium* exists if there are a price vector and an allocation vector that clear the open markets in the spectrum under the above maximization assumptions on households, producers, and marketmakers. In addition, I require that potential marketmakers on closed markets foresee only negative returns to entry.

There are two examples that may help illustrate these ideas, and these examples will demonstrate the kinds of market pathologies that can arise even without market power. In the first case, there will be in equilibrium too few open markets for Pareto efficiency in the presence of complementary goods. The second illustrates that too many markets may be open as well. This case occurs when there are market setup costs, and there is substitutability among some of the goods.

Example 1: Endogenous missing markets
The first example involves quasiconcave differentiable utility functions, but violates the simultaneous reservation price property of Hart

(1980).[5] Let there be two consumers with three goods and the following utilities and endowments:

$$U^1 = \left(c_{11}c_{21}\right)^{1/2} + \left(1/2\right)c_{31}; \qquad \omega^1 = \left(1, 0, 2\right)$$

$$U^2 = \left(c_{12}c_{32}\right)^{1/2} + \left(1/2\right)c_{22}; \qquad \omega^2 = \left(1, 2, 0\right)$$

These two functions are concave since they are the sums of concave functions. A complete market competitive equilibrium is $p_1 = p_2 = p_3 = 1$, with $\sigma_{hk} = 1$ and $c_{hk} = 1$, all h, k.

If the market in good 2 is closed, there is no incentive for a market in good 3 to open. Person one is the sole owner of good 3 and has no desire for good 1 when he cannot buy good 2, so no amount of money will induce person one to reduce his consumption of good 3. A similar argument shows that without an open market in good 3, person two cannot be induced to part with good 2, so the market in that good will not open.

If there were a merger of the two marketmakers, the externalities would be internalized and the market failure would vanish. However, in a complex system of markets without a rich variety of communication channels, the two marketmakers are unlikely to find each other. These are precisely the circumstances where incomplete markets are a likely outcome of private calculation, and some government coordination is desirable.

Example 2: Complete markets can be Pareto inefficient (with transactions costs)

Two consumers have identical concave utilities given by

$$U = \log c_1 c_2 + \min\left(c_3, c_4\right).$$

Endowments are $\omega^1 = (1, 1, 3, 2)$, $\omega^2 = (1, 1, 2, 3)$

The markets in goods 1 and 2 operate without cost. The markets in goods 3 and 4 operate with identical setup costs of technologies of 0.1 of units of good 1 and 0.1 units of good 2 for any positive level of transactions. Consumers own equal shares of the marketmakers. A complete markets equilibrium allocation here is $c^1 = c^2 = (0.9, 0.9, 2.5, 2.5)$. Each person is getting utility of $2 \log 0.90 + 2.5 = 2.289$ in equilibrium.

One can show that marketmaker 4 would open even if the market in good 3 were closed and vice versa. If any one market is open in this

---

[5] This is not a counterexample to his Proposition 4, as the utility functions are not strictly increasing at zero consumption.

example, the other market will also open. Therefore the only nontrivial market equilibrium is the complete markets equilibrium.

Now suppose the market in good 4 were closed by fiat. It turns out that in this "restricted market equilibrium,"[6] the first person has utility $2 \log 1.233 + 2 = 2.419$, whereas the second person has $2 \log 0.666 + 3 = 2.595$, where the allocations are $c^1 = (1.233, 1.233, 2, 2)$ and $c^2 = (0.666, 0.666, 3, 3)$. One can also show that marketmaker 4 would make a profit by opening, if he were allowed to do so. In sum, both are better off than in the free entry complete markets equilibrium. Fewer markets are better.

4   The model

There are goods $h = 1, \ldots, H$. There is a *market spectrum*, σ, an H-dim vector. $\sigma_h = 0$ means the market is *closed*, no trades are possible in h. Similarly $\sigma_h = 1$ means the market is *open* for trade in h, and prices for good h are quoted on that market.

Let Σ = set of permissible market spectra, and let Σ be contained in the set of all possible combinations of 0's and 1's in an H-dimensional vector. Since the market structure can be incomplete, I must specify the agents' market information set: They know which markets are open and they know which markets are closed. As in Foley (1970), agents may buy or sell on open markets. I make an explicit distinction between a good that is bought versus a good that is sold. When some z_h^i is negative, the consumer is trying to sell commodity h. When z_h^i is positive, the consumer is trying to buy commodity h. The situation is reversed for producers: y_h^j is positive if and only if the producer is trying to sell. In general, the same good will have a buying price higher than a selling price. The difference between a buying price and a selling price can occur in a general competitive equilibrium because of transactions costs.

4.1   Consumers

Consumers are indexed by $i = 1, \ldots, n$. They have endowments ω^i, net trades z^i and closed convex consumption sets $X^i \subseteq R_+^H$. They have strictly quasiconcave C^3 utility functions $U^i(\omega^i + z^i)$. Consumers are competitive: They take buying and selling prices as given. They also take the market spectrum σ as given. Thus, (p^b, p^s, σ) is taken parametrically. Define as the *market consumption set*:

---

[6] That is to say, the allocation that would result from optimizing behavior with market 4 shut down.

$$Z^i(\sigma) = \left\{ z^i \middle| \omega^i + z^i \in X^i \text{ and } \quad z^i_h = 0, \text{ if } \quad \sigma_h = 0 \right\}$$

The consumer maximizes

$$U^i(\omega^i + z^i) \text{ subject to:}$$

$$z^i \in Z^i(\sigma), \text{ so that } z^i_h = 0 \quad \text{if} \quad \sigma_h = 0$$

$$p^b z^{i+} - p^s z^{i-} = \sum \theta_{ij} \pi^j$$

where $z^{i+} = \max(z^i_h, 0)$ is the vector of bought goods, $z^{i-} = -\min(z^i_h, 0)$ is the vector of sold goods, where π^j is the dividend paid by firm j, θ_{ij} is the proportion of shares in j owned by i, and j varies across producing and marketmaking firms.

The solution to this maximization yields a *consumer's desired net trade function*:

$$z^i(p^b, p^s, \sigma) \quad i = 1, \ldots, n.$$

4.2   Producers

Producers are competitive: They also take (p^b, p^s, σ) as given. Define a *market net trade set for firm j*:

$$Y^j(\sigma) = \left\{ y^j \in Y^j \middle| y^j_h = 0 \text{ if } \sigma_h = 0 \right\}$$

where Y^j = production technology (a subset of R^H that contains 0 is strictly convex within its relative interior, and so forth). Let y^{j+} and y^{j-} be defined in the same manner as that for z^{i+} and z^{i-}. Then total profits for firm j are $\pi^j \equiv \text{Max } p^s y^{j+} - p^b y^{j-}$, given (p^b, p^s, σ). The firms then choose y^j to maximize π^j subject to $y^j \in Y^j(\sigma)$.

Call the solution $y^j(p^b, p^s, \sigma)$ the *firm's desired net trade function*.

4.3   Marketmakers

Marketmakers operate on only one market, with perfect partial equilibrium knowledge of demands, supplies, and open markets. They know nothing outside of their own market. The sequence of transactions is this: First, units of account are used to trade with sellers of commodity h at the exchange rate of p^s_h per unit of h. Then the units of commodity h so acquired are bought by the ultimate buyers of commodity h for p^b_h units of account. Marketmaker h's total purchases of good h are equal to the total sales to him of good h by consumers and firms, s_h. Marketmaker h's only revenues are derived from his total sales of good h, which is equal to the total amount bought from him by consumers and firms, b_h. There are no inventories held by the marketmaker, so necessarily $b_h \leq s_h$. There are transactions costs associated with each market h: for each market transaction volume $s_h = b_h$; there are associated transactions input vectors $t^h \in R^H$ which make s_h feasible as a market h volume of trade, $(s_h, t^h) \in T^h$. Transactions costs are incurred by the marketmaker in the form of labor and other materials required to seek buyers and sellers and to monitor subsequent transactions. It does not matter for real transactions costs what unit of account is used. The set T^h is called the *transactions technology for commodity h*.

Given a list of the open markets, define a *market transactions technology*

$$T_h(\sigma) \equiv \left\{ (s_h, t^h) \in T_h \big| t_k^h = 0 \text{ if } \sigma_k = 0 \right\}.$$

It is assumed that the marketmaker buys inputs competitively on open markets. Let the cost function of marketmaker h be denoted $C^h(s_h, p^b, \sigma)$ $= \text{Min}\{(p^b \cdot t^h | (s_h, t^h) \in T^h(\sigma)\}$. The solution to this cost minimization problem is denoted $t^h(s_h, p^b, p^s, \sigma)$.

The profit function of the marketmaker as a simple function of the quantities of purchases, sales, and transactions costs is defined as

$$\pi^h \equiv p_h^b b_h - p_h^s s_h - p^b t^h$$

Assumption T1: *The market for commodity 1 is always open, $\sigma_1 = 1$, for all $\sigma \in \Sigma$. Furthermore, commodity one is always desired and it has zero transactions costs.*

Remark: *This is an assumption about the existence of a commonly traded commodity (perhaps commodity money, serving as unit of account). Without such an assumption, trivial equilibria with $\sigma = 0$ could be pervasive, and other complications would arise.*

Assumption T2: *If there is no trading at a profit maximum on an open market h, the marketmaker shuts it down. It is closed and no trading is possible in h.*

Remark: *This is automatically true if there are positive transactions costs. If there are none, and there is no activity on the market, there are two ways of making zero profits: open and inactive, or* *closed altogether. I assume the marketmaker simply closes his market in this instance.*

There are two polar cases of marketmaker information and incentives examined here: monopoly and perfect competition. I consider both realistic. In some cases, such as NASDAQ stocks, there can be 20 or even 200 marketmakers. In other financial markets, there may be only one. For a recent product innovation, or in small countries, there may be only one potential marketmaker. In still other cases, one would expect oligopolistic firms within a market. There may be Nash behavior across markets when significant interdependencies are recognized (see Makowski and Ostroy [1995] for related work on this). I will explore these cases in future work.

A   Monopolistic marketmakers

Although a detailed analysis of monopoly marketmakers is outside the scope of this chapter, it might be instructive to look briefly at this case. Consumers and firms are perfectly competitive.

Monopoly Assumption: The (potential) marketmaker in h makes a calculation of his profits in a monopolistic partial equilibrium fashion. He knows partial equilibrium demand (buyers) and supply (sellers) as functions of p_h^b, p_h^s, and σ_h. Let $-h \equiv (1, 2, \ldots h - 1, h + 1, \ldots)$. These functions are expressed as:

$$(1) \quad b_h\left(p_h^b, p_h^s, \sigma_h; p_{-h}^b, p_{-h}^s, \sigma_{-h}\right) \equiv \sum_j z_h^{j+}\left(p_h^b, p_h^s, \sigma_h; p_{-h}^b, p_{-h}^s, \sigma_{-h}\right)$$
$$+ \sum_j y_h^{j-}\left(p_h^b, p_h^s, \sigma_h; p_{-h}^b, p_{-h}^s, \sigma_{-h}\right)$$
$$+ \sum_k t_h^k\left(p_h^b, p_h^s, \sigma_h; p_{-h}^b, p_{-h}^s, \sigma_{-h}\right)$$

$$(2) \quad s_h\left(p_h^b, p_h^s, \sigma_h; p_{-h}^b, p_{-h}^s, \sigma_{-h}\right) \equiv \sum_j z_h^{j-}\left(p_h^b, p_h^s, \sigma_h; p_{-h}^b, p_{-h}^s, \sigma_{-h}\right)$$
$$+ \sum_j y_h^{j+}\left(p_h^b, p_h^s, \sigma_h; p_{-h}^b, p_{-h}^s, \sigma_{-h}\right)$$

Monopoly profits are defined as

$$(3) \quad \Pi^h\left(p_h^b, p_h^s, \sigma_h; p_{-h}^b, p_{-h}^s, \sigma_{-h}\right) \equiv p_h^b b_h\left(p_h^b, p_h^s, \sigma_h; p_{-h}^b, p_{-h}^s, \sigma_{-h}\right)$$
$$- p_h^s s_h\left(p_h^b, p_h^s, \sigma_h; p_{-h}^b, p_{-h}^s, \sigma_{-h}\right)$$
$$- C_h\left(s_h\left(p_h^b, p_h^s, \sigma_h; p_{-h}^b, p_{-h}^s, \sigma_{-h}\right), p^b\right)$$

The marketmaker maximizes profits Π^h with respect to the variables under his control and subject to the constraint that purchases cannot be greater than sales:

$$\varrho^h\left(p_{-h}^b, p_{-h}^s, \sigma_{-h}\right) \equiv$$

$$\underset{\left(p_h^b, p_h^s, \sigma_h\right)}{\text{Max}} \Pi^h(\cdot) \text{ s.t. } b_h\left(p_h^b, p_h^s, \sigma_h; p_{-h}^b, p_{-h}^s, \sigma_{-h}\right)$$

$$\leq s_h\left(p_h^b, p_h^s, \sigma_h; p_{-h}^b, p_{-h}^s, \sigma_{-h}\right) \tag{4.1}$$

If Π^h is always negative for positive σ_h, then maximum profit occurs at shutdown with 0 profits and $b_h = s_h = 0$. A monopolistically competitive equilibrium $(p^{b*}, p^{s*}, \sigma^*)$ occurs when all agents are optimizing as above and when all open markets clear and no monopoly marketmaker foresees a profit on closed markets. Monopolistic equilibria are not efficient, but they may still be Pareto ranked.

B   Free-entry perfectly competitive marketmakers
In contrast to the case of monopoly marketmakers is the case of perfect competition.

Competitive Assumption: *For all k', the marketmaker in k' takes prices p_k and market states σ_k as given for all $k \neq k^+$.*

Remarks: This case parallels Foley's (1970) model of transactions costs, in which there are also some stimulating paragraphs on market formation. One can think of a single competitor as a single marketmaker who is fighting potential competitors. If there were no transactions costs, then $p^b = p^s$ in equilibrium.

The competitive marketmaker in market h knows only the price vectors and the list of open markets (p^b, p^s, σ) and his own costs. With this information, he maximizes profit with respect to $s_h = b_h$ and σ_h. Let

$$\pi^h \equiv \left(p_h^b - p_h^s\right)s_h - C_h\left(s_h; p^b, p^s, \sigma\right)$$

$$\varrho^h\left(p^b, p^s, \sigma\right) \equiv \text{Max } \pi^h \text{ subject to } b_h \leq s_h \tag{4.2}$$

If the first expression in (4.2) is always negative when $s_h > 0$ and $\sigma_h = 1$, then shutdown occurs and the profit maximum occurs at 0 with b_h

$= s_h = 0$. If $\sigma_h = 1$, then free entry by all marketmakers would imply zero profits and price-taking behavior.

5   Market formation equilibrium

An equilibrium with open and closed markets will happen only when no marketmaker has an incentive to open another market and when no marketmaker desires to close an open market.

> **Definition:** *A market formation equilibrium (MFE) is a list of buying and selling prices and a market spectrum $(p^{b*}, p^{s*}, \sigma^*)$ such that:*
>
> (a)   *Given $(p^{b*}, p^{s*}, \sigma^*)$, consumers maximize U^i subject to the budget constraint and $z^i \in Z^i(\sigma^*)$.*
>
> (b)   *Given $(p^{b*}, p^{s*}, \sigma^*)$, producers maximize π^j subject to $y^j \in Y^j(\sigma^*)$.*
>
> (c)   *Open markets h with $\sigma_h^* = 1$ are exactly those in which positive activity earns nonnegative profits for the marketmakers at $(p^{b*}, p^{s*}, \sigma^*)$.*
>
> (d)   *Closed markets h with $\sigma_h^* = 0$ are exactly those in which positive activity earns negative profits for the marketmakers at $(p^{b*}, p^{s*}, \sigma^*)$. A marketmaker in any commodity h with $\sigma_h^* = 0$ finds a profit maximum only when $b_h^* = s_h^* = 0$, that is, profits are negative whenever b_h and s_h are positive.*
>
> (e)   *Markets clear subject to σ_h^*:*
>
> $\sigma_h^* = 1$ *implies* $b_h^* \leq s_h^*$ *and* $p_h^{b*} (s_h^* - b_h^*) = 0$. *At the same time, $\sigma_h^* = 0$ implies $b_h^* = s_h^* = 0$. Further, for all commodities h, $\Sigma_j z_h^{j*} + \Sigma_j y_h^{j*} + \Sigma_k t_h^{k*} = 0$, unless $p_h^{b*} = 0$.*

I will say a *competitive market formation equilibrium* occurs when all marketmakers are perfectly competitive firms at an MFE allocation. A *monopolistic market formation equilibrium* occurs when all marketmakers are monopolistically competitive at an MFE allocation.

> **Definition:** *A complete competitive markets equilibrium is a competitive market formation equilibrium with $\sigma^* = (1, 1, \ldots, 1)$.*

> **Definition:** *An inactive market h at prices and market spectrum (p^b, p^s, σ) is one in which $\sigma_h = 1$, but b_h and s_h are zero.*

6 Welfare economics

Now consider generalizing Examples 1 and 2 above.

> **Proposition 1:** *There are competitive market formation equilibria in which a missing market occurs endogenously. Further, there can be coordination failures.*

> *Proof:* Example 1. QED.

> **Proposition 2:** *Complete markets may not be Pareto efficient if there are setup costs to marketmaking.*

> *Proof:* Example 2. QED.

> **Proposition 3:** *A competitive complete markets equilibrium without transactions setup costs is Pareto efficient.*

> *Proof:* As Foley (1970) points out, this case is equivalent to a standard competitive equilibrium. He proves this by distinguishing between the same commodity when it is bought by a consumer from the case when the same commodity is sold by a (presumably different) consumer. But, the first welfare theorem tells us that a standard competitive equilibrium is Pareto efficient. QED.

I now turn to the issue of the Pareto inefficient equilibrium failure of markets to exist in a more general case. Critical to this failure are market complementarities. One appealing definition of complementarities is similar to that of strategic complements in the literature.[7] It says that if the marketmaker in k were to increase the amount available of good k, then the marketmaker in h would benefit, and vice versa.

> **Definition:** *Goods h and k are strategic market complements[8] if and only if for all (p^b, p^s, σ), an increase in the market volume of k raises the marginal profits*

$$\Pi^{h'} \equiv \frac{\partial \pi^n}{\partial s_h}$$

---

[7] There are no strategic interactions here in the competitive case.

[8] See, for example, Milgrom and Roberts (1990).

*of the marketmaker in h with respect to its own market volume
$s_h = b_h$. Similarly, increases in the market volume of good h must
raise marketmaker k's marginal profits.*

It turns out, however that a different condition is needed for coordination failure to occur. The following definition requires that, without
trading possibilities for good h, potential buyers of k will not accept the
prices necessary to cover transactions costs and reservation prices of
sellers and vice versa.

Definition: *Goods h and k are market complements at $(p^b, p^s,
\sigma)$ if and only if $\sigma_h = 0$ implies that $\pi^k < 0$ for any positive s_k and
$\sigma_k = 0$ implies that $\pi^k < 0$ for any positive s_h.*

The theorem below establishes that missing markets can happen
under conditions of market complementarity. First, I show that there can
be an allocation under open markets that dominates an allocation when
markets are closed. This is true regardless of complementarity, but
depends on a lack of setup costs and the desirability of commodities.

Proposition 4:   *Suppose that marketmakers are competitive and
that there are no setup costs to transactions. Suppose also that the
market for h is open and active when an additional market for
some commodity k is open and active, but not when k is closed
and vice versa. Then, there is an allocation with h and k open that
is Pareto superior to any allocation with h and k closed.*

Proof: For any consumer i, and at any point in i's consumption
set, define the marginal rate of substitution of good h for good
1 in the usual way:

$$\text{MRS}_{h1}^i = -\frac{\partial z_1^j}{\partial z_1^i} \qquad \text{when} \qquad du_i = 0$$

that is, as a slope of an indifference surface in the $h1$ plane.
At an equilibrium with $\sigma_h = 0$, it must be that profit π^k is nonpositive for the marketmaker in k in the neighborhood of zero
trades in h. At the endowment point, there will generally be a
difference between the individual slopes of the indifference
curves between goods h and 1. Since profits are negative in
this region, none (that is, over all i, j) of these gaps $\text{MRS}_{h1}^i -
\text{MRS}_{h1}^j$ is sufficiently large to cover the marginal transactions
costs Δ_h in market h. In other words, the gap between the
highest price anyone would pay and the lowest price at which

anyone would sell is below the marginal transactions cost at 0 volume.

If the market for k were open and trades took place, then by assumption, profits for market h would now be positive and that market would open. Positive profits mean that the gap between some of the MRS_{h1}^i's is now large enough to cover the marginal transactions costs Δ_h in market h. There are now mutually beneficial trades in market h because $\mathrm{MRS}_{h1}^i > \mathrm{MRS}_{h1}^j + \Delta_h$, where person i is a buyer and person j is a seller.   QED.

The following coordination failure result appeals to market complementarity to satisfy the assumptions of Proposition 4.

> **Theorem:** *Suppose that goods h and k are market complements. Then there is no equilibrium with market h closed and market k open, or vice versa. The only equilibrium possibilities are with both markets closed or with both open. If there are no setup costs, there is an allocation with h and k open that is Pareto superior to an equilibrium with the h and k markets closed.*
>
> *Proof:* Let σ be any vector with $\sigma_k = 0$. By market complementarity, profit for the marketmaker in h is negative at all market volumes for h, unless there is a shutdown of the market. Again by market complements, the potential marketmaker in k sees only negative profits by opening. By symmetry, if the market in h is closed, the marketmaker in k also sees negative profit for any positive activity level for market k. Market "k" will therefore also be closed in equilibrium.
>
> The only equilibrium possibilities are with both open or with both closed. If there are no transactions setup costs, the equilibrium with both markets closed is Pareto dominated by an allocation possible when both markets are open by Proposition 4.
> QED.

7   Conclusions and future research

The introduction of initially incomplete markets with endogenous market formation leads to several new observations about competitive markets. Purely competitive behavior by all economic agents can be Pareto inefficient, even without restrictions on the final number of markets. Missing markets can arise with or without perfect competition. Complementarities seem to be the main culprit here. However, the presence of setup costs is another source of Pareto inefficiency. Example 2 shows that, socially, it is too costly to market all substitutable goods, yet these markets may be individually profitable.

I chose the partial equilibrium assumption about marketmakers because it is more realistic in many instances, and because it retains some of the myopic informational spirit of competitive equilibrium. The behavior of the marketmaker who has partial equilibrium information could be competitive or imperfectly competitive. Competitive behavior can be justified on the usual grounds that there are many competitors, at least potentially. It must be recalled, however, that the marketmaker might face a setup cost technology, which is incompatible with competition. Even the normal case of U-shaped cost curves is incompatible with competition if the increasing returns are large relative to the size of the market. One of the goals of future research in this area should be to shed some light on markets with setup costs to transactions. See Heller (1972) for an early attempt involving approximate equilibria.

Even without complementarities of the usual sort, coordination failure with endogenous markets is common. For example, suppose there are N types of consumers, and there is no production.[9] Type n consumer owns just type n good and nothing else. This type of consumer gains utility solely from good $n + 1$. Within a type, every consumer is identical. Thus, a type n trader sells all his type n good to consumers of type $n - 1$. He then spends all his resultant income on good $n + 1$. This is a closed chain if type N consumers only want to buy good 1 and type 1 consumers only sell to type N. Assume that there are no transactions costs and all markets are initially open. It is clear that a Pareto efficient competitive equilibrium exists in which all markets are open, buying prices equal selling prices, and consumers of type n sell all their endowment on market n and use all the proceeds to buy good $n + 1$. It is easily seen that there is a price vector at which supply equals demand for each good. For example, if there are equal numbers of consumers in each type and if every type had the same quantity of endowment as any other type, a vector of ones is an equilibrium price vector.

Now consider the role of marketmakers in the economy. Their presence leads to other equilibria. For example, suppose that by some historical accident the market for good n is closed at the outset. There is now zero demand for good $n + 1$, and that market closes so there is no demand for good $n + 2$, and so forth. There is a chain reaction, and the economy settles down to autarky, the worst outcome. This is a classic case of coordination failure.

---

[9] Production may easily be added to the example.

Now take the case of setup costs. A marketmaker will not be open for business in good n unless there is sufficient volume for him to pay his setup costs. If there are sufficiently different costs, or if there are different numbers of traders in each type, some marketmakers will lose money no matter what, whereas others might make a profit if some other markets were open. But as seen above, no marketmaker will find it profitable to open, so long as even one market is closed. So long as transactions costs are not too large, a social planner could find it efficient to open all markets simultaneously, even though some markets are not sustainable in equilibrium. This case of equilibrium inefficiency is not one of coordination failure, since there are no other equilibria by construction.

For the next example, assume that profits are all regulated to be zero. Where do the transactions cost goods come from? Assume that only one good is needed to set up a market, and it is the same good for each market. Suppose further that this good is owned by all the consumers in sufficient quantity to cover the setup costs. Suppose they gain zero utility from it. In that case, there is a Pareto efficient equilibrium in which all markets are open. There is another equilibrium, however, in which all markets are closed, and so there is zero demand for the transaction good. The consumer has zero income and so zero demand. This, too, is a classic case of coordination failure.

Sufficient conditions for all market formation equilibria to be fully competitive equilibria is a subject for future work. I conjecture that, under some conditions, a market formation equilibrium might be Pareto efficient if all its closed markets were inactive when opened simultaneously. It might be thought that Pareto efficiency would also occur if all markets were open in equilibrium, but Example 2 shows this is false in the presence of market setup costs. Research also needs to be done on the conditions for the existence of a market formation equilibrium. The role for the size of the economy in the existence and Pareto efficiency questions is also important, particularly with setup costs.

References

Allen, F., and D. Gale. 1988. Optimal security design, *Review of Financial Studies 1*, 3:229–63.

Allen, F., and D. Gale. 1990. Incomplete markets and incentives to set up an options exchange, Geneva Papers on Risk and Insurance, *Risk Insurance*, 15:17–46.

Allen, F., and D. Gale. 1994. *Financial Innovation and Risk Sharing.* Cambridge, MA: MIT Press.

Arrow, K. J. 1969. The organization of economic activity: issues pertinent to the choice of market vs. non-market allocation. In *The Analysis of Public Expenditure: The PPB System*, Joint Economic Committee. Washington, DC: Government Printing Office, pp. 47–64.

Bisin, A. 1992. General equilibrium economies with imperfectly competitive financial intermediaries. Mimeo, University of Chicago.

Bisin, A. 1994. General equilibrium and endogenously incomplete financial markets. Mimeo, MIT.

Duffie, D., and R. Rahi. 1995. Financial market innovation and security design: an introduction. Journal of Economic Theory, 65:1–42.

Durlauf, S. N. 1992. Nonergodic economic growth. *Review of Economic Studies*, 60(2):349–66.

Foley, D. 1970. Economic equilibrium with costly marketing. *Journal of Economic Theory*, 2:276–96.

Hahn, F. 1971. Equilibrium with transactions costs. *Econometrica*, 39:417–40.

Hahn, F. 1990. Some remarks on missing markets. Mimeo, Cambridge University.

Hart, O. 1980. Perfect competition and optimal product differentiation. *Journal of Economic Theory*, 22:279–312.

Heal, G. Price and market share dynamics in network industries, this volume.

Heller, W. P. 1972. Transactions with set-up costs. *Journal of Economic Theory*, 4(3):465–78.

Heller, W. P. 1986. Coordination failure in complete markets with applications to effective demand. In *Equilibrium Analysis: Essays in Honor of Kenneth J. Arrow, Vol. II*, ed. W. P. Heller, R. M. Starr, and D. A. Starrett. Cambridge University Press.

Heller, W. P., and D. A. Starrett. 1976. On the nature of externalities. In *Theory and Measurement of Economic Externalities*, ed. S. Lin. New York: Academic Press.

Makowski, L. 1980. Perfect competition, the profit criterion and the organization of economic activity. *Journal of Economic Theory*, 22:222–42.

Makowski, L., and J. Ostroy. 1995. Appropriation and efficiency: A revision of the first theorem of welfare economics. *American Economic Review*, 85:808–27.

Milgrom, P., and J. Roberts. 1990. Rationalizability, learning and equilibrium in games with strategic complementarities. *Econometrica*, 58(6):1255–78.

Pesendorfer, W. 1995. Financial innovation in a general equilibrium model. *Journal of Economic Theory*, 65:79–116.

Rosenstein-Rodan, P. 1943. Problems of industrialization of Eastern and Southeastern Europe. *Economic Journal*, 53:202–11.

Scitovsky, T. 1954. Two concepts of external economies. *Journal of Political Economy*, 62:70–82.

CHAPTER 13

Toward a general theory of
social overhead capital

Hirofumi Uzawa

1   Introduction

Social overhead capital constitutes a vital element of any society. It is
generally classified into three categories: natural capital, social infrastructure, and institutional capital. These categories are neither exhaustive nor exclusive, but they illustrate the nature of the functions
performed by social overhead capital and the social perspective associated with them.

Natural capital consists of natural resources such as forests, rivers,
lakes, wetlands, coastal seas, oceans, water, soil, and above all the earth's
atmosphere. They all share the common feature of being regenerative,
subject to intricate and subtle forces of the ecological and biological
mechanisms. They provide all living organisms, particularly human
beings, with the environment in which it is possible to sustain their lives
and to regenerate themselves. However, rapid economic development
and population growth in the last several decades, with the accompanying vast changes in social conditions, have altered the delicate ecological
balance of natural capital to such a significant extent that its effective-
ness has been lost in many parts of the world.

Social infrastructure is another important component of social overhead capital. It consists of social capital such as roads, bridges, public
mass transportation systems, water, electricity, and other public utilities,
communication and postal services, sewage and fire-fighting facilities,
among others. Social overhead capital may also include institutional
capital, such as hospitals, educational institutions, judicial and police
systems, public administrative services, financial and monetary institu-

This article was prepared in 1992 as the Beijer Institute Discussion Paper Series No. 13.

tions, and so forth. It provides members of society with services crucial in maintaining human and cultural life.

Social overhead capital is in principle not appropriated by individual members of the society, but held as common property, managed by social institutions of various kinds. These institutions maintain social overhead capital and distribute equitably the services derived from it. Thus, it is of crucial importance in the theory of social overhead capital to find the institutional management of social overhead capital that is optimum from the social point of view. The present chapter formulates an analytical framework in which the economic implications of social overhead capital are examined and explores the conditions under which the intertemporal allocation of social overhead capital and privately owned scarce resources is dynamically optimum from the social point of view.

The problem of dynamic optimality was originally discussed by Ramsey (1928) and Hotelling (1931). It was revived as the theory of optimum economic growth in the 1960s, particularly by Cass (1965), Koopmans (1965), Dasgupta and Heal (1979), and others. In reference to the context of environmental economics, however, it was Mäler (1974) who first formulated the intertemporal general equilibrium model in which economic implications of the environment could be fully explored, and then developed a detailed analysis of the pattern of intertemporal allocations of scarce resources including the growth and depletion of the environment that are dynamically optimum from the social point of view. Since then, there have been many contributions to the optimum theory of economic growth and environmental quality. The dynamic models of social overhead capital introduced in this chapter are largely within the framework of the optimum theory of environmental quality á la Mäler.

One of the intricate problems inherent in social overhead capital theory concerns the phenomenon of externalities. Since the classic treatment of Pigou (1925), economists have been puzzled by the phenomenon of externalities, but they put it aside as peripheral and not worthy of serious consideration. Concern with environmental issues has, however, changed economic thinking, and a large number of articles have appeared where the issue of externalities occupies a central place, from both the theoretical and empirical points of view. The analytical treatment of externalities formulated in this chapter is adopted from that introduced in Uzawa (1974), where two kinds of externalities, static on the one hand and dynamic on the other, were recognized with respect to the services derived from the stock of social overhead capital.

The introduction of the general model of social overhead capital is preceded by simple analyses of two types of social overhead capital, the natural environment and social infrastructure.

The natural environment, or rather natural capital, has been subject to an extensive examination in the literature, particularly with respect to the fisheries and forestry commons. Analysis of the fisheries commons was initiated by Gordon (1954) and Scott (1955), and was later extended to a general treatment within the framework of modern capital theory by Schaefer (1957), Crutchfield and Zellner (1962), Clark and Munro (1975), and Tahvonen (1991), among others.

The simple dynamic model of the natural environment deals primarily with the case of the fisheries commons. Uzawa (1974) used it to examine the theory of the tragedy of the commons, as advanced by Hardin (1968).

The model of the natural environment developed in Section 2 may be applicable to the dynamics of the forestry commons as well. The dynamics of the forestry commons has also been extensively analyzed in the literature. Wicksell (1901) developed the core of modern capital theory with an analysis of forests as the prototype. The most recent contribution to forestry economics was made by Johansson and Löfgren (1985); the basic premises of the dynamic model of natural capital introduced are an application of their work.

Section 3 formulates a simple dynamic model to discuss the social infrastructure. Social infrastructure, another important component of social overhead capital, exhibits a characteristic aspect distinct from natural capital. Society generally allocates a significant portion of its scarce resources to the construction and maintenance of social overhead capital. A central issue in the dynamic theory of social infrastructure is to find the criteria by which scarce resources are allocated between investment in infrastructure on the one hand, and production of goods and services on the other.

The dynamic models introduced in Sections 2 and 3 below are general equilibrium versions of those formulated in Uzawa (1992), where the phenomena of externalities are not explicitly discussed. The dynamically optimal allocation of scarce resources occurs when the imputed prices associated with the accumulation and use of social overhead capital are used as signals in the allocative process. Privately owned scarce resources, and goods and services produced by private economic units, are allocated through the mechanism of competitive market institutions.

When we include all the social overhead capital in a particular nation, the social institutions fiduciarily entrusted with their management constitute the Government in the broadest sense. The aggregate expenditures incurred by all these social institutions are nothing but the governmental expenditures, either on the current account or on the capital account. Thus, the problem we address is that of devising an institutional framework in which the ensuring governmental activities are dynamically optimal from the social point of view.

2   The natural environment as social overhead capital

We assume that the stock of the natural environment is measured in terms of homogeneous quantity, as with the fisheries and forestry commons. Let us denote by V_t the stock of the natural environment at time t, where the time suffix t will occasionally be omitted for the sake of expository brevity. The rate at which the stock V_t changes over time, to be denoted by $\dot{V}_t$, is primarily determined by two factors, ecological on the one hand and anthropogenic or economic on the other.

The rate of change in the stock V of the natural environment which is ecologically determined will be denoted by $\mu(V)$. The function $\mu(V)$ defines a curve as in Figure 1, where the abscissa measures the stock V of the natural environment and the ordinate measures the rate of change in V, $\dot{V}/V$. We assume there are two critical levels of the stock, $\underline{V}$ and $\overline{V}$, at which the stock of the natural environment remains stationary; that is,

$$\mu\left(\underline{V}\right) = \mu\left(\overline{V}\right) = 0$$

Either $\underline{V} = 0$, as with some forestry commons, or $\overline{V} = +\infty$ as with open oceans.

To see how the second, economic factor concerning the change in stock V of the natural environment is determined, we work within the framework of the theory of activity analysis. Let us denote the vector of activity levels by $a = (a_j)$, where a_j denotes the level of activity j. We assume that activities j comprise all possible productive activities carried out by members of the economy. The natural environment is assumed to be depleted by the quantity ξ_j when activity j is operated at a unit level. The total quantity of the natural environment to be depleted, x, is then given by

$$X = \xi_t a = \sum_j \xi_j a_j$$

where $\xi = (\xi_j)$ denotes the vector of technological coefficients concerning the depletion of the natural environment.

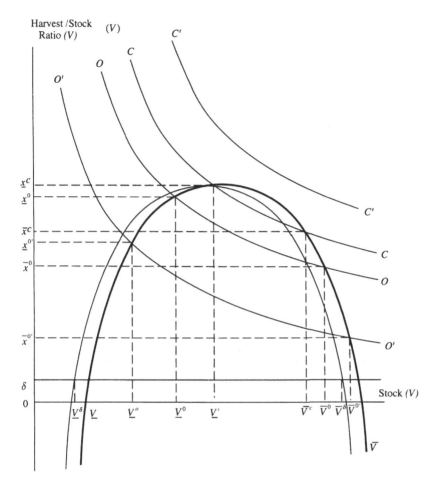

Figure 1. Ecological and economic rates of change in the stock of the natural environment.

The change in the stock of the natural environment is described by the following dynamic equation:

$$\dot{V}_t = \mu(V_t)V_t - X_t \tag{2.1}$$

where

$$X_t = \xi a_t \tag{2.2}$$

and a_t is the vector of activity level at time t.

We have to specify the quantities of privately owned resources employed when the economic activities are carried out at the levels represented by the vector of activity levels a_t. Privately owned scarce resources are generically denoted by l and the quantity of resources of type l required for activity j at the unit level is given by a_{lj}. When the endowment of scarce resources in the economy is given by the vector $K = (K_l)$, then a vector of activity levels $a_t = (a_{jt})$ is feasible if, and only if, the following conditions are satisfied:

$$a_t \geq 0, \quad Aa_t \leq K \tag{2.3}$$

where $A = (a_{lj})$ is the matrix of the coefficients of resource requirements.

The quantities of consumption goods produced are determined by the vector of activity levels. Consumption goods are denoted generically by i, and we assume that activity j at its unit level produces consumption goods of type i by the quantity c_{ij}. Then the vector of consumption goods, $c_t = (c_{it})$, produced by the vector of activity levels a_t, may be expressed as:

$$c_t = Ca_t \tag{2.4}$$

where $C = (c_{ij})$ is the matrix of the coefficients of outputs.

The role of the natural environment as a crucial factor in the determination of the living standard is now expressed by the specification that the utility function involves not only vectors of consumption goods but also the stock of the natural environment. Thus, the level of the social utility at time t, to be denoted by u_t, may be expressed as follows:

$$u_t = u\left(c_t, V_t\right) = u\left(c_t\right)\phi\left(V_t\right) \tag{2.5}$$

where $u(c)$ and $\phi(V)$ are, respectively, the positive, strictly concave functions of the vector of consumption goods c, and the stock of the natural environment V. The form of the utility function as expressed by (2.5) presupposes it is separable with respect to c and V. In what follows, we assume that

$$\gamma = \frac{\phi'\left(V\right)V}{\phi\left(V\right)} \tag{2.6}$$

is a constant between 0 and 1, taking a suitable measurement for the stock of the natural environment, if necessary.

The competitive equilibrium at time t may now be obtained if we find a price vector of consumption goods, $p_t = (p_{it})$, and a vector of activity levels, $a_t = (a_{jt})$, such that feasibility conditions (2.3) and (2.4) are satisfied,

$$u_c(c_t, V_t) \quad \text{and} \quad p_t \quad \text{are proportional,} \tag{2.7}$$

and $p_t c_t$ is maximized among all feasible vectors of activity levels.

Such a competitive equilibrium is shown uniquely to exist. The conditions for competitive equilibrium are satisfied for the pair of vectors of consumption goods c_t and of activity levels a_t which maximize the utility function $u(c, V)$ subject to the constraints (2.3) and (2.4). Let a_t^c and c_t^c be the vectors, respectively, of activity levels and of consumption goods at the competitive equilibrium at time t.

The dynamic equation (2.1) may now be written as:

$$\frac{\dot{V}_t}{V_t} = \mu(V_t) - \frac{X_t^c}{V_t} \tag{2.8}$$

where $X_t^c = \xi a_t^c$.

Since the rate at which the natural environment is depleted at the competitive equilibrium is determined independently of the stock of the natural environment, X_t^c / V_t may be depicted by the downward sloping curve CC as indicated in Figure 1. It generally intersects with the $\mu(V)$ curve at two points, with corresponding levels of the stock of the natural environment, $\underline{V}^C$ and $\overline{V}^C$. The CC curve may intersect with the $\mu(V)$ curve at more than two points, resulting with more than two values of V^C. In such cases, the highest value of $\overline{V}^C$ will be used. In addition, the CC curve may have no point of intersection with the $\mu(V)$ curve, as is indicated by the $C'C'$ curve in Figure 1.

It is easily seen from the figure that the upper critical level $\overline{V}^C$ is the long run stationary level of the stock of the natural environment for the competitive case, whereas the lower critical level $\underline{V}^C$ is an unstable stationary state. If the stock of the natural environment V_t is less than $\overline{V}^C$, but larger than $\underline{V}^C$, then it approaches $\overline{V}^C$; if V_t is larger than $\overline{V}^C$, then it again steadily approaches $\overline{V}^C$.

When the CC curve does not have a common point with the $\mu(V)$ curve, as with the $C'C'$ curve, then the stock of the natural environment V_t tends to decline steadily to approach the state of extinction, $V = 0$. This is the case Hardin (1968) referred to as the tragedy of the commons. It occurs when the endowments of privately owned scarce resources are relatively abundant compared with the ability of the natural environment to regenerate itself. Even when there is a stable, long run stationary level $\overline{V}^C$, the question arises: Is the time-path of the stock of the natural environment under competitive arrangements optimum from the viewpoint of the society as a whole?

We consider the case where the criterion for the dynamic optimum is defined in terms of the Ramsey–Cass–Koopmans utility integral

$$\int_0^\infty U_t e^{-\delta t} dt \tag{2.9}$$

where $U_t = u(c_t, V_t)$ is the utility level at time t and δ is the rate of discount, assumed to be a positive constant.

A time-path (c_t, a_t) of vectors of consumption goods c_t and of activity levels a_t is defined as dynamically optimum if it is feasible, that is, conditions (2.3) and (2.4) are satisfied, and the utility integral (2.9) is maximized among all feasible time-paths, where the stock of the natural environment V_t changes over time according to the dynamic equation (2.1) with the given initial condition V_o and the rate of depletion X_t is related to the vector of activity levels a_t in terms of the constraint (2.2).

In order to characterize the dynamically optimum time-path, we introduce the imputed price of the stock of the natural environment at each time t, to be denoted by λ_t. It is defined as the discounted present value of the marginal increases in the social utility in the future due to the marginal increase in the stock of the natural environment at time t. A simple calculation shows that the imputed price λ_t satisfies the following equation:

$$\lambda_t = \int_t^\infty u(c_\iota)\phi(V_\iota)e^{-\int_t^\iota (\delta - \mu(V_s) - \mu'(V_s)V_s)} d\iota$$

which, by differentiating with respect to t, yields

$$\frac{\dot{\lambda}_t}{\lambda_t} = \left[\delta - \mu(V_t) - \mu'(V_t)V_t\right] - \frac{u(c_t)\phi'(V_t)}{\lambda_t}$$

On the other hand, the optimum vector of activity levels a_t at time t is determined so that the imputed real income

$$H_t = u(c_t)\phi(V_t) + \lambda_t\left[\mu(V_t)V_t - X_t\right]$$

is maximized subject to the constraints (2.2), (2.3), and (2.4).

The structure of the dynamically optimum time-path may be more easily analyzed if we introduce the following imputed price:

$$\pi_t = \frac{\lambda_t}{\phi(V_t)}$$

The optimum vector of activity levels a_t^0 at time t is then obtained by maximizing

$$u(c_t) - \pi_t X_t$$

subject to the constraints (2.2), (2.3), and (2.4).

The dynamic equation for the new imputed price π_t may be written as:

$$\frac{\dot{\pi}}{\pi} = \left[\delta - \hat{\mu}(V)\right] - \gamma \frac{\dfrac{u(c^0)}{\pi} - X^0}{V} \tag{2.10}$$

where $a^0 = a_t^0$ is the vector of activity levels which maximizes

$$u(c) - \pi X \tag{2.11}$$

subject to the constraints

$$c = Ca, \quad X = \xi a \qquad a \geq 0 \qquad Aa \leq K \tag{2.12}$$

The coefficient γ in equation (2.10) is defined by (2.6) and assumed to be a positive constant, and $\hat{\mu}(V)$ is defined by

$$\hat{\mu}(V) = (1 + \gamma)\mu(V) + \mu'(V)V \tag{2.13}$$

The dynamic equation (2.10) for the imputed price, together with the equation for the stock of the natural environment

$$\frac{\dot{V}}{V} = \mu(V) - \frac{X^0}{V} \tag{2.14}$$

describes the time-path of (π, V) which corresponds to the dynamically optimum time-path of vectors of consumption goods c^0 and of activity levels a^0. One has only to choose among them the time-path for which the transversality conditions are satisfied:

$$\lim_{t \to \infty} \pi_t V_t e^{-\delta t} = 0 \tag{2.15}$$

Before we analyze the phase diagram of the system of differential equations, (2.10) and (2.14), a property concerning the relationships between imputed price π and the optimum vectors of consumption goods and activity levels may be noted. Suppose the imputed price is changed from π to $\pi + \Delta\pi$, and the corresponding changes in the optimum vector of consumption goods and optimum depletion are respectively from c to $c + \Delta c$ and from X to $X + \Delta X$. Since both (c, X) and $(c + \Delta c, X + \Delta X)$ are feasible, the following inequalities hold:

$$\left(u + \Delta u\right) - \pi\left(X + \Delta X\right) \le u - \pi X,$$
$$u - \left(\pi + \Delta\pi\right)X \le \left(u + \Delta u\right) - \left(\pi + \Delta\pi\right)\left(X + \Delta X\right)$$

Adding these two inequalities, we obtain

$$\Delta\pi\Delta X \le 0$$

Hence, the optimum level of the depletion of the natural environment, X^o, is decreased as the imputed price of the natural environment, π, increases. Similarly, it can be shown that, as the imputed price π increases,

$$\frac{u(c^o)}{\pi} - X^o \text{ decreases.}$$

We first examine the conditions under which the stock of the natural environment V remains stationary, that is,

$$\mu(V) = \frac{X^o}{V} \tag{2.16}$$

Since the rate of depletion X^o associated with the optimum vector of activity levels a^o is determined independently of the stock of the natural environment, the right-hand side of the equation (2.16) may be depicted by the downward sloping curve, as illustrated by the OO curve in Figure 1. The OO curve generally intersects with the $\mu(V)$ curve at two points, with the corresponding levels of the stock of the natural environment, $\underline{V}^o$ and $\overline{V}^o$. As the imputed price π increases, the rate of depletion V^o associated with the optimum vector of activity levels X^o is decreased, resulting in the downward shift of the OO curve, as indicated in Figure 1. Hence, the lower critical level $\underline{V}^o$ is decreased, while the upper critical level $\overline{V}^o$ is increased. The particular case where the imputed price is 0 corresponds to the competitive equilibrium, that is, the CC curve. On the other hand, as the imputed price π tends to infinity, the OO curve approaches the abscissa. Hence, $\underline{V}^o \to \underline{V}$ and $\overline{V}^o \to \overline{V}$. The relationships

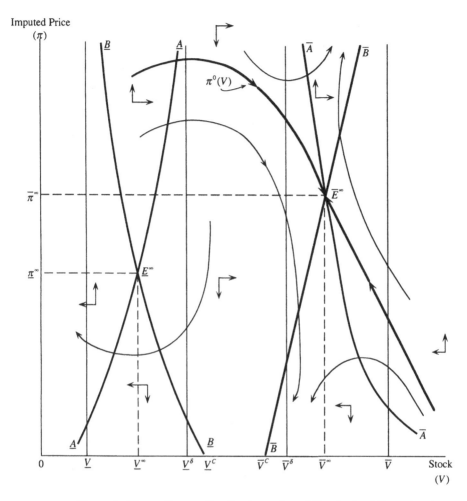

Figure 2. Phase diagram for the dynamics of the stock of the natural environment, 1.

between imputed price π and the stock of the natural environment V for which the stationarity condition (2.16) is satisfied may now be depicted by two curves, $\underline{BB}$ and $\overline{BB}$, in Figure 2, where the abscissa measures the stock of the natural environment V and the ordinate the imputed price π. If (π, V) lies in the region above these two curves, V tends to increase, whereas, if it lies in the regions below them, V tends to decrease, as indicated by the arrowed lines in Figure 2.

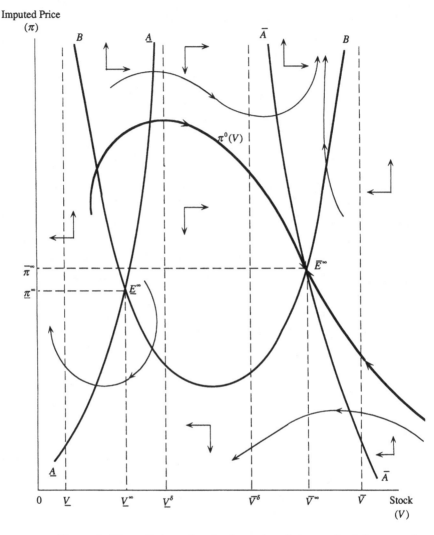

Figure 3. Phase diagram for the dynamics of the stock of the natural environment, 2.

In the case where the competitive equilibrium does not have a point of intersection with the $\mu(V)$ curve, as with the $C'C'$ curve in Figure 1, the phase diagram for the stock of the natural environment V may be depicted by the single curve BB, as illustrated in Figure 3.

The phase diagram for the imputed price π may be similarly obtained. The dynamic equation (18.10) shows that the imputed price π remains stationary if and only if the following conditions are satisfied:

$$\delta - \hat{\mu}(V) = \gamma \frac{\dfrac{u(c^o)}{\pi} - X^0}{V} \tag{2.17}$$

The left-hand side of the equation (2.17) is depicted by two curves, $\underline{GG}$ and $\overline{GG}$, in Figure 4, where the abscissa measures the stock of the natural environment V and the ordinate measures the rate of change in V. The two critical levels of the stock of the natural environment, $\underline{V}\delta$ and $\overline{V}\delta$, are obtained from the following conditions:

$$\hat{\mu}(\underline{V}\delta) = \hat{\mu}(\overline{V}\delta) = \delta$$

For a given level of the imputed price π, the right-hand side of the equation (18.17) is depicted by the downward sloping curve, as illustrated by the HH curve in Figure 4. The HH curve generally intersects with the $\underline{GG}$ and $\overline{GG}$ curves at two points, with the corresponding levels of the stock of the natural environment, $\underline{V}\pi$ and $\overline{V}\pi$. It is easily seen from Figure 4 that, as imputed price π becomes higher, the lower critical level $\underline{V}\pi$ is increased and the upper critical $\overline{V}\pi$ is decreased, respectively approaching $\underline{V}\delta$ and $\overline{V}\delta$ as imputed price π becomes infinity. Thus the combinations of (π,V) for which the conditions (2.17) are satisfied are described by the $\underline{AA}$ and $\overline{AA}$ curves in Figure 2 or Figure 3. The imputed price tends to increase if (π,V) lies above these two curves, while it tends to decrease if it lies below these curves, as indicated by the arrowed lines in Figure 2 or Figure 3.

There are two stationary points, $\underline{E}^\infty$ and $\overline{E}^\infty$, with corresponding levels of imputed price and stock of the natural environment, $\underline{\pi}^\infty$, $\underline{V}^\infty$, and $\overline{\pi}^\infty$, $\overline{V}^\infty$. Solution paths to the pair of dynamic equations, (2.10) and (2.14), are indicated by the arrowed curves in Figure 2 or Figure 3. Hence, there exist a pair of solution paths which converge to the stationary state $\overline{E}^\infty$, as indicated by the heavy arrowed curves. The functional form for these stable solution paths may be denoted by $\pi^o(V)$. Then, the optimum time-path will be obtained if, at each time t, the imputed price of the stock of the natural environment is given at the level $\pi_t = \pi^o(V_t)$, and the vectors of activity levels and consumption goods, a_t and c_t, are determined accordingly.

It is seen from either Figure 2 or Figure 3 that the long-run stationary level of the stock of the natural environment, $\overline{V}^\infty$, is higher than the

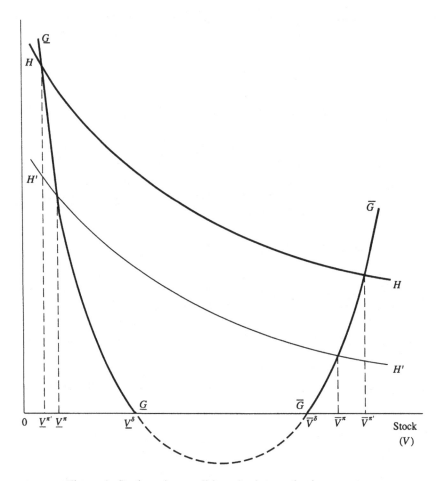

Figure 4. Stationarity conditions for imputed price.

competitive stationary level, $\overline{V}^c$, but is lower than the ecologically sustainable level of the stock of the natural environment, $\overline{V}$. The long-run stationary level of the stock of the natural environment thus obtained represents an optimum balance between the productive gains harvested from the resources of the natural environment on the one hand and the loss in the social welfare due to the depletion of the natural environment on the other. Thus, the stable long-run stationary level, $\overline{V}^\infty$, may be defined as the long-run sustainable stock of the natural environment which is optimum from the social point of view. The optimum sustainable long-run stock of the natural environment may be, as outlined above, obtained in terms of the imputed price of the stock of the natural environment which is charged to the members of the society according to the quantities of the stock of the natural environment depleted by their economic activities.

The simple dynamic model of the natural environment we have developed in this section shows that the optimum sustainable stock of the natural environment may not be attained through the allocative mechanism of market institutions. Under competitive arrangements, for example, even when the phenomenon of the tragedy of the commons may not occur, the long-run level of the stock of the natural environment at the competitive equilibrium inevitably is lower than the optimum sustainable level, thus implying a loss in the long-run level of the social welfare.

The institutions of the commons have historically been set up to solve the problems of the optimum use of the resources from the natural environment. Some of the more successful historical and traditional commons have been studied in detail. Among them, the Japanese common-property arrangements concerning the fisheries rights of the seas, both offshore and distant, may be cited among the most efficient and well managed.

3   Social infrastructure as social overhead capital

In the previous section, we formulated a simple dynamic model concerning the depletion of the natural environment due to economic activities, and derived the conditions under which the allocative mechanism involving the use of the natural environment as factors of production is dynamically optimum. This section concerns the problems of social infrastructure and formulates a dynamic model where the role of social infrastructure as social overhead capital is explicitly brought out.

We assume that social infrastructure may be measured in terms of the homogeneous quantity. The stock of social infrastructure at time t will be denoted by V_t, time suffix t again being conveniently omitted. It is assumed to depreciate at a certain technologically determined rate, say μ per annum.

The stock of infrastructure is depleted due to economic activities conducted in the economy. The economic activities in relation to the production of consumption goods are represented by a vector of activity levels, $a = (a_j)$, where activities are denoted by j. The rate at which the stock of social infrastructure is depleted due to economic activities is specified in a manner similar to that used for the natural environment.

The rate of depletion X_t at time t is related to the vector of activity levels a_t at time t:

$$X_t = \xi a_t \tag{3.1}$$

where $\xi = (\xi_j)$ is the vector specifying the stock of the natural environment depleted by economic activities. The quantities of privately owned resources employed by economic activities are given by Aa_t, where $A = (a_{lj})$ is the matrix of input coefficients.

The stock of social infrastructure may be increased by employing scarce resources in the construction of its physical and institutional components. Let us denote such activities generically as s, and represent their activity levels by a vector, $b = (b_s)$. If we denote by $\eta = (\eta_s)$ the vector specifying the quantities of social infrastructure newly contracted by such activities, then the increase in the stock of social infrastructure at time t may be given by

$$Y_t = \eta b_t \tag{3.2}$$

The quantities of privately owned scarce resources required for investment activities in social infrastructure are specified by the matrix $B = (b_{ls})$. The vector of inputs of privately owned scarce resources required for the vector of activity levels b_t is given by Bb_t.

The change in the stock of social infrastructure is specified by the dynamic equation

$$\dot{V}_t = Y_t - X_t - \mu V_t \tag{3.3}$$

with the given initial condition V_o.

For vectors of activity levels b_t and a_t to be feasible, the following conditions have to be satisfied:

$$b_t \quad a_t \geq 0 \quad Bb_t + Aa_t \leq K \tag{3.4}$$

where $K = (K_l)$ is the vector of endowments of privately owned scarce resources.

As for the specifications concerning the production of consumption goods and the nature of the social utility function, we use a formulation similar to the case of the natural environment. The vector of consumption goods $c_t = (c_{it})$ produced by vector of activity levels $a_t = (a_{jt})$ is given by

$$c_t = Ca_t \tag{3.5}$$

where $C = (c_{ij})$ is the matrix of output coefficients; the social utility u_t at time t is given by

$$u_t = u(c_t, V_t) = u(c_t)\phi(V_t) \tag{3.6}$$

where $u(c)$ and $\phi(V)$ are both positive, strictly concave functions respectively of c and V, and the γ defined by (2.6) is a constant.

A time-path of vectors of activity levels and consumption goods (b_t, a_t, c_t) is defined as dynamically optimum if it is feasible in the sense that feasibility conditions (3.1–3.5) are satisfied, and it maximizes the Ramsey–Cass–Koopmans utility integral (2.9) among all feasible time-paths. As with the natural environment, the structure of dynamically optimum time-paths may be characterized in terms of the imputed price of the stock of social infrastructure.

Let λ_t denote the imputed price at time t of the stock of social infrastructure. Then the definition of imputed price implies

$$\lambda_t = \int_t^\infty u(c_\iota)\phi'(V_\iota)e^{(\delta+\mu)(\iota-t)}d\iota \enspace .$$

which, by differentiation with respect to time t, yields

$$\frac{\dot{\lambda}_t}{\lambda_t} = (\delta + \mu) - \frac{u(c_t)\phi'(V_t)}{\lambda_t} \tag{3.7}$$

The optimum vectors of activity levels and consumption goods, (b_t, a_t, c_t) at each time t may be obtained by maximizing the imputed real income

$$H_t = u(c_t)\phi(V_t) + \lambda_t(Y_t - X_t - \mu V_t)$$

subject to the feasibility conditions (3.1), (3.2), (3.4), and (3.5).

The new imputed price π_t is now introduced to simplify our analysis:

$$\pi_t = \frac{\lambda_t}{\phi(V_t)}$$

Then, (b_t, a_t, c_t) is optimum if and only if it maximizes the real income in terms of the new imputed price π_t:

$$H_t = u(c_t) + \pi_t(Y_t - X_t)$$

subject to the feasibility conditions (3.1), (3.2), (3.4), (3.5), and (3.6).

An argument analogous to that for the natural environment shows that, as imputed price π_t becomes higher, the net addition to the stock of social infrastructure, $Y_t - X_t$, is increased, while imputed real income per imputed price, $u(c_t)/\pi_t + (Y_t - X_t)$, is decreased.

The dynamic equations for the stock of social infrastructure V_t and the new imputed price π_t can be derived from (3.3) and (3.7):

$$\frac{\dot{V}}{V} = \frac{Y - X}{V} - \mu \tag{3.8}$$

$$\frac{\dot{\pi}}{\pi} = \delta + \left(1 + \gamma\right)\mu - \gamma \frac{\dfrac{u(c)}{\pi} + \left(Y - X\right)}{V} \tag{3.9}$$

The dynamically optimum time-path may be obtained if we find the solution paths (V_t, π_t) to the dynamiç system, (3.8) and (3.9), for which the transversality conditions (2.15) are satisfied.

Let us first examine the conditions under which the stock of social infrastructure remains stationary. The stock of social infrastructure V_t remains stationary if and only if the right-hand side of dynamic equation (3.8) is zero, that is,

$$V = \frac{Y - X}{\mu} \tag{3.10}$$

Since $Y - X$ is determined independently of V, the right-hand side of (3.10) may be depicted by the upward sloping curve, as illustrated by the EE curve in Figure 5, where the stock of social infrastructure V is measured along the abscissa, while the ordinate measures imputed price π. The EE curve intersects with the ordinate at a positive distance from the origin, while, as π becomes infinity, the EE curve asymptotically approaches the vertical line with the distance, $(\overline{Y} - \overline{X})/\mu$, from the ordinate. The value of $(\overline{Y} - \overline{X})$ is obtained by maximizing $(Y - X)$ subject to the constraints (3.1), (3.2), (3.4).

When (π, V) lies above the EE curve, the right-hand side of equation (3.8) becomes positive, implying that $\dot{V} > 0$, whereas when it lies below the EE curve, $\dot{V} < 0$.

The phase diagram for imputed price π may be similarly obtained. Imputed price π remains stationary if and only if the following conditions are satisfied:

$$V = \gamma \frac{\dfrac{u(c)}{\pi} + (Y - X)}{\delta + (1 + \gamma)\mu} \tag{3.11}$$

Since the numerator of the right-hand side of (3.11) is independent of V and decreases as imputed price π is increased, the right-hand side of (3.11) may be depicted by the downward sloping curve, FF, as illustrated in Figure 5. As imputed price π becomes infinity, the FF curve asymptotically approaches the vertical line whose distance from the ordinate

equals $\gamma \dfrac{\overline{Y} - \overline{X}}{\delta + (1 + \gamma)\mu}$.

When (π, V) lies above the FF curve, the imputed price π tends to increase; when it lies below the FF curve, it tends to decrease, as indicated by the arrowed lines in Figure 5.

Solution paths to the pair of dynamic equations, (3.8) and (3.9), are the structure as indicated by the arrowed curves in Figure 5. There always exist a pair of solution paths both of which converge to the stationary point (π^∞, E^∞). Such solution paths are represented by the functional relationships $\pi = \pi^o(V)$. The dynamically optimum time-path may be obtained if, at each time t, the imputed price $\pi_t = \pi^o(V_t)$ is used in the allocation of privately owned resources between the production of consumption goods and investment in social infrastructure. The resulting time-path of the stock of social infrastructure then becomes dynamically optimum.

The stationary long-run level V^∞ of the stock of social infrastructure is determined in relation to the given parameters concerning the technological conditions, the availability of privately owned scarce resources, and the intertemporal preference ordering. An increase in the social rate of discount δ implies that the FF curve in Figure 5 shifts downward, resulting in a decrease in the long-run level V^∞ of the stock of social infrastructure, with an accompanying decrease in the imputed price π^∞. On the other hand, an increase in the sensitivity parameter δ implies that the FF curve shifts upward, resulting in increases in both the long-run level V^∞ of the stock of social infrastructure and imputed price π^∞.

An increase in the endowments of privately owned scarce resources or an improvement in technological conditions will result in a shift to the right-hand direction of both the EE and FF curves. Hence, the long-run stationary level V^∞ of the stock of infrastructure becomes higher, while the imputed price π^∞ may be either decreased or increased.

Imputed Price
(π)

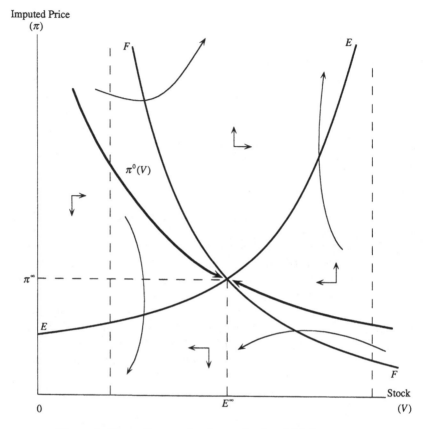

$\pi^0(V)$

π^∞

E^∞

Stock
(V)

0

Figure 5. Phase diagram for the stock of social infrastructure.

In the simple dynamic model concerning the accumulation of social overhead capital, we have assumed that the technological conditions and the availability of privately owned scarce resource remain constant, independent of the accumulation of the stock of social infrastructure. The phenomena of technological progress induced by the availability of social infrastructure and the accompanying increase in investment activities in the stock of privately owned scarce resources may be regarded as central issues in the theory of social infrastructure, particularly within the context of developing nations. Similarly, the problems of designing institutional frameworks in which the optimum allocation of both social overhead capital and privately owned scarce resources may be realized are crucial in any attempt toward practical implementations of the theory of social overhead capital we have developed in this chapter. With these qualifications in mind, we explore further the theoretical implications of the analysis developed in this and previous sections.

4   Externalities and imputed prices

In the formulation of the dynamic models of natural capital and social infrastructure, as developed in the previous sections, we have not taken due account of the phenomenon of externalities in the processes of consumption and production involving social overhead capital. In this section, we extend the analysis introduced in Uzawa (1974) to cover the situation where social overhead capital exhibits a significant degree of externalities with respect to both consumption and production activities in the economy.

Let us denote by V_t the stock of natural capital at time t, as in Section 2, and by $\mu(V)$ the ecological rate of growth in V. It is assumed that the $\mu(V)$ function is represented by a curve as illustrated in Figure 1.

It is assumed that there exist a number of producing units in the economy, generically denoted by β, and the vector of activity levels for producers β is denoted by $a\beta = (a_j\beta)$, where j generically represents activities at the disposal of producers. The stock of social overhead capital is depleted by production activities. It is assumed that the vector of activity levels $a\beta$ involves the depletion of natural capital by the quantity $X\beta = X\beta(a\beta)$.

The quantities of consumption goods produced by β are denoted by the vector of consumption goods, $Y\beta = (Y_i\beta)$, where i generically refers to consumption goods. The production functions are written as $Y\beta = Y\beta(a\beta)$, where, for the sake of brevity, the values and the functions are denoted by the same symbols.

The processes of production require the input of privately owned factors of production. The vector of factors of production employed by β will be denoted by $K\beta(a\beta) = (K_l\beta(a\beta))$, where l refers to privately owned factors of production.

The social institution in charge of the maintenance and regeneration of social overhead capital is also engaged in productive activities. The vector of activity levels with respect to social overhead capital will be denoted by $a\alpha$. The quantities of the stock of natural capital to be regenerated and depleted by vector of activity levels is specified respectively by $Y\alpha = Y\alpha(a\alpha)$ and $X\alpha = X\alpha(a\alpha)$; the quantities of factors of production employed are given by $K\alpha = K\alpha(a\alpha)$.

We assume that the endowments of factors of production are given by $K = (K_l)$, to remain constant throughout the following discussion. The feasibility conditions then are given by

$$K\alpha(a\alpha) + \sum \beta K\beta(a\beta) \le K \qquad (4.1)$$

On the other hand, the aggregate quantity of the stock of natural capital to be depleted is given by

$$X = X\alpha(a\alpha) + \sum \beta X\beta(a\beta) \qquad (4.2)$$

There are two kinds of externalities, static and dynamic. The static externalities occur when the marginal productivities of privately owned factors of production are decreased as the aggregate quantity of the stock of natural capital to be either depleted as harvests or utilized as factors of production is increased. On the other hand, the dynamic externalities are observed when the decline in the stock of natural capital induces the changes in the conditions of marginal productivities of factors of production.

We first discuss the phenomenon of static externalities, which will be handled by introducing the aggregate quantity of the stock of natural capital, X, as a relevant variable in both the production functions and the resource requirement functions. It is assumed that the quantities of consumption goods produced by producer β are given by

$$Y\beta = Y\beta(a\beta, X)$$

and the resource requirement functions are written as

$$K\beta = K\beta(a\beta, X)$$

where the conditions of external diseconomies are expressed by

$$Y_X\beta < 0 \qquad K_X\beta > 0 \qquad Y_{XX}\beta < 0 \qquad K_{XX}\beta > 0$$

Similar specifications will be made for the sector in charge of natural capital. It is assumed that

$$Y\alpha = Y\alpha(a\alpha, X) \qquad K\alpha = K\alpha(a\alpha, X),$$

$$Y_X\alpha < 0 \qquad K_X\alpha > 0 \qquad Y_{XX}\alpha < 0 \qquad K_{XX}\alpha > 0$$

The feasibility conditions (4.1) now may be written as

$$Ka\big(aa, X\big) + \sum \beta K\beta\big(a\beta, X\big) \le K \tag{4.3}$$

The standard neoclassical assumptions are made for the technological conditions in both the private and public sectors of the economy. The production functions, $Ya = Ya(aa, X)$ and $Y\beta = Y\beta(a\beta, X)$, are all assumed to be positive valued, strictly quasi-concave, homogeneous of order one, and continuously twice-differentiable with respect to (aa, X) and $(a\beta, X)$ respectively, together with the following conditions:

$$Ya\big(0, X\big) = 0 \qquad Y_{aa}a\big(aa, X\big) > 0$$
$$Y\beta\big(0, X\big) = 0 \qquad Y_{a\beta}\beta\big(a\beta, X\big) > 0$$

Similar assumptions are made for the resource requirement functions. It is assumed that $Ka(aa, X)$ and $K\beta(a\beta, X)$ are positive valued, strictly quasi-convex, homogeneous of order one, and continuously differentiable with respect to (aa, X) and $(a\beta, X)$, respectively, together with the conditions:

$$Ka\big(0, X\big) = 0 \qquad K_{aa}a\big(aa, X\big) > 0$$
$$K\beta\big(0, X\big) = 0 \qquad K_{a\beta}\beta\big(a\beta, X\big) > 0$$

The change in the stock of natural capital is now given by the following dynamic equation:

$$\dot{V}_t = \mu\big(V_t\big)V_t + Y_t a - X_t \tag{4.4}$$

with the initial condition V_o.

We must now specify how the output of consumption goods is distributed among the individual members of the economy. It is assumed that the aggregate income is distributed among members of the economy in such a manner that a certain well-defined social utility function is maximized. We also assume that the external effects the stock of natural capital may have on the level of real income are expressed by the specification that the level of social utility depends on the stock of natural capital as well as on the aggregate quantities of consumption goods produced in the economy. The level of social utility at time t, U_t, is written as:

$$U_t = U\big(C_t, V_t\big) \tag{4.5}$$

where

$$C_t = \sum \beta Y \beta\left(a_t \beta, X_t\right) \tag{4.6}$$

Before we discuss the dynamically optimum path of economic activities involving both the allocation of privately owned resources and the regeneration and depletion of natural capital, we examine the structure of competitive equilibrium and its implications for the long-run state of the stock of natural capital.

Let the prices of consumption goods and privately owned factors of production, measured in a certain accounting unit, be represented by price vectors, $p = (p_{ji})$ and $r = (r_l)$, respectively. Under the competitive hypothesis, each producer β will choose the vector of activity levels $a\beta$ which maximizes his net profits:

$$pY\beta\left(a\beta, X\right) - rK\beta\left(a\beta, X\right) \tag{4.7}$$

where the aggregate quantity of natural capital depleted, X, is assumed to be a given parameter for each producer β.

Under the competitive hypothesis, there is no incentive for the regeneration of natural capital, and $a\alpha = 0$, $Y\alpha = 0$. The feasibility conditions (4.3) are simply written as

$$\sum \beta K\beta\left(a\beta, X\right) \le K \tag{4.8}$$

On the other hand, the demand conditions imply that the prices of consumption goods are proportional to the levels of marginal utilities. That is,

$$U_c \sim p \tag{4.9}$$

where the symbol indicates the proportionality of two vectors.

The prices of consumption goods and factors of production at the competitive equilibrium are obtained if they satisfy the equilibrium conditions (4.8) and (4.9), while the maximizing conditions of the net profits (4.7) are realized. Under certain conditions concerning the production functions and resource requirement functions, the competitive equilibrium always exists and is uniquely determined. Instead of going into detail, we take it for granted that the competitive equilibrium uniquely exists, and the price vectors at the competitive equilibrium are denoted by $p(0)$ and $r(0)$, with the corresponding vectors of activity levels $a\beta(0)$. The level of social utility at the competitive equilibrium is given by

$$U(0) = U\left(C(0)\right)$$

where the dependency upon the stock of natural capital is, for the time being, omitted, and

$$c(0) = \sum \beta Y \beta \left(a\beta(0) \, X(0) \right)$$

and

$$X(0) = \sum \beta X \beta \left(a\beta(0) \right)$$

In view of the external diseconomies in the use of the stock of natural capital incorporated into the formulation of our model, it is straightforward to see that the allocation of scarce resources at the competitive equilibrium is not statically optimum, in the sense that it is possible to find another pattern of resource allocation involving the allocation of privately owned factors of production and the use of the stock of natural capital which would result in a higher level of social utility $U(C)$. The nonoptimality of the competitive equilibrium exists because no charges are made for the use of the stock of natural capital, although it is scarce from the social point of view. We introduce a pricing scheme according to which each producer is charged an amount proportional to the quantity of the stock of natural capital depleted by his activities and we see how the level of social utility may be affected by the introduction of such a scheme.

Let us denote by θ the price charged to each producer for the unit quantity of the stock of natural capital depleted by his activities. The net profits for producer β then will be given by

$$pY\beta(a\beta, X) - rK\beta(a\beta, X) - \theta X\beta(a\beta) \tag{4.10}$$

instead of (18.35) as in the case of competitive equilibrium.

The net profits (18.38) are maximized when the following marginality conditions are satisfied:

$$pY_{a\beta}\beta = rK_{a\beta}\beta + \theta X_{a\beta}\beta \tag{4.11}$$

where $(a\beta, X)$ are omitted for the sake of brevity.

The new equilibrium associated with the pricing scheme, θ, is specified by $p(\theta)$, $r(\theta)$, and $a\beta(\theta)$. Then, in addition to the profit maximizing conditions (4.11), we have

$$X(\theta) = \sum \beta X \beta(\theta)$$
$$\sum \beta K \beta(\theta) = K$$

which, by differentiation with respect to θ, yield:

$$X'(\theta) = \sum \beta X^{\beta'}(\theta) \tag{4.12}$$

$$\sum \beta K^{\beta'}(\theta) = 0 \tag{4.13}$$

since the endowments of privately owned factors of production are assumed to remain constant.

We should like to see how the level of social utility

$$U(\theta) = U(C(\theta)) \qquad C(\theta) = \sum \beta Y \beta(a\beta(\theta) X(\theta)) \tag{4.14}$$

changes when the rate of charge θ changes. We differentiate (4.14) with respect to θ to obtain

$$\begin{aligned}
U'(\theta) &\sim p\left[\sum \beta Y_{a\beta} \beta a^{\beta'}(\theta) + Y_X \beta X'(\theta)\right] \\
&= \sum \beta\left[rK_{a\beta} \beta a^{\beta'}(\theta) + \theta X_{a\beta} \beta a^{\beta'}(\theta)\right] + \sum \beta p Y_X \beta X'(\theta) \\
&= \sum \beta\left[-rK_X \beta a^{\beta'}(\theta)\right] + \theta X'(\theta) + \sum \beta p Y_X \beta X'(\theta) \\
&= \left[\theta + \sum \beta\left(p Y_X \beta - rK_X \beta\right)\right] X'(\theta).
\end{aligned}$$

Hence, we have the following equality:

$$\frac{dU(\theta)}{d\theta} \sim (\theta * - \theta)\left(-\frac{dX(\theta)}{d\theta}\right) \tag{4.15}$$

where $\theta*$ is the quantity defined by

$$\theta * = \sum \beta\left[-p Y_X \beta + rK_X \beta\right] \tag{4.16}$$

The $\theta*$ as defined by (4.16) corresponds to the concept of marginal social costs associated with the use or depletion of the stock of natural capital. It expresses the aggregate of the marginal losses incurred by all members of the economy due to the marginal increase in the quantity of the use or depletion of the stock of natural capital, within the context of the static environment. It should not be identified with the concept of marginal social costs in the dynamic context, to be introduced later.

The equality (4.15) implies that, when the rate θ is lower than the marginal social cost θ^*, then the level of social utility $U(\theta)$ is increased, as the rate of charge θ is increased, whereas, when the rate θ is higher than θ^*, an increase in the rate θ tends to lower the level of social utility. When the rate θ of charge is equal to the magnitude of marginal social costs θ^*, the resulting allocation of resources is optimum in the sense that the level of social utility $U(\theta)$ is maximized. This is simply the principle of marginal social cost pricing applied to the use of natural capital. It may be noted that the competitive equilibrium corresponds to the case where $\theta = 0$.

However, the level of social utility $U(\theta)$ is only maximized when the pricing scheme is used in the allocation of the resources to be obtained from the given stock of natural capital, while privately owned scarce resources are allocated in a competitive market. The question naturally arises: Is it possible to find an alternative allocation of scarce resources where the level of social utility would be higher than that achieved through the principle of marginal social cost pricing? The answer to this question is no, as implied from the basic premises on which our model has been constructed. In order to see this, let us consider the following optimum problem:

Find vectors of activities $(a\beta)$ which maximize the level of social utility $U(C)$ subject to the constraints that

$$C = \sum \beta Y \beta(a\beta, X) \tag{4.17}$$

$$\sum \beta K \beta(a\beta, X) \le K \tag{4.18}$$

$$X = \sum \beta X \beta(a\beta, X) \tag{4.19}$$

This optimum problem is solved in terms of the Lagrange method. Let p, r, and θ be, respectively the Lagrange unknowns associated with the constraints (4.17), (4.18), and (4.19), and let the Lagrangian form be defined by

$$
\begin{aligned}
L(a\beta, X, p, r, \theta) = U(C) &+ p\left(\sum \beta Y \beta(a\beta, X) - C\right) \\
&+ r\left(K - \sum \beta K \beta(a\beta, X)\right) \\
&+ \theta\left(X - \sum \beta X \beta(a\beta)\right)
\end{aligned} \tag{4.20}
$$

Then the optimum solution is obtained by the first-order conditions with respect to the Lagrangian form (4.20):

$$U_c = p \tag{4.21}$$

$$pY_{a\beta}\beta - rK_{a\beta}\beta - \theta X_{a\beta}\beta = 0 \tag{4.22}$$

$$\theta + \sum \beta p Y_X \beta - \sum \beta r K_X \beta = 0 \tag{4.23}$$

together with the constraints (4.17), (4.18), and (4.19), where, however, (4.18) is satisfied with equality.

We can easily see that optimum conditions (4.17–4.19) and (4.21–4.23) are identical to those for the equilibrium conditions for the pricing scheme with the rate of charge equal to the marginal social cost θ^*. The marginal social cost for the use of the stock of natural capital now may be identified with the imputed price of the stock of natural capital, which will be effectively utilized in bringing about the allocation of scarce resources, both privately owned factors of production and natural capital, which is optimum from the static point of view. In the next few sections, we extend our analysis to incidences of the regeneration and depletion of natural capital, examined in terms of the optimum criteria involving not only the current welfare effect, but also the welfare of future generations.

5   Optimum investment in natural capital

In the previous section, we formulated a model of natural capital as social overhead capital and saw how the allocation optimum from the static point of view may be attained in terms of the concept of imputed prices. We did not consider, however, the influence the regeneration and depletion of the stock of natural capital might have on the allocative processes and social welfare of the economy, although the dynamic aspect is incorporated in the basic equation (4.4), reproduced here for convenience:

$$\dot{V}_t = \mu(V_t)V_t + Y_t a - X_t \tag{4.4}$$

where $\mu(V)$ is the ecological rate of growth in the stock of natural capital, and $Y_t a, X_t$ are respectively the rates at which the stock of natural capital is either regenerated or depleted.

The rate of depletion of the stock of natural capital, X_t, is determined by the economic activities undertaken by members of society, including the social institution in charge of natural capital:

$$X_t = Xa(a_t a) + \sum \beta X \beta(a_t \beta) \tag{5.1}$$

where $a_t a$, $a_t \beta$ denote the vectors of activity levels at time t.

On the other hand, the rate of regeneration of the stock of natural capital, $Y_t a$, is solely determined by the social institution in charge of natural capital:

$$Y_t a = Ya\big(a_t a, X_t\big) \tag{5.2}$$

At the competitive equilibrium, there is no incentive for the economy to allocate scarce resources to regenerate natural capital. The same is true for the static optimum where each member of society pays charges based on the imputed price, in the static sense, for the depletion of the stock of natural capital brought about by his or her activities.

When, however, one looks at the problems of the allocation of scarce resources from the dynamic point of view, the regeneration and depletion of the stock of natural capital play a crucial role, primarily because the basic premises postulated for the structure of the social utility function, as formalized in (4.5):

$$U_t = U\big(C_t, V_t\big) \tag{4.5}$$

where the aggregate vector of consumption goods, C_t, is given by

$$C_t = \sum \beta Y \beta\big(a_t \beta, X_t\big) \tag{4.6}$$

The regeneration and depletion of the stock of natural capital today have direct implications for the levels of social utility for all future generations.

The criteria for dynamic optimality are formulated in terms of the Ramsey–Cass–Koopmans utility integral, introduced in previous sections:

$$U = \int_0^\infty U_t e^{-\delta t} dt$$

where the social rate of discount δ is assumed to be positive and constant.

Analysis of the problem of dynamic optimum involves rather tedious calculation. We therefore focus our attention on a simple case which retains most of the crucial elements of our analysis. This is the case where the social utility function (4.5) is separable with respect to the aggregate vector of consumption goods C and the stock of natural capital V, as previously assumed. The social utility function is assumed to have the following form:

$$U_t = u(C_t)\phi(V_t) \tag{5.3}$$

where $u(C)$ and $\phi(V)$ are positively valued, strictly concave, and continuously twice-differentiable with respect to C and V, respectively. It is also assumed that $U(C,V)$ is concave with respect to (C,V) and that

$$\gamma = \frac{\phi'(V)V}{\phi V}$$

is constant, as in the previous sections.

The endowments of privately owned factors of production are $K = (K_l)$, assumed to remain constant. The feasibility conditions (4.3) are reproduced:

$$K\alpha(a_t\alpha, X_t) + \sum \beta K\beta(a_t\beta, X_t) \le K \tag{4.3}$$

A time-path of vectors of activity levels, $(a_t\alpha, a_t\beta)$, is defined as dynamically optimum, if it is feasible, that is, (4.4), (5.1), (5.2), (4.6), and (4.3) are satisfied, and it maximizes the Ramsey–Cass–Koopmans utility integral (4.2) among all feasible time-paths of vectors of activity levels.

The dynamically optimum time-path of vectors of activity can be characterized in terms of the imputed price of the stock of natural capital at each time t, to be denoted by λ_t.

A calculation similar to the one explained in Section 2 derives the following basic equation for the dynamics of imputed price λ_t:

$$\frac{\dot{\lambda}_t}{\lambda_t} = \delta - \mu(V_t) - \mu'(V_t)V_t - \frac{u(C_t)\phi'(V_t)}{\lambda_t} \tag{5.4}$$

On the other hand, imputed price λ_t is used in defining the concept of real income:

$$H_t = u(c_t)\phi(V_t) + \lambda_t(Y_t\alpha - X_t) \tag{5.5}$$

The optimum vectors of activity levels $(a_t\alpha, a_t\beta)$ are obtained by maximizing real income (5.5) subject to the feasibility constraints (5.1), (5.2), (4.6), and (4.3).

Let p, r, and θ denote, respectively, the Lagrange unknowns associated with the constraints (4.6), (4.3), and (5.1). Then the Lagrangian form becomes

$$L(a\alpha, a\beta, X, p, r, \theta) = U(C)\phi(V) + \lambda\big(Y\alpha(a\alpha, X) - X\big)$$
$$+ p\Big(\sum \beta Y \beta(a\beta, X) - C\Big)$$
$$+ r\Big(K - K\alpha(a\alpha, X) - \sum \beta K \beta(a\beta, X)\Big)$$
$$+ \theta\Big(X - X\alpha(a\alpha, X) - \sum \beta X \beta(a\beta, X)\Big)$$

$$(5.6)$$

The first-order conditions are:

$$U_c = p \tag{5.7}$$

$$\lambda Y_{a\alpha}\alpha = rK_{a\alpha}\alpha + \theta X_{a\alpha}\alpha \tag{5.8}$$

$$pY_{a\beta}\beta = rK_{a\beta}\beta + \theta X_{a\beta}\beta \tag{5.9}$$

$$\theta = \lambda + \big(-\lambda Y_X \alpha + rK_X \alpha\big) + \sum \beta\big(-pY_X \beta + rK_X \beta\big) \tag{5.10}$$

The condition (5.7) means that the aggregate pattern of consumption is so arranged that the utility level is maximized subject to the budgetary constraints. The condition (5.8) is realized when the value based on the imputed price of the stock of natural capital is assigned to the regenerative activities of the social institution in charge of natural capital. It must pay, as must other productive agencies, a sum corresponding to the imputed value of the depletion of the stock of natural capital incurred by its activities.

The marginality condition (5.9) is nothing but the standard profit maximization condition, where the depletion of the stock of natural capital is evaluated based on its static imputed price.

The condition (5.10) states that the imputed price equals the marginal social cost associated with the use of natural capital, θ^*, to be defined by

$$\theta^* = \lambda + \big(-\lambda Y_X \alpha + rK_X \alpha\big) + \sum \beta\big[-pY_X \beta + rK_X \beta\big] \tag{5.11}$$

The assumptions concerning the production and regenerative functions assure us that the optimum vectors of activity levels at each time t, $(a_t\alpha, a_t\beta)$, are uniquely determined once the dynamic imputed price λ_t of the stock of natural capital at time t is known. The determination of the dynamic imputed price λ_t may be more easily analyzed if we replace it with the imputed price in terms of $\phi(V_t)$ introduced in the previous sections. Let the new imputed price π_t be defined by

$$\pi_t = \frac{\lambda_t}{\phi(V_t)}$$

Then the dynamic equations (4.4) and (5.4) may be rewritten as follows:

$$\frac{\dot{V}}{V} = \mu(V) - \frac{X - Y\alpha}{V} \tag{5.12}$$

$$\frac{\dot{\pi}}{\pi} = \hat{\mu}(V) - \gamma \frac{\dfrac{u(C)}{\pi} - (X - Y\alpha)}{V} \tag{5.13}$$

where the time suffix is omitted, and

$$\hat{\mu} = \delta + (1 + \gamma)\mu(V) + \mu'(V)$$

The optimum vectors of activity levels at time t, $(a_t\alpha, a_t\beta)$, are now determined as the optimum solution to the following maximizing problem:

Maximize

$$u(C) - \pi_t(X - Y\alpha) \tag{5.14}$$

subject to the constraints (5.1), (5.2), (4.6), and (4.3).

This maximization problem is defined independently of the stock of natural capital V_t, and the optimum vectors of activity levels, $(a_t\alpha, a_t\beta)$, are uniquely determined, depending on the new imputed price π_t alone. An argument similar to those presented in Section 2 shows that, as the new imputed price π_t becomes higher, the net rate of accumulation of the stock of natural capital, $Y\alpha - X$, increases, while the level of real income measured in terms of π_t,

$$\frac{u(C)}{\pi} - (X - Y\alpha)$$

tends to be decreased.

The dynamically optimum time-path of vectors of activity levels may now be obtained if one finds the solutions to the pair of differential equations, (5.3) and (5.4), for which the transversality conditions (2.15) are satisfied.

The structure of the optimum trajectories, therefore, is identical to those of the simple cases discussed in Section 2, and the phase diagrams introduced there are directly applicable to the present situation.

The phase diagrams have different structures, depending on whether the competitive equilibrium has a point in common with the $\mu(V)$ curve. Figure 2 illustrates the phase diagrams for the case where the competitive equilibrium intersects with the $\mu(V)$ curve, with the corresponding levels of the stock of natural capital, $\underline{V}^\infty$ and $\overline{V}^\infty$. The upper critical level $\overline{V}^\infty$ represents the stable, long-run stationary level of the stock of natural capital, to which the competitive equilibrium converges as time goes to infinity. It is decisively lower than the ecologically sustainable level of the stock of natural capital, $\overline{V}$, which is characterized by the condition that $\mu(\overline{V}) = 0$.

In Figure 2, the combinations of V and π, for which V remains stationary are depicted by two curves, $\underline{BB}$ and $\overline{BB}$, whereas, the $\underline{AA}$ and $\overline{AA}$ curves represent the stationarity for π. The solution paths to the pair of differential equations, (18.54) and (18.55), are typically illustrated by the arrowed curves in Figure 2. The stable pair of solution paths which converge to the stationary state $\overline{E}^\infty$, as denoted by the functional notation $\pi^o(V)$, gives us the optimum trajectory. The imputed price for the stock of natural capital generally increases as the stock of natural capital declines, as is seen from the trajectory in Figure 2. The long-run stationary level of the stock of natural capital, $\overline{V}^\infty$, is higher than the competitive level $\overline{V}^c$, but lower than the ecologically sustainable maximum level $\overline{V}^\infty$. It may be noted that $\overline{V}^\infty$ is higher than another critical level $\overline{V}\delta$, which is defined by $\hat{\mu}(\overline{V}\delta) = 0$.

Figure 3 illustrates the phase diagrams for the case where the competitive equilibrium does not have a common point with the $\mu(V)$ curve, as is the case with the $C'C'$ curve in Figure 1. The stock of natural capital steadily declines at the competitive equilibrium, eventually approaching the state of extinction. The combinations of V and π, for which the stock of natural capital V remains stationary, are depicted by the single curve, $\underline{BB}$. It intersects with the $\underline{AA}$ and $\overline{AA}$ curves at two points, $\underline{E}^\infty$ and $\overline{E}^\infty$, with the corresponding levels of the stock of natural capital, $\underline{V}^\infty$ and $\overline{V}^\infty$. The optimum trajectory may be obtained by the stable pair of solution paths converging to the upper critical level $\overline{V}^\infty$. The structure of the dynamically optimum path is analyzed similarly to the previous case.

We have thus seen, by applying the standard technique of the optimization theory, that the management of natural capital dynamically optimum from the social point of view may be attained through the devices of two imputed prices, static on the one hand and dynamic on the other. The static imputed price expresses the extent to which the marginal increase in the depletion of the stock of natural capital leads to marginal losses to all the members of the society, including those activities related to the regeneration of the stock of natural capital. On the other hand, the dynamic imputed price of the stock of natural capital at each time t measures the extent of the marginal increases in the levels of social utility for future generations due to the marginal increase in the stock of natural capital at time t. It is expressed as the discounted present value of the marginal increases in future levels of social utility, and it is the basis for the evaluation of regenerative activities.

The static imputed price assures that the optimum level of the depletion of the stock of natural capital is attained, and the dynamic imputed price serves as an effective instrument in terms of which the optimum level of investment in natural capital may be obtained. In the analysis presented here, it is assumed that no significant administrative costs are involved in implementing the pricing scheme, with respect to both static and dynamic circumstances, and that the introduction of such a pricing scheme does not have an effect on technological and institutional conditions. In any practical application of the optimum criteria introduced here, however, a system of institutional arrangements concerning property ownerships, regulatory measures, tax and subsidy instruments, and other measures have to be devised to substitute effectively for the pricing scheme to approximate the long-run optimum, as in numerous cases of the historical and traditional commons, particularly those of the fisheries, forestry, and agricultural commons in Southeast Asian countries.

6   A general dynamic model of social overhead capital

In this section, we formulate a general dynamic model of social overhead capital with particular reference to social infrastructure, as introduced in Section 4.

The society is assumed, as specified in Section 4, to be composed of private economic units, to be generically denoted by β and a social institution, α, which is fiduciarily entrusted with the management of social overhead capital. Private economic units are engaged in the production of consumption goods which are consumed by individual members of the society, denoted by v. Productive activities require the services provided by the existing stock of social overhead capital as well as the employment of privately owned factors of production. The output of consumption goods produced by each economic unit β is specified by the production function, $Y\beta = Y\beta(a\beta)$, where $a\beta$ denotes the vector of activity levels undertaken by β. The quantities of privately owned scarce resources required are given by $K\beta(a\beta)$; the services derived from social overhead capital are given by $K\beta(a\beta)$.

A social institution is engaged in the regeneration or construction of social overhead capital. Its production function $Ya = Ya(aa)$ specifies the quantity of the stock of social overhead capital regenerated or newly produced, whereas the resource requirement functions are denoted by $Ka(aa)$. The social institution also uses the services of social overhead capital, specified by $Xa(aa)$.

The total quantity of the services of social overhead capital X is given by

$$X = Xa(aa) + \sum \beta X \beta(a\beta)$$

In the previous sections, the phenomenon of static externalities inherent in the use of social overhead capital is expressed by the specification that the production functions and resource requirement functions for private economic units and social institution a involve the total quantity of the services of social overhead capital X. The crucial properties are that, as X is increased, the output of consumption goods and newly produced social overhead capital is decreased and the required quantities of privately owned factors of production are increased. In a more general case of social overhead capital, these functions involve the existing stock of social overhead capital as well. Hence, they may be respectively written as follows:

$$Ya(aa, X, V), \quad Ka(aa, X, V), \quad Y\beta(a\beta, X, V), \quad K\beta(a\beta, X, V)$$

where V denotes the existing stock of social overhead capital.

The aggregate quantities of consumption goods produced are given by

$$C_t = \sum \beta Y_t \beta(a_t \beta, X_t, V_t) \tag{6.1}$$

while the feasibility conditions for privately owned factors of production are given by

$$Ka(a_t a, X_t, V_t) + \sum v Kv(a_t v, X_t, V_t) + \sum \beta K\beta(a_t \beta, X_t, V_t) \le K \tag{6.2}$$

where K stands for the endowment vector of factors of production privately owned.

The activities of each member of the society are again represented by vectors of activity levels, typically denoted by av. It is assumed that activ-

ities by members of the society also require the services of social overhead capital as well as the input of consumption goods. The quantities of
services derived from social overhead capital and the input of consumption goods required for vector of activity levels are respectively
denoted by $Xv = Xv(av)$ and $Cv(av, X, V)$.

The total quantity of services of social overhead capital utilized is
rewritten as

$$X_t = X\alpha(a_t\alpha) + \sum v Xv(a_t v) + \sum \beta X\beta(a_t\beta) \tag{6.3}$$

The availability conditions for consumption goods imply

$$C_t = \sum v Cv(a_t v, X_t, V_t) \tag{6.4}$$

For each member, the utility level Uv is assumed to be determined by
the vector of activity levels av, together with the total quantity of services of social overhead capital being utilized X and the existing stock
of social overhead capital V; in functional form

$$U_t v = Uv(a_t v, X_t, V_t) \tag{6.5}$$

We assume that utility levels are measured in terms of an interper-
sonally comparable unit, so that the social utility may be defined by

$$U_t = \sum v Uv(a_t v, X_t, V_t) \tag{6.6}$$

The following analysis may be applied to the general situation where
the social utility U is expressed by a well behaved social welfare function $W(\ldots, Uv, \ldots)$, but, for expository brevity, the discussion is carried
out in terms of the simple case (6.6).

Standard assumptions are made concerning the production functions,
resource requirement functions, and utility functions. Since the following analysis depends crucially on some of these properties, they are
reproduced here, some at the risk of repetition.

The production functions $Y\beta(a\beta, X, V)$ and $Y\alpha(a\alpha, X, V)$ are positive
valued, homogeneous of order one, strictly quasi-concave, continuously
twice-differentiable with respect to $(a\beta, X, V)$ and $(a\alpha, X, V)$, and

$$Y_{a\beta}\beta > 0, \quad Y_X\beta < 0, \quad Y_V\beta > 0, \quad Y_{XX}\beta < 0, \quad Y_{VV}\beta < 0$$

similarly for $Y\alpha$.

On the other hand, the resource requirement functions $K\beta(a\beta, X, V)$
and $K\alpha(a\alpha, X, V)$ are positive valued, homogeneous of order one, strictly

quasi-convex, continuously twice-differentiable with respect to ($a\beta$, X, V) and ($a\alpha$, X, V), and

$$K_{a\beta}\beta > 0, \quad K_X\beta > 0, \quad K_V\beta < 0, \quad K_{XX}\beta > 0, \quad K_{VV}\beta > 0$$

and similarly for $K\alpha$.

The functions $X\beta(a\beta)$ and $X\alpha(a\alpha)$ are positive valued, homogeneous of order one, strictly quasi-concave, continuously twice-differentiable with respect to $a\beta$ and $a\alpha$, and

$$U_{a\beta}\beta > 0, \quad X_{aa}\alpha > 0$$

Some of the assumptions above may be relaxed with respect to the inequality signs in the following analysis. However, they are assumed here mainly to avoid unnecessary complications.

As for the utility functions Uv (av, X, V), they are assumed to be positive valued, strictly quasi-concave, and continuously twice-differentiable with respect to (av, X, V), and

$$U_{av}v > 0, \quad U_Xv < 0, \quad U_Vv > 0$$

It is also assumed that the indifference surfaces are all homothetic, so that

$$Uv\left(av, X, V\right) = Uv\left(av, X\right)\phi\left(V\right)$$

where $av = \dfrac{av}{V}, x = \dfrac{X}{V}$. (To simplify the exposition, the same notations av are used for two purposes. Similarly for $a\beta$, $a\alpha$.)

In the analysis below, we assume that the quantity

$$\gamma = \frac{\phi'\left(V\right)V}{\phi\left(V\right)}$$

is constant. It is easily seen that $0 < \gamma < 1$.

The intertemporal preference ordering for the social utility is now assumed to be represented by the Ramsey–Cass–Koopmans utility integral:

$$\int_0^\infty U_t e^{-\delta t} dt \tag{6.7}$$

where U_t is the level of social utility (6.6) at time t, and δ is the rate of discount, assumed to be positive.

In order to complete the construct of the dynamic model, we need to specify the rate at which the stock of social overhead capital V_t changes over time. It is composed of two factors, the first related to the regeneration or new construction of social overhead capital and the second to the depletion of the stock of social overhead capital due to ecological and economic conditions. The change in the stock of social overhead capital due to the regeneration and new construction is given by $Y_t\alpha = Y\alpha(a_t\alpha, X_t, V_t)$; the stock of social overhead capital is depleted by the quantity $\mu(X_t, V_t)$. We assume that the function $\mu(X, V)$ is convex, and homogeneous of order one with respect to (X, V). Hence, it may be written as

$$\mu\left(X, V\right) = \mu\left(x\right)V, \qquad x = \frac{X}{V}$$

where $\mu(x)$ satisfies the following conditions:

$$\mu\left(0\right) = 0, \qquad \mu\left(x\right) > 0, \qquad \mu'\left(x\right) > 0, \qquad \mu''\left(x\right) > 0$$

The basic dynamic equation is now written as:

$$\dot{V}_t = Y\alpha\left(a_t\alpha, X_t, V_t\right) - \mu\left(X_t, V_t\right) \tag{6.8}$$

with the given initial condition V_o.

A time-path of vectors of activity levels and stock of social overhead capital, $(a_tV, a_t\beta, a_t\alpha, V)$, is defined to be dynamically optimum if it is feasible, that is, it satisfies (6.1–6.6) and (6.8), and it maximizes the Ramsey–Cass–Koopmans utility integral (6.7) among all feasible time-paths.

The concept of the imputed price of the stock of social overhead capital is again used to find the time-path which is dynamically optimum. Let λ_t be the imputed price at time t, and the real income at time t be defined by

$$H_t = \sum vUv\left(a_tv, X_t, V_t\right) + \lambda_t\left(Y_t\alpha - \mu\left(X_t, V_t\right)\right) \tag{6.9}$$

The optimum vectors of activity levels $(av, a\alpha, a\beta)$ are determined in such a manner that real income H_t is maximized subject to feasibility conditions (6.1–6.5). Let p_t, r_t, and θ_t be, respectively, the Lagrange multipliers, that is, the static imputed prices associated with (6.1–6.5), (6.2), and (6.3). Then the first-order conditions for the Lagrangian form become:

$$U_{av}v = pC_{av}v + \theta X_{av}v \tag{6.10}$$

$$pY_{a\beta}\beta = rK_{a\beta}\beta + \theta X_{a\beta}\beta \tag{6.11}$$

$$\lambda Y_{a\alpha}\alpha = rK_{a\alpha}\alpha + \theta X_{a\alpha}\alpha \tag{6.12}$$

$$\theta = \sum v\left(-U_X v + pC_X v\right) + \sum \beta\left(-pY_X \beta + rK_X \beta\right)$$
$$+ \left(-\lambda Y_X \alpha + rK_X \alpha\right) + \lambda\mu_X \tag{6.13}$$

together with the feasibility conditions themselves.

Note that the feasibility conditions and the marginality conditions are in general stated in terms of the inequalities instead of the equalities as stated here. However, it can be shown that a slight modification of the assumptions concerning the production functions and resource requirement functions assures us that they are satisfied with the equality sign.

The right-hand side of equation (6.12) corresponds to the concept of the marginal social cost θ^* associated with the use or depletion of the stock of social overhead capital, and the condition (6.12) is the mathematical expression of the principle of marginal social cost pricing.

Before the dynamic equation for imputed price λ_t is derived, we simplify the static optimization problem above with the help of the homogeneity assumptions concerning the relevant functions. Let us first introduce variables per stock of social overhead capital in the following way:

$$av = \frac{av}{V}, \quad a\beta = \frac{a\beta}{V}, \quad a\alpha = \frac{a\alpha}{V}, \quad x = \frac{X}{V},$$
$$xv = \frac{Xv}{V}, \quad x\beta = \frac{X\beta}{V}, \quad x\alpha = \frac{X\alpha}{V}$$

where time suffix t is omitted.

Then the static optimization problem may be reduced to the following: Maximize real income

$$\sum vuv\left(a_t v, x\right)\phi(V) + \lambda\left\{ya\left(a\alpha, x\right) - \mu(x)\right\}V \tag{6.14}$$

subject to the constraints that

$$\sum vcv\left(av, x\right) \le \sum \beta y\beta\left(a\beta, x\right) \tag{6.15}$$

$$ka\left(a\alpha, x\right) + \sum \beta k\beta\left(a\beta, x\right) \le k \tag{6.16}$$

$$x = \sum vxv\big(av\big) + \sum \beta x\beta\big(a\beta\big) + xa\big(aa\big) \tag{6.17}$$

where $k = \dfrac{K}{V}$, and $y\beta(a\beta, x)$, $k\beta(a\beta, x)$, ..., are the corresponding functions with respect to variables per stock of social overhead capital V.

The constraints for this optimization problem becomes independent of V, except for (6.16), which is affected by changes in V through $k = K/V$. The imputed price associated with the constraints (6.16) is denoted by $\lambda\pi$.

The dynamic equation for imputed price λ_t is now expressed by

$$\dot{\lambda} = \delta - \left\{ \sum vuv\big(av, x\big)\phi'\big(V\big) + \lambda\big[ya\big(aa\big) - \mu\big(X\big)\big] - \lambda rk\right\} \tag{6.18}$$

The dynamic equation for the stock of social overhead capital may be written as

$$\frac{\dot{V}}{V} = ya\big(aa, x\big) - \mu\big(x\big) \tag{6.19}$$

The dynamically optimum time-path $(a_t v, a_t \beta, a_t a, V)$ may be obtained if one finds a solution path of the pair of differential equations, (6.18) and (6.19), for which the transversality conditions

$$\lim_{t \to \infty} \lambda_t V_t e^{-\delta t} = 0$$

are satisfied.

The solution paths to (6.18) and (6.19) are more easily analyzed if the new imputed price

$$\pi_t = \lambda_t \frac{V_t}{\phi\big(V_t\big)}$$

is introduced. The dynamic equation for the new imputed price π_t, to be obtained from (6.18) and (6.19), is given by

$$\frac{\dot{\pi}}{\pi} = \delta - \left\{ \gamma\left\{ \frac{1}{\pi}\sum vuv\big(av, x\big) + \big(ya\big(aa, x\big) - \mu\big(x\big)\big)\right\} - rk\right\} \tag{6.20}$$

In terms of the new imputed price π_t, the static optimization problem above is slightly modified. Instead of maximizing (6.14), the maxim is now written as

$$\frac{1}{\pi} \sum vuv\big(av, x\big) + \big\{ya\big(aa, x\big) - \mu\big(x\big)\big\}$$

The maximum value of this optimization problem depends on imputed price π and $k = K/V$, written in the functional form: $g(\pi, k)$. It is easily seen that $g(\pi, k)$ is concave with respect to k, $g\pi(\pi, k) < 0, r = g_k(\pi, k)$, and $g(\pi, k) - rk$ is an increasing function of k; hence it is decreased as V is increased ($k = K/V$). An argument like that in Section 2 shows that, as imputed price π becomes higher, $\Sigma vuv(av, x)$ is decreased, while $ya(aa, x) - \mu(x)$ is increased. These properties are used to analyze the phase diagrams for the pair of basic dynamic equations, (6.19) and (6.20).

Let us first examine the conditions under which V remains stationary, that is, the right-hand side of dynamic equation (6.19) vanishes. Since $ya - \mu(x)$ is increased as π increases, it may be depicted by the upward sloping curve, AA, as in Figure 6, where π is measured along the abscissa. An increase in V decreases $k = K/V$, and the AA curve correspondingly shifts downward, resulting in an increase in the level of π, at which $ya - \mu(x) = 0$. The conditions for the stationarity of V are expressed by the upward sloping curve EE in Figure 5, where V is measured along the abscissa and π along the ordinate. If (π, V) lies on the left side of the AA curve, V tends to be increased; on the right side, V tends to be decreased.

The conditions for the stationarity of imputed price π are slightly more complicated. Imputed price π remains stationary if and only if

$$\delta = \gamma g\big(\pi, k\big) - rk \tag{6.21}$$

Since the right-hand side of equation (6.21) is generally a decreasing function of V, where $k = K/V$, it may be represented by the downward sloping curve, BB, where the abscissa measures V. There are exceptional cases when $\gamma g(\pi, k) - rk$, particularly when γ is close to 0. The analysis below, however, is applied with slight modifications.

The intersection of the BB curve with the horizontal line with the distance δ from the abscissa gives the level of the stock of social overhead capital V at which imputed price π remains stationary. As imputed price π is increased, the BB curve shifts downward, thus resulting in a decrease in V at which condition (6.21) is satisfied. Hence, the combinations of (π,

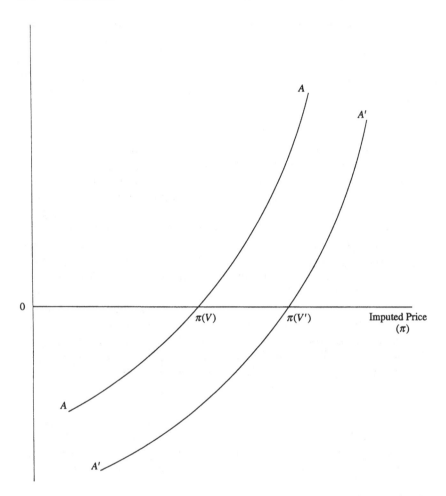

Figure 6. Stationarity conditions for the stock of social overhead capital.

V) at which dynamic equation (6.20) is stationary are depicted by the downward sloping curve, *FF*, in Figure 5. When (π, V) lies above the *BB* curve, $\dot{\pi} > 0$; when it lies below the *BB* curve, $\dot{\pi} < 0$, as indicated by the arrowed lines.

The solution paths to the pair of dynamic equations, (6.19) and (6.20), are now illustrated by the arrowed curves in Figure 5. The pair of solution paths which converge to the long-run stationary state, $\overline{E}^{\infty}$, gives us the time-path of imputed price $\pi_t = \pi^o(V_t)$, for which the transversality conditions are satisfied.

Thus we have shown that the structure of dynamically optimum time-paths of vectors of activity levels and the stock of social overhead capital, $(a_t\alpha, a_t\beta, a_t\nu, V_t)$, for the general dynamic model of social overhead capital is identical with the case of the simple model of social infrastructure. The qualifications and remarks concerning the practical applications of our abstract model are equally valid for the general situation.

7   Competitive equilibrium and social overhead capital

In the previous sections, we formulate a dynamic model of social overhead capital and examine the pattern of resource allocation over time, including both privately owned scarce resources and services derived from social overhead capital, which is dynamically optimum from the social point of view. The analysis has been confined, however, to the case where there is only one type of social overhead capital, either natural capital or social infrastructure. In this section, we extend our analysis to consider the general circumstances where several types of social overhead capital are involved in the processes of economic activities.

The basic premises and relevant variables introduced in the previous sections remain valid here, except for those concerning social overhead capital. Social overhead capital here comprises several distinct kinds of resources and constitutes the physical component of the natural capital or social infrastructure. The stock of social overhead capital at each time t, V_t, is not a scalar quantity, but a vector with as many components as the number of different types of social overhead capital. A number of social institutions fiduciarily entrusted with the management of social overhead capital are generically denoted by α. Each social institution may be either in charge of a particular type of social overhead capital or entrusted with the management of several kinds of social overhead capital. Similar kinds of social overhead capital such as natural capital, forests, rivers, lakes, and so forth, may be managed by a number of social institutions.

The aggregate quantities of social overhead capital either used up or depleted at each time t by economic activities are represented by a vector X_t:

$$X_t = \sum \nu X\nu\left(a_t\nu\right) + \sum \alpha X\alpha\left(a_t\alpha\right) + \sum \beta X\beta\left(a_t\beta\right) \qquad (7.1)$$

The concepts of dynamic optimality and imputed price are introduced to the general case, as discussed in the previous section. However, the dynamic optimization problem now involves a calculus of variation problems with many state variables, and the existence of dynamically optimum time-paths requires assumptions of a complicated mathematical nature. In the present context, we postulate that the dynamically optimum time-path of the accumulation or decumulation of social overhead capital uniquely exists, characterized by a vector of imputed prices at each time t, λ_t.

We begin our discussion with a more detailed description of the property ownership arrangements. The endowments of privately owned factors of production, denoted by a vector K in the previous section, are owned by individual members of the society. Each individual v is assumed to own factors of production, Kv. The economic units engaged in productive activities are also owned by individual members. Each individual v is assumed to own shares of economic unit β, $s_{v\beta}$. Thus, individual v is entitled to receive $s_{v\beta}\pi\beta$ out of producer β's profits

$$\Pi\beta = pY\beta - rK\beta - \theta X\beta \tag{7.2}$$

where p and r are, respectively, the prices of consumption goods and of the use of privately owned factors of production prevailing in the market, whereas θ is the rate of charge for the use of social overhead capital. In a purely competitive situation, θ equals 0; in the optimum case, θ is equated to the marginal social cost θ^*, which, in the present context, is defined by

$$\theta^* = \sum v\left(-\frac{U_Xv}{\varepsilon} + PC_Xv\right) + \sum\beta\left(-PY_X\beta + rK_X\beta\right) + \sum\alpha\left(-PY_X\alpha + rK_X\alpha\right) \tag{7.3}$$

ε is the coefficient required to convert the utility unit to the measure in terms of market price.

It is assumed that

$$\sum vKv = K \tag{7.4}$$

and

$$s_{v\beta} \geq 0 \qquad \sum vs_{v\beta} = 1$$

Each individual v's income Yv is given by

$$Yv = \sum\beta s_{v\beta}\prod\beta + rKv \tag{7.5}$$

When each individual v's taxes for his income are Tv, then the pattern of consumption he chooses is given by that which maximizes his utility $Uv(Cv, X, V)$ subject to the budget constraints

$$pCv + \theta Xv = Yv - Tv \tag{7.6}$$

Adding the equations (7.2) and (7.6) over β and v, and noting (6.1–6.4) and (7.4–7.6), we obtain

$$T + \theta X = rK\alpha + \theta X\alpha \tag{7.7}$$

where T is the total tax revenue

$$T = \sum vTv \tag{7.8}$$

The left-hand side of equation (7.7) expresses the total receipts of the governmental sector, while the right-hand side expresses the total expenditure incurred in the regenerative or investing activities concerning social overhead capital.

The analysis developed in the previous section shows that there exist price vectors, p and r, the rate of charge for the use of social overhead capital, θ, and a system of tax subsidy arrangements, Tv, such that each producer β maximizes his profit $\pi\beta$, each individual v maximizes his utility subject to his budget constraint (7.6), and the governmental sector minimizes its expenditure to maintain the dynamically optimum level of investment in social overhead capital; the rate of charge for the use of social overhead capital equals marginal social cost θ^*. Thus we have shown that the dynamically optimum time-path of allocation of privately owned scarce resources and of the use and accumulation (or decumulation) of social overhead capital may be attained within the institutional framework of competitive equilibrium when the principle of marginal social pricing is applied to the use of services of social overhead capital and investment in social overhead capital is maintained at a level corresponding to the dynamically imputed price of the stock of social overhead capital.

In the dynamic analysis of social overhead capital, we emphasize the regeneration and investment activities of the social institutions in charge of it. The analysis is easily extended to handle those activities directly concerned with providing the services of social overhead capital to members of the society. One has only to introduce a new vector of activity levels, $b\alpha$, which represents the levels of activities related to the provision of services derived from the given stock of social overhead capital.

The quantity of services provided by ba is expressed by $X(ba)$, privately owned factors of production are employed by the quantities $\overline{K}(ba, X, V)$, and the feasibility conditions (6.20) may be replaced by

$$\overline{K}\alpha(ba) + K\alpha(aa) + \sum \beta K\beta(a\beta) + \sum \nu K\nu(a\nu) \le K \qquad (7.9)$$

where the dependency on (X, V) is not explicitly written out.

The standard assumptions are made with respect to $X\alpha(ba)$ and $\overline{K}\alpha(ba)$. The new constraint is introduced:

$$X = X(ba) \qquad (7.10)$$

with the associated imputed price η_t at time t.

The concept of the static marginal social cost for the use of social overhead capital is now modified:

$$\theta* = \eta + \sum \nu(-U_X\nu + pC_X\nu) + \sum \beta(-pY_X\beta + rK_X\beta)$$
$$+ (-\lambda Y_X\alpha + rK_X\alpha) + \lambda \mu_X \qquad (7.11)$$

and the optimum for ba is determined by the condition that

$$\eta X\alpha(ba) - r\overline{K}\alpha(ba) \qquad (7.12)$$

is maximized.

The expenditures incurred in relation to ba, $r\overline{K}_X\alpha$, correspond to the governmental expenditures on the current account, whereas the expenditures with respect to aa are those on capital account. The analysis of social overhead capital developed here may provide us with the framework within which it is possible to examine economic implications of governmental activities in general.

Appendix: On the sufficiency of Pontryagin's Maximum Principle

Pontryagin's Maximum Principle has been extensively utilized, without, however, explicitly specifying the conditions under which the solution paths are dynamically optimal. In this appendix, I give a mathematical proof for the statements concerning the sufficiency of Pontryagin's Maximum Principle as utilized here.

The problems of finding the dynamically optimal time-paths discussed in this chapter may in the most general form be stated as follows:

Let $a = (a_j)$ be the vector of activity levels and V be the stock of social overhead capital, both at time t, where the time suffix is omitted unless an explicit reference is required. The level of social utility U_t at time t is given by

$$U_t = u(a_t)\phi(V_t) \tag{A.1}$$

where both functions $u(a)$ and $\phi(V)$ are assumed to be positive-valued, continuously twice-differentiable, monotone, and strictly quasi-concave. The elasticity of function $\phi(V)$ with respect to V is assumed to be constant, say γ:

$$\frac{\phi'(V)V}{\phi(V)} = \gamma$$

so that

$$\phi(V) = V\gamma$$

Note that both functions $u(a)$ and $\phi(V)$ are concave, but the product, $u(a)\phi(V)$, is not necessarily a concave function with respect to (a, V). However, we assume that $u(a)$ is homothetic with respect to a, in the sense that the marginal rates of substitution remain constant along any ray from the origin. Hence,

$$u(\theta a) = \theta^\alpha u(a), \qquad \text{for all} \qquad a \geq 0 \qquad \text{and} \qquad \theta > 0$$

with a certain positive constant α.

Therefore, the social utility function may be written as

$$U = u(a)\phi(V) = u\left(V^{\frac{\gamma}{\alpha}} a\right) \tag{A.2}$$

The dynamic equation for the stock of social overhead capital is generally written as

$$\dot{V}_t = f(a_t, V_t) \tag{A.3}$$

where the function $f(a, V)$ is assumed to be continuously twice-differentiable, homogeneous of order one, and concave with respect to (a, V).

The resource requirement functions are denoted by $g(a, V)$, and the endowment vector of privately owned scarce resources are given by $K = (K_t)$, where it is assumed that

$$K > 0, \quad \text{i.e.} \quad K_t > 0 \quad \text{for all } t$$

Then the feasibility conditions are written as

$$g(a_t, V_t) \leq K \tag{A.4}$$

where the nonnegativity of the vector of activity levels a is not explicitly mentioned.

We assume that the resource requirement functions $g(a, V)$ are positive-valued, continuously twice-differentiable, homogeneous of order one, and concave with respect to (a, V). It is also assumed that

$$g(0, V) = 0$$

Hence, there exists a vector of activity levels a^*, namely 0, such that

$$g(a^*, V) < K \tag{A.5}$$

which plays an important role in the analysis below.

The dynamic optimality problem is now stated as follows:

To find a time-path (a_t, V_t) feasible in the sense that the dynamic equation (A.3) is satisfied with the given initial condition V_o, and resource requirement conditions (A.4) are satisfied at each time t, and it maximizes the utility integral:

$$\int_0^\infty u(a_t)\phi(V_t)e^{-\delta t}dt \tag{A.6}$$

among all feasible time-paths, where the rate of discount δ is assumed to be a positive constant.

The necessary conditions are given by Pontryagin's Maximum Principle. Suppose there exists a feasible time-path (a_t^o, V_t^o) which is dynamically optimal. Then there necessarily exists a time-path of imputed price λ_t which is a continuous function of time t and the following conditions are satisfied: At each time t, a_t^o maximizes the Hamiltonian

$$H_t = u(a_t)\phi(V_t^o) + \lambda_t f(a_t, V_t^o) \tag{A.7}$$

subject to the resource constraints (A.4)

$$\dot{\lambda}_t = \frac{\partial H_t}{\partial V_t} + \delta\lambda_t \tag{A.8}$$

and

$$\lim_{t\to\infty} \lambda_t V_t^o e^{-\delta t} = 0 \tag{A.9}$$

the last conditions being referred to as the transversality conditions.

Let us first note certain implications of conditions (A.7). Since the assumption (A.5) is satisfied, there exists a vector of (static) imputed prices, r_t, for the endowments of privately owned factors of production such that $r_t > 0$, and (a_t^o, V_t) is a nonnegative saddle-point of the Lagrangian:

$$L_t = u(a_t)\phi(V_t) + \lambda_t f(a_t, V_t^o) + r_t\{K - g(a_t, V_t^o)\}$$

(See, for example, Arrow, Hurwicz, and Uzawa [1958] *Studies in Linear on a Non-linear Programming*, Stanford University Press, pp. 32–7.)

Hence, conditions (A.7) may be reformulated as

$$u_a(a_t^o)\phi(V_t^o) + \lambda_t f_a(a_t^o, V_t^o) - r_t g_a(a_t^o, V_t^o) \le 0 \tag{A.10}$$

with equality whenever $a_t^o > 0$;

$$g_a(a_t^o, V_t^o) \le K \tag{A.11}$$

with equality whenever $r_t > 0$.

The dynamic equation (A.8) may be simply rewritten as

$$\dot{\lambda}_t = \delta\lambda_t - \{u(a_t^o)\phi'(V_t^o) + \lambda_t f_V(a_t^o, V_t^o) - r_t g_V(a_t^o, V_t^o)\} \tag{A.12}$$

Before we examine the sufficiency of the Pontryagin's conditions for the cases discussed in Uzawa (1992), we give a simple proof for the standard case where the maximand $u(a)\phi(V)$ is a concave function of (a, V).

Proposition A1: *In addition to the assumptions made above, suppose $u(a)\phi(V)$ is a concave function of (a, V). Then the time-path (a_t^o, V_t^o) for which conditions (A.7–A.9) are satisfied is dynamically optimum.*

Proof: Before we proceed with the proof of Proposition 1, consider a well-hnown property concerning concave functions. If a function $f(a, V)$ is concave with respect to (a, V), the following inequality holds:

$$f\left(a^{o}, V^{o}\right) - f\left(a, V\right) \geq f_{a}\left(a^{o}, V^{o}\right)\left(a^{o} - a\right) + f_{V}\left(a^{o}, V^{o}\right)\left(V^{o} - V\right)$$

(A.13)

If $f(a, V)$ is strictly quasi-concave, the inequality (A13) holds with a strict inequality sign for $(a^{o}, V^{o}) \neq (a, V)$.

Let us define

$$\psi\left(a, V\right) = \int_{0}^{\infty}\left[u\left(a_{t}\right)\phi\left(V_{t}\right) + \lambda_{t}\left\{f\left(a_{t}, V_{t}\right) - \dot{V}_{t}\right\}\right.$$
$$\left. + r_{t}\left\{K - g\left(a_{t}, V_{t}\right)\right\}\right]e^{-\delta t}dt$$

where λ_{t} is the time-path of imputed prices whose existence is guaranteed by Pontryagin's Maximum Principle.

Then, applying (A.13) to $\psi(a, V)$, we obtain

$$\psi\left(a^{o}, V^{o}\right) - \psi\left(a, V\right) \geq \int_{0}^{\infty}\left[u_{a}\left(a_{t}^{o}\right)\phi\left(V_{t}^{o}\right)\left(a^{o} - a\right)\right.$$
$$+ u\left(a_{t}^{o}\right)\phi'\left(V_{t}^{o}\right)\left(V_{t}^{o} - V_{t}\right) + \lambda_{t}\left\{f_{a}\left(a_{t}^{o}, V_{t}^{o}\right)\left(a_{t}^{o} - a_{t}\right)\right.$$
$$+ f_{V}\left(a_{t}^{o}, V_{t}^{o}\right)\left(V_{t}^{o} - V_{t}\right)\right\} - \lambda_{t}\left(\dot{V}_{t}^{o} - \dot{V}_{t}\right)$$
$$\left. - r_{t}\left\{g_{a}\left(a_{t}^{o}, V_{t}^{o}\right)\left(a_{t}^{o} - a_{t}\right) + g_{V}\left(a_{t}^{o}, V_{t}^{o}\right)\left(V_{t}^{o} - V_{t}\right)\right\}\right]e^{-\delta t}dt$$

with strict inequality for $(a^{o}, V^{o}) \neq (a, V)$.

Hence, in view of conditions (A.10–A.12), we have

$$\psi\left(a^{o}, V^{o}\right) - \psi\left(a, V\right)$$
$$\geq \int_{0}^{\infty}\left\{\left(-\dot{\lambda}_{t} + \delta\lambda_{t}\right)V_{t}^{o} - V_{t}\right) + \lambda_{t}\left(\dot{V}_{t}^{o} - \dot{V}_{t}\right)e^{-\delta t}dt$$
$$\doteq \lambda_{t}\left(V_{t}^{o} - V_{t}\right)e^{-\delta t}\Big|_{0}^{\infty} \quad \left[\text{transversality conditions } (A.9)\right]$$

with strict inequality for $(a^{o}, V^{o}) \neq (a, V)$.

Therefore, considering conditions (A.4) and (A.11), we have

$$\int_0^\infty u\!\left(a_t^o\right)\!\phi\!\left(V_t^o\right)\!e^{-\delta t}\,dt > \int_0^\infty u\!\left(a_t\right)\!\phi\!\left(V_t\right)\!e^{-\delta t}\,dt$$

for all feasible $(a, V) \neq (a^o, V^o)$.   QED.

The cases discussed in Uzawa (1992) are easily handled in terms of Proposition A1. We have

Proposition A2: *In addition to the conditions assumed above, the utility function $u(a)$ is assumed to be homothetic. Then, the time-path (a_t^o, V_t^o) for which conditions (A.7–A.9) are satisfied is dynamically optimal.*

Proof: The utility function may be written in the form given in (A.2). By introducing new variables

$$\hat{V}_t = V_t V_t^{\frac{\gamma}{\alpha}} = V_t^{\frac{\alpha+\gamma}{\alpha}}, \qquad a_t = V_t^{\frac{\gamma}{\alpha}} a_t$$

the optimum problem may be reformulated as follows:
To find the time-path $(\hat{a}, \hat{V}_t)$ which maximizes the utility integral

$$\int_0^\infty u\!\left(\hat{a}_t\right)\!e^{-\delta t}\,dt$$

subject to the constraints:

$$\hat{V} = \frac{\alpha + \gamma}{\alpha} f\!\left(\hat{a}_t, \hat{V}_t\right)$$

where $\hat{K} = \hat{V}_t^{\frac{\gamma}{\alpha+\gamma}} K$.

Since the functions $u(\hat{a})$ and $f(\hat{a}, \hat{V})$ are concave with respect to $(\hat{a}, \hat{V})$ and $\hat{K}_t$ is concave with respect to $\hat{V}$, Proposition A1 with a slight modification may be applied to the optimum problem thus formulated. It is easily seen that Pontryagin's Maximum Principle applied to the modified optimum problem results in the optimal solution to the original problem.   QED.

References

Berkes, F., ed. 1989. *Common Property Resources: Ecology and Community-based Sustainable Development.* London: Balhaven Press.

Cass, D. 1965. Optimum economic growth in an aggregative model of capital accumulation. *Review of Economic Studies*, 32:233–40.

Clark, C. W., and G. R. Munro. 1975. The economics of fishing and modern capital theory. *Journal of Environmental Economics and Management*, 2:92–106.

Crutchfield, J. A., and A. Zellner. 1962. *Economic Aspect of the Pacific Halibut Fishery*. Washington, D.C.: U.S. Government Printing Office.

Dasgupta, P. S., and G. M. Heal. 1974. The optimal depletion of exhaustible resources. *Review of Economic Studies*, Special Issue on Exhaustible Resources.

Dasgupta, P. S., and G. M. Heal. 1979. *Economic Theory and Exhaustible Resources*. Cambridge: Cambridge University Press.

Gordon, H. S. 1954. The economic theory of common property resources: The fishery. *Journal of Political Economy*, 62:124–42.

Hardin, G. 1968. The tragedy of the commons. *Science*, 162:1243–8.

Hotelling, H. 1931. The economics of exhaustible resources. *Journal of Political Economy*, 39(2)(April):137–75.

Johansson, P.-O., and K.-G. Löfgren. 1985. *The Economics of Forestry and Natural Resources*. Oxford and New York: Basil Blackwell.

Koopmans, T. C. 1965. On the concept of optimum economic growth. *Semaine d'Etude sur le Rôle de l'Analyse Économétrique dans la Formulation de Plans de Development*, pp. 225–87. Paris.

Mäler, K.-G. 1974. *Environmental Economics: A Theoretical Inquiry*. Baltimore and London: Johns Hopkins University Press.

McCay, B. J., and J. M. Acheson, eds. 1987. *The Question of the Commons: The Culture and Economy of Communal Resources*. Tucson: University of Arizona Press.

Pigou, A. C. 1925. *The Economics of Welfare*. Macmillan.

Ramsey, F. P. 1928. A mathematical theory of saving. *Economic Journal*, 38:543–59.

Schaefer, M. B. 1957. Some considerations of population dynamics and economics in relation to the management of commercial marine fisheries. *Journal of the Fisheries Research Board of Canada*, 14:669–81.

Scott, A. D. 1955. The fishery: The objectives of sole ownership. *Journal of Political Economy*, 63:116–24.

Tahvonen, O. 1991. On the dynamics of renewable resource harvesting and population control. *Environmental and Resource Economics*, 1:97–117.

Uzawa, H. 1974. Sur la théorie économique du capital collectif social. *Cahier du Séminaire d'économetrie*, 103–22. Translated in *Preference, Production, and Capital: Selected Papers of Hirofumi Uzawa* (1988). New York and Cambridge: Cambridge University Press, pp. 340–62.

Uzawa, H. 1992. The tragedy of the commons and the theory of social overhead capital. The Beijer Institute of Ecological Economics Discussion Paper.

Wicksell, K. 1901. *Föreläningar i Nationalekonomi, Häfte 1*. Lund: Gleerups. Translated as *Lectures on Political Economy, Vol. I: General Theory*, ed. L. Robbins. (1934) London: George Routledge.

CHAPTER 14

On population externalities and
the social rate of discount

David A. Starrett

The social rate of discount[1] plays a central role in applied welfare economics, governing such decisions as the amount of public investment,
interventions in private capital markets, and the size of intergenerational
transfers. Ever since the social choice theory literature began to evolve
into practical models of government planning, there has been a lively discussion concerning the appropriate social rate and reasons why it should
or should not deviate from the private (market) rate. Kenneth Arrow
was an early and frequent contributor to this literature along with many
others;[2] on the occasion of Arrow's Festschrift, I attempted to summarize a number of elements in the debate. Since that time, the subject
seems to have receded somewhat from prominence, the prevailing
opinion being that value judgments must ultimately be invoked and that
economic theory cannot resolve such matters.

I would like to take this opportunity to reopen the subject, not
because I think there is anything really new to say about the underlying
value judgments, but because this is a context in which these judgments
can be illuminated most starkly. I address the issue of population crowding and the appropriate way to measure its social costs.

The literature identifies one crowding externality in particular as
being important to the population question: the "global commons." To
the extent that access to such common resources is essential to well-
being, an extra person imposes external costs by crowding other people
out. By way of introduction, we provide a general set-up for measuring
this externality and argue that if the global commons were interpreted
broadly to include all the earth's fixed factors, the associated external

---

[1] A more technical exposition of some of these issues can be found in Starrett (1992).

[2] See Arrow (1966), (1982). A nice summary of the issues can be found in Krutilla and
Fisher (1975).

cost of an extra person would be quite substantial. However, many of the associated resources (land, minerals) are not common property but privately owned and the presumption (at least from economic theory) is that markets will internalize the associated externalities. Our central contention in this chapter is that even if markets work perfectly, this conclusion depends critically on equating the social rate of discount with the market rate of interest and consequently counting future people less than current people. If instead, people are counted equally, a large external cost reemerges.

1   Fixed factors and the global commons

The main argument for a population externality (on the standard of living) relies on diminishing returns to fixed factors. (We formalize this argument later.) This argument is in a state of disrepute among some economists due to its abuse at the hands of the "club of Rome,"[3] who invoked it with a vengeance by assuming away substitution possibilities. However, the theoretical foundations of the argument are perfectly valid in a general production framework; legitimate controversy is confined to the issue of how quickly diminishing returns set in and measurements of the argument's importance.

The logical argument for elements of diminishing returns is based on the view that any fixed technology must exhibit constant returns to scale at sufficiently large scales. The argument is that at sufficiently large scales the best way to expand scale further is through replication and that this option is always available. For our purposes, it is enough that the world economy be a sufficiently large scale in this sense; that is, if we had a second "earth" exactly like the first, we could do no better than replicate (specialization at that scale has no benefits).

Thinking now of the earth as a fixed factor, it follows logically under maintained assumptions that we will observe diminishing returns (from a fixed technology) to increasing population. Consequently, increased population can only be offset by improvements in the technology. The current debate over population issues focuses on the extent to which the benefits of technical change can continue to overcome the detrimental effects of population increase. Although this debate is obviously quite important, its resolution is not crucial to the question of concern here. As long as technological progress is independent of population size (a proposition that seems reasonable in a world of our size where research and development (R and D) effort is widely duplicated), the presence of

---

[3] See, for example, Meadows et al. (1972).

externality will not depend on whether or not technical progress occurs.[4] With or without such progress, output per person will be lower with extra population than without it.

To get some feel for the orders of magnitude involved, we study a simple example that serves to isolate the effect of fixed factors on welfare. The framework here is one in which a single consumption good (Y) is produced from labor (L) and the fixed factor (T) only. Drawing on the argument made earlier we assume without loss of generality that the production function $F(L,T)$ exhibits constant returns to scale.

When the fixed factor is treated as a nonexcludable good (the global commons), all people are assumed to have equal access to it. Ignoring for now differences in ability, we take this to mean that each person receives the average product of labor (output per person).[5] Given constant returns to scale overall, and a fixed common size (T) each additional person will lower the average product of labor and consequently, the decision to have an extra child confers negative externalities on everyone else. This externality can be thought of as representing added congestion on the common and as such is well understood.[6]

For comparison purposes, we develop an expression for the size of this externality. When one extra person is added to an initial labor supply of L^o, output per person falls by

$$F\big(L^o,T\big)\big/L^o - F\big(L^o + 1,T\big)\big/\big(L^o + 1\big)$$

Since this cost is incurred by L^o people the *global external cost* (GEC) is

$$GEC = F\big(L^o,T\big) - \big[L^o/L^o + 1\big]F\big(L^o + 1,T\big)$$
$$\approx \big[F\big(L^o,T\big) - L^o F_L\big(L^o,T\big)\big]\big/\big[L^o + 1\big]$$
$$= \big[TF_T\big(L^o,T\big)\big]\big/\big[L^o + 1\big]$$

---

[4] It is possible that the direction of technical progress might be influenced by population. For example, once population pressure gets extreme, efforts may shift more in the direction of augmenting the fixed factor (as exemplified by the "green revolution"). This factor might mitigate the crowding externality somewhat.

[5] In much of the sequel we treat everyone as alike. Obviously, if there are differences in things like ability, different people will generate different levels of externalities. Here we are concerned with average aggregative effects so we ignore these differences.

[6] For a general discussion of common property externalities, see Baumol and Oates (1975).

where the approximate equality is derived from a first-order Taylor's expansion and the last equality follows from Euler's equation for functions homogeneous of degree one.

Thus, we see that the externality imposed is equal to the "value" per person of the global commons. Is this a large or small number? Ultimately this question is empirical and cannot be answered on the basis of theory alone. However, it is worth pointing out a certain fallacy of composition that can lead intuition astray. There is little doubt that the addition of a single person will have a very small effect on the average product of labor. Consequently if there is allocation symmetry, there will be a practically negligible effect on any other single individual (and the impact would surely go to zero as the number of people grows without bound). But the *aggregate* impact certainly need not be negligible in this sense. In particular, for the Cobb–Douglas production function, GEC is a constant fraction of per capita output (measured by the "land" parameter), independent of population size.

Only a small fraction of this cost is borne by a particular family deciding on an extra child. Let us look at the family incentive to have a child; here we treat the net benefits of a child as measured by its consumption and ignore any noneconomic satisfaction that might be derived. Net family benefit (NFB) is measured as

$$NFB = \left[\ell^o + 1\right]\left[F\left(L^o + 1, T\right)/\left(L^o + 1\right)\right] - \ell^o\, F\left(L^o, T\right)/L^o$$
$$\simeq F\left(L^o + 1, T\right)/\left[L^o + 1\right] - \ell^o\, T F_T\left(L^o, T\right)/\left[L^o\left(L^o + 1\right)\right]$$

where ℓ^o represents the initial family size. The first term in NFB is the consumption of the new child; whether this should be counted as a social as well as a private benefit depends on the welfare treatment of the unborn. But regardless of our feelings about that question, the second is only a fraction of the global external cost. And this will be a negligible fraction as long as the family is small relative to the population at large.

Note that if T is taken as a proxy for all fixed factors, the external cost surely would be a significant fraction of income; if this cost were imposed as a tax, we would expect a substantial effect on incentives to have children.[7] Therefore, it seems quite important to determine the extent to which private ownership of fixed factors serves to internalize this externality.

---

[7] Since our current context is static in nature, income is the relevant measure of total resources here. We soon turn to an explicitly dynamic version.

With private ownership, the fixed factors are assets that are managed by owners and transferred from one generation to the next through market transactions or bequests. Therefore, we need to look at dynamic intergenerational models.

2 Motives for intergenerational transfer

For our purposes, it is useful to classify models on a spectrum according to the degree and motivation for voluntary transfers between generations. At one extreme is the *dynasty* model in which the transfers are determined by a single family decision maker (patriarch) maximizing a "family" objective function.[8] At the opposite extreme is the pure *life-cycle* model in which there are no voluntary transfers so that all fixed factor assets must be sold from one generation to the next. In between, there are a number of *overlapping generation* variants in which some transfers take place as bequests but there is some residual conflict of interest among generations.[9]

The dynasty model treats parents and all their descendants as a single optimizing unit faced with a resources constraint that aggregates all resources controlled by the "family." When markets are complete, the constraint on become collapses single wealth constraint and the dynamic model becomes formally equivalent to a purely static one. If the fixed factor is privately owned, all intergenerational family size issues are fully internalized. The patriarch will see that if an extra person is added to the family then "land" owned by the family must be spread over more people and he will weigh this cost against benefits. To the extent that the incidence of this cost tends to fall on the future, parents can leave larger bequests to spread the burden optimally. There are no externalities (other families see no change in their return per person from the fixed factor) and the issue of the appropriate social rate of discount is moot; the social rate must be equal to the private rate since the family will automatically use the latter to spread resources across time "optimally." Nerlove studied a model of this sort and was among the first to show formally that there was no population externality in the dynasty model with private ownership of all fixed factors. We do not reproduce this model explicitly here but comment on its relevance shortly. It remains true in the dynasty model that population generates

[8] As pointed out by Barro, this model does not require that the patriarch actually make all decisions, only that he leave bequests optimally from the family perspective.

[9] Divergent points of view on this matter are given by Kotlikoff (1988) and Modigliani (1988). See Bernheim (1988) for a general discussion of these models and a survey of attempts to distinguish empirically among them.

a crowding externality on the global commons; in that case, all families see a reduction in output per person when any family adds to the population.

When bequests are not "fully optimal" as required by the dynasty model, members of the various generations must be treated as distinct agents in welfare economics and what bequests do occur convey an external effect on the recipient. These externalities have implications for population policy but are not directly relevant to the discounting issues of central concern here (see Starrett [1992] for further discussion).

3   A single asset life cycle model

Let us turn to a model in which there are no obvious nonmarket externalities between generations, namely the life cycle model with no bequests. In this situation, productive assets become the store of value that people acquire and hold as part of their life cycle saving. Obviously in a fully disaggregated dynamic model there are many types of productive assets that fill this role (physical capital, renewable and exhaustible resources to name a few). Here, we focus on the simplest case where land is the only such asset, leaving more general analysis for future research.

The simplest equilibrium model that can incorporate these features was first studied by Calvo (1978). People live two periods, working only in the first. They save during that period and spend the proceeds during the second (retirement) period. The fixed factor (land) is the only available asset, so young people save by purchasing it from the old. Calvo used this model to study indeterminacies of competitive equilibrium in infinite horizon models. We make enough assumptions here to eliminate potential indeterminacy and see how the resulting equilibria vary with population choices.

3.1   Production

As before, there are two factors of production: Labor (L) and Land (T). A single consumption good is produced from a time-invariant constant returns to scale production function $F(L,T)$. Competitive conditions are assumed so that each factor is paid the value of its marginal product. Letting output be the current value numeraire, W_t, R_t be the current value returns to labor and land respectively, and writing the factor ratio as $\ell_t = L_t/T$, we can summarize the equilibrium production relationships with a pair of functions: $W_t = W(\ell_t)$, $R_t = R(\ell_t)$, where $W' < 0$ and $R' > 0$.

3.2   Households

There is no labor-leisure margin so (normalizing individual labor supply to one) each householder born in date t will earn income W_t and must decide how to divide it between early consumption and saving. Thus, she faces a problem of the form

$$\text{Max } U\!\left(c^1, c^2\right)$$

subject to

$$c^1 = W_t - s \qquad c^2 = s\!\left[1 + r_t\right]$$

where r_t stands for the rate of return on savings. This problem determines a savings function of the form $s_t = S(W_t, 1 + r_t)$. All households are assumed alike and clearly there must be L_t of them born at date t.

3.3   Equilibrium

Since land is the only asset, the rate of return on savings will be determined from its flow payout plus realized capital gains.[10] Letting q_t stand for the current value land price at date t, we have

$$r_t = \frac{q_{t+1} - q_t}{q_t - R_t} + \frac{R_t}{q_t - R_t} \qquad \text{and} \qquad \varrho_t = 1 + r_t = \frac{q_{t+1}}{q_t - R_t}$$

Since all land must be held by the young generation, the equilibrium condition on that market at date t takes the form

$$L_t S\!\left(W_t, \frac{q_{t+1}}{q_t - R_t}\right) = \left(q_t - R_t\right)T$$

Given a population policy, this dynamic equation determines the price path through time. Calvo discovered a potential indeterminacy in solutions to this equation, but we ignore these here and assume a unique solution.[11] Cohort welfare in turn depends on this solution through the indirect utility functions:

---

[10] We use the convention here that all flow transactions take place at the beginning of the period.

[11] Two assumptions are required for uniqueness. First, there must be perfect foresight so that the equilibrium price path can be extended into the indefinite future. Second, income effects cannot be too important.

$$V_t = V\left(W_t, \frac{q_{t+1}}{q_t - R_t}\right)$$

In this (admittedly quite stark) model, the productivity of the fixed factor accrues to people only as a rate of return to savings (since land is not collectively owned or passed by bequest, it can only be acquired in an act of saving). A population increase will lead to a relative increase in the return to land which will in turn raise the equilibrium interest rates. Each generation is thereby induced to discount the future more, since it is relatively cheap to provide for it. We explore the implications of this relationship below.

4   Pecuniary externalities and the first welfare theorem

There are propositions in the theory of welfare measurement that suggest externalities should be absent from the model just introduced (and generalizations of it). In any complete markets model, effects that work themselves out entirely through changes in prices represent pure transfers: Agents on one side of the market gain by exactly the same amount as agents on the other side lose.[12] This proposition is a version of the First Welfare Theorem: If the income distribution is "optimal" and there are no nonmarket externalities, competitive equilibrium achieves the first-best outcome. Since population choice affects only prices, the proposition would appear to apply to the Calvo model. The transfer mechanism here is carried out through the price of land; it is easy to show that the sale price of land will go up in response to an increase in population, benefiting the sellers (parents) at the expense of buyers (children).[13]

To emphasize the role played by discounting, let us examine the way in which the markets "eliminate" externalities here. How can it be that no one loses on balance given that output per person must fall just as it does when the fixed factor is common property? Part of the answer derives from the new dynamic aspects of the problem. Since old people do not work, the ratio of work force to *population* actually goes up during the first period of extra population. Consequently, output per population may go up in this period even though it must go down in the subsequent

---

[12] This proposition has many incarnations, going back at least as far as Meade (1955). For a recent exposition of the subject and references to the earlier literature, see Starrett (1988), Chapter 9.

[13] See Starrett (1992) for a rigorous demonstration of this proposition in a somewhat more general context.

period. And notice that these same statements will be true whether or not the fixed factor is common property. Therefore, a sufficiently high discount rate could make people indifferent to the corresponding changes in consumption per person per period.

Unfortunately, this cannot be the whole story since it is quite possible that output per population may go down in both periods. This will happen if the labor-land ratio gets high enough so that F_L falls below F/N, where N stands for the total population. As long as $F_L \to 0$ when $L/T \to \infty$, we would eventually find ourselves in that range with a sufficiently large labor supply. In this circumstance, everyone would be worse off in the global commons world yet somehow no one is worse off on balance in the private property world.

The resolution of this puzzle again involves discounting. The discount rate must get high enough to induce the young to save a positive amount of their first period income which consists of *labor income only*. The more serious are crowding effects on the fixed factor, the lower the marginal product of labor (determining labor income) and the more pronounced this discounting effect must become. (We demonstrate the relationship analytically for steady states, momentarily.) The saving undertaken by an extra person generates a surplus that can be used to marginally increase someone's consumption in the associated period. Consumption must fall (by relatively more) in subsequent periods, but as long as discounting is high enough, measured welfare need not fall.

5   The social rate of discount and equity considerations

It is well known that the price-neutrality proposition ignores equity considerations. If the losers on one side of a market are more socially deserving (at the margin) than the gainers on the other, then there is a consequent net social loss. Such a situation may apply here. As we just saw, it is the offspring generation that loses at the expense of the parent generation; effects through the sale price of land are equal and opposite, but they still matter more to the children (whom they affect in the first period of life) than to the parents (whom they affect in the second, discounted, period of life). Consequently, if we choose to count children and parents equally in the social accounting, the parents' decision to have a child generates a negative externality if we take all social objectives into account. Only if we "socially discount" children at the private rate of interest do the price effects fully cancel.

If we count people equally, a net social cost reemerges which looks surprisingly similar in magnitude to that found before. Now, the global external cost would be measured as the cost to the young from price increase (ΔqT) minus the *discounted* benefit to the old ($\Delta qT/(1+r)$). In steady state, $r = R/(q-R)$ so we have

$$GEC = RT\frac{\Delta q}{q} \cong \varepsilon\frac{RT}{L}$$

where ε stands for the elasticity of land price with respect to population increase.

Thus, we see that only if we socially discount the future at the private interest rate (which is ultimately determined by the importance of fixed factors in generating crowding) is the population externality internalized here. We think it is difficult to justify social discounting in the context of these sorts of policy issues. Our model "justifies" new population on the grounds that the extra workers can generate a small short term gain during their productive time although a relatively heavy cost is paid in the future. As long as the future is sufficiently discounted, there is no net social cost. However, the overall quality of life definitely declines over time and we think this constitutes a legitimate external cost.[14]

The issues are even more dramatically illustrated if we consider a permanent long run change in population size. That is, suppose someone in cohort $t-1$ has an extra child who is expected also to have an extra child, and so forth. If we were initially in a steady state, the price system will adjust in one period to the new steady state. The steady state price of land will go up, and in fact will rise by more than the short run price increase. Exactly the same calculations we did before now imply that *each* generation following cohort $t-1$ suffers a welfare loss (relative to the previous cohort's gain), whose size has the same general form as before.

Consequently, if all cohorts were really counted equally, *no* finite benefit could justify extra population. These types of calculations force us to confront paradoxes associated with zero discounting (whereby we are forced to count the future as "infinitely" more important than the present); nonetheless, it seems difficult to defend the position that the appropriate size of external cost is "zero."

6   Zero discounting and the paradox of infinity

It is well known that zero discounting generates logical problems for welfare economics, problems that must be confronted if we are to defend

---

[14] There will be no actual decline if technological improvement is sufficiently rapid, but as discussed earlier, there will still be an external cost in that people will be worse off than they would have been without the extra population.

successfully positions taken above.[15] The difficulties can be expressed in a number of different ways:

1 If we attempt to employ zero discounting over an infinite horizon, no finite time period gets any "weight" in decision making.

2 There is no "appropriately continuous" welfare indicator that will accurately reflect zero social discounting.

3 In models that admit physical capital, consistent application of zero discounting implies that we should impose forced saving (and investment) on the current generation until the private rate of return is lowered to zero.

In the specific context discussed earlier, there is an even more dramatic implication, namely:

4 If people are to be consistently counted equally as of the first period of their lives, yet allowed to discount future values within their lifetimes, then straight lump sum transfers from old to young are always justified as long as the private rate of return is greater than zero.

Given these observations, it seems clear that zero discounting cannot and should not be applied blindly to guide all social decisions. But then, we must ask: Are there both *reasonable* and *consistent* frameworks for employing zero discounting in a discriminating way? Here we suggest a framework and argue that it fills the bill.

Our framework is perhaps best motivated by the homily: "Today is the first day of the rest of your life." We suggest that other things (such as income or employment status) being equal, society should treat the people alive at a moment of time on equal footing (as if each were "newborn"). We combine this view with the position that people of the future should be on equal footing as well, yet individuals discount at the private interest rate within their lifetimes.

Before attempting to be more specific, we explore this concept and its implications in broad outline. First, we observe that if this framework is employed over time it involves a time inconsistency. In particular, our attitude toward the transfer of $1 from tomorrow's young prople to tomorrow's old is different *today* than it will be *tomorrow*; in the first situation the transfer looks bad whereas in the second, it is a wash.

Whenever there is time inconsistency the underlying framework

---

[15] These problems were first identified and discussed by Koopmans (1972, 1974).

cannot be applied uniformly to all choices since that would lead to intransitive decisions. For example, we could (a) take $1 today from the young, and give $1 + δ tomorrow to the young; (b) tomorrow, take $1 + δ from the young and give $1 + 2$\delta$ to the old; (c) give today's young $1 - δ and require them to pay $1 + 2$\delta$ tomorrow (when they are old). All three of these transactions would increase social welfare under our framework as long as δ is small relative to the private interest rate,[16] yet the final net outcome makes everyone (weakly) worse off.

From the above reasoning some conclude that there is no place for time inconsistent objectives. However, we think they can still be justified as long as they are applied in restricted contexts where the inconsistencies are inconsequential. Here we suggest a partial ordering in which the "allowed" set of comparisons cannot generate intransitivities.

7   A criterion for equitable intervention

We seek rules to guide government action or intervention in a mixed economy setting; the environment is characterized by a *status quo* equilibrium in which all private markets clear and corresponding prices are functions of publicly chosen variables and other parameters. Our rules will be stated as guidelines for approving government actions or interventions (hereafter referred to as *projects*) relative to this status quo.

To each project, we associate an *action date (t)*, namely that time at which that project makes its first change in status quo variables. Each household alive at such a date is assumed to have a "forward looking" indirect utility function whose arguments include variables of the underlying equilibrium and (possibly) past decisions. We assume that these functions are internally time consistent; for example, in the case of additively separable direct utility, they are defined via the Bellman recursive equation. The collection of households born in date s is referred to as *cohort s*. For household h from cohort s alive at date t, we represent the corresponding indirect utility as $V_t^{hs}(.)$; for cohorts born in the future ($s > t$), we specify $V_t^{hs}(.) = V_t^{hs}(.)$, that is, we measure utility as of the beginning of life. Since the action date is held fixed in much of what follows, we frequently suppress the index t in the sequel.

Any proposed project will induce a change in utilities for affected households. For simplicity, we assume that projects are small enough so that we can think of these changes as "first order." These we normalize in standard fashion using the marginal utility of wealth at the action date

[16] The precise condition is $(1 + 2\delta)/(1 - \delta) < 1 + r$, or $\delta < r/(3 + r)$.

(or first period of life for future cohorts) and represent as $\delta V^{hs}/\lambda^h$. Our acceptance criteria require that a certain weighted sum of these utility changes be positive, the weights to be determined according to equity principles specified below:

1   All members of a given cohort are weighted equally; consequently, we work with the cohort welfare increment: $\delta W^s = \Sigma_h \delta V^{hs}/\lambda^h$.
2   All households alive at the date of action (t) are weighted equally; using β to represent weights, $\beta^s = 1, s \le t$.
3   Any *net costs* imposed on a future cohort are undiscounted; if $s > t$ and $\delta W^s < 0$, then $\beta^s = 1$.
4   Any *net benefits* conferred on a future cohort are discounted at the private rate; if $s > t$ and $\delta W^s > 0$. then $\beta^s = \varrho(s,t)$, the private discount factor for numeraire date s evaluated at date t.

Given these principles, a project (a) would be evaluated according to $\delta Z(a) \equiv \Sigma_s \beta^s \delta W^s(a)$.

Before exploring consequences, we discuss the rationale for these principles. According to (1), we consider all lump sum transfers among members of a given cohort as welfare neutral. This stipulation serves to isolate the issues of intergenerational equity that particularly concern us. The second principle guarantees that *all transfers* at the date of action are welfare neutral; in particular, direct transfers from old to young are not seen as welfare improving.

Principles (3) and (4) distinguish between benefits and costs imposed on the future. Benefits are treated as if they were private bequests, thus discounted at the private rate, whereas costs are undiscounted. Since the public conferring of benefits is an alternative to private bequests, (4) is in the nature of a consistency condition. Principle (3) captures our view of intergenerational equity and creates no conflict with private preferences since negative bequests are infeasible, and the young have no access to capital markets before they are born.

It should be obvious from previous discussion that these principles are not consistent with a welfare criterion that ranks all projects. That is, we cannot use δZ as a consistent criterion for welfare change. However, we propose to use it only as a criterion for welfare improvement from the given status quo. That is, we propose the rule: Accept project (a) if $\delta Z(a) \equiv \Sigma_s \beta^s \delta W^s(a) > 0$, and show that this constitutes a consistent rule for action.

Claim: *If $\delta Z(a) > 0$ and $\delta Z(b) > 0$, and all private discount rates are nonnegative, then $\delta Z(a \& b) > 0$.*

Proof: Let c represent the project a & b and introduce the notation:

$$x^+ = \max\{x, 0\} \qquad \left[note\ x = x^+ + x^- \right]$$
$$x^- = \min\{x, 0\}$$

Then, for any project, we can write

$$\delta Z(.) = \sum_{s \leq t} \delta W^s(.) + \sum_{s > t} \delta W^s(.)^- + \sum_{s > t} \varrho(s, t) \delta W^s(.)^+ \qquad \text{QED.}$$

Now, from well known properties of x^+ and x^-, there exist numbers $\varepsilon^s \geq 0$ such that

$$\delta W^s(c)^+ = \delta W^s(a)^+ + \delta W^s(b)^+ - \varepsilon^s$$

and   all s

$$\delta W^s(c)^- = \delta W^s(a)^- + \delta W^s(b)^- + \varepsilon^s$$

Consequently,[17]

$$\delta Z(c) = \delta Z(a) + \delta Z(b) + \sum_{s > t} \left(1 - \varrho(s, t) \right) \varepsilon^s \geq \delta Z(a) + \delta Z(b)$$

where the last inequality follows from our assumption of nonnegative private discount rates. Therefore, if projects (a) and (b) pass our test, so does (c).

Thus, as a criterion for positive action, our test passes a consistency check and generates a legitimate partial ordering that is a refinement of the Pareto partial ordering. As with any such partial ordering, the planner must be creative in packaging projects to find combinations that will pass the test (recall the compensation of losers by gainers in the Pareto improvement test). Moreover, our test leaves some degree of indeterminacy that must be resolved before the rules can be fully operational. One issue here involves the choice of action date. In standard applied welfare economics, the date of evaluation is irrelevant; changing that date merely multiplies all relevant quantities by a common discount factor. However, in our present context, we have seen that the date of evaluation does matter.

---

[17] Since all projects are assumed to be of first order, we do not need to worry about the order of project introduction in making these calculations.

Our choice of action date seems appropriate as it entails using weights that are deemed equitable to those people alive when the decision must be made. This choice also happens to have the property that it maximizes the chance that any particular project will be accepted. To see this, note that the only effect of postponing an evaluation date is to (possibly) lower the relative weight placed on a negative cost term; this will happen when a "future" cohort incurring costs becomes a "current" cohort.[18]

A second indeterminacy issue involves the choice of a status quo. It is well known that the status quo matters in the context of "limited action rules" of the type proposed here; we give an example in the context of population choice momentarily. Consequently, if the present definition of equity is to be operational, it must include rules for choosing a "justifiable" status quo. We think of the issue here as one of specifying the scope of individual freedoms: What decisions can an individual make without having to submit those choices to collective review? This question is important in broader contexts, but takes on extra significance in light of the aforementioned indeterminacy.

8 Population policy and directions for future research

It is easy to see that our equity criterion can justify imposing a "child tax" on prospective parents in the labor-land model considered earlier. When (1) markets are complete, (2) bequests do not occur, and (3) all future effects are discounted, we saw that the population decision induces no externalities. However, if the costs imposed on future unborn cohorts are to be undiscounted, there is a positive external cost, and the extra child is justified under our criteria only if the private benefits to having this child outweigh this cost. Thus a family would face the correct social incentives only if a tax were imposed at the rate of these costs. And recall that the external cost is relatively large in this case, being commensurate with that when the fixed factor is common property. This conclusion does require that the status quo be set so as not to include the child and that the associated decision be deemed subject to collective review. Note that if the status quo is redefined to include the child, a social initiative to delete it would not pass our approval test (in this case, no net costs are imposed on the future so current costs exactly cancel future benefits).

---

[18] Note however, that we might still want to package projects that take place in the future with "current" projects in the search for a passing combination.

320   **D. A. Starrett**

Obviously various value judgments are involved here and many would argue that this type of interference is never justified. However, we believe that the equity principles set forth above are compelling and worthy of further study. In subsequent work, we will provide a more systematic discussion and defense of improvement rules based on partial orderings and will explore their implications for social intervention in a wide range of decision problems where public action (or regulation) is subject to debate.

References

Arrow, K. 1966. Discounting and public investment criteria. In *Water Research*, ed. A. V. Kneese and S. C. Smith. Baltimore: Johns Hopkins Press.
Arrow, K. 1982. The rate of discount on public investments with imperfect capital markets. In *Discounting for Time and Risk in Energy Policy*. Washington, DC: Resources for the Future.
Arrow, K., and A. Fisher. 1974. Preservation, uncertainty and irreversibility. *Quarterly Journal of Economics*, 88(2):312–19.
Barro, R. 1974. Are government bonds net wealth? *Journal of Political Economy*, 82(6):1095–117.
Baumol, W., and W. Oates. 1975. *The Theory of Environmental Policy*. Englewood-Cliffs, NJ: Prentice-Hall.
Bernheim, B. D. 1988. Ricardian equivalence: An evaluation of theory and evidence. Working paper, NBER, Harvard University.
Calvo, G. 1978. On the indeterminacy of interest rates and wages with perfect foresight. *Journal of Economic Theory*, 19(2):34–7.
Dasgupta, P., and G. Heal. 1979. *Economic Theory and Exhaustible Resources*. Cambridge University Press.
Ehrlich, P., A. Ehrlich, and J. Holdren. 1977. *Ecoscience, Population, Resources and the Environment*. New York: W. H. Freeman.
Koopmans, T., P. A. Diamond, and R. Williamson. 1964. Stationary utility and time perspective. *Econometrica*, 32(1–2):82–100.
Koopmans, T. 1972. Representation of preference orderings over time. In *Decision and Organization*, ed. M. McGuire and R. Radner. Amsterdam: North Holland, Chap. 4.
Koopmans, T. 1974. Some observations on "optimal" economic growth and exhaustible resources. In *Economic Structure and Development: Essays in Honor of Jan Tinbergen*, ed. H. C. Bos, H. Linnemann, and P. de Wolff. Amsterdam: North Holland, 239–55.
Kotlikoff, L. 1988. Intergenerational transfers and savings. *Journal of Economic Perspectives*, 2(2):41–58.
Krutilla, J., and A. Fisher. 1975. *The Economics of Natural Environments*. Washington, DC: Resources for the Future.
Mäler, K-G. 1990. Sustainable development. Unpublished manuscript, Stockholm School of Economics.
Meade, J. 1955. *Trade and Welfare*. London: Oxford University Press.
Meadows, D. 1979. *The Limits to Growth*. New Ycrk: Universe Books.

Modigliani, F. 1988. Present, Past, and Future. *Journal of Economic Perspectives*, 2(4):49–58.
Nerlove, M. 1987. *Household and Economy: Welfare Economics of Endogenous Fertility*. New York: Academic Press.
Starrett, D. 1988. *Foundations of Public Economics*. Cambridge: Cambridge University Press.
Starrett, D. 1992. On the social costs of global crowding. SITE Technical Report No. 46, Stanford University.

CHAPTER 15

Trade and welfare

Tito Cordella, Enrico Minelli, and
Heracles Polemarchakis

The argument for international trade is that in a competitive equilibrium with trade all individuals gain in utility, compared to domestic autarky.

Ever since the modern formulation of gains from trade by Samuelson (1939) and the identification of competitive equilibrium allocations with Pareto optimal allocations by Arrow (1951), it has been recognized that the argument requires transfers across individuals. In a world economy which consists of many countries, and in which each country is a collection of possibly heterogeneous individuals, domestic autarky refers to a competitive equilibrium allocation of each country in isolation, though not of each individual in isolation. A competitive allocation with trade across countries need not entail an improvement in the utility of every individual.

Transfers of commodities or revenue balance across individuals. Domestic transfers balance across individuals within each country. They are thus a restricted class of transfers of evident interest for policy.

Are domestic transfers sufficient for Pareto gains from trade? An affirmative answer was given by Grandmont and McFadden (1972). Consider a competitive equilibrium allocation for each country, the autarkic allocation, and a competitive equilibrium allocation for the world economy obtained after the domestic reallocation of commodities associated with the autarkic allocation. By a revealed preference argument, each individual is at least as well off in this competitive equilibrium allocation for the world economy as in autarky. Evaluating the

This text presents research results of the Belgian program on Interuniversity Poles of Attraction initiated by the Belgian State, Prime Minister's Office, Science Policy Programming. The scientific responsibility is assumed by its authors.

This work was supported in part by SPES grants No. CT91-5021, No. CT91-0066, No. CT91-5047, and No. CT91-0057 from the Commission of the European Communities. We wish to thank Paolo Siconolfi for helpful comments.

domestic reallocation of commodities at the competitive equilibrium prices for the world economy determines domestic transfers of revenue sufficient for Pareto gains from trade.

In a recent article, Cordella and Ventura (1992) showed that the argument fails if domestic transfers of commodities are implemented after trade in world markets.

We argue here that domestic transfers of commodities or revenue implemented before trade in world markets need not suffice for Pareto gains from trade. Our argument complements the argument of Grandmont and McFadden, although contradicting its conclusion.

In the absence of strong monotonicity and strictly positive endowments, which is natural, the existence of competitive equilibrium is ensured when the economy is resource related. This means that any subset of individuals is endowed with commodities that could increase the utility of the complementary subset of any feasible allocation (McKenzie [1959a, 1959b]). Resources relatedness is thus a property of the preferences as well as of the endowments of individuals. Even if the world economy is resource related as is every country in isolation, the world economy may fail to be resource related after the endowments are modified to coincide with an autarkic equilibrium allocation. A competitive equilibrium following the domestic transfer of commodities may then fail to exist, and the argument of Grandmont and McFadden cannot proceed.

When, following the transfer of commodities associated with domestic autarky, resource relatedness fails, and competitive equilibria fail to exist, two possibilities arise: Either an alternative transfer of commodities or revenue exists which leads to Pareto gains from trade, or some individual loses in utility with international trade relative to domestic autarky for all redistributions of commodities or revenue compatible with equilibrium.

We construct an example illustrating both possibilities.

1 The example

A world economy, $\mathbf{W}$, has individuals $h = 1,2,3$, and commodities $l = 1, \ldots 4$. The world economy is divided into countries, $\mathbf{A}$ and $\mathbf{B}$, each a subset of individuals. In particular, $\mathbf{A} = \{1,2\}$ and $\mathbf{B} = \{3\}$.

The utility functions and endowments of individuals are as follows:
For country $\mathbf{A}$,

$$u^1 = x_1 + x_3 + \min\{1 + \delta, x_4\}, \quad x \geq 0, \quad w^1 = (1,1,1,1)$$
$$u^2 = x_2, \quad\quad\quad\quad\quad\quad\quad\quad\quad\; x \geq 0, \quad w^2 = (1,1,0,0)$$

and for country $\mathbf{B}$,

$$u^3 = x_1, \quad x \geq 0, \quad w^3 = \left(1, 1, 1, \varepsilon\right)$$

with

$$0 \leq \delta < \varepsilon < \frac{1}{2}$$

The world economy, as well as the economy of every country, satisfies standard conditions for the existence and optimality of competitive equilibrium allocations: The preferences of individuals described by their consumption sets and utility functions are continuous and convex, and display local nonsatiation, and, most important, in conjunction with their endowments, they satisfy resources relatedness. An economy satisfies resources relatedness if and only if, for any nontrivial partition of the set of individuals, $\mathbf{H}$, into two, nonempty subsets, $\mathbf{H}_1$ and $\mathbf{H}_2$, and for any feasible allocation, $x^{\mathbf{H}} = \{x^h : h \in \mathbf{H}\}$, there exists an individual $h \in \mathbf{H}_2$ such that $u^h(x^h + \Sigma_{h_1 \in \mathbf{H}_1} w^{h_1}) > u^h(x^h)$.

Since in both countries, and hence in the world economy as well, at least one individual has a utility function strictly monotonically increasing in the consumption of commodity $l = 1$, we treat it throughout as numeraire: $p_1 = 1$.

The autarkic equilibrium in country $\mathbf{A}$ is unique and obtains at prices

$$p^{\mathbf{A}} = \left(1, 1, 1, 1\right)$$

and the associated allocation of commodities and utilities is

$$x^{1,\mathbf{A}} = \left(2, 0, 1, 1\right), \quad u^{1,\mathbf{A}} = 4$$
$$x^{2,\mathbf{A}} = \left(0, 2, 0, 0\right), \quad u^{2,\mathbf{A}} = 2$$

whereas in country $\mathbf{B}$ the unique autarkic equilibrium prices are

$$p^{\mathbf{B}} = \left(1, 0, 0, 0\right)$$

and the associated allocation of commodities and utilities is

$$x^{3,\mathbf{A}} = \left(1, 1, 1, \varepsilon\right), \quad u^{3,\mathbf{B}} = 1$$

The equilibrium for the world economy $\mathbf{W}$ is unique and obtains at prices

$$p^{\mathbf{W}} = \left(1, \frac{1}{2}, 1, 0\right)$$

and the associated allocation of commodities and utilities is

$$x^{1,W} = \left(\frac{1}{2}, 0, 2, 1 + \varepsilon\right), \quad u^{1,W} = \frac{7}{2} + \delta$$

$$x^{2,W} = \left(0, 3, 0, 0\right), \quad u^{2,W} = 3$$

$$x^{3,W} = \left(\frac{5}{2}, 0, 0, 0\right), \quad u^{3,W} = \frac{5}{2}$$

Individual $h = 1$ is worse off with trade compared with autarky:

$$u^{1,W} = \frac{7}{2} + \delta < 4 = u^{1,A}$$

Feasible allocations for the world economy such that all individuals are strictly better off than at the competitive equilibrium with autarky indeed exist; for example, the allocation

$$x^{1,W} = \left(2 - k, 0, 2, 1 + \varepsilon\right) \quad u^{1,W} = 5 + \delta - k$$

$$x^{2,W} = \left(0, 3, 0, 0\right) \quad u^{2,W} = 3$$

$$x^{3,W} = \left(1 + k, 0, 0, 0\right) \quad u^{3,W} = 1 + k$$

for

$$0 < k < 1 + \delta$$

Furthermore, each such allocation can be obtained as a competitive equilibrium with transfers of commodities or, more simply, revenue,

$$\tau^{1,W} = \frac{3}{2} - k, \quad \tau^{2,W} = 0 \quad \tau^{3,W} = k - \frac{3}{2}$$

and prices,

$$p^W = \left(1, \frac{1}{2}, 1, 0\right)$$

These, however, are not domestic transfers. They do not balance across individuals within each country.

The question arises: Are there domestic transfers for which an associated competitive equilibrium allocation improves the utility of every individual compared to autarky?

Let τ be the transfer of revenue from individual $h = 2$ to individual $h = 1$ in country **A** – it is pedantic to write $\tau^1 = \tau$ and $\tau^2 = -\tau$ – while no transfer occurs within country **B** which consists of one individual. Since individual $h = 2$ is the only one to demand commodity $l = 2$ and he demands only that commodity, his revenue equals the aggregate expenditure of commodity $l = 2$ or $1 + p_2 - \tau = 3p_2$. Thus $2p_2 = 1 - \tau$, which implies that only transfers

$$\tau < 1$$

are possibly compatible with competitive equilibria.

Following a domestic transfer of revenue $\tau < 1$ in country $\mathbf{A}$, the equilibrium for the world economy $\mathbf{W}$ is unique and obtains at prices

$$p^{\mathbf{W}} = \left(1, \frac{1 - \tau}{2}, 1, 0\right)$$

and the associated allocation of commodities and utilities is

$$x^{1,\mathbf{W}} = \left(\frac{1 + \tau}{2}, 0, 2, 1 + \varepsilon\right) \quad u^{1,\mathbf{W}} = \frac{7 + \tau}{2} + \delta$$
$$x^{2,\mathbf{W}} = \left(0, 3, 0, 0\right) \quad u^{2,\mathbf{W}} = 3$$
$$x^{3,\mathbf{W}} = \left(\frac{5 - \tau}{2}, 0, 0, 0\right) \quad u^{3,\mathbf{W}} = \frac{5 - \tau}{2}$$

For $\delta \in (0, 1/2)$, a transfer $\tau \in (1 - 2\delta, 1)$ yields a competitive equilibrium at which all individuals gain in utility compared to autarky.

For $\delta = 0$, no domestic transfer yields a competitive equilibrium at which all individuals gain in utility compared to autarky.

It is instructive to see that the argument of Grandmont and McFadden fails, for $\delta = 0$ as well as for $\delta \in (0, 1/2)$. Consider, as Grandmont and McFadden suggest, the world economy but with initial endowments for individuals in country $\mathbf{A}$

$$w^1 = \left(2, 0, 1, 1\right)$$
$$w^2 = \left(0, 2, 0, 0\right)$$

If $p_2 > 0$ there is an excess supply of commodity $l = 2$ equal to 1, the endowment of individual $h = 3$, which is not compatible with market clearing. The only individual who could absorb this excess, individual $h = 2$, has no endowment of another commodity to offer in exchange. If $p_2 = 0$, the optimization problem of individual $h = 2$ has no solution, which, again, is not compatible with market clearing. Grandmont and McFadden evidently make assumptions which fail in our example and which guarantee that competitive equilibria for the world economy exist when the domestic transfer of commodities equates the initial endowments of individuals with their allocation at the autarkic competitive equilibrium.

It is interesting that, even when the transfer suggested by Grandmont and McFadden fails to yield equilibria and a fortiori to yield a Pareto improvement in welfare relative to domestic autarky, other such transfers may exist. In our example, they do for $\delta \in (0,1/2)$ but not for $\delta = 0$.

2 Conclusion

The characterization of minimal sufficient conditions for the existence of domestic transfers such that, with international trade, every individual gains in utility compared to domestic autarky, is a controversial subject.

References

Arrow, K. J. 1951. An extension of the basic theorems of classical welfare economics. In *Proceedings of the second Berkeley symposium on mathematical statistics and probability*, ed., J. Neyman. University of California Press, 507–32.

Cordella, T., and L. Ventura. 1992. A note on redistribution and gains from trade. *Economics Letters,* 39:449–53.

Grandmont, J.-M., and D. McFadden. 1972. A technical note on classical gains from trade. *Journal of International Economics*, 2:109–205.

McKenzie, L. 1959a. On the existence of general equilibrium for a competitive economy. *Econometrica*, 27:54–71.

McKenzie, L. 1959b. On the existence of general equilibrium: Some corrections. *Econometrica*, 29:247–8.

Samuelson, P. A. 1939. The gains from international trade. *Canadian Journal of Economics*, 5:195–205.

CHAPTER 16

History as a widespread externality in some Arrow–Debreu market games

Peter J. Hammond

1   Introduction

Among Kenneth Arrow's many highly significant and widely cited contributions to economic science are his path-breaking essays on the two
fundamental efficiency theorems of welfare economics (Arrow, 1951), on
the role of securities in the allocation of risk-bearing (Arrow, 1953; 1964),
and the joint article with Gérard Debreu (Arrow and Debreu, 1954) on
the existence of general competitive or Walrasian equilibrium. There is
also the joint monograph by Arrow and Hahn (1971).[1] Of these, the first
article uses what has since become the standard definition of Walrasian
equilibrium, possibly modified by lump-sum redistribution of wealth, and
related equilibrium to Pareto efficient allocations. The second article
defines what it means to have a complete set of securities markets in a
sequence economy with uncertainty. The third proves the existence of
equilibrium under what have since become almost standard assumptions.
And the monograph with Frank Hahn explores not only the main ideas

---

[1] According to Intriligator (1987), the first three articles mentioned above were cited
respectively 59, 264 (including references to the French version, which was published
first), and 117 times during the period 1966–83; when ranked by their frequency of cita-
tion, that made them, respectively, the twenty-sixth, eighth, and fifteenth items in Arrow's
list of publications. Apart from the second article, therefore, these are far from being the
most frequently cited of Arrow's works during that period. The first ranked item, *Social
Choice and Individual Values*, was cited no fewer than 1203 times; the second ranked,
Arrow and Hahn (1971), was cited 561 times during the same period. This last figure may
reflect the significance of Arrow's work in general equilibrium theory more accurately
than the less frequent citations of the articles cited in the opening text. These may have
become classics to the extent that they are not frequently cited, just as few modern physicists or mathematicians bother to cite the works of Newton, although many rely on ideas
derived from his work. It should be added that *Essays in the Theory of Risk-Bearing*,
which includes a reprint of Arrow (1953, 1964), was also frequently cited.

328

in general competitive analysis, but also much of the progress in making it applicable to real economic phenomena.

An important feature of Arrow and Debreu (1954) is its conscious use of explicitly game-theoretic ideas, previously found in the related paper by Debreu (1952).[2] A generalization of the usual notion of a game is involved, since there is an auctioneer whose strategy choice determines the price vector. Given this choice, agents are then constrained to choose net trades within their budget sets. Thus the strategic choice of the auctioneer limits the strategies the other players are allowed to choose.

This chapter presents an easy modification of this generalized game so that it becomes a game in the usually accepted sense, with agents free to choose strategies within a specified fixed strategy set that is independent of what other players may choose. The important feature of the Arrow–Debreu market game presented in Section 2 is that agents are free to make demands that violate their budget constraints. If they do so, however, they will be reduced to autarky. This is evidently a strong enough sanction to make budget constraints self-enforcing. Thus the game has a set of slightly restricted "straightforward" Nash equilibria[3] in which net trades satisfying the budget constraints are announced by all agents, including even those who have zero net trade in equilibrium and so would have nothing to lose by violating their budget constraints. It is not surprising that the set of all such equilibria corresponds exactly to the set of Walrasian equilibria, as did the Nash equilibria of the generalized game which Arrow and Debreu considered.

In order to discuss the efficiency theorems of welfare economics, one should consider a redistributive agency as an extra player, whose objective is to maximize some Paretian Bergson social welfare function. Then it is evidently necessary to consider Walrasian equilibria relative to different possible systems of lump-sum wealth redistribution. For those expected to pay lump-sum taxes, the threat of autarky may not suffice to make their budget constraints self-enforcing. Instead of a zero net trade, however, any arbitrary net trade within the budget set will suffice to deter violations of the budget constraint. Section 3 explains this.

The main purpose of this chapter, however, is not to present these trivial and not very exciting results on true games whose straightforward Nash equilibria implement desirable Walrasian equilibria. Rather, it is to point out some problems in applying the standard Arrow–Debreu methodology to intertemporal economic models. The games formulated

---

[2] It should be noted, however, that the 1954 essay by Arrow and Debreu was cited as motivating the work reported in Debreu (1952).

[3] That is, one where players have no incentive to misrepresent their characteristics.

above raise the issues of what happens if markets cannot be prevented from reopening in later periods and if a benevolent welfare maximizing government cannot commit itself in advance not to make transfers at later dates. It turns out that the Nash equilibria which correspond to Walrasian equilibria can easily be subgame imperfect, in the sense that they require incredible responses by the auctioneer or redistributive agency to trading agents' deviations from the equilibrium path (see Selten, 1965; 1973; 1975). Nor do these subgame imperfections result from an artifice of the particular game formulations set out in Sections 2 and 3: Exactly the same imperfections would arise in any other game whose Nash equilibrium outcomes were Walrasian equilibrium allocations.

To substantiate these claims, the heart of the chapter presents two simple models of an intertemporal economy lasting for two periods. The first of these involves only two agents, one of whom is a mine owner with the power to influence second period prices by choosing how much of a single exhaustible resource stock to extract in the first period, and how much to leave in the ground for later use as an input to production in the second period. The two-period market game in which reopening markets is impossible has the usual Walrasian equilibrium of an Arrow–Debreu economy. But if the mine owner believes that markets cannot be prevented from reopening in the second period, the only subgame perfect equilibrium will involve higher extraction in the first period, lower in the second period, since in this way the mine owner can exercise monopoly power. Perversely, this manipulation of the market economy makes the mine owner worse off. Section 4 demonstrates this.

An economy with a continuum of negligibly small agents will evidently not be subject to such manipulation, even in subgame perfect equilibrium. When a redistributive agency enters the economy, however, individual agents have the power to exploit its benevolence in a dramatic fashion. Section 5 considers a counterpart of the model in Section 4, but with a continuum of agents and also a benevolent government. The essentially unique subgame perfect equilibrium requires almost every mining firm to use up its entire resource stock in the first period, leaving nothing to produce in the second period. The point is that optimal redistribution in the second period implies complete equality so that the mean output from using all resource stocks is shared equally by all. This destroys any incentive for mine owners to save by keeping some of their resource stock for the second period. In fact, redistribution in the second period makes holding back resource stock for the future an activity equivalent to the private provision of a public good, or creation of a "widespread externality" in the sense of Hammond, Kaneko, and

Wooders (1989). Such an externality affects everybody, and depends on the distribution of individual decisions in the population, even though each individual has negligible influence on its creation. As Section 5 also argues, the only policy remedies which work are those recognizing that there really is a public good problem.

It could be argued that welfare maximizing lump-sum redistribution is impractical anyway. I have elsewhere claimed that it is generally incentive incompatible (Hammond, 1979; 1987), especially when small coalitions can manipulate the economic system by exchanging goods on the side. But as Tesfatsion (1986) was careful to point out, previous analyses of the "time inconsistency" or incredibility of public policy were usually conducted in models where first-best optimal policy was infeasible for one reason or another. In her article and in the example of Section 5 below, this is emphatically not the case.

Nevertheless, the main lesson of Section 5 is that, even when instruments of more realistic government policy are affected by the current state or history of the economy, as they surely should be, and if this state is influenced by individuals' decisions, then history becomes like a privately supplied public good or widespread externality. The typical presumption is that any such externality or public good will be inefficiently supplied, so the fact that government intervention in the economy will be desirable later on provides a rationale for intervention now, in order to treat this public good problem. This lesson appears to remain valid in a wide range of circumstances.

Issues this discussion raises are whether general equilibrium theory has anything interesting to say about public policy in intertemporal economies and whether anything valid remains from the many apparently interesting analyses offered in the past, especially by macroeconomists. Many macroeconomic models, however, have contained only a single "representative" agent, for whom there can never be any problem with public goods. One welcome feature of some recent work on endogenous growth is precisely that, even though it often retains a continuum of identical representative agents, it does nevertheless allow public good problems to arise – though through technological externalities rather than through policy reactions to economic states influenced by earlier private decisions.

As for past work by microeconomists on intertemporal general equilibrium theory, surprisingly little of the literature has sought to explain the scope for and influence of public policy. There seem to have been problems enough anyway, including finding a role for money and understanding why markets are incomplete. Many special models have been used to consider particular issues of intertemporal economic policy – pension and social security systems, the appropriate social rate of discount on public investment projects, the role of the national debt and its significance, the relative merits of income versus expenditure taxes, and so forth. What is lacking is any general framework as broad as those that appear in Arrow (1951) and Arrow and Debreu (1954), as well as those in the static analysis of the public sector due to Diamond and Mirrlees (1971). In other words, we lack what is needed for a systematic general treatment of all relevant aspects of intertemporal economic policy, and especially of how different policy instruments interact with each other. Filling this need is a serious undertaking that has yet to be attempted. The concluding Section 6 does, however, venture a brief sketch of what the most important ingredients for such a treatment are likely to be. The emphasis should turn away from frameworks such as the famous complete contingent commodity model of Debreu (1959, Chapter 7; also discussed in Arrow and Hahn [1971, Section 5.6]), which aims to determine the entire future course of economic history all at one go. Instead the framework should be closer to the well-known Arrow (1953, 1964) model of a securities market, with the equilibrium allocation determined sequentially by looking one period ahead within each successive period, or to the Hicksian theory of temporary equilibrium. An early modern discussion of the latter can be found toward the end of a much lesser known article by Arrow (1971) and in Arrow and Hahn (1971, Chapter 6).

Section 7 contains some brief concluding remarks.

2   A first simple Arrow–Debreu market game

2.1   Defining the game

Consider an economy with a finite set of private agents I and a finite set of commodities G, so that $\Re^G$ is the commodity space. Suppose that each agent $i \in I$ has a set $X^i \subset \Re^G$ of feasible net trades, and a utility function $u^i: X^i \to \Re$ representing i's preferences over net trade vectors. Assume that the no trade or autarky vector $0 \in X^i$ for all $i \in I$, and that i's preferences are locally nonsatiated – that is, the utility function u^i has no local maximum. Let $\mathbf{X}^I$ denote the Cartesian product $\Pi_{i \in I} X^i$ of the trading agents' feasible sets.

Suppose, too, that there is an auctioneer, denoted by superscript A, whose role is to clear markets by choosing a normalized commodity price vector p in the simplex

$$\Delta := \left\{ p \in \Re^G \middle| \forall g = 1, \ldots, G \; p_g \geq 0; \; \sum_{g=1}^{G} p_g = 1 \right\}$$

The price vector p announced by the auctioneer will help determine the net trade vector $t^i \in X^i$ that each agent $i \in I$ actually obtains from the economy as a function $t^i(s^i, p)$ of i's strategy choice $s^i \in X^i$, to be thought of as a net trade demand, as well as a function of p. Specifically, it is assumed that

$$t^i\left(s^i, p\right) = \begin{cases} s^i & \text{if } ps^i \leq 0 \\ 0 & \text{otherwise} \end{cases}$$

This definition ensures that $pt^i(s^i, p) \leq 0$ for all $p \in \Delta$ and all $s^i \in X^i$.

Agent i's payoff as a function of the strategy profile $(\mathbf{s}^I, p)$ is accordingly given by $v^i(\mathbf{s}^I, p) := u^i(t^i(s^i, p))$. Thus agents are allowed to have the net trade vectors they each demand as long as these lie within their budget sets, but agents whose demands violate their budget constraints are reduced to autarky.

The specification of the game is completed by defining the auctioneer's payoff function as $v^A(\mathbf{s}^I, p) := p \sum_{i \in I} s^i$, which is just the value at prices p of the aggregate net demand vector for all agents $i \in I$. Note that $v^A(\mathbf{s}^I, p) \geq p \sum_{i \in I} t^i(s^i, p)$; a sufficient condition for equality is that all agents $i \in I$ satisfy their budget constraints $p s^i \leq 0$.

Finally, therefore, the market game is the collection

$$\left\langle I \cup \{A\}, \mathbf{X}^I \times \Delta, \left\langle v^h \right\rangle_{h \in I \cup \{A\}} \right\rangle$$

consisting of the set of players, their allowable strategies, and their payoff functions.

2.2 Equivalence of straightforward Nash and Walrasian equilibria

Let us now consider some obvious properties of the best response $\hat{s}^i$ in the market game by an agent $i \in I$ to any price vector p chosen by the auctioneer, and of the resulting net trade vector $\hat{t}^i := t^i(\hat{s}^i, p)$. One has $pt^i(s^i, p) \leq 0$ and also $u^i(\hat{t}^i) \geq u^i(t^i(s^i, p))$ for all $s^i \in X^i$. This implies that $p\hat{t}^i \leq 0$. Also, for all $s^i \in X^i$ that satisfy $ps^i \leq 0$ one has $t^i(s^i, p) = s^i$ and so $u^i(\hat{t}^i) \geq u^i(s^i)$. Thus each agent's best response $\hat{s}^i$ yields a net trade vector $\hat{t}^i = t^i(\hat{s}^i, p)$ equal to a Walrasian net trade vector at the price vector p. Because of local nonsatiation it must also be true that $p\hat{t}^i = 0$.

In fact, $\hat{s}^i$ will equal $\hat{t}^i$ except in the special case when $\hat{t}^i = 0$ because autarky happens to be an optimal net trade for agent i at prices p; then

$\hat{s}^i$ could be zero or any net demand vector satisfying $p\hat{s}^i > 0$. I limit my attention to "straightforward" best responses and corresponding Nash equilibria, for which $\hat{s}^i = 0$ in this case.

It is now fairly easy to show that any straightforward Nash equilibrium of this game gives rise to a Walrasian equilibrium of the exchange economy, and vice versa. Suppose first that $(\hat{\mathbf{x}}^I, \hat{p})$ is a Walrasian equilibrium of the exchange economy. Since each agent's net demand vector $\hat{x}^i$ must maximize $t^i(x^i)$ subject to $x^i \in X^i$ and $\hat{p}x^i \leq 0$, it must be a best response to $\hat{p}$ in the market game. Since $\Sigma_{i\in I}\hat{x}^i \leq 0$ while $\hat{p}\Sigma_{i\in I}\hat{x}^i = 0$, it is also true that $\hat{p}\Sigma_{i\in I}\hat{x}^i \geq p\Sigma_{i\in I}\hat{x}^i$ for all $p \in \Delta$. Thus $\hat{p}$ is a best response by the auctioneer to the profile of net demands $\hat{\mathbf{x}}^I$ in the market game.

Conversely, suppose that $(\hat{s}^I, \hat{p})$ is a straightforward Nash equilibrium of the market game. We have already seen that each agent i's strategy $\hat{s}^i$ yields a Walrasian net trade vector $\hat{t}^i := t^i(\hat{s}^i, \hat{p}) = \hat{s}^i$ at the price vector $\hat{p}$, and also that $\hat{p}\hat{t}^i = 0$ for all $i \in I$. So, since $\hat{p}$ is the auctioneer's best response to the net demand profile $\hat{s}^I$, it must be true that $p\Sigma_{i\in I}\hat{t}^i \leq \hat{p}\Sigma_{i\in I}\hat{t}^i = 0$ for all $p \in \Delta$. This implies that $\Sigma_{i\in I}\hat{t}^i \leq 0$, and also implies the "rule of free goods" according to which any good which is in excess supply in equilibrium must have a zero price. In particular, $(\hat{t}^I, \hat{p})$ must be a Walrasian equilibrium of the exchange economy.

3   A market game with redistribution

For Arrow's (1951) second fundamental efficiency theorem of welfare economics to be valid at general Pareto efficient allocations in economies where not all agents are identical, lump-sum redistribution of wealth must be allowed. Moreover, this second theorem acquires most of its interest when applied to the maximum of any Paretian Bergson social welfare function. Accordingly, a new market game is now considered, with an additional *redistributive player* R whose strategy is to choose any wealth distribution function $\mathbf{m}^I(\cdot): \Delta \to \Re^I$ with levels $\langle m^i(p)\rangle_{i\in I}$ large enough to ensure that every agent $i \in I$ has a nonempty budget set $B^i(p)$: $= \{x^i \in X^i \mid px^i \leq m^i(p)\}$ for all $p \in \Delta$, while also satisfying the obvious restriction that $\Sigma_{i\in I} m^i(p) = 0$. Note that it is generally impossible to ensure nonemptiness of each budget set $B^i(p)$ unless each m^i is allowed to depend on p in this way.

The auctioneer and the trading agents function in much the same way as they did in the market game of Section 2. The only difference is that each net trade function $t^i(s^i, p)$ must now be redefined to include the function $m^i(\cdot)$ as an extra argument and to make the new budget constraint $px^i \leq m^i(p)$ become self-enforcing. To this end, for each $i \in I$ and each

$p \in \Delta$ let $\bar{x}^i(p)$ be any fixed net trade vector in the nonempty budget set $B^i(p)$, and let the value of the new function be

$$t^i\left(s^i, p, m^i(\cdot)\right) = \begin{cases} s^i & \text{if } ps^i \leq m^i(p) \\ \bar{x}^i(p) & \text{otherwise} \end{cases}$$

The only remaining feature before the new market game

$$\left\langle I \cup \{A, R\}, \mathbf{X}^I \times \Delta \times S^R, \left\langle v^h \right\rangle_{h \in I \cup \{A,R\}} \right\rangle$$

becomes fully specified as the redistributor's payoff function v^R. This is taken to be $v^R := W(\langle u^i(t^i) \rangle_{i \in I})$ for some Paretian Bergson social welfare function W.

Arguing as in Section 2, given any equilibrium wealth distribution rule $\hat{\mathbf{m}}^I(\cdot)$, define a straightforward Nash equilibrium as one in which any agent $i \in I$ who enjoys a net trade vector no better than $\bar{x}^i(p)$, and so has nothing to lose from violating the budget constraint $ps^i \leq \bar{m}^i(p)$, in fact chooses to respect this constraint. Then the set of straightforward Nash equilibria of this market game must give allocations that coincide with the set of Walrasian equilibria relative to this rule. Furthermore, suppose that the allocation $\hat{x}^I$ maximizes the welfare function $W(\langle u^i(x^i) \rangle_{i \in I})$ subject to the feasibility constraints $x^i \in X^i$ (all $i \in I$) and $\Sigma_{i \in I} x^i \leqq 0$, and that this optimal allocation can be achieved by facing each trader with the budget constraint $\hat{p}x^i \leq \hat{p}\hat{x}^i$ for a suitable price vector $\hat{p} \in \Delta$ because Arrow's (1951) second efficiency theorem applies. Then at least one straightforward Nash equilibrium of this new market game must yield an outcome of the form $(\hat{x}^I, \hat{p}, \hat{\mathbf{m}}^I(\cdot))$, where the wealth distribution functions satisfy $\hat{m}^i(p) \equiv p\hat{x}^i$ for all $i \in I$ and all $p \in \Delta$. The reason is that trading agents and the auctioneer are all choosing straightforward best responses as in Section 2, whereas the redistributor cannot possibly do better than reach the equilibrium first-best allocation $\hat{x}^I$ by adjusting the wealth distribution rule to achieve some other straightforward equilibrium and so some other feasible allocation. On the other hand, if there are multiple Walrasian equilibria relative to the equilibrium wealth distribution rule $\hat{\mathbf{m}}^I(\cdot)$, not every straightforward Nash equilibrium need be a welfare optimum which maximizes W, because, as Samuelson (1974) and Bryant (1994) point out, the trading agents and the auctioneer could together steer the economy to a suboptimal equilibrium even after an optimal wealth distribution rule has been set up. This alternative equilibrium must be Pareto efficient, but the distribution of real wealth could still be suboptimal.

4   A simple economy with an exhaustible resource

4.1   The model

Consider a simple economy which lasts for two periods ($t = 1, 2$) and in which there are two agents. There are three goods – one consumption good, the stock of a single exhaustible resource, and labor. The first agent is a working miner who consumes c_t units of the consumption good and has an inelastic supply of n_t units of labor in each period t. This worker's preferences for two-period consumption streams are assumed to be represented by the utility function

$$u(c_1, c_2) \equiv \ln c_1 + \ln c_2$$

The second agent is the owner and manager of the mine, who uses the worker's labor in order to mine the resource whose initial stock is S_0 at the beginning of period 1. In each of the two periods, the quantity e_t of this resource is combined with ℓ_t units of labor to produce y_t units of output of the single consumption good according to the constant returns to scale Cobb–Douglas production function

$$y_t = e_t^\gamma \ell_t^{1-\gamma}$$

where $0 < \gamma < 1$. The mine owner's consumption or dividend in period t is denoted by d_t, and his preferences for two-period consumption streams are assumed to be represented by the same utility function

$$v(d_1, d_2) \equiv \ln d_1 + \ln d_2$$

4.2   Intertemporal Walrasian equilibrium

The usual two-period intertemporal Walrasian equilibrium in this economy occurs when an "auctioneer" at the beginning of the first period sets prices for both periods to clear all markets, knowing what the mine worker and mine owner will later supply and demand for each possible price system which the auctioneer might choose. This Walrasian equilibrium can be found by choosing a Pareto efficient allocation which maximizes the weighted welfare sum

$$\alpha u(c_1, c_2) + (1 - \alpha) v(d_1, d_2)$$

for some suitable value of α satisfying $0 \le \alpha \le 1$. The relevant feasibility constraints are

$$c_t + d_t \le y_t = e_t^\gamma \ell_t^{1-\gamma} \quad \text{and} \quad \ell_t \le n_t \quad (t = 1, 2) \qquad e_1 + e_2 \le S_0$$

Introducing nonnegative Lagrange multipliers p_t for the shadow price of the consumption good and w_t for that of labor in period t ($t = 1, 2$), and ϱ for the shadow price of the resource stock, the relevant Lagrangean becomes

$$\mathcal{L} \equiv \sum_{t=1}^{2} \left[\alpha \ln c_t + (1 + \alpha)\ln d_t - p_t\left(c_t + d_t - e_t^{\gamma} \ell_t^{1-\gamma}\right) \right.$$
$$\left. - w_t\left(\ell_t - n_t\right) \right] - \varrho\left(e_1 + e_2 - S_0\right)$$

The first order conditions for an optimum therefore are the six equations

$$\frac{\alpha}{c_t} = \frac{1 - \alpha}{d_t} = p_t \qquad p_t(1 - \gamma)e_t^{\gamma} \ell_t^{-\gamma} = w_t$$
$$p_t \gamma e_t^{\gamma-1} \ell_t^{1-\gamma} = \varrho \qquad (t = 1, 2)$$

together with equality versions of the five inequality constraints that define a feasible allocation. These first order conditions imply that

$$p_t y_t = p_t\left(c_t + d_t\right) = \alpha + (1 - \alpha) = 1$$

and also that

$$w_t n_t = w_t \ell_t = (1 - \gamma)p_t y_t = (1 - \gamma) \qquad \varrho e_t = \gamma p_t y_t = \gamma$$

for each of the two periods $t = 1, 2$. The last equation implies that $e_1 = e_2$. The optimal allocation is therefore

$$e_t = \frac{1}{2}S_0 \qquad y_t = \left(\frac{1}{2}S_0\right)^{\gamma} n_t^{1-\gamma} \qquad c_t = \alpha y_t \qquad d_t = (1 - \alpha)y_t$$

for each of the two periods $t = 1, 2$. The associated shadow prices are

$$p_t = 1/y_t \qquad w_t = (1 - \gamma)/n_t \qquad \varrho = 2\gamma/S_0$$

To achieve a Walrasian equilibrium, the welfare weight α should be chosen so that both agents just satisfy their respective budget constraints. By Walras' Law, it is enough to look at either agent on his own. In fact, it is easier to consider the mine worker, whose Walrasian budget constraint

$$p_1 c_1 + p_2 c_2 = w_1 n_1 + w_2 n_2$$

is exactly satisfied when $\alpha = 1 - \gamma$. The intertemporal Walrasian equilibrium therefore consists of the production plan and the price system given above, together with the consumption allocation

$$c_t = (1 - \gamma)y_t \qquad d_t = \gamma y_t$$

for each of the two periods $t = 1, 2$. Note that $p_t c_t = w_t n_t$ in each of the two periods separately. This implies that the mine worker neither saves nor borrows during the first period. Because of aggregate budget balance, the mine owner does not save or borrow either, so there is no need for an asset market of any kind. The only form of saving in the economy comes from the mine owner deciding not to exhaust his stock of the resource all in one period. Finally, note for future reference that the mine owner's utility in this Walrasian equilibrium is given by

$$v^W = 2\ln\left[\gamma\left(\frac{1}{2}S_0\right)^\gamma\right] + (1 - \gamma)\ln(n_1 n_2)$$

4.3   Subgame perfect equilibrium

The above intertemporal Walrasian equilibrium was calculated on the presumption that the "auctioneer" in the first period makes irreversible decisions regarding prices for both periods. It is as though his plans were being submitted to the "umpire" whom von Neumann and Morgenstern (1953) exploited as a device to help understand the normal rather than the extensive form of a game. Their idea was that, in the normal form of a game, the umpire carries out the players' strategies on their behalf. There is thus no opportunity for changing plans part way through the extensive form of a game, so subgame perfection is never an issue. Von Neumann and Morgenstern claimed that considering only the normal form would never lose any generality. Yet the work by Selten (1965; 1973; 1975) and many successors on subgame perfect equilibria in extensive form games that are not two-person zero-sum has made this claim completely untenable – at least for Nash equilibria, which almost everybody now agrees need to be refined.[4]

In the Walrasian equilibrium model of an intertemporal economy, we must therefore ask whether the auctioneer's initially planned prices will actually emerge later on, if such prices are not irreversible commitments. For the model just considered, it turns out that they will not, if the mine owner chooses to leave a stock of the resource which differs from the intertemporal equilibrium level $S_1 = \frac{1}{2}S_0$ at the end of the first period. And if the mine owner foresees this, he will want to exploit his power to affect market prices.

---

[4] Arrow and Debreu wrote when Nash equilibrium was still a novel concept, long before Selten's fundamental work, and even longer before that work had its deserved impact.

Consider a slightly different version of the above intertemporal economy in which there are:

´1 First period markets for consumption, labor, and an Arrow security for delivering consumption in the second period
2 Second period markets for consumption and labor

Suppose trade takes place in an extensive game of complete information in which the players are the auctioneer, the mine owner, and the mine worker, and the order of moves is as follows:

1 At the beginning of the first period the auctioneer sets prices for consumption and labor in the first period, and for the Arrow security, to clear markets in full knowledge of what the mine owner and mine worker will supply and demand at each possible price vector which he might set.
2 The mine owner and mine worker exchange contracts for first period labor supply, first period consumption, and the Arrow security, taking the auctioneer's price system as given, and then execute the first period part of those contracts – that is, the mine owner extracts as much as he wishes of his stock of the resource, hires what he wants of the mine worker's labor up to the limit of the worker's supply, and then produces output of which some is sold to the mine worker and the rest is consumed by the mine owner – in addition, Arrow securities may be traded.
3 At the beginning of the second period, and fully aware of what has happened in the first period, the auctioneer sets prices for consumption and labor in the second period in order to clear markets after the Arrow security contracts have been honored, in full knowledge of what the mine owner and mine worker will supply and demand at each possible price vector which he might set.
4 The mine owner and mine worker exchange contracts for second period labor supply and consumption, taking both the auctioneer's price system and the need to honor the Arrow security contracts as given, and then execute those contracts.

Suppose that, at the beginning of the second period of a two-period economy, the mine owner's resource stock is S_1. Suppose, too, that any Arrow security transactions during the first period have the effect of adding a units net of consumption to the worker, and b to the mine owner. It must be true that $a + b = 0$ in order to have the Arrow security market clear in the first period. Then any Walrasian equilibrium in the second period involves the auctioneer setting the real wage w_2/p_2 equal to $(1 - \gamma) S_1^\gamma n_2^{-\gamma}$, which is the marginal product of labor. From this and the worker's budget constraint $p_2 c_2 = w_2 n_2 + p_2 a$, it follows that

$$p_2\left(c_2 - a\right) = w_2 n_2 = p_2\left(1 - \gamma\right) S_1^\gamma n_2^{1-\gamma} = \left(1 - \gamma\right) p_2 y_2$$

The unique Walrasian equilibrium for the second period alone therefore consists of the allocation

$$c_2 = \left(1 - \gamma\right) S_1^\gamma n_2^{1-\gamma} + a = \left(1 - \gamma\right) y_2 + a$$
$$d_2 = \gamma S_1^\gamma n_2^{1-\gamma} + b = \gamma y_2 + b$$

and the price system defined by the real wage given above. Note how the equilibrium allocation is a function of a, b, and S_1.

Suppose the worker and mine owner both understand this dependence and use their power to manipulate prices in the second period by means of suitable actions in the first period. Then the worker will choose the variables c_1 and a to maximize his anticipated utility, which is

$$\ln c_1 + \ln\left[\left(1 - \gamma\right)\left(S_0 - e_1\right)^\gamma n_2^{1-\gamma} + a\right] \equiv \ln c_1 + \ln\left[\left(1 - \gamma\right) y_2 + a\right]$$

subject to the budget constraint

$$p_1 c_1 + ra = w_1 n_1$$

Here r denotes the price of the Arrow security.

If we use λ to denote the shadow price associated with the worker's budget constraint, the first order conditions for utility maximization become

$$\frac{1}{c_1} = \lambda p_1 \qquad \frac{1}{\left(1 - \gamma\right)\left(S_0 - e_1\right)^\gamma n_2^{1-\gamma} + a} = \frac{1}{\left(1 - \gamma\right) y_2 + a} = \lambda r$$

After multiplying each side of the budget constraint by λ, recognizing that it must hold with equality, and then substituting from the above first order conditions, we obtain

$$\lambda w_1 n_1 = \lambda\left(p_1 c_1 + ra\right) = 2 - \lambda\left(1 - \gamma\right) ry_2$$

This implies that $1/\lambda = \frac{1}{2}[w_1 n_1 + (1 - \gamma) ry_2]$. So substituting for $1/\lambda$ back in the first order conditions gives the worker's expenditures

$$p_1 c_1 = \frac{1}{2}\left[w_1 n_1 + \left(1 - \gamma\right) ry_2\right] \qquad ra = \frac{1}{2}\left[w_1 n_1 - \left(1 - \gamma\right) ry_2\right]$$

on first period consumption and the Arrow security. These are functions of the first period price vector (p_1, w_1, r) and also of future output y_2 which depends on the mine owner's choice of e_1. Notice that expenditure on present and on future consumption is determined as in the linear expenditure system, but with $(1 - \gamma)ry_2$ already committed to expenditure on second period consumption, in effect, and with $w_1 n_1$ as exogenous wage income.

On the other hand, the mine owner will choose the variables d_1, e_1, ℓ_1 and b to maximize his anticipated utility, which is

$$\ln d_1 + \ln\left[\gamma\left(S_0 - e_1\right)^\gamma n_2^{1-\gamma} + b\right] \equiv \ln d_1 + \ln\left(\gamma y_2 + b\right)$$

subject to the budget constraint

$$p_1 d_1 + rb = p_1 e_1^\gamma \ell_1^{1-\gamma} - w_1 \ell_1 = p_1 y_1 - w_1 \ell_1$$

If we use μ to denote the shadow price associated with the mine owner's budget constraint, the first order conditions for utility maximization become

$$\frac{1}{d_1} = \mu p_1 \qquad \frac{1}{\gamma\left(S_0 - e_1\right)^\gamma n_2^{1-\gamma} + b} = \frac{1}{\gamma y_2 + b} = \mu r$$

and

$$w_1 = p_1\left(1 - \gamma\right)e_1^\gamma \ell_1^{-\gamma} = \left(1 - \gamma\right)p_1 y_1/\ell_1$$

$$\frac{\gamma^2\left(S_0 - e_1\right)^{\gamma-1} n_2^{1-\gamma}}{\gamma\left(S_0 - e_1\right)^\gamma n_2^{1-\gamma} + b} = \mu p_1 \gamma e_1^{\gamma-1} \ell_1^{1-\gamma}$$

After multiplying each side of the budget constraint by μ, recognizing that it must hold with equality, and then substituting from the above first order conditions, we obtain

$$\mu\left(p_1 y_1 - w_1 \ell_1\right) = \mu\left(p_1 d_1 + rb\right) = 2 - \mu\gamma ry_2$$

This implies that $1/\mu = \frac{1}{2}(p_1 y_1 - w_1 \ell_1 + \gamma ry_2)$. Substituting for $1/\mu$ back in the first order conditions gives the mine owner's conditional expenditures

$$p_1 d_1 = \frac{1}{2}\left(p_1 y_1 - w_1 \ell_1 + \gamma ry_2\right) \qquad rb = \frac{1}{2}\left(p_1 y_1 - w_1 \ell_1 - \gamma ry_2\right)$$

on consumption and the Arrow security. These are functions of the first period price vector (p_1, w_1, r), of the labor input ℓ_1, and also of the output stream y_1, y_2 which depends on the mine owner's choice of e_1. As with the mine worker, these functions represent an instance of the linear expenditure system.

Now we impose the Arrow security market clearing condition $a + b = 0$. It implies that

$$0 = 2r(a + b) = w_1 n_1 - (1 - \gamma)ry_2 + p_1 y_1 - w_1 \ell_1 - \gamma ry_2 = p_1 y_1 - ry_2$$

where the last equality comes from using the market clearing condition $\ell_1 = n_1$ in order to simplify. Because $w_1 = p_1(1 - \gamma)y_1/n_1$, it follows that equilibrium price ratios are determined by the two equations

$$w_1 n_1 = (1 - \gamma)p_1 y_1 = (1 - \gamma)ry_2$$

This implies, however, that in any equilibrium the conditional demands are

$$c_1 = (1 - \gamma)y_1 \qquad a = 0 \qquad \text{and} \qquad d_1 = \gamma y_1 \qquad b = 0$$

Thus asset markets play no role whatsoever in the equilibrium allocation.

Note, too, that

$$1/\mu = \frac{1}{2}(p_1 y_1 - w_1 \ell_1 + \gamma ry_2) = \frac{1}{2}[p_1 y_1 - (1 - \gamma)p_1 y_1 + \gamma p_1 y_1] = \gamma p_1 y_1$$

because $b = 0$, the first order condition for the mine owner's optimal choice of e_1 simplifies to

$$\frac{\gamma}{S_0 - e_1} = \mu p_1 \gamma e_1^{\gamma - 1} \ell_1^{1-\gamma} = \frac{\mu p_1 \gamma y_1}{e_1} = \frac{1}{e_1}$$

which implies that $e_1 = S_0/(1 + \gamma)$. This contrasts with the rate of extraction $e_1 = \frac{1}{2}S_0$ which, as previously shown, is required for any intertemporally Pareto efficient allocation. Since $0 < \gamma < 1$, the mine owner who tries to exploit his monopoly power always uses an amount of the resource stock which, from the point of view of intertemporal Pareto efficiency, is too much in the first period and too little in the second.

To complete the description of this new subgame perfect equilibrium in which the mine owner exploits his market power, notice that

$$d_1 = \gamma y_1 = \gamma e_1^\gamma \ell_1^{1-\gamma} = \gamma \left(\frac{S_0}{1 + \gamma}\right)^\gamma n_1^{1-\gamma}$$

and

$$c_1 = (1 - \gamma)y_1 = (1 - \gamma)\left(\frac{S_0}{1 + \gamma}\right)^\gamma n_1^{1-\gamma}$$

The corresponding equilibrium real wage is then

$$\frac{w_1}{p_1} = \frac{c_1}{n_1} = (1 - \gamma)\left(\frac{S_0}{1 + \gamma}\right)^{\gamma} n_1^{-\gamma}$$

The remaining stock of the exhaustible resource at the beginning of the second period is therefore

$$S_1 = S_0 - e_1 = S_0 - \frac{S_0}{1 + \gamma} = \frac{\gamma S_0}{1 + \gamma}$$

The resulting equilibrium allocation in the second period is therefore

$$c_2 = (1 - \gamma)y_2 = (1 - \gamma)S_1^{\gamma}\ell_2^{1-\gamma} = (1 - \gamma)\left(\frac{\gamma S_0}{1 + \gamma}\right)^{\gamma} n_2^{1-\gamma}$$

$$d_2 = \gamma y_2 = \gamma\left(\frac{\gamma S_0}{1 + \gamma}\right)^{\gamma} n_2^{1-\gamma}$$

Finally, the mine owner's utility from this subgame perfect equilibrium is

$$v^P := \ln d_1 + \ln d_2 = \ln\left[\gamma\left(\frac{S_0}{1 + \gamma}\right)^{\gamma} n_1^{1-\gamma}\right] + \ln\left[\gamma\left(\frac{\gamma S_0}{1 + \gamma}\right)^{\gamma} n_2^{1-\gamma}\right]$$

$$= 2\ln\left[\gamma\left(\frac{S_0}{1 + \gamma}\right)^{\gamma}\right] + \ln\left(n_1^{1-\gamma}\gamma^{\gamma} n_2^{1-\gamma}\right)$$

Notice therefore that the mine owner's utility net gain from this subgame perfect equilibrium with monopoly power, $v^P - v^W$, is given by

$$2\ln\left[\gamma\left(\frac{S_0}{1 + \gamma}\right)^{\gamma}\right] + \ln\left(n_1^{1-\gamma}\gamma^{\gamma} n_2^{1-\gamma}\right) - 2\ln\left[\gamma\left(\frac{1}{2}S_0\right)^{\gamma}\right]$$

$$- (1 - \gamma)\ln(n_1 n_2) = -2\ln(1 + \gamma) + \gamma\ln\gamma + 2\gamma\ln 2$$

$$= \gamma\ln\left[\frac{4\gamma}{(1 + \gamma)^2}\right] = \gamma\ln\left[1 - \frac{(1 - \gamma)^2}{(1 + \gamma)^2}\right] < 0$$

The mine owner always loses in the end by being manipulative. At first this seems surprising, because one might think that the mine owner can always revert to the nonmonopolistic intertemporal Walrasian equilibrium simply by selecting the rate of exploitation of the natural resource $e_1 = \frac{1}{2}S_0$ appropriate for that equilibrium. This is false, however, for the interesting reason that, in the first period of this subgame perfect monopolistic equilibrium, the auctioneer foresees the mine owner's manipulation and so sets prices in a way which denies him the intertemporal Walrasian equilibrium stream of resource rents and so of consumption.

4.4   Continuum economies

This fully worked out example is intended only to illustrate what is perhaps obvious: Once agents foresee how market clearing prices in the future depend on their current actions, they will wish to exploit their monopoly power over such future prices. This problem does not arise, however, in continuum economies with each agent having negligible power to influence future prices. The next section of this chapter is concerned with such economies. It shows how redistributive policies of the kind presumed in the second efficiency theorem of welfare economics can nevertheless create new subgame perfection problems of their own.

5   Redistribution in a simple continuum economy

5.1   An intertemporal welfare optimum

We now consider an economy with a continuum of identical workers and another continuum of identical mine owners. Suppose each worker and each mine owner is identical to the worker and to the mine owner, respectively, in the two agent economy of Section 4. Suppose the proportions of workers and of mine owners in the economy are μ and $1 - \mu$ respectively. Suppose, too, that the government of this economy chooses a symmetric allocation to all the workers and mine owners which maximizes the appropriately weighted sum

$$W := \mu\left(\ln c_1 + \ln c_2\right) + \left(1 - \mu\right)\left(\ln d_1 + \ln d_2\right)$$

of the utilities of the typical worker and mine owner. The physical feasibility constraints are that

$$\mu c_t + \left(1 - \mu\right)d_t \leq \left(1 - \mu\right)y_t = \left(1 - \mu\right)e_t^\gamma \ell_t^{1-\gamma}; \quad \ell_t \leq n_t$$

for both time periods $t = 1, 2$, and that

$$e_1 + e_2 \leq S_0$$

With shadow prices p_t for consumption, w_t for labor, and ϱ for the exhaustible resource, the appropriate Lagrangean can be written as

$$\mathcal{L} = \sum_{t=1}^{2} \Big\{ \mu \ln c_t + \big(1 - \mu\big)\ln d_t - p_t\big[\mu c_t + \big(1 - \mu\big)d_t$$
$$- \big(1 - \mu\big)e_t^{\gamma}\ell_t^{1-\gamma}\big] - w_t\big(\ell_t - n_t\big) \Big\} - \varrho\big(e_1 + e_2 - S_0\big)$$

The first-order conditions for an optimum thus include, for $t = 1, 2$, the equations

$$\frac{1}{c_t} = p_t = \frac{1}{d_t} \qquad \big(1 - \mu\big)p_t\frac{\big(1 - \gamma\big)y_t}{\ell_t} = w_t \qquad \big(1 - \mu\big)p_t\frac{\gamma y_t}{e_t} = \varrho$$

Together with the resource constraint $\mu c_t + (1 - \mu)d_t = (1 - \mu)y_t$, the first two of these equations imply that

$$\big(1 - \mu\big)p_t y_t = \mu p_t c_t + \big(1 - \mu\big)p_t d_t = \mu + \big(1 - \mu\big) = 1$$

Since it must be true that $\ell_t = n_t$ for any optimum, we also have

$$w_t n_t = 1 - \gamma \qquad \varrho e_t = \gamma$$

From this and the constraints it follows that the welfare optimal allocation is given by

$$e_1 = e_2 = \frac{1}{2}S_0 \qquad y_t = \Big(\frac{1}{2}S_0\Big)^{\gamma} n_t^{1-\gamma} \qquad c_t = d_t = \big(1 - \mu\big)y_t$$

This involves a perfectly egalitarian allocation of consumption. Moreover, half the stock of the resource in every mine is used up in each of the two periods, as in Section 4.1.

Finally, this optimal allocation can be decentralized by means of markets in which suitably normalized prices for consumption and labor in each of the two periods are the Lagrange multipliers $p_t = 1/(1 - \mu)y_t$ and $w_t = (1 - \gamma)/n_t$ which were found above.

5.2 Subgame perfect policy

This optimum effectively presumes that the government is committed to its redistribution policy in advance, and that each mine owner also commits himself to keep half his resource stock until the second period. If such commitments are impossible, however, a subgame imperfection arises. For suppose that the government bases its second period optimal redistributive policy on what the mine owners have already chosen in the first period. In this economy, what consumption was in the first period is irrelevant to the second period decisions. The optimal second period policy involves maximizing the second period welfare integral

$$W_2 : = \mu \int \ln c_2 + \left(1 - \mu\right) \int \ln d_2$$

subject to the resource constraints

$$y_2 \leq \left(1 - \mu\right)e_2^{\gamma}\ell_2^{1-\gamma} \qquad e_2 \leq S_1$$

for each mine separately, and subject to the overall resource constraints

$$\mu\bar{c}_2 + \left(1 - \mu\right)\bar{d}_2 \leq \left(1 - \mu\right)\bar{y}_2 \qquad \left(1 - \mu\right)\bar{\ell}_2 \leq \mu n_2$$

Here $\bar{c}_2$ denotes the mean level of $\bar{c}_2$ among the population of mine workers, whereas $\bar{d}_2$, $\bar{y}_2$, and $\bar{\ell}_2$ denote the mean levels of d_2, y_2, and ℓ_2 respectively among the population of mine owners. Note that asymmetric allocations are now being considered, as is appropriate when issues of subgame perfection arise. Since all mine workers have identical exogenous supplies of labor, there is no need to write $\bar{n}_2$.

Obviously it is optimal for all mine workers and all mine owners to have the same consumption levels $c_2 = d_2 = \bar{c}_2 = \bar{d}_2$. Also, an optimal allocation of labor is one that maximizes mean output $\int e_2^{\gamma}\ell_2^{1-\gamma}$ per mine by equalizing labor's marginal product $(1 - \gamma)e_2^{\gamma}\ell_2^{-\gamma}$ in each mine. Because $e_2 = S_1$ is required in (almost) every mine for mean output to be maximized, for this special case labor should be supplied to each mine in proportion to its available resource stock S_1. This implies that

$$\ell_2 = \mu S_1 n_2 / \left(1 - \mu\right)\bar{S}_1 = S_1 \bar{\ell}_2 / \bar{S}_1$$

where $\bar{S}_1$ denotes the mean level of resource stock per mine, and $\bar{\ell}_2$ is the mean labor supply per mine, which must equal $\mu n_2/(1 - \mu)$. So optimal output in each mine is

$$y_2 = S_1^{\gamma}\left[S_1 \bar{\ell}_2/\bar{S}_1\right]^{1-\gamma} = S_1\left(\bar{\ell}_2/\bar{S}_1\right)^{1-\gamma}$$

which implies that optimal mean output per mine is $\bar{y}_2 = \bar{S}_1^{\gamma}\bar{\ell}_2^{1-\gamma}$.

The welfare optimal distribution of this second period mean output is then given by

$$c_2 = \bar{c}_2 = d_2 = \bar{d}_2 = \left(1 - \mu\right)\bar{y}_2$$

for each mine worker and each mine owner respectively.

Note in particular how the allocation of consumption to each mine owner in the second period is completely independent of how much resource stock he has available in that period. Not surprisingly, therefore, each mine owner has every incentive to exhaust his resource stock entirely in the first period, in case markets are used in an attempt to decentralize the intertemporal optimal allocation. With d_2 fixed, each mine owner chooses ℓ_1 and e_1 in the first period to maximize current consumption d_1 subject to the budget constraint

$$p_1 d_1 \leq p_1 y_1 - w_1 \ell_1 = p_1 e_1^\gamma \ell_1^{1-\gamma} - w_1 \ell_1$$

and the resource constraint $e_1 \leq S_0$. The mine owner's optimum clearly involves having $e_1 = S_0$. After all, by exhausting his stock of the resource immediately, each mine owner can maximize his first period resource rents without forfeiting any second period consumption. If mine owners correctly foresee the optimal second period redistributive policy of the government, therefore, it is a dominant strategy for them all to exhaust their resource stocks in the first period. This would imply that output must fall to zero in the second period, yielding minus infinite utility for all agents.

Even if markets are not used to arrange net trade vectors in the first period, in many cases it is still a dominant strategy for each mine owner to exhaust his resource stock immediately. For instance, suppose that the prescribed net trade to some mine owner consisted of a net payment of t_1 units of consumption in exchange for receiving ℓ_1 (> 0) units of labor – that is, the net trade vector is $(-t_1, \ell_1)$. Then, by using e_1 units of the resource stock in the first period, the mine owner's consumption stream would become

$$\left(d_1, d_2\right) = \left(e_1^\gamma \ell_1^{1-\gamma} - t_1, \bar{d}_2\right)$$

where $\bar{d}_2$ is independent of his personal decisions. The corresponding utility is

$$v\left(d_1, d_2\right) = \ln d_1 + \ln \bar{d}_2 = \ln\left(e_1^\gamma \ell_1^{1-\gamma} - t_1\right) + \ln \bar{d}_2$$

which is clearly maximized by choosing $e_1 = S_0$. This is indeed the dominant strategy of each mine owner – or, to be more accurate, of each mine owner who is allowed to use a positive amount of labor in the first period.

5.3   *A market for the resource stock*

Since resource stocks are being excessively exploited, a standard economists' remedy might be to create a market for them, just as it is often thought that excessive exploitation of fishery stocks or of a common could be overcome through making those resources private property. Yet such a policy is of no help here, and would actually create chaos even in the first period. Every agent would want to take an indefinitely large short position in the market for the resource stock during the first period, knowing that this would have no bearing on the allocation of consumption in the second period. Suppose that in the first period there were perfect markets for consumption, labor supply, and the resource stock, with prices p_1, w_1, and r_1 respectively. Let S_1^O and S_1^W denote the net holdings of the resource stock at the end of the first period by the typical mine owner and the typical mine worker respectively.

In this first period, each mine worker will choose his planned consumption stream c_1, c_2, and his position S_1^W in the resource market to maximize utility $u(c_1, c_2) \equiv \ln c_1 + \ln c_2$ subject to the budget constraint

$$p_1 c_1 + r_1 S_1^W \leq w_1 n_1$$

The mine worker also faces the constraint that $c_2 = \bar{c}_2$, completely independent of what he chooses in the first period, because of the government's second period redistribution policy. Then there is no optimal policy in the first period unless $r_1 = 0$. For, since it must be true that $p_1 > 0$, the mine worker can make c_1 arbitrarily large by having $S_1^W \to -\infty$ if $r_1 > 0$, and $S_1^W \to +\infty$ if $r_1 < 0$.

The position of each mine owner is little different. Since second period consumption $d_2 = \bar{d}_2$ is not influenced at all by his decisions, he will choose d_1, e_1, ℓ_1, y_1, and his position S_1^O in the resource market to maximize utility $v(d_1, d_2) \equiv \ln d_1 + \ln \bar{d}_2$ subject to the production constraint $y_1 \leq e_1^\gamma \ell_1^{1-\gamma}$, the resource constraint $e_1 \leq S_0$, and finally the first period budget constraint

$$p_1 d_1 + r_1 S_1^O \leq y_1 - w_1 \ell_1 + r_1 \left(S_0 - e_1 \right)$$

Once again there is no optimal policy unless $r_1 = 0$. For, since it must be true that $p_1 > 0$, the typical mine owner can make d_1 arbitrarily large by having $S_1^O \to -\infty$ if $r_1 > 0$, and $S_1^O \to +\infty$ if $r_1 < 0$.

Only if $r_1 = 0$ can there be equilibrium in the resource market, but the resource market has no role to play. This implies that we are back with the same equilibrium as before, with each mine owner choosing $e_1 = S_0$ and so exhausting the resource stock in the first period.

5.4   Remedial policy

This disastrous outcome of total immediate exhaustion of the resource stock arises because optimal redistributive policy in the second period has the effect of converting output in the second period, and so the resource stock at the end of the first period, into a kind of privately provided public good or widespread externality. No matter how much resource stock a mine owner retains, his consumption in the second period is always the same. This encourages mine owners to "ride free" by exhausting all their stocks in the first period, to enjoy the largest possible resource rent.

Recognizing that a public good or externality problem has arisen suggests various kinds of policy remedies. Obviously direct controls like rationing could work in principle, with each mine owner being allowed to use no more than half his resource stock in the first period. Alternatively, one could subsidize resource retention or penalize excessive resource use. This could involve a subsidy s being imposed on each unit of resource saving, with a corresponding tax rate s on each unit of excessive resource use. Specifically, each mine owner is faced with the new first period budget constraint

$$p_1 d_1 \leq p_1 e_1^{\gamma} \ell_1^{1-\gamma} - w_1 \ell_1 + s \left(\frac{1}{2} S_0 - e_1 \right)$$

as well as the earlier resource constraint $e_1 \leq S_0$. The subsidy rate s will be set so that each mine owner wants e_1 to be at its efficient level of $\frac{1}{2}S_0$ when maximizing d_1 subject to this budget constraint. Bearing in mind that $p_1 = 1/(1 - \mu) y_1$ is the price of output and consumption in the first period which sustains an intertemporal optimum, this requires that

$$s = p_1 \gamma e_1^{\gamma-1} n_1^{1-\gamma} = \gamma p_1 y_1 / e_1 = \gamma / (1 - \mu) y_1 = 2\gamma / (1 - \mu) S_0$$

In effect, this amounts to having the government buy out the right to use each mine in the first period for the sum of $s \cdot \frac{1}{2} S_0 = \gamma/(1 - \mu)$, which could be regarded as the value of that half of its total stock which will be depleted during the first period. Since in each period mean resource rents per head of population are $\varrho e_t = \gamma$, this also represents each mine owner's share of these rents. Thereafter each mine owner is allowed to lease back half his mine in the first period in exchange for royalty payments at the rate s on each unit of resource depletion.

It would not do, however, to have the government pay for the whole resource stock of each mine, with a view to allowing each mine owner to save some of the proceeds in order to finance his own second period consumption. This would not work because the government's optimal second period redistribution policy always ignores completely any asset holdings held at the start of that period. If there were some kind of perfect capital market on which mine owners could save for future consumption, each of them would like not only to spend immediately all the compensation paid by the government for using the mine, but also to borrow indefinitely large sums in the first period knowing that these would be repaid, in effect, by the government's optimal redistribution program in the second period. The government, therefore, in the first period should buy the right to use the resource stock for the first period only. Trying to set up any kind of normal capital market of the kind economists have become accustomed to advocating would be nothing short of disastrous in this model.

6   Sequential economic policy analysis

6.1   Subgame imperfections

Although formally correct, the fundamental efficiency theorems of welfare economics do not explicitly consider the subgame perfection of a competitive market mechanism in an intertemporal setting. With a small number of agents in a static economy, one can imagine reaching competitive equilibrium through a game in which there is an omniscient auctioneer who sets prices that clear all markets, and by allowing agents to trade as they wish at these prices. In an intertemporal economy, however, unless there are many agents, or unless there is complete separation between the economies in different periods, some individuals will be able to manipulate equilibrium prices in the "subeconomies" which begin in later periods. As the example of Section 4 shows, they can do this by adjusting their previous investment plans or any other earlier economic decisions which affect preferences or feasible sets in the subeconomy. Thus, unlike static economies, there are conceptual difficulties in considering competitive market economies unless there is a continuum of agents whose investment and other decisions have a negligible effect on later prices.

It is not really surprising that competition requires many agents. Rather, the surprise is that, in a single period economy, it may be compatible with having only a few agents. More deeply troubling, however, is the subgame imperfection that accompanies lump-sum redistribution even in continuum economies. This is similar to a phenomenon noticed by Tesfatsion (1986) in particular, though related to earlier work by Kydland and Prescott (1977; 1980), Calvo (1978), Fischer (1980), and many others on the time inconsistency of macroeconomic policy. In a static economy, and under the usual conditions ensuring the validity of Arrow's second efficiency theorem of welfare economics, a benevolent government that wishes to maximize some Paretian Bergson social welfare function can do so by instituting complete perfectly competitive markets along with an optimal redistribution of income by means of lump-sum transfers. With many periods, however, such optimal redistribution in any subeconomy will typically depend on the past decisions of economic agents. If the benevolent welfare objective is sufficiently egalitarian, for instance, it will mandate lump-sum taxes on those who have saved a great deal in the past to finance transfers to those who have left themselves with little or no wealth. Agents who understand this dependence will see that their incentives to save, to invest, or to create future wealth for themselves are all seriously blunted by the egalitarian redistributive policies which the government will pursue later. The example of Section 5 illustrated this.

One may well object that the redistributive policy contemplated in that example is clearly absurd precisely because it destroys all incentives to save, to invest, or to conserve resource stocks. Nevertheless, that policy, as in Tesfatsion (1986), is just the logical implication of the government's first-best welfare maximization in the second period economy. The absurd policy of this example fulfills its purpose – namely, to show that subgame imperfections arise even in standard first-best welfare economics, when one tries to apply it to simple intertemporal settings. This is true even for "perfect" markets, without public goods, externalities, distortionary taxes, asymmetric information, or any other form of "market failure." The point is that the prospect of what will appear in the future to be nondistortionary lump-sum redistribution actually functions now as "taxes on history." Such taxes typically distort individual decisions to "supply history." In this simple example, "history" was just the distribution of resource stocks left in each mine at the end of the first period.

In the more realistic case where lump-sum compensation is impossible, Dixit and Norman (1980; 1986) were still able to demonstrate the gains from trade, using commodity (and income) tax adjustments to compensate losers. Related results are in Hammond and Sempere (1995).

This example, and the one in the previous section, do nothing to contradict the usual Arrow–Debreu theory, even in an intertemporal setting. That theory remains valid when trading plans, prices, and lump-sum transfers can all be fixed *now*, remaining unchanged at all future times. Yet what is so special about "now," which allows trading plans, prices, and lump-sum transfers to be set at this time and remain fixed for ever thereafter? Why are the trading plans, prices, and lump-sum transfers for the future not those set some time ago in the past? And, if changes to past plans are allowed now, what will happen when a new "now" comes around a little while later? Do trading plans, prices, and lump-sum transfers remain at the levels being planned now, or will they respond to changed circumstances if individuals happen to deviate from their original (Nash equilibrium) trading plans? Since changes in trading plans do induce changes in the prices needed to maintain equilibrium, as considered in Section 4, or in the transfers needed for distributive justice, as considered in Section 5, subgame imperfections cannot just be assumed away. The Arrow–Debreu theory remains logically consistent, but its plausibility as a description of an ideally functioning intertemporal economy disappears almost completely.

6.2   Sequential allocations

The above discussion points to the conclusion that, even in a simple two period sequence economy, each period's equilibrium prices and economic policy variables will typically all depend on the state of the economy at the beginning of the period. Here "state" is to be understood in its Markovian sense, as a sufficient statistic for all the past history of the economy, so knowledge of the state is enough to know everything relevant for the future of the economy. Recent work in general equilibrium theory has begun to consider equilibrium Markov processes (see Duffie et al., [1994] and Stokey and Lucas, with Prescott, [1989]), but much remains to be done. However, it seems to me that much can still be learned from models with finite horizons or even just two periods. These allow the technical problems of recursion in general infinite horizon Markov processes to be avoided while an appropriate conceptual framework is still being formulated.

This dependence of policy variables and equilibrium prices on the current state of the economy suggests the need for an approach to intertemporal economics rather different from that of Irving Fischer (1907; 1930), Hicks (1946), and Debreu (1959). Their apparatus of "dated commodities" or "dated contingent commodities" is reminiscent of the "open loop" policy in control theory, in that it specifies what will happen at each future date in a model with certainty, and at each future "date-event" when there is uncertainty. The proposal here is to consider instead the equivalent of "closed loop" policies, describing what single period allocation will come about as a function of the state at the start of that period. We may call these "sequential allocations." Such a description of the outcome of the economic system is more general because it allows consideration of what will happen off any equilibrium path of our dynamic model. The discussion of Section 6.1 points to the need for a richer formulation of this kind.

Sequential allocations like this can be considered in a rather general stochastic overlapping generations model with a continuum of agents having bounded lifetimes. Each agent can be both a consumer and a producer. There can be both aggregate and idiosyncratic uncertainty. Each agent can have a personal "history" or state described in part by personal capital stocks. But the personal state can also include any other variables affecting preferences, consumption, and production possibilities, and so forth. Then there will be a Markov process determining the same agent's personal history one period later, conditional on consumption, production, labor supply, and other economic decisions in the current period. Such personal state variables can capture the effects of age, health, family circumstances, education, and so forth. Each agent's idiosyncratic Markov process can also be affected by an aggregate state which can represent the physical environment, together with aspects of the economic system, public goods, and so forth. The "history" or state of the economy as a whole is described by this systemic state variable, together with the entire frequency distribution of individual agents' personal states in the population of all living agents. This will be called the "macro state," for obvious reasons.

There are some technical problems in the formulation of such a model. There will be a continuum of individuals who, conditional on the evolution of the macro state, have personal states following stochastically independent Markov processes. In particular, if we consider just one period, and neglect the macro state for a moment, there will be a continuum of independent random variables describing the individuals' personal states. As Gale (1979), Feldman and Gilles (1985), and Judd (1985) in particular have pointed out, this leads to nonmeasurable sample functions describing the empirical distribution in the population.

This should not be surprising. An American taxpayer's social security number gives no information about his or her height, and we can think of the function from social security number to height as approximately the realization of a continuum of independent random variables. The function is extremely irregular, and not measurable in the limit as one goes to a continuum of individuals. Yet the joint distribution of Americans' social security numbers and heights is no doubt rather close to the product of two independent distributions – one a well-defined distribution of social security numbers, and another of people's heights.

This suggests a simpler escape from the technical problem of nonmeasurability than that presented by resorting to finitely additive charges (Feldman and Gilles, 1985), nonstandard analysis (Anderson [1991], Section 5), or alternative integrals (Bewley [1986]). Instead of a fixed population of individual labels and then random personal states for each, one can consider instead a joint distribution of both individual labels and personal states. For large enough populations the strong law of large numbers applies and tells us that frequency distributions will match probability distributions.

A similar construction based on joint distributions can be used for the continuum of individual stochastic processes used in the model described informally here. The result is a description of a sequence economy that appears to be immensely rich, capable of embracing many dynamic phenomena. It is also a step toward generalizing the Arrow–Debreu model so it becomes a collection of interacting dynamic processes, rather than just a means of allocating resources once and for all.

6.3   Sequential competitive equilibria

Within the sequential model described above, it is natural to think of a sequential competitive equilibrium as a process specifying the price vector in each period as a function of the macro state, and also specifying each agent's allocation as a function of both the macro state and the agent's own personal state. This would be for an equilibrium without lump-sum transfers. The second efficiency theorem, however, forces us to consider equilibria with transfers. These equilibria typically specify how much each agent is allowed to spend each period on current goods and services, as a function of both the macro state and the personal state. Note that such transfers can substitute for all financial markets (including those for credit, futures, insurance, and so forth) because such markets are no more than a device for reallocating claims to current expenditure between agents in different time periods and contingently upon different events. Where there are traded financial assets, their holdings should be included in the description of each agent's personal state. Then each agent will be faced with a separate budget constraint for each period, and for each macro state and personal state that could occur at the start of that period.

Sequential equilibria of this kind raise many issues. One obvious question concerns their existence. Standard techniques should be able to prove existence of an equilibrium in each subeconomy that depends only on the macro state at the beginning of the subeconomy. It is by no means obvious, however, even in the two period case, that later equilibria can be selected in a way that depends only on the macro state at the beginning of these later subeconomies. Typically, therefore, it may be necessary to allow the entire history of previous macro states to affect what equilibrium prices emerge in each subeconomy. Then each macro state would have to be expanded to include within its description a complete history of all previous macro states. Some reduction in the dimensionality of the relevant state space may well be possible, however.

The presence of transfers or of other instruments of government economic policy, and their dependence on the macro state, is an important new feature of such sequential models. In particular, the macro state includes the interpersonal distribution of personal states, which in turn is affected by the distribution of individual agents' consumption, saving, investment, production, and work decisions in all previous periods. As remarked in Section 1, this makes the macro state into a kind of "widespread externality," the public good aspect of the macro state in intertemporal models mentioned in Section 6.1.

6.4   Sequential policy analysis

The example of Section 5 shows the need to consider more carefully how the dependence of future government policy on past actions by agents affects those agents' incentives. However, it also shows how limited may be the ability of governments to pursue redistributive programs, even in the absence of information failures and other obstacles to ideal lump-sum redistribution. Issues of "time (in)consistency" or, more exactly, of subgame (im)perfection, arise not only in macroeconomics and not only when there are "distortionary" taxes or public goods – they are inherent in intertemporal models of an economic system. It is more interesting, perhaps, that the above example also shows how any individual decision in an intertemporal economy has a public good aspect, because of the predicted reaction of government policy to earlier decisions by individual agents. This vital feature seems to be missing from all but a very few of the intertemporal models that have been used for policy analysis, especially those used by microeconomists. For some of the exceptions, see Rogers (1986), Staiger and Tabellini (1987), Klein (1987), Chari (1988), Stokey (1989; 1991), Karp and Newbery (1989), Maskin and Newbery (1990), and Bliss (1991). Macroeconomists, on the other hand, are very familiar with the "Lucas critique" concerning the government's policy reactions (Lucas [1976]), but do not seem to have brought out all its public good aspects.

Another limitation of the literature on public finance is that much of it appears to consider only rather inflexible policies. Examples include a permanent change in income tax rates, a permanent and constant new tax on fuels which produce carbon dioxide when burnt, a permanent and irreversible move toward freer trade or market integration, and so forth. Yet sequential economies call for sequential policies that depend on the macro state. Previous sections of this chapter have considered sequential lump-sum redistribution. It is natural for policy economists to consider sequential commodity and income taxes, sequential regulation of industry, sequential policies to combat pollution, and so forth. And for economic theorists to consider sequential budget decentralizations of incentive compatible sequential allocation mechanisms, and sequential rules for providing public goods.

Sequential policies of this kind play an important role in macroeconomic discussion of issues like stabilization policy. It is surely time to embody them in microeconomic policy models. In real economies, they are inevitable. Even a government which tries to ignore fluctuations in the macroeconomy, and maintains constant tax rates and public expenditure programs regardless of the state of the business cycle, will find itself balancing its finances and meeting its budget deficit with a countercyclical level of borrowing. In other words, unless there is no uncertainty whatsoever, its borrowing policy at least will be sequential, in the sense of depending on the macro state.

This is a simple observation, yet it has profound implications. Following Sen (1972), Hammond (1986; 1990) pointed out the need for a balancing policy to accompany any public (or private) sector project or tax reform. Unlike the private sector which is usually modeled as balancing its finances optimally, the public sector usually relies on unspecified tax or borrowing policies to meet any shortfall it may experience. Yet these balancing policies are a crucial part of a project or tax reform – in Hammond (1986) there are nontrivial cases where the only immediate effect of a project is to generate a surplus for the government, a surplus which will only benefit individuals once it is spent in some useful way (including the possibility of reducing existing tax revenue requirements). This is the balancing part of the policy. And, as should be clear from the argument of the previous paragraph, this balancing policy will have to depend on the macro state, as well as on the size of the increased deficit or surplus that has to be balanced. A similar phenomenon applies to the gains from increased production efficiency, from trade liberalization, or from forming a customs union. To achieve the Pareto improvements claimed in most textbooks, the gainers from such "supplyside" policies have to pay lump-sum compensation to the losers – to those who have human or physical capital invested irreversibly in industries which cease to be competitive, for instance. This lump-sum compensation depends on what the individual's net trade would have been in the absence of a reform. In a sequential economy, there has to be something equivalent to a lump-sum adjustment to each individual's budget constraint in each period, and for each macro and personal state in each period. Moreover, each such adjustment depends on what the individual would have consumed and produced in that period, for that macro and personal state. We are back with sequential lump-sum transfers.

In the more realistic case where lump-sum compensation is impossible, Dixit and Norman (1980, 1986) were still able to demonstrate the gains from trade, using commodity (and income) tax adjustments to compensate losers. In a static model we show how to generate Pareto improvements by instituting a total freeze on consumer prices, wages, and dividends, combined with poll subsidies and perfectly flexible tax rates. This leaves producer prices free to adjust so as to clear all markets. In a sequential setting, the corresponding policy requires freezing consumer prices, wages, and dividends at levels they would have had, as functions of the macro state, in the absence of any reform. Obviously there are enormous practical difficulties in determining what these would have been, let alone in arranging the required freeze. This leads us to regard the possibility of Pareto gains as largely illusory. Instead, one should be evaluating combinations of sequential supply side policy reforms together with imperfect sequential policies that lighten the burden on the most deserving losers.

There is no reason why only balancing or compensating policies should be sequential. Public sector projects can often be improved by making them more responsive to changes in the macro state – for example, by concentrating on projects for (re)constructing a country's infrastructure during periods when the economy would otherwise be in recession, or by adapting the intensity of (re)training programs to the level of unemployment. The same is true of tax policies. Economic policy as a whole is almost inevitably sequential. Good economic policy will take into account the sequential nature of the economy; models for evaluating policy must then also be sequential.

This chapter starts by formulating two Arrow–Debreu market games whose straightforward Nash equilibria are Walrasian. Both games have an auctioneer setting prices to maximize net sales value. In the second an additional redistributive agency maximizes welfare through optimal lump-sum transfers. In intertemporal economies, however, it is shown that subgame imperfections can arise because agents understand how current decisions such as those determining investment influence either future prices (with finitely many agents) or future redistribution (even in continuum economies). The latter observation undermines the second efficiency theorem of welfare economics in sequential environments. When the state of the economy affects future policy, it functions like a "widespread externality."

Some readers may find it odd that I should contribute a chapter to this volume pointing out some limitations of the Arrow–Debreu methodology, but my enjoyable interaction with Kenneth Arrow over many years makes me keenly aware that nobody is readier than he to accept that there are such limitations, or readier to adapt the Arrow–Debreu framework to overcome them. Unfortunately, limitations of space and time prevent me from exploring here how an equilibrium theory of sto-

·

chastic allocation processes retains much of the formalism and essential insights of Arrow's pioneering work on the role of securities markets in a simple sequence economy, at the same time overcoming the subgame imperfections noted here.

7   Acknowledgments

It is a great pleasure to record that I have had the privilege of knowing Kenneth Arrow, and of receiving his encouragement for my research efforts, since the very early 1970s. I have also enjoyed being a colleague since 1979 when we both arrived in the Stanford Economics Department (Kenneth for his second spell in the department).

This chapter was essentially completed while the author was Benjamin Meaker Visiting Professor at the University of Bristol during June 1993, its final version while he was supported by an Alexander von Humboldt Foundation Research Award, and visiting the Center for Economic Studies at the University of Munich. My thanks to these institutions for supporting this and other research endeavors as well as to Christopher Bliss, Graciela Chichilnisky, and Mark Salmon for comments and suggestions.

The chapter was presented to the meeting of the Society for the Advancement in Economic Theory held on the Greek island of Cephalonia in May 1993, and to the August 1993 Econometric Society European Meeting in Uppsala, Sweden. Parts had previously been included in European University Institute Working Paper ECO No. 90/14 (September 1990) entitled "Intertemporal Objectives," and in "Recursive Efficiency in Sequential Economies," written in October 1991 and revised in February 1992.

Section 5 builds on ideas due to Leigh Tesfatsion (1986) in particular, to whom I owe an apology for originally doubting the validity of her results. For their patient attention as I began formulating some of the concepts used here, I am grateful to Jean-Michel Grandmont and Frank Hahn. For helpful discussion I am indebted to Paul Grout, Louis Makowski, Margaret Meyer, James Mirrlees, Klaus Nehring, Martine Quinzii, Debraj Ray, Joaquim Silvestre, Bernt Stigum, and other members of the mathematical economics or theory seminars at Nuffield College, Oxford, at El Colegio de México, and at the Universities of Siena, Barcelona, Oslo, California at Davis, and Bristol, as well as to Christopher Bliss and Mark Salmon. None of the above is responsible for any remaining confusion, nor for my inability to heed all their good advice.

References

Anderson, R. M. 1991. Non-Standard Analysis with Applications to Economics. In *Handbook of Mathematical Economics*, Vol. IV, ed. W. Hildenbrand and H. Sonnenschein. Amsterdam: North-Holland, Chapter 39, pp. 2145–208.

Arrow, K. J. 1951. An extension of the basic theorems of classical welfare economics. In *Proceedings of the Second Berkeley Symposium on Mathematical Statistics and Probability*, ed. J. Neyman. Berkeley: University of California Press, pp. 507–32; reprinted in Arrow (1983), Chapter 2, pp. 15–45.

Arrow, K. J. 1953, 1964. Le rôle des valeurs boursières pour la répartition la meilleure des risques. In *Econométrie*. Paris: Centre National de la Recherche Scientifique, pp. 41–8; translation of English original, The role of securities in the optimal allocation of risk-bearing, later published in *Review of Economic Studies*, 31:91–6; reprinted in Arrow (1983), Chapter 3, pp. 48–57.

Arrow, K. J. 1971. The firm in general equilibrium theory. In *The Corporate Economy: Growth, Competition, and Innovative Potential*, ed. R. Marris and A. Wood. London: Macmillan, and Cambridge, MA: Harvard University Press, pp. 68–110; reprinted in Arrow (1983), Chapter 8, pp. 156–98.

Arrow, K. J. 1983. *Collected Papers of Kenneth J. Arrow*, Vol. 2: *General Equilibrium*. Cambridge, MA: Belknap Press of Harvard University Press.

Arrow, K. J., and G. Debreu. 1954. Existence of an equilibrium for a competitive economy. *Econometrica*, 22: 265–90; reprinted in Arrow (1983), Chapter 4, pp. 59–91 and in Debreu (1983), Chapter 4, pp. 68–97.

Arrow, K. J., and F. Hahn. 1971. *General Competitive Analysis*. San Francisco: Holden-Day.

Bewley, T. 1986. Stationary monetary equilibrium with a continuum of independently fluctuating consumers. In *Contributions to Mathematical Economics*, in Honor of Gérard Debreu, ed. W. Hildenbrand and A. Mas-Colell. Amsterdam: North-Holland, pp. 79–102.

Bliss, C. J. 1991. Adjustment, compensation and factor mobility in integrated markets. In *Unity with Diversity in the European Economy: The Community's Southern Frontier*, ed. C. J. Bliss and J. B. de Macedo. Cambridge: Cambridge University Press.

Bryant, W. D. A. 1994. Misrepresentations of the second fundamental theorem of welfare economics: Barriers to better economic education. *Journal of Economic Education*, 25:75–80.

Calvo, G. A. 1978. On the time consistency of optimal policy in a monetary economy. *Econometrica*, 46:1411–28.

Chari, V. V. 1988. Time consistency and optimal policy design. *Federal Reserve Bank of Minneapolis: Quarterly Review*, 12 (4, Fall):17–31.

Debreu, G. 1952. A social equilibrium existence theorem. *Proceedings of the National Academy of Sciences*, 38:886–93; reprinted in Debreu (1983), Chapter 2, pp. 50–8.

Debreu, G. 1959. *Theory of Value: An Axiomatic Analysis of Economic Equilibrium*. New York: John Wiley.

360   **P. J. Hammond**

Debreu, G. 1983. *Mathematical Economics: Twenty Papers of Gerard Debreu.* Cambridge University Press.

Diamond, P., and J. Mirrlees. 1971. Optimal taxation and public production, I and II. *American Economic Review*, 61:8–27, 261–78.

Dixit, A., and V. Norman. 1980. *Theory of International Trade.* Welwyn, Herts., UK: James Nisbet.

Dixit, A., and V. Norman. 1986. Gains from trade without lump-sum compensation. *Journal of International Economics*, 21:99–110.

Duffie, D., J. Geanakoplos, A. Mas-Colell, and A. McLennan. 1994. Stationary Markov equilibria. *Econometrica*, 62:745–81.

Feldman, M., and C. Gilles. 1985. An expository note on individual risk without aggregate uncertainty. *Journal of Economy Theory*, 35:26–32.

Fischer, S. 1980. Dynamic inconsistency, cooperation, and the benevolent dissembling government. *Journal of Economic Dynamics and Control*, 2:93–107.

Fisher, I. 1907. *The Rate of Interest: Its Nature, Determination, and Relation to Economic Phenomena.* New York: Macmillan.

Fisher, I. 1930. *The Theory of Interest.* New Haven: Yale University Press.

Gale, D. M. 1979. Large economies with trading uncertainty. *Review of Economic Studies*, 46:319–38.

Hammond, P. J. 1979. Straightforward individual incentive compatibility in large economies. *Review of Economic Studies*, 46:263–82.

Hammond, P. J. 1986. Project evaluation by potential tax reform. *Journal of Public Economics*, 30:1–36.

Hammond, P. J. 1987. Markets as constraints: Multilateral incentive compatibility in continuum economies. *Review of Economic Studies*, 54:399–412.

Hammond, P. J. 1990. Theoretical progress in public economics: A provocative Assessment. *Oxford Economic Papers* (Special Issue on Public Economics), 42:6–33.

Hammond, P. J., M. Kaneko, and M. H. Wooders. 1989. Continuum economies with finite coalitions: Core, equilibrium, and widespread externalities. *Journal of Economic Theory*, 49:113–34.

Hammond, P. J., and J. Sempere. 1995. Limits to the potential gains from economic integration and other supply-side policies. *Economic Journal*, 105, 1180–204.

Hicks, J. R. 1939; 2nd ed., 1946. *Value and Capital.* Oxford: Oxford University Press.

Intriligator, M. D. 1987. The impact of Arrow's contribution to economic analysis. In *Arrow and the Foundations of the Theory of Economic Policy*, ed. G. R. Feiwel. London: Macmillan; New York: New York University Press, Chapter 30, pp. 683–91.

Judd, K. 1985. The law of large numbers with a continuum of random variables. *Journal of Economic Theory*, 35:19–25.

Kaneko, M., and M. H. Wooders. 1989. The core of a continuum economy with widespread externalities and finite coalitions: From finite to continuum economies. *Journal of Economic Theory*, 49:135–68.

Karp, L., and D. Newbery. 1989. Intertemporal consistency issues in depletable resources. Centre for Economic Policy Research, Stanford University Discussion Paper No. 346.

Klein, D. 1987. The microfoundations of time inconsistency under a benevolent rule. GEA Working Paper 87-01, New York University; revised as The microfoundations of rules vs. discretion (1988).

Kydland, F. E., and E. C. Prescott. 1977. Rules rather than discretion: The inconsistency of optimal plans. *Journal of Political Economy*, 85:473–91.

Kydland, F. E., and E. C. Prescott. 1980. Dynamic optimal taxation, rational expectations, and optimal control. *Journal of Economic Dynamics and Control*, 2:79–91.

Lucas, R. E., 1976. Econometric policy evaluation: A critique. In *The Phillips Curve and Labor Markets, Carnegie-Rochester Conference Series on Public Policy*, ed. K. Brunner and A. H. Meltzer. Amsterdam: North-Holland, pp. 19–46; reprinted in R. E. Lucas, *Studies in Business Cycle Theory*. Cambridge, MA: M.I.T. Press 1981.

Maskin, E., and D. M. Newbery. 1990. Disadvantageous oil tariffs and dynamic consistency. *American Economic Review*, 80:143–56.

Neumann, J. von, and O. Morgenstern. 1943; 3rd ed., 1953. *Theory of Games and Economic Behavior*. Princeton: Princeton University Press.

Rogers, C. A. 1986. The effect of distributive goals on the time inconsistency of optimal taxes. *Journal of Monetary Economics*, 17:251–69.

Samuelson, P. A. 1974. A curious case where reallocation cannot achieve optimum welfare. In *Public Finance and Stabilization Policy*, ed. W. L. Smith and J. C. Culbertson. Amsterdam: North-Holland.

Selten, R. 1965. Speltheoretische behandlung eines oligopolmodells mit nachfrageträgheit. *Zeitschrift für die gesamte Staatswissenschaft*, 121:301–24, 667–89.

Selten, R. 1973. A simple model of imperfect competition, where 4 are few and 6 are many. *International Journal of Game Theory*, 2:141–201.

Selten, R. 1975. Re-examination of the perfectness concept for equilibrium points of extensive games. *International Journal of Game Theory*, 4:25–55.

Sen, A. K. 1972. Control areas and accounting prices: An approach to economic evaluation. *Economic Journal*, 82:486–501.

Staiger, R. W., and M. Tabellini. 1987. Discretionary trade policy and excessive protection. *American Economic Review*, 77:823–37.

Stokey, N. L. 1989. Reputation and time consistency. *American Economic Review, Papers and Proceedings*, 79:134–9.

Stokey, N. L. 1991. Credible public policy. *Journal of Economic Dynamics and Control*, 15:627–56.

Stokey, N. L., and R. E. Lucas (with E. C. Prescott). 1989. *Recursive methods in economic dynamics*. Cambridge, MA: Harvard University Press.

Tesfatsion, L. 1986. Time-inconsistency of benevolent government economies. *Journal of Public Economics*, 31:25–52.

CHAPTER 17

Redistribution by a representative democracy and distributive justice under uncertainty

Peter Coughlin

1 Introduction

In his 1972 Nobel lecture, Kenneth Arrow observed that "general competitive equilibrium above all teaches us the extent to which a social allocation of resources can be achieved by independent private decisions coordinated through the market" (1973, p. 228). He then added: "But, as has been stressed, there is nothing in the process which guarantees that the distribution be just." This led him to conclude, "thus even under the assumptions most favorable to decentralization of decision making, there is an irreducible need for a social or collective choice on distribution."

In *The Limits of Organization* (1974), Arrow stated: "With regard to distributive justice, . . . it is perfectly possible to defend the proposition that through one action or another (and we think here usually of taxation and redistribution), we can change the distribution of income as we wish. . . . But of course we are here taking away from one and giving to another. We have a straight conflict situation, not one that can be resolved by . . . jointly improving the welfare of each individual" (1974, p. 24). This observation squarely placed redistribution via government in the class of social choices for which (he had already argued) "criteria we associate with 'distributive justice' have to be called into play" (p. 20). This view has been echoed elsewhere, in, for example, Edmund Phelps's entry on "distributive justice" for *The New Palgrave: A Dictionary of Economics*: "Distributive justice is largely about redistributive taxation and subsidies" (1987, p. 886).

Most economists accept the view that the distribution of income should reflect an identifiable and defensible principle of justice (for

362

discussions of established principles of justice, see Sen [1974; 1987; 1990]). Some have argued, however, that having redistribution be a social or collective choice made by the government in a representative democracy does not accomplish this goal. Prominent among these scholars is James Buchanan, the 1986 Nobel laureate in economics.

This chapter investigates the assertion by Buchanan and other public choice economists that redistribution via government in a representative democracy does not reflect an identifiable and defensible principle of distributive justice. The assertion is specifically examined in the context of the models of representative democracy developed in the public choice literature. The first major conclusion is that, when it is assumed that voting is fully determined by candidates' redistributive strategies, the assertion is valid. The second major conclusion is that when (instead) it is assumed that candidates are uncertain about voters' choices and use an econometric model like the logit model, the assertion is not valid. This establishes that public choice theory does *not* lead us inexorably to the dismal conclusions about redistribution via government that have been asserted by Buchanan and others.

2   *The Calculus of Consent*

In *The Calculus of Consent*, Buchanan and his co-author Gordon Tullock wrote, "The amount of redistribution that unrestrained majority voting will generate will tend to be greater than that which the whole group of individuals could conceptually agree on as 'desirable' at the time of constitutional choice" (1962, p. 194). In a subsequent article, Buchanan harshly criticized the view that "the redistribution that 'should' be performed at various levels of government is that which individuals, acting through their collective entities, local and central, expressly prefer." In particular, he wrote: "outcomes that reflect some 'true' amalgamation of individual preferences are not, of course, possible to attain. Political outcomes emerge from the workings of institutions, themselves imperfect, that exhibit stochastic variety and, on occasion, internal inconsistency" (Buchanan [1974, p. 39]). In his book *Freedom in Constitutional Contract*, Buchanan insisted that "Once chosen, the fiscal structure should not be subject to year-to-year manipulation and change by shifting coalitions" (1977, p. 210).

Buchanan's views were subsequently developed more fully in a chapter on "Distributive Justice and Distributive Politics" in his book *The Reason of Rules: Constitutional Political Economy*, written with Geoffrey Brennan. Brennan and Buchanan set out "to take political institutions more or less as we know them and ask . . . whether there is any theoretical presumption that political processes generate greater 'distributive justice' than, say, a predominantly market-oriented regime" (1985, p. 118). This objective, quite naturally, led them "to investigate the nature of the pressures on distributional outcomes that arise from electoral processes" (p. 128). Identifying the particular institutions whose workings were of primary concern, they stated: "Those pressures necessarily reflect the nature of the institutional setting, of which electoral competition under simple majority rule is a major (and many would argue predominant) feature" (pp. 128–9). Pinpointing the main issue that they set out to resolve, they said, "The substantive issue is whether there is any reason to believe that distributive justice will be secured" (p. 129).

Brennan and Buchanan summarized their main conclusion about this important issue as follows: "The central message of the ... analysis undertaken ... is that ordinary majoritarian politics is a highly imperfect mechanism for securing distributive justice" (pp. 127–8). They saw this conclusion as one that argues for constraining the redistributive power of representative democracies: "All this suggests the possibility of lifting the determination of the redistributive or transfer budget out of the jurisdiction of in-period majoritarian politics and making it a matter of explicit constitutional compact" (p. 132). Brennan and Buchanan also raised the prospect that adopting this alternative arrangement might lead to there being *no* redistribution: "There is available, at the constitutional level, a wider set of options, and the means chosen for achieving more equitable outcomes need not necessarily involve interpersonal transfers" (p. 132).

A clear summary of this result was provided in John Broome's review of their book:

[O]ne of their main practical conclusions ... is that political processes are unlikely to improve on the free market in distributing income ..., so ... there should be rules outlawing or regulating attempts at redistribution. (1988, p. 282)

The central question in *this* essay is whether the "economic theory of politics" (as Buchanan [1984, p. 11] has dubbed the Public Choice literature) necessarily draws us to Buchanan's critical view of redistribution via government in representative democracies. Do the established models in the Public Choice literature inexorably lead us to conclude that the redistribution which takes place in representative democracies fails to be "just," as this term is used in political philosophy and welfare economics (see, for instance, Sen (1987, 1990)). In addressing this question, I will adopt Buchanan's methodological view that "the normative implications of public choice theory ... can stand on their own, and they can be allowed to emerge as they will or will not from the positive analysis" (Buchanan 1984, p. 12). Thus we will be looking at the issue at hand from two separate (albeit related) perspectives: (1) a "positive perspective" which assesses what redistribution can be expected in a representative democracy, and (2) a "normative perspective" which addresses the question "Can the expected redistribution be considered just?"

This essay specifically addresses positive models of representative democracy that have been developed in the Public Choice literature and surveyed by Dennis Mueller (1976; 1979; 1989). I consider how a widely used collective choice procedure – determining the income distribution indirectly by electoral competition between politicians – fares from the normative perspective of distributive justice. Is the distributional outcome from electoral competition just?

Section 3 uses Brennan and Buchanan's "extremely simple, highly abstract model of majority rule" (1985, p. 118) to motivate the somewhat more complicated model of electoral competition under majority rule discussed in the ensuing sections. Section 4 discusses the implications of having candidates who believe the choices voters make are fully determined by the candidates' redistributional proposals. Section 5 discusses the implications of having political candidates uncertain about the choices voters will make and who, therefore, use an econometric model (namely, the logit model) to predict the voters' behavior. Sections 4 and 5 pay special attention to whether the outcomes from such elections can be viewed as reflecting an identifiable and defensible principle of distributive justice. The final section (Section 6) summarizes the chapter and provides some concluding remarks.

3   A model of redistribution by representative democracies

Following Brennan and Buchanan I make a simplifying assumption which generalizes their assumptions. The set of voters is divided into m groups (each voter being in exactly one group). Θ will denote the set of groups in the electorate; $g(\theta)$ will denote the (positive) proportion of the set of voters contained in any given group θ. It is easy to see that this formulation includes, as a special case, the possibility that each "group" is simply one person. It should be noted that the approach of dividing an electorate into groups is not special to this model. It has also been used by James Enelow and Melvin Hinich (1984, Chap. 5), Assar Lindbeck and Jorgen Weibull (1987), and others.

Brennan and Buchanan's model includes each of the following features. First: "In order to focus solely on the distributional consequences of majority rule" they "assume that the only thing government does is make transfers" (1985, p. 118). Second: They assume that each voter votes. Third: They assume that "there is no altruism; all aim to maximize their own real incomes" (1985, p. 118). That is, a given voter prefers distribution x to distribution y if and only if x provides him (or, alternatively, his group) with more income than y does. Fourth: They assume that "all transfers are 'lump sum,' that is, total income can be redistributed at will without loss. Aggregate money income (and the aggregate wealth stock) are totally unaffected by the transfer process" (1985, p. 119).

The model specified here retains these four features. I also assume that the governmental transfers are specifically transfers of income (rather than, say, ones that could potentially involve transfers of wealth as well). Y will denote the total amount of income in the society.[1]

Just as in the analysis by Brennan and Buchanan, the collective decision considered here is made at the "postconstitutional" stage – that is, the social choice is made according to the rules specified at an earlier time. We assume that, at the constitutional stage, it was decided that each group, θ, would receive at least some (positive) amount k_θ, which, as the notation suggests, might vary from group to group. I also assume that Y exceeds the sum of the legal minima for the groups. It is thus assumed that at least some of the groups have predistribution incomes exceeding their legal minima, so some transfers are possible. The postdistribution income for group θ is denoted by s_θ. A feasible (or legally permissible) income distribution is denoted by $s = s_1, \ldots, s_m$. It is denoted by a vector whose components specify the postdistribution incomes for the m groups in the electorate.

One potential interpretation of the legal minima for the groups is that they are the values in the "natural distribution" that would arise in "a genuinely anarchistic order" (Buchanan 1975, p. 58). Under this interpretation, the assumed inequality would be expected to hold – since, as Buchanan (1975) emphasizes, the total income available in a purely anarchistic setting can be expected to be far below what can be achieved in a society with an effective government. The inequality is also appropriate with many other potential interpretations of the legal minima.

If a group could be left with no income, then the members of the group (either alone or with the members of other groups that could potentially be left indigent) might very well choose to rebel, or to refuse to work,

---

[1] Similar formulations of the set of possible income distributions for a society have been used by Kenneth Arrow (1969; 1981), Amartya Sen (1973; 1974), and others.

or to start or enter an "underground economy" in which the government cannot easily tax their income away. Thus if, at the constitutional stage, people were concerned about whether the government's decisions would be accepted or about maintaining the political system to be adopted, there would be good reasons for legal minima to be present.

As noted above, the model specified here will retain Geoffrey Brennan and James Buchanan's (1985) assumption that the preferences on the set of possible income distributions are such that "there is no altruism; all aim to maximize their own real incomes." Indeed, a number of scholars – including Gordon Tullock (1983) and Assar Lindbeck (1985) – have argued that income redistribution by government takes place primarily because certain groups in the economy (such as farmers or government employees) want to have income transferred to them and have enough votes to make it happen. The specific "selfish voter" case we consider makes use of the "Bernoulli assumption" about preferences for income (see, for instance, Arrow [1963, p. 39; 1970, pp. 22–3] or Shubik [1984, p. 15]). In particular, we assume that voter i has the following utility function on S: $U_i(s) = U_\theta(s) = \alpha_\theta + \beta_\theta \cdot \log\{s_\theta\}$, where (1) θ is the group that contains i, (2) α_θ and β_θ are scalars (that is, real numbers), (3) $0 < \beta_\theta < 1$, and (4) $\log\{x\}$ denotes the natural logarithm of x. Since the legal minima for the groups' incomes are positive (that is, there is no group which gets nothing), each voter's utility function is defined at each feasible income distribution s (since, in particular, this property of the model assures that, for each group θ, $\log\{s_\theta\}$ is defined at each s).

As noted in the introduction, Brennan and Buchanan identified "electoral competition under simple majority rule" as "a major (and many would argue predominant) feature" of the "institutional setting" which determines the redistribution that takes place via government in a representative democracy. Brennan and Buchanan approximated the electoral competition by considering binary choices (for the voters) between possible distributions. Here the electoral competition is modeled more explicitly, by assuming that (1) there are two candidates, $c = 1, 2$, (2) each candidate c chooses a position ψ_c in the set S of feasible income distributions, and (3) each candidate wants to maximize his or her expected plurality.

Let us assume that the probability that a given voter i votes for a particular candidate c can be written as $P_i^c(\psi_1, \psi_2) = P_\theta^c(\psi_1, \psi_2)$, where θ is the group that contains i. In other words, it is being assumed that each group satisfies the homogeneity assumption that all the voters in the group have the same "selection probability" and that this probability is a function of the distributional positions chosen by the two

candidates. As the notation suggests, this probability may be different
for different choices of the group, θ, and for different choices of the candidate, c.[2]

The assumptions made above directly imply that the candidates' decisions constitute a two-person, zero-sum game (with the zero-sum feature
specifically reflecting the fact that, as one candidate gains in expected
vote, the other one necessarily declines in expected vote by the exact
same amount).[3] Following the standard approach in Game Theory, a pair
of candidate positions will be in equilibrium if and only if neither candidate could increase his expected plurality by unilaterally changing his
position. Any such pair will, accordingly, be called an "electoral equilibrium." If an equilibrium exists, it identifies the positions the candidates
can be expected to select.

Finally, to convert this model of electoral competition into a model
of the redistribution that takes place via government in a representative democracy, we assume – as in Brennan and Buchanan's (1985)
analysis, and throughout the public choice literature on representative
democracy surveyed by Mueller (1976; 1979; 1989) – that the position
selected by the winning candidate (before election day) will become the
actual income distribution in the society when he takes office.

4   Voting determined by distributional preferences

Geoffrey Brennan and James Buchanan assume that all voters "cast their
votes in accordance with their interests" (1985, p. 118). Using the notation introduced in the preceding section, we can state this assumption as:
For each voter i and each candidate c,

$$P_i^c(\psi_1, \psi_2) = P_\theta^c(\psi_1, \psi_2) = \begin{cases} 1 \ if \ U_\theta(\psi_c) > U_\theta(\psi_k) \\ 1/2 \ if \ U_\theta(\psi_c) = U_\theta(\psi_k) \\ 0 \ if \ U_\theta(\psi_c) < U_\theta(\psi_k) \end{cases} \quad (4.1)$$

where k is the "other" candidate. That is, in words, a voter will choose
candidate 1 if he thinks that 1's redistributional position will benefit his

[2] The assumptions listed above specify the model discussed in the remainder of this paper.
The model, it is important to point out, is one that I have already analyzed (Coughlin
[1992, Chap. 2]). As a consequence, in what follows we use results already established.
Since proofs of these results have already been published in my book, there is no
need to provide proofs here. Rather, we concentrate entirely on discussing the issues at
stake.

[3] Other references that explicitly treat candidate decisions as a two-person, zero-sum game
include Enelow and Hinich (1984), Shubik (1984), and Ordeshook (1986).

group more than 2's position will, and vice versa. If the voter's utility for the two candidates' redistributional positions is equal, the probability of choosing either is one-half. As Brennan and Buchanan point out, this formulation of the candidates' expectations about voters' choice behavior "follow[s] conventional public-choice practice" (1985, p. 118) in that it matches the approach used in most of the election models surveyed by Mueller (1976; 1979; 1989). When Brennan and Buchanan (1985) made this assumption, they immediately raised some doubts as to whether it is an appropriate assumption (see their footnote 5 on p. 118) but they did not pursue the implications of their doubts in their analysis. This section discusses what follows when one assumes (as do Brennan and Buchanan [1985]) that the candidates' expectations about the voters' choices satisfy equation (6.1). I return to Brennan and Buchanan's doubts about the appropriateness of this assumption in the next section.

With the candidate expectations under consideration, there is no electoral equilibrium when there are three or more groups and no single group contains half or more of the voters (see Coughlin [1992, p. 35]). Since (with the expectations under consideration) – in general – there is no equilibrium, the answer to the question "What income distribution can be expected?" is given by the answer to the broader question "What outcome can be expected when there is no electoral equilibrium?" Peter Aranson summarized the answer as follows: When an electoral "equilibrium simply does not exist . . . the election outcome appears random. If one candidate is the first to announce a clear policy proposal, his opponent can always find a winning strategy" (1981, p. 292).

What does this answer imply for the view that redistributions carried out by governments in representative democracies do not reflect an identifiable and defensible principle of justice? The answer to this closely related question is contained in the following statement by Aranson, which addresses the broader question of just what a candidate can reasonably be claimed to be advocating when he adopts a strategy that maximizes his expected plurality:

Perhaps candidates really wish to advocate what they believe to be the "public interest" as revealed by the "democratic process," which identifies the collective "wisdom" of the electorate. Candidates with such a belief in the electoral process would hold that a public policy achieving the approval of the majority of the electorate is the public policy that wins elections and is identical to the public interest. If a pure strategy equilibrium exists, these candidates have no problem. But if it does not, then they cannot possibly know what the public interest is. (1981, pp. 296–7)

Combining Aranson's statement with the fact that (with the candidate expectations under consideration) there is no electoral equilibrium, one concludes that the income distributions selected by winning candidates lack a clear and defensible normative rationale. This tells us that, when the candidate expectations under consideration are added to the model of redistribution in a representative democracy specified in Section 3, we are inexorably led to the conclusion that (in the resulting model) redistribution via government definitely does not reflect an identifiable and defensible principle of justice. Thus, in the model of governmental redistribution under considered here, when the candidates believe the voters' choices are fully determined by their redistributional positions, Buchanan's critical view of redistribution via government in a representative democracy is valid.

5   Candidate uncertainty and electoral equilibria

If ψ_1 and ψ_2 are taken to be two alternative "consumption bundles" for a consumer in the market (rather than, as in this chapter, alternative distributions of income), then the standard assumptions used in microeconomic models of markets imply that equation (4.1) will describe the behavior that can be expected if the consumer has a choice between ψ_1 and ψ_2. It is, therefore, tempting to think that there is no need to investigate any alternative assumptions about the candidates' expectations of the voters' choices – and that, as a consequence, the negative conclusion at the end of Section 4 is the end of the story.

There are, however, two good reasons for considering alternatives to the assumption expressed by equation (4.1). First, a number of Public Choice scholars have argued that individual choice behavior in voting may differ from individual choice behavior in the market. The first to argue for this view was James Buchanan (1954). More recently, Buchanan and Brennan (1984) have elaborated on and developed his original arguments more fully. In their more recent article, they conclude that "even the most enthusiastic defender of a method that presumes voters to vote preferences over outcomes ... must acknowledge the possibility of an independent source of 'noise,' attributable to the logical gap between voter action and voter preference" (1984, p. 199). Second, even if choice behavior in voting is exactly like choice behavior in the market, as Peter Ordeshook has pointed out, "candidates are rarely certain about voter preferences. ... Information from public opinion surveys is not error-free and is best represented as statistical" (1986, p. 179). Thus there are clear reasons to think that candidates may be convinced that factors other than the voters' utilities for income distributions will enter into the voters' choices, and that these other factors may be ones the candidates cannot readily observe (as in standard econometric models of choice).

These observations suggest that a natural line of inquiry in this context is to address the question: What are the implications of assuming (1) that candidates are uncertain about the choices voters will make (because of the possibility that unobservable factors will affect those choices) and (2) that candidates will, therefore, use an econometric model to describe voters' behavior? As in my earlier analysis of elections and income redistribution (Coughlin [1992]), the particular statistical model I consider is the best known and most widely used qualitative response model in econometrics: the logit model.

Following the standard approach used in logit models,[4] let us assume that voter i's utility for candidate c being elected is an unobservable (or latent) variable that can be written as $u_i(\psi_c) = U_\theta(\psi_c) + \varepsilon_{ic}(\psi_c)$, where θ is the group that i is in, and $\varepsilon_{ic}(\psi_c)$ is a random variable. The random variable specifically reflects the "noise" between what the candidates know about the voters' preferences for particular income distributions and the voters' actual choice on election day.

Assuming that voter i's choices correspond to his "complete" utility function u_i (rather than to the utility function U_i, which measures his preferences on redistributional reputations, but leaves out other relevant factors) means that equation (4.1) gets replaced by the following (analogous) equation:

$$P_i^c(\psi_1, \psi_2) = \begin{cases} 1 \ if \ u_i(\psi_c) > u_i(\psi_k) \\ 1/2 \ if \ u_i(\psi_c) = u_i(\psi_k) \\ 0 \ if \ u_i(\psi_c) < u_i(\psi_k) \end{cases} \tag{5.1}$$

Taken together with the definition of $u_i(\psi_c)$ and $u_i(\psi_k)$ (that is, with the earlier specification of i's unobservable utility for the two candidates' being elected), equation (6.2) directly implies that the probability that i will vote for c can be written as

$$P_i^c(\psi_1, \psi_2) = \begin{cases} 1 \ if \ \varepsilon_{ic}(\psi_c) - \varepsilon_{ik}(\psi_k) > U_\theta(\psi_k) - U_\theta(\psi_c) \\ 1/2 \ if \ \varepsilon_{ic}(\psi_c) - \varepsilon_{ik}(\psi_k) = U_\theta(\psi_k) - U_\theta(\psi_c) \\ 0 \ if \ \varepsilon_{ic}(\psi_c) - \varepsilon_{ik}(\psi_k) < U_\theta(\psi_k) - U_\theta(\psi_c) \end{cases}$$

$$\tag{5.2}$$

[4] See, for instance, Daniel McFadden's survey article (1982).

where, as before, θ is the group that voter i is in and k is the index for the "other" candidate. Once the assumption that unobservable factors enter into the voters' choices has been cast in this form, it becomes clear that for the selection probabilities for a given voter i to be fully specified, the only thing to be added at this point is an appropriate assumption about the distribution of the random variable $\varepsilon_{ic}(\psi_c) - \varepsilon_{ik}(\psi_k)$. Since we are using the logit model here, we are specifically assuming that this random variable has a logistic distribution.

With the candidate expectations now under consideration, a unique electoral equilibrium exists and is the pair of candidate positions (ψ_1^*, ψ_2^*) at which $\psi_1^* = \psi_2^*$, and their common position maximizes (using the notation defined in Section 3) the following weighted sum of the voters' Bernoulli utility functions on the set of feasible income distributions:[5]

$$\sum_{\theta \in \Theta} \left[\alpha_\theta + \beta_\theta \cdot \log\{s_\theta\} \right] \cdot g(\theta) \tag{5.3}$$

This conclusion implies that the income distribution which maximizes (5.3) is the income distribution that can be expected in any representative democracy in which the assumptions in Section 3 and this section's assumption about the candidates' expectations are satisfied.

Explicitly solving for the maximum of (6.4)[6] reveals that the income distribution that can be expected is one in which the amount that a group j will get will be influenced by whether (again, making use of the notation introduced in Section 3) the inequality

$$\frac{\beta_\theta \cdot g(\theta)}{\sum_{\zeta \in \theta} \beta_\zeta \cdot g(\zeta)} \cdot Y > k_j \tag{5.4}$$

holds for the group. The equilibrium income distribution itself can be described as follows. First, if the inequality in (5.4) does not hold for a given group (that is, the income level on the left-hand side of (5.4) does not exceed the legal minimum for the group), then the corresponding constraint $s_\theta \geq k_\theta$ becomes binding; the group, therefore, gets what it is required to get by law – and nothing more. Second, for each remaining group (that is, for each group for whom the income level on the left-hand side of (5.4) exceeds k_j), the income that it will get is

$$s_\theta = \frac{\beta_\theta \cdot g(\theta)}{\sum_{\zeta \in A} \beta_\zeta \cdot g(\zeta)} \cdot \left[Y - \sum_{\zeta \in B} k_\zeta \right] \tag{5.5}$$

---

[5] See Coughlin (1992, pp. 38, 52–7).   [6] See Coughlin (1992, pp. 54–6).

Thus the proportion of the remaining income that will go to that group is the "normalized" product of the coefficient β_j from its utility function and its size (that is, the ratio of $\beta_j \cdot g(j)$ to the sum $\Sigma_{\theta \in A}\{\beta_\theta \cdot g(\theta)\}$).

One important implication of these results is that (this time around) the relevant portion of Aranson's statement quoted at the end of the preceding section is the portion that applies when an electoral equilibrium exists. As a consequence, this time around, his statement tells us that the income distribution the candidates select can be interpreted as what is in the public interest, as revealed by the democratic process. This implication follows in particular because (since an electoral equilibrium exists) the model is one in which the outcome does not "exhibit stochastic variety and, on occasion, internal inconsistency" and, hence, is free of the characteristics which Buchanan (1974) argued are inappropriate for an institution that is going to carry out redistribution.

These results also have another important implication. Kenneth Arrow wrote:

In the prescription of economic policy normative questions of distributive justice inevitably arise. The implicit basis of economic policy judgment is some version of utilitarianism. (1985, p. 140)

Amartya Sen similarly observed:

[I]n traditional welfare economics, when the notion of justice has been invoked, it has typically been seen only as a part of a bigger exercise, viz., that of social welfare maximization. (1987, p. 1039)

Solving (5.3) maximizes a Benthamite social welfare function (in particular, one which uses the voters' utility functions on the set of possible income distributions). Therefore, solving (5.3) is clearly an identifiable and defensible principle of justice. Therefore, since a representative democracy will select an income distribution which maximizes (5.3), a representative democracy selects an income which reflects an identifiable and defensible principle of justice.

6   Conclusion

This chapter has investigated whether Public Choice Theory leads us inexorably to the conclusion that, as Brennan and Buchanan (1985) suggested, redistribution via government in a representative democracy does not reflect an identifiable and defensible principle of distributive justice. I addressed this normative question in the context of the positive models of representative democracy developed in the Public Choice literature.

The first step in the analysis is the specification of a model of redistribution in a representative democracy. The first major conclusion is about the model obtained by assuming that voting is fully determined by the voters' preferences on income distributions. In this first case, redistribution by representative democracies *does not* reflect an identifiable and defensible principle of justice, as in the conclusions reached by Brennan and Buchanan (1985). The second major conclusion is for the alternative model of representative democracy where candidates are uncertain about the choices voters will make and use a logit model for voters' choices. In this alternative case, redistribution via government *does* reflect an identifiable and defensible principle of justice.

Finally, returning to the central question in this chapter: The second major conclusion clearly implies that the answer is "No, Public Choice Theory does not inexorably lead us to the conclusion that redistribution via government in a representative democracy fails to reflect any identifiable and defensible principle of justice." It is now clear that the Public Choice literature does not support any sweeping normative assessment that either declares that redistribution via government in a representative democracy always reflects an identifiable and defensible principle of distributive justice or declares that it always fails to do so. Rather, any such assessment necessarily fails to reflect accurately either what happens when "on the one hand" voting is fully determined by the voters' preferences on income distributions or when "on the other hand" political candidates are uncertain about the choices voters will make and, therefore, use an econometric model (such as a logit model) of voter choice behavior.

References

Aranson, P. 1981. *American Government: Strategy and Choice*, Cambridge, MA: Winthrop Publishers.

Arrow, K. 1963. *Social Choice and Individual Values* 2nd ed. New York: Wiley.

Arrow, K. 1969. Tullock and an existence theorem. *Public Choice*, 6:105–11.

Arrow, K. 1970. *Essays in the Theory of Risk Bearing*. Amsterdam: North-Holland.

Arrow, K. 1973. General economic equilibrium: Purpose, analytic techniques, collective choice. *Les Prix Nobel en 1972*, Stockholm: Nobel Foundation, pp. 253–72.

Arrow, K. 1974. *The Limits of Organization*, New York: Norton.

Arrow, K. 1981. Optimal and voluntary income distribution. In *Economic Welfare and the Economics of Soviet Socialism*, ed. S. Rosefielde. Cambridge, UK: Cambridge University Press, pp. 267–88.

Arrow, K. 1985. Distributive justice and desirable ends of economic activity. In *Issues in Contemporary Macroeconomics & Distribution*, ed. G. Feiwel. Albany: State University of New York Press, pp. 134–56.

Brennan, G., and J. Buchanan. 1984. Voter choice: Evaluating political alternatives. *American Behavioral Scientist*, 28:185–201.

Brennan, G., and J. Buchanan. 1985. *The Reason of Rules: Constitutional Political Economy*. Cambridge, UK: Cambridge University Press.

Broome, J. 1988. Review of *The Reason of Rules: Constitutional Political Economy* by Geoffrey Brennan and James Buchanan. *Economica*, 55:282–3.

Buchanan, J. 1954. Individual choice in voting and the market. *Journal of Political Economy*, 62:334–43.

Buchanan, J. 1974. Who should distribute what in a Federal system? In *Redistribution Through Public Choice*, ed. H. Hochman and G. Peterson. New York: Columbia University Press, pp. 22–42.

Buchanan, J. 1975. *The Limits of Liberty: Between Anarchy and Leviathan*. Chicago: University of Chicago Press.

Buchanan, J. 1977. *Freedom in Constitutional Contract*. College Station: Texas A&M Press.

Buchanan, J. 1984. Politics without romance: A sketch of positive Public Choice Theory and its normative implications. In *The Theory of Public Choice – II*, ed. J. Buchanan and R. Tollison. Ann Arbor: University of Michigan Press, pp. 11–22.

Buchanan, J., and G. Tullock. 1962. *The Calculus of Consent*. Ann Arbor: University of Michigan Press.

Coughlin, P. 1992. *Probabilistic Voting Theory*. Cambridge, UK: Cambridge University Press.

Enelow, J., and M. Hinich. 1984. *The Spatial Theory of Voting*. Cambridge, UK: Cambridge University Press.

Lindbeck, A. 1985. Redistribution policy and the expansion of the public sector. *Journal of Public Economics*, 28:309–28.

Lindbeck, A., and J. Weibull. 1987. Balanced-budget redistribution as the outcome of political competition. *Public Choice*, 52:273–97.

McFadden, D. 1982. Qualitative response models. In *Advances in Econometrics*, ed. W. Hildenbrand. Cambridge, UK: Cambridge University Press, pp. 1–37.

Mueller, D. 1976. Public choice: A survey. *Journal of Economic Literature*, 14:395–433.

Mueller, D. 1979. *Public Choice*. Cambridge UK: Cambridge University Press.

Mueller, D. 1989. *Public Choice II*. Cambridge, UK: Cambridge University Press.

Ordeshook, P. 1986. *Game Theory and Political Theory*. Cambridge, UK: Cambridge University Press.

Phelps, E. 1987. Distributive justice. In *The New Palgrave: A Dictionary of Economics*, Volume 1, ed. J. Eatwell et al. London: Macmillan, pp. 886–8.

Sen, A. 1970. *Collective Choice and Social Welfare*. San Francisco: Holden-Day.

Sen, A. 1973. *On Income Inequality*. Oxford: Clarendon.

Sen, A. 1974. Rawls versus Bentham: An axiomatic examination of the pure redistribution problem. *Theory and Decision*, 4, pp. 301–10.

Sen, A. 1987. Justice. *The New Palgrave: A Dictionary of Economics*, Volume 2, ed., J. Eatwell et al. London: Macmillan, pp. 1039–43.

Sen, A. 1990. Justice: Means versus freedom. *Philosophy and Public Affairs*, 19, pp. 111–21.

Shubik, M. 1984. *A Game Theoretic Approach to Political Economy*. Cambridge, MA: MIT Press.

Tullock, G. 1983. *Economics of Income Redistribution*. Boston: Kluwer.

Author index

377

Subject index

agents: in Arrow–Debreu economy, 67; called marketmakers, 237–9, 242–6, 250–1; information partition by, 53–4; in overlapping generations with sequential allocations model, 352–4; in process of equilibria with transfers, 354–5; in sequence economy, 67

airline industry: cost minimizing structure of routes in, 218–19; value-added networks in reservation systems, 192

allocation of goods: autarkic and world competitive equilibrium, 322–7; in consumer–producer coalition, 30–1; in Walrasian economy, 80n9

Arrow–Debreu economy: applying intertemporal models to, 329–30; equilibrium in, 126–7; futures markets in, 101; inability to hedge price risks in, 73–9; informational role of prices in, 53; market game with redistribution, 334–5; price expectations in, 67; with price uncertainty, 10–11, 31, 75–95; as sequential model of uncertainty, 97; simple market game, 332–4; uncertainty in, 72–9

Arrow–Debreu equilibrium allocation, 132–8

Arrow futures market, 236–7

auctioneer: in Arrow–Debreu economy, 77; in economy with price uncertainty, 77–8, 87; Walrasian, 74

autarky, domestic, 322–7

bandwagon effects, 192–3, 204
Black–Scholes option pricing model, 111

capital: social and institutional, 253–4; social overhead capital, 253

capital, natural *See also* stock of natural capital: dynamic model of, 255; optimum investment in, 280–6; as part of social overhead capital, 253

catastrophe futures and bundles, 13, 131
centralization, 10–11, 14

commodities: allocation and reallocation in autarkic and world trade scenarios, 322–7; in resource allocation under certainty and uncertainty, 45–6; as state-contingent claims, 91–2

commodity markets, Arrow–Debreu, 100–1

commons, global: measurement of, 308–9; as nonexcludable good, 307–8; population crowding externality on, 309–10

competition, perfect and monopolistic, 239
complexity theory, 129

consumers: of information goods, 28–35; in market formation model, 241–2

consumption: state-dependent utility of, 55

contracts: insurance, 50, 61; mutual insurance contracts, 13, 127–31, 137–8; price-dependent, 58–60

coordination: options market as substitute for, 111; sunspots as devices for, 68

coordination failure: conditions in market equilibrium for, 247–50; in market innovation models, 236

costs. *See also* transaction costs: average and marginal cost pricing, 175, 195–201, 205–9, 214; in choice of optimal policy related to new

386   **Subject index**

uncertainty (*cont.*)
33–6; in terms of exogenous states of
nature (Arrow), 99–101
uncertainty, endogenous: defined, 11; faced
by economic agents (Kurz), 101–2;
literature on, 46–7; motivating, 73–4;
role of options in hedging against,
102–4; source of, 101
uncertainty, exogenous: difference from
endogenous uncertainty, 101; hedging
for efficent allocation of risk, 102–4;
and incomplete options markets, 112;
options in state-contingent markets
for, 103–4; source of, 101
unemployment: equilibrium rate of, 144; in
intertemporal model of shirking, 13–14,
264–80
utility: with autarkic and international
trade, 322–7; price-dependent, 55–6;
social utility function of natural capital,
281; state-dependent, 55; von
Neumann–Morgenstern, 125

value: of a firm, 21–2; information theory
of, 26; set-valued expectations, 10
value-added networks (VANs): airline
reservation systems as, 192; average
cost pricing solution, 175; with
diverse set of users, 211–13;

emergence of markets through,
14–15; with identical users, 200–211;
Nash equilbrium usage patterns,
202–9; as natural monopoly, 191–2,
202–3, 213–14; price and market
share, 205–9; Reuters FX monitor
and SWIFT as examples of, 191–2
voters: in model of income distribution,
365–8; selection probability in electoral
competition, 367–70; self-interest of
(Brennan and Buchanan), 368–72
voting: determined by distributional
preferences, 368–72; individual choice
behavior in, 370–3; redistribution by
majority, 363

Walrasian equilibria: of Arrow–Debreu
economy, 330, 333–4; intertemporal,
336–8; in market game with
redistribution, 335; Nash equilibria
correponding to, 329–30, 336–44;
standard definition of, 328; subgame
perfect equilibrium in intertemporal,
338–44
welfare economics: efficiency theorems of,
328–9, 350, 354; in market formation,
247–51; social rate of discount in
applied, 312–13; zero discounting,
314–16